W9-BCG-994

ATLANTIC LEGACY

E
69.1
M52
1969

Atlantic Legacy

Essays in American-European Cultural History

by Robert O. Mead

1969
New York   New York University Press
London   University of London Press Limited

216974

COPYRIGHT © 1969 BY NEW YORK UNIVERSITY
LIBRARY OF CONGRESS CATALOG CARD NUMBER: 68–16831
MANUFACTURED IN THE UNITED STATES OF AMERICA

To F. L. M.

Thus, in the beginning, all the world was America.
—John Locke

⚓ PREFACE ⚓

The ideas and reflections gathered here are the fruit of more than a decade's residence in Europe, and more than twice that in the United States. Like most Americans (and like most Europeans) I was early taught that my particular country was the center of the world, the hub of the universe, and, with a suitable dose of patriotism instilled, that it was the Leibnizian best of all possible worlds. I still believe this to be mainly so, although not so firmly after having lived a while on both sides of the Atlantic waterway.

Although almost all Americans, unless their skin was red, had come from Europe (or Africa or Asia), Europe was cast out of mind and the New Life started in its own context, unproved, with its own particular challenges. The European connection was sloughed off in everyday life much as the crab loses its shell as it grows larger. Europe was left behind as the new American empire was created; what remained in the American common mind was a confabulation of myths handed down, often bitter memories, often a recollection of semifeudal economic oppression. America held out the key to anyone who wanted to open the door to the promised land. After so many people had used the key the door was slammed shut and the key hung inside; the Attorney General came to act like a new Peter at the gates of paradise.

The immigration restriction was made about the time I happened into the world, and my wife also, although she was on the "other side" of the Atlantic. By that time the American character which was two hundred years in the making, more or less, had largely been formed. In that time, too, the United States had built a respectable national history with several external wars (as of now we have been enemies to just about everybody), a Civil War (which is still being fought), the conquest of the Western frontier (still unconquered in Hollywood studios), an agricultural revolution (resulting in surpluses that cost billions of dollars to store and were found difficult even to *give* away to the half-starved of the world), and a technological-industrial revolution (which about half the world condemns as the worst excess of bourgeois capitalist bandits, and under which the sky is definitely not the limit for new exploitation).

This story of the building of America and its national character is known, if not understood, by almost every American. It is taught in schools and colleges and universities as most national history is taught—dates, battles, kings or presidents, peace treaties, social and economic struggles rattling down the passage of time. What was going on in other countries at the same time is largely ignored, unless there happens to be a meeting point, such as a war or a nonstop solo flight to a place called Le Bourget, which is fully written up and documented and put away for the idle curious a century hence. American history is presented as a miraculous chronicle of a happy few who were able to jump into the Ark before Europe was engulfed, headed west, and, as Lincoln said, "created a new land" under a Puritan God. Eyes turned to the Western frontier; Americans were preoccupied with new deeds. Americans and their historians seemed to forget that Europe was still there.

In fact, Europe was not only still there, but was also very much in America itself. Thinking itself cut loose from the European entanglement by the war of independence, America expanded—trade with Europe continued to grow, immigration of Europeans increased, the American mercantile fleet became the largest in the world by 1845, the cultural connection expanded with American intellectuals and artists going to Europe to study and work, Europeans visited the United States, and Europeans invested huge sums in land companies, industry, and commerce, and later in railroads spanning the continent. The Atlantic, instead of being an ocean barrier the cold tides of which would wash away European footprints from the American strand, became the effective channel of communication between the Old World and the New. The Atlantic became the interior lake of Western civilization.

Europe, on the other hand, at least conservative Europe holding political power and exercising control over schools and universities, press, and pulpit, felt itself best rid of the United States except as a convenient dumping ground for an excess population prone to turbulence and revolt. Radical-Republican-Democratic America, fighting within itself for full nationhood and unification out of many disparate regions, bitter factional and political quarrels, slavery, teeming half-built cities amidst vast wastes, a rugged, uncouth, and uncultivated population with pretentions that theirs was the best of all possible worlds—all this was to be kept isolated from an orderly and civilized Europe. Chateaubriand, who had visited America and idealized America in *Atala* and *Natchez,* was able to write in 1824 that American political principles were "directly at variance with those of every power." In *Une idylle tragique* Paul Bourget has a French aristocrat say: "The Americans and I, we hardly understand one another. The pointless energy of these people exhausts me, even in thinking about it. And how many of them there are, how many!"

Then, when the bourgeois liberals came to power in Europe, they looked upon American industrial expansion—and a political system with universal suffrage that hardly coincided with their own particular political style—as a direct challenge to their interests. The image of the American ideal was taken up mostly by the radical reformers, such as Cobden and Bright, utopian socialists like St. Simon and Cabet, and by those family relatives of emigrants who received letters and money from America.

With the exception of some brilliant studies such as those of Tocqueville and Bryce, an almost indigestible mass of travelers' reports strangely entwined myth and reality about the United States, the mythology often gaining credence over reality, even to our own day. Essentially, people found what they wanted to find in a foreign country. Lawrence did not describe the real Arabia any more than Lafcadio Hearn described the real Japan, or Chateaubriand the real America.

The American view of Europe is much the same; for the American, Europe has too many "foreigners" in its midst who even have trouble speaking English, much like the unhappy Russian immigrant to the United States who wrote to a New York Russian newspaper: "The Americans are bad people. You speak to them in the plainest Russian language, and you even add a word or two of English for their benefit, and they still do not understand a thing!"

The systematic study of America as a dynamic and integral force in the Western world has been long ignored in European universities, and little of its history and literature has been taught. This does not mean that the United States was intentionally excluded, but rather that university education throughout the nineteenth and well into the twentieth century was classical and selective, training the upper classes to the service of the state and the professions. It was so selective that as late as 1914 English history beyond 1837 was not taught at Oxford. Furthermore, A. S. Namier, appointed professor of English literature at Oxford in 1885, never discussed literature written after the Norman Conquest. When he announced a course on Chaucer, he was teased for his recognition of the "decadents."

Within the last two generations, Europe has willy-nilly learned much about America in schools and universities, from personal contacts, and all the mass media. And America has sprung its isolationist chains and has become aware of what is going on in Europe. There is still much myth, but there is even more reality. A new class of interpreters is appearing. By this I do not mean simply linguists, although they may be that, but people such as journalists, writers, teachers, film producers, cultural and press attachés, transatlantic businessmen, and others who are able to understand the *ingenium et mores* of other Atlantic peoples and explain them to their own. This is a dangerous business, and is exceedingly hard to do. It is like putting on someone else's shoes and pretending they are comfortable, when often they

are not. Then the interpreter has to jump into a third pair of shoes and try
to explain what he has learned in a manner understandable to his compatriot. In "What Paul Bourget Thinks of Us," Mark Twain observed that the
interpreter should be able to reveal us to ourselves so that we can shape
our lives more rationally, but more often he explains people to himself.
After all, it is a little hard and rather silly to explain the bug to the bug,
or to other bugs of the same species.

We shall look at some aspects of the transatlantic cultural relation, of
the quickening communication of people and ideas back and forth across our
"interior lake." I am aware that what is here is ambitious in design but
modest in detail, with no pretence to elaborate learning. I have written a
rather personal book, and I have often made assertions because I believe
them to be true, rather than burdening them with the weight of independent
authorities. Sometimes there may be an air of impertinence, sometimes cen-
sorious, sometimes too casual, but it is a serious subject that should not
be treated frivolously.

Attention has been devoted to various writers and artists in developing
the Atlantic theme of a cultural push-pull between Europe and America.
As a student of the history of ideas I have attempted to reflect their more
socially oriented thinking, simply because I believe that the writer or artist
is the best mirror of a period. He is the most sensitive interpreter of the
changing social seas about him, I would even say more so than the vocal
politician or less vocal businessman, by whom, let us freely admit, the
Atlantic stream is largely dominated. The observations and thoughts of our
writers and artists are presented as though they are "interpretations" of the
social interplay. It is difficult, of course, to draw the line: where I contrast
Teddy Roosevelt as the Man of Action with Henry Adams as the Man of
Thought, another could as easily discuss T. R. the writer with H. A. the
diplomat, *homo faber* rather than *homo sapiens*. It is a matter of shadings,
and for the sake of contrast I have highlighted certain aspects of a transatlantic person to the extent perhaps of putting the rest of him in too feeble
or too dim a light.

Of one thing I am convinced, and that is that on both sides of the
great water we have failed to take into our several accounts the Atlantic
Ocean itself as *mare nostrum*. It remains a psychological block for many, but
it is our most precious sea lane to American-European understanding. I do
not want to be unnecessarily romantic about the sea, yet Romain Gary, the
distinguished French novelist and former consul at San Francisco, is with me
when he writes:

> Listen to the murmur as the tide rises and the ocean comes closer. If the
> sky seems hollow now that the stars are gone, let heaven hide in

emptiness, for we are not alone. There is a might here, a reassuring promise, almost a certitude—and no matter how far we throw away our hope, the sea will always find it and bring it back to us intact.

This little book of compounded prejudices would not have been possible without the intimate collaboration of two persons, French and American, which is explanation in itself of what I am driving at.

Robert O. Mead
New York City

ᴄ᷎ᴀ ACKNOWLEDGMENTS ᴇ᷎ᴏ

There are many others who have written on the transatlantic relation, whether political, diplomatic, social, or cultural, and if I have pretensions to anything it is simply the coordination of those readings that have come to me and seemed most impressive and which are cited in the bibliography. Many of my thoughts have been better expressed in such books written by my former professor Jacques Barzun, and by Alfred Kazin, Frederick J. Hoffman, and my friends Louis Hartz, Eric Goldman, and Edmund Wilson.

And how can one avoid mentioning such charming people as Gilbert Chinard, André Maurois, Henri Peyre, and André Siegfried in their efforts to translate the Atlantic relation? My colleagues at New York University— Oscar Cargill and Leon Edel—have taught me much in their interpretations of European-American thinking. The immense efforts of one person to make John Bull and Uncle Sam understand each other somewhat better have, I hope, been accomplished by Mr. S. Gorley Putt, O.B.E. His own writings and gentle help have been inestimable.

To all of those writers preceding me in what I should like to think of as a grateful task, my many thanks for showing me the way.

Finally, no two people have been more loyal and dedicated in the publication of this book than John Hammond and Sandra Cherry of the New York University Press, to whom I extend continuing friendship and deep thanks.

It has not been my intention to document these little essays heavily. However, the reader may wish to go a bit further into a particular subject mentioned. Consequently, those citations which I thought either too obscure to find easily, or those which are so well known that they should not be missed, are included at the end of each chapter. The more general works I have cited only when they are first mentioned, or with the appearance of other works by the same author.

There are many bibliographies on the transatlantic relation, which may be found almost anywhere; the one at the end of this book is my own selected choice out of an immense body of writings.

Excerpts from Oscar Cargill's *Intellectual America: Ideas on the March*, copyright ©
1941 by The Macmillan Company. Reprinted by permission of The Macmillan Company
and Oscar Cargill.

George Braziller, Inc.—from *Character and Opinion in the United States* by George
Santayana; reprinted with permission of the publisher.

Excerpts from Henri Peyre's *Observations on Life, Literature and Learning in America*,
copyright © 1961 by Southern Illinois University Press. Reprinted by permission of
Southern Illinois University Press.

Excerpts reprinted by permission of Coward-McCann, Inc. from *Jefferson: The Scene
of Europe, 1784–1789* by Marie Kimball. Copyright © 1950 by Coward-McCann, Inc.

Excerpts from Saint-John Perse's *Oeuvre Poétique II*, copyright © 1960 by Editions
Gallimard. Reprinted by permission of Editions Gallimard.

Excerpts from Harold Laski's *The American Democracy*, copyright © 1948 by The
Viking Press, Inc. Reprinted by permission of The Viking Press, Inc.

Excerpt from Archibald MacLeish's *America Was Promises*, copyright © 1939 by
Duell, Sloan and Pearce. Reprinted by permission of Duell, Sloan and Pearce, affiliate
of Meredith Press.

Excerpt from Archibald MacLeish's "Frescoes for Mr. Rockefeller's City" in *The
Collected Poems of Archibald MacLeish*, copyright © 1962 by Archibald MacLeish.
Reprinted by permission of Houghton Mifflin Company.

Excerpts from Archibald MacLeish's "Einstein" and "Hamlet" in *Poems, 1924–1933*,
copyright © 1933 by Archibald MacLeish. Reprinted by permission of Houghton
Mifflin Company.

Excerpts from Ezra Pound's "Hugh Selwyn Mauberly," and "The Age Demanded" in
Personae, copyright © 1926, 1954 by Ezra Pound. Reprinted by permission of New
Directions Publishing Corporation.

Excerpts from Ezra Pound's "Stark Realism" in *Pavannes and Divagations*, copyright ©
1958 by Ezra Pound. Reprinted by permission of New Directions Publishing
Corporation.

Excerpt from T. S. Eliot's *Selected Essays*, copyright © 1950 by Harcourt, Brace &
World, Inc. Reprinted by permission of Harcourt, Brace & World, Inc.

Excerpts from Van Wyck Brooks' *The Ordeal of Mark Twain*, copyright © 1920 and
The Pilgrimage of Henry James, copyright © 1925 by E. P. Dutton & Co. Inc.
Reprinted by permission of E. P. Dutton & Co. Inc.

Excerpts from Van Wyck Brooks' *From the Shadow of the Mountain*, copyright ©
1961 by E. P. Dutton & Co. Inc. Reprinted by permission of E. P. Dutton & Co. Inc.

Excerpts from Sinclair Lewis' *Dodsworth*, copyright © 1947 by Harcourt, Brace &
World, Inc. Reprinted by permission of Harcourt, Brace & World, Inc.

Excerpts from E. E. Cummings' "you shall above all things" in *Poems 1923–1954*,
copyright © 1954 by E. E. Cummings. Reprinted by permission of Harcourt, Brace &
World, Inc.

Excerpts from Philip Rahv's *The Discovery of Europe*, copyright © 1960 by Houghton Mifflin Company. Reprinted by permission of Houghton Mifflin Company.

Excerpt from John Dos Passos' *Manhattan Transfer*, copyright © 1953 by Houghton Mifflin Company. Reprinted by permission of Houghton Mifflin Company.

Excerpts from Henry Longfellow's *The Complete Poetical Works of Longfellow*, ed., Horace E. Scudder, copyright © by Houghton Mifflin Company. Reprinted by permission of Houghton Mifflin Company.

Excerpts from William Dean Howells' *The Rise of Silas Lapham*, copyright © 1937 by Houghton Mifflin Company. Reprinted by permission of Houghton Mifflin Company.

Excerpts from Henry Seidel Canby's *Turn West, Turn East*, copyright © 1951 by Houghton Mifflin Company. Reprinted by permission of Houghton Mifflin Company.

Excerpts from Camille Ferri-Pisani's *Prince Napoleon in America, 1861*, copyright © 1959 by Indiana University Press. Reprinted by permission of Indiana University Press.

Excerpt from Jacques Barzun's *God's Country and Mine*, copyright © 1954 by Jacques Barzun. Reprinted by permission of Atlantic-Little, Brown and Company.

Excerpts from Alan Valentine's *1913: America Between Two Worlds*, copyright © 1962 by The Macmillan Company. Reprinted by permission of The Macmillan Company.

Excerpts from *Sinclair Lewis: an American Life* by Mark Schorer, copyright © 1961 by Mark Schorer. Used by permission of McGraw-Hill Book Company.

Excerpts from Edmund Wilson's *Europe Without Baedeker*, copyright © 1966 by Edmund Wilson. Reprinted by permission of Edmund Wilson and Farrar, Straus & Giroux.

Excerpts from *As Others See Us: The United States Through Foreign Eyes*, edited by Franz M. Joseph, copyright © 1959 by Princeton University Press. Reprinted by permission of Princeton University Press.

Excerpt from Robinson Jeffers' "Shine, Perishing Republic" in *The Selected Poetry of Robinson Jeffers*, copyright © 1959 by Robinson Jeffers. Reprinted by permission of Random House, Inc.

Excerpts from Allen Tate's "Ode to Our Young Pro-Consuls of the Air" in *Poems, 1922–1947*, copyright © 1948 by Charles Scribner's Sons. Reprinted by permission of Charles Scribner's Sons.

Excerpts from Ernest Hemingway: *Three Novels of Ernest Hemingway: The Sun Also Rises. A Farewell to Arms. The Old Man and the Sea*. Reprinted by permission of Charles Scribner's Sons.

Excerpts from Jacques Maritain's *Reflections on America*, copyright © 1958 by Charles Scribner's Sons. Reprinted by permission of Charles Scribner's Sons.

Excerpts from Malcolm Cowley's *Exile's Return*, copyright © 1951 by The Viking Press, Inc. Reprinted by permission of The Viking Press, Inc.

Excerpts from André Siegfried's *America at Mid-Century*, copyright © 1955 by Harcourt, Brace & World, Inc. Reprinted by permission of Harcourt, Brace & World, Inc.

CONTENTS

↩ INTRODUCTION ↪

The transit of culture across the Atlantic has long been a concern of intellectual historians. From the founding of the first settlements to the present, it has been a continuing process, fascinating as it has modified from era to era, bringing mutations and enrichment. Various phases and facets of this process have been the subject of monographs, but overall syntheses and evaluations have been relatively few—hence the importance of this fine historical survey. Drawing upon the monographic literature, and frequently going beyond it to provide insights and observations of his own, Robert O. Mead has written an overview which contributes to our understanding of the European cultural legacy to America. It is notable for its breadth, its erudition, and especially its felicity of style.

Mead was an essayist of rare talent who poured his life experience into this book. He was himself representative of that generation of young Americans who discovered Europe after the Second World War. A graduate of George Washington University who earned his Ph.D. in European cultural history at Columbia University, Mead spent the 1950's in Europe, first as an assistant director of the Salzburg Seminar in American Studies, and then as director of the program for American students at the University of Paris. At Salzburg, with charm, wit, and unending generosity and enthusiasm, he helped introduce young Europeans to American culture—and in the process came himself to attain an unusual knowledge and appreciation for European civilization. During his years in Paris, Mead was a warm, sympathetic, and expert guide to Americans in search of a French education. Later, in the United States, he further employed these same qualities to introduce European students to American university life. Through these years his knowledge of European culture and its significance to America grew, and his judgments matured. It is tragic that his death, while this book was in process of publication, has cut short his career of service and scholarship. In consequence, this book stands as a memorial to his unique qualities of mind, warmth of heart, and largeness of spirit. Mead was in his own career an embodiment of much that has been best in the Atlantic legacy.

Frank Freidel

July 11, 1969

ATLANTIC LEGACY

ᮠ CULTURAL WAVES ᮡ

*Et c'est la Mer qui vint à nous sur les degrés de
pierre du drame:*

*Avec ses Princes, ses Régents, ses Messagers vêtus
d'emphase et de métal, ses grands Acteurs aux yeux
crevés et ses Prophètes à la chaine, ses Magiciennes
trépignant sur leurs socques de bois, la bouche
pleine de caillots noirs, et ses tributs de Vierges
cheminant dans les labours de l'hymne.*

*Avec ses Pâtres, ses Pirates et ses Nourrices
d'enfants-rois, ses vieux Nomades en exil et ses
Princesses d'élégie, ses grandes Veuves silencieuses
sous les cendres illustres, ses grands Usurpateurs
de trônes et Fondateurs de colonies lointaines, ses
Prébendiers et ses Marchands, ses grands Con-
sessionaires de provinces d'étain, et ses grands
Sages voyageurs à dos de buffles de rizière.*

—Saint-John Perse*

Five centuries of cultural waves have washed each side of the Atlantic, each
new tide bringing or taking away new ideas, ideas changed by the sea water.
Ideas and people sift back and forth, storm-tossed by revolutions and persecutions. In the holds of great cargo ships are crates with innocent labels:
Coca-Cola, General Motors, Dior, Haig's. Ships are laden with soldiers or
students, tourists bearing cameras and *How-to-Say-It in Five Languages,* professors and intellectuals in cabin-cribbed and confined class. Prime ministers
and diplomatic secretaries, elegant and evasive, worried and harried, sail in
first-class loneliness to and fro with little parcels of ideas and prejudices.

The sea is contained by both Europe and America. Should one dike
crumble, the other is left high and dry. As Europe goes, morally and spiritually, so goes the world. Europeans and Americans are locked together like
Dante's lovers in purgatory's miasmic swamp. Donne wrote:

* From *Oeuvre Poétique II,* copyright © 1960 by Editions Gallimard. Reprinted
by permission of the publisher.

. . . should chance or envies Art
Divide these two, whom nature scarce did part?
Since both have th' enflaming eyes
And both the loving heart,

Water stincke soon, if in one place they bide,
And in the vast sea are more putrifi'd:
But when they kisse one banke, and leaving this
Never looke backe, but the next banke does kisse,
Then are they purest; Change is the nursery
of unsicke, joy, life, and charity.

The fresh salt air of the Atlantic clears our clouded heads and purifies our thinking. Ideas surface like whitecaps bursting here and there on the heavy swell of the sea. Our European-American relationship becomes a family problem.

Daily we chew over the old rags of prejudice and rage, of envy and scorn, and we are left with a bitter aftertaste. America is young, vigorous, progressive; Europe is old, tired, decadent. America is raw and crude and innocent and puerile and susceptible; Europe is dark and profound and wise and wary and scheming. America is practical, experimental, promising; Europe is helpless, reactionary, doomed. America and Europe are still shrouded in the mists of their own delusions and for their common good must thoughtfully chart a course into the waves of the future.

The United States has been torn between its own oceanic insularity and its messianic dreams. America has a tradition of escape and outward success —it escaped from Europe and succeeded in achieving its own nationhood, but its absolutist national morality led it again and again to make efforts to convince the world overseas of its message. It is frustrated and retreats when the letter is not read. Americans either flee from the world or embrace it too ardently. The American credo is difficult to define and harder still for others to understand or appreciate, for the American tradition is unique and non-revolutionary. Europe has emerged from its social revolutions, while Asia and Africa are now undergoing them.

Tocqueville did not overestimate the contribution of natural riches or industrial wealth to the success of American liberal democracy but, pointing equally to the ideal climate and natural wealth of South America, noted that no other nations on the earth were more miserable. He saw the American democratic success as mainly due to laws but more particularly to customs.[1] We may wonder whether the American experience is of any use to Africa or Asia, or even Europe for that matter. Joyce Cary's *An American Visitor* shows the damage that can be done by an unthinking American in Africa by exercising well-intentioned but misguided authority. What may be good for General Motors may be good for America, but it does not follow that what is good for America is good for the rest of the world.

The American is essentially not a revolutionist because he believes that he is already on the right track. Seventeenth-century William Stoughton in his *New England's True Interest* wrote that "if any people have been lifted up to advantages and privileges we are the people. . . . We have had the eye and hand of God working everywhere for our good. Our adversaries have had their rebukes and we have had our encouragements and a wall of fire around us." The American likes to think that he is moving along with destiny, much as Communists think they have all the right solutions to human problems. Americans think that they constantly improve as they go along, much as Franklin Roosevelt tinkered under the hood during the Depression. American idealism is nothing if it does not bring about a practical transformation.

The Americans did not have to *écraser l'infâme* with their revolution; in fact, 1776 was not a real social revolution; it is better described as a war of independence and as a continuation of European intrigue after the Seven Years War. Royal governors were simply replaced by elected governors. Tocqueville wrote in his introduction on the United States:

there is no country in the world where the great social revolution of which I speak seems to have almost its natural limits; it took place there in a simple and easy manner, or, rather, we can say that the country has seen the results of the democratic revolution which is happening amongst us, without having had the revolution itself.

If feudalism was not present in America, it was impossible to return to it after the Revolution. America had no Metternich or Charles X. It is an interesting sidelight that both Marx and Engels explicitly noted that America escaped the feudal stage of development, but that America might even so achieve a socialism similar to Europe's. "America," said Tocqueville, "has least in its breast the germs of revolution." America escaped feudalism on the right and escaped socialism on the left. The American liberal character could forge a path right down the middle in what came to be known as the "American Way of Life."

Americans had all been uprooted from their several soils and ancestries and plunged into one vortex whirling in a space otherwise emtpy. America had to be made before it could be lived in, which created the pioneer, the booster, the gambler, and the hot pistol. American frontier freedom gave a personal detachability. The American is easily lavish with money, for if you lose all, you are still yourself. The American is cheerfully experimental without need for critics or carping advice. The American copes with novel situations and has enough optimism to start anew in the face of failure, to hit the road. America received a kind of selection from Europe: all the colonists and frontiersmen were voluntary exiles from labor laws, corn laws, and poor laws which had filled the highways and byways with mendicants and vagrants in the painful changing of the old European order. An act of the English Parliament of 1663 authorized justices of the peace to send rogues, vagrants, and "sturdy beggars" to the American colonies. The colonies vigorously protested, but were ignored by the Crown.

The fortunate, the deeply rooted, and the lazy remained at home; the dissatisfied or adventurous or unwanted crossed the Atlantic. A lady of the French court sent a young man to Benjamin Franklin with the recommendation that "if you have in your country the secret of reforming a detestable creature who is the chief torment of his family, I beg you to send over the bearer of this letter. You will be performing a miracle worthy of yourself." [2] The young man went over, fought, and died during the Revolution. The Golden West was glorified to induce migration; America was exaggerated to Europe; Zenith had to be better than New York, and New York must be better than Paris or London.

The English, Dutch, and Swedes had begun to form this American character in the seventeenth century, followed by the German and the Scotch-Irish in the eighteenth century. The Scotch-Irish fed through Pennsylvania, and, not content with staying in the already settled towns, pushed to the foothills of the Alleghenies and the Blue Ridge Mountains and established a frontier line from Massachusetts to the Carolinas. The Scotch-Irish always remained in the forefront of the westward-moving frontier, real pioneers.

In 1683 religious refugees from the Rhineland established Germantown, near Philadelphia. They were followed by Mennonites, Dunkers, and Moravians. With characteristic German zeal, they established rich farms, excellent schools and colleges, and a lively press. After the devastation of the Palatinate during the French and Spanish wars, many peasants came to the colonies sponsored by Queen Anne. The revocation of the Edict of Nantes in 1685 started a large migration of French Huguenots to South Carolina, Virginia, New York, Rhode Island, and Massachusetts. Irish Catholics joined their fellow English Catholics in Maryland. By the time of the Revolution, American cities had become the most cosmopolitan in the world.

By 1776 there was a well-delineated American conscience, to be further defined by the revolutionary heroes. In 1774 the *Gazette de France* noted that

navigators who have studied the northern continent state that an inner spirit for liberty is inseparable from the soil, the skies, the forests and the lakes which keeps this vast and still new and from resembling other parts of the universe. They are persuaded that every European transported to those climates will contract this particular character.

Americans did not become simple rustics enjoying their liberty. A spirit of cosmopolitanism continued, as may be seen from some random examples. Benjamin Thompson (Count Rumford) married Lavoisier's widow and was offered command of West Point and the post of inspector-general of the army by John Adams, but he refused, both to stay in Europe as a British knight and count of the Holy Roman Empire and to continue his scientific research. Benjamin West was president of the Royal Academy for almost thirty years. Before going to London, West had first spent four years in Rome supported by Lord Hamilton; he was also under the influence of Winckelmann. Arriving in London, George III gave him a studio in the palace and read Livy to him as he painted. The monarch named him historical painter to the Crown and gave him a pension of a thousand pounds a year. He was well liked by the artistic colony and was the friend of Horace Walpole, Burke, and Samuel Johnson, the same Dr. Johnson who could say at the outbreak of the Revolution that he was willing to think well of all mankind except an American. Among West's students were Copley, the Peales, Gilbert Stuart, Trumbull, Washington Allston, and Thomas Sully.

The international career of John Trumbull is particularly interesting as an example of transatlantic cultural exchange. Son of the governor of Connecticut, he was aide-de-camp to Washington, and then deputy adjutant-general to Gates' army. After an argument with John Hancock, he resigned his post and returned to paint in Boston, meanwhile petitioning the British secretary of state to be allowed to study under West in London. The petition was approved; he left for France, where Franklin gave him a letter of introduction to West.

Shortly after his arrival in England he was arrested as a spy, in 1780, as a reprisal for the execution of Major André. He spent a pleasant eight months in a room of the warden's house, and his guard served as butler and valet. Burke and Charles James Fox came to visit him. He was finally released, with West and Copley bearing surety for him, and returned to America via Holland, but failed to achieve success with his painting. Connecticut, his father told him, was not Athens, so Trumbull went again to London to work in West's studio.

At Jefferson's invitation West went to Paris in 1785 and stayed at his home. For several years he returned to Paris to paint Franco-American revolutionary heroes and to perfect his knowledge of painting and architecture. At the time of the outbreak of the French Revolution he declined Jefferson's offer to become his secretary, went to New York for three unprofitable years, and then returned to London as secretary to John Jay. After the conclusion of the Jay Treaty he stayed on to carry out its execution. In 1804 he returned to New York, but the Embargo Act four years later cut off his patrons' resources, so he again went back to London and reestablished his clientele there. With the Treaty of Ghent and the close of the Napoleonic Wars, Trumbull returned to the United States to spend the rest of his life quietly as president of the American Academy of Fine Arts and with a lifetime annuity from Yale University.

John Singleton Copley, after a year's study in Rome, settled in England to become one of the most celebrated painters of the day; he became a member of the Royal Academy as a result of his historical paintings, such as *The Death of Chatham,* which was inspired by West's *Wolfe.* His son became lord chancellor with the title of Lord Lynhurst.

Gilbert Stuart returned to the United States after seventeen years in England. Thomas Jefferson and Benjamin Franklin, as related below, became well-known international figures. Benjamin Rush, founder of American medicine and signer of the Declaration, studied in England, Scotland, and Paris.

Book culture was the principal culture available to colonial America, and America treasured its books as much as a medieval monastery treasured its palimpsests. From the very beginning of colonial life, learning was highly prized. Between 1630 and 1690 there were as many university graduates of Oxford and Cambridge in New England as in old England. The colonial gentleman was cultured, corresponded with Europe, and sent his children to Europe to be educated. Not only the colonial Southern gentleman and the New England Puritans kept up the intellectual contact. The Roman Catholics of Maryland sent their children to the "English" schools on the Continent: Paris, Louvain, Douai, and Rome. The Quakers and Moravians through travel and correspondence maintained their Old World connections.

Talleyrand suggested in 1794 that a bank be set up in London with branches in continental Europe for American tourists—a sort of early American Express Company.

> It is easy to observe that they indulge more than ever in traveling, either to form commercial connections with Europe, or to enjoy the luxury and pleasure of the old world, or to imitate the English in the habit of completing by tours the education of all rich young men. Because of the position of America there are no short trips for an American; often they plan to tour several European countries.

This has a peculiarly contemporary ring.

The Atlantic coastal towns maintained a lively cosmopolitanism against the westward-moving frontier spirit. They imported learning, styles, ideas, social systems, and customs. From the tedium of colonial life Americans turned to Europe for fresh intellectual and mercantile supplies and kept up the idea that they were a part of European life, while the expanding Western frontier, thrust on its own resources, became ignorant and distrustful of the Atlantic-oriented Eastern cities. The frontier became more "American," less European, and the continued westward march tended to develop a cultural dichotomy in American life. The Midwest frequently showed little in common with the littoral Eastern states.

Sadly, Dutch and French cultural influences waned, the Dutch leaving in 1664 and the French after 1765. The *Evangeline* of Longfellow, for example, described the removal of the French Acadians to Louisiana to become "Cajuns." The Huguenots continued to emigrate to America, often over five thousand a year, but they were mostly absorbed into the predominantly Anglo-Saxon cultural mores. The French *coureur des bois* vanished from the American scene, gone with the Indian to the Happy Hunting Ground, the cowboy to the Last Roundup, leaving behind only a legend.

The disappearance of the patroons from the Hudson River Valley spelled the final disappointment to those yearning for an aristocratic estate. Thomas Hutchinson's hope for a local aristocracy was dashed by Samuel Adams and the Boston Tea Party, and Hutchinson's correspondence on this subject was scathingly exposed by Benjamin Franklin. It is true that there were men such as Daniel Leonard, loving aristocratic luxury and ostentation, who argued from Hobbes and ignored the Revolution of 1688 in his articles signed "Massachusettensis," but he wound up as a judge in isolated Bermuda. Most American Tories were expelled or emigrated to Canada, the West Indies, or England. Out of a population of 3.5 million over 100,000 Tories left the United States, and despite the 1783 treaty with England their property was confiscated. Thus the possibility of an American aristocracy virtually disappeared with the Revolution and in the South received its *coup de grâce* with the Civil War.

The Southern gentlemen described in Thackeray's *The Virginian* had aristocratic pretensions, but they were only agrarian capitalists. Henry Adams wrote of them that they were "stupendously ignorant of the world. As a class, the cotton-planters were mentally one-sided, ill-balanced, and provincial to a degree rarely known," and from them one could "learn nothing but bad temper, bad manners, poker, and treason." [3] The Southern "aristocrat" still continues to chew on the cud of a fictionalized past, and it is a mistake to read into the Civil War a crusade of roundhead New England Puritans against the flower of Southern chivalry. Likewise, the industrial capitalist of the nineteenth and twentieth centuries had to buy his

daughter a European title or himself a European castle to satisfy the aristocratic desire. In American society one could not be avowedly antidemocratic;
one could only hope to put the brake on democracy's forward march. Both
Emerson and Twain, for example, loved aristocracy secretly but praised
democracy openly. Twain wrote that "there are princes which I cast in the
Echte princely mold, and they make me regret—again—that I am not a
prince myself. It is not a new regret but a very old one. I have never been
properly and humbly satisfied with my condition." If he liked aristocracy
he illogically hated monarchy: "Monarchy? Why is it out of date? It
belongs to the state of culture that admires a ring in your nose, a head full
of feathers and your belly painted blue." [4]

The lack of an American aristocracy became a problem for the Whig
liberals who had only windmills to joust at, no Bolingbroke or Bossuet to
criticize. The aristocratic pretensions of Alexander Hamilton seemed fraudu-
lently ludicrous to John Adams. Hamilton was but "the bastard brat of a
Scotch pedlar." According to Adams, "talent, birth, virtues, services, sacri-
fices" did not count in American society, only money. Significantly, universal suffrage was introduced in America long before it was in other
nations, and the public school system tended to enforce equality, to resist
domination by any elite. American society was not to be based on inherited
qualities of birth, class, or race, and the consequent emphasis of equality
primarily stressed achievement—the American race to succeed.

Europe never lost interest in America nor in its American cousins.
While Americans were studying Locke (eventually they were to become
absolutist Lockeans par excellence) and Montesquieu, Europeans were fascinated by the new mythology of America. The American was the closest thing
to the *Bon Sauvage* of Rousseau, developing in perfect simplicity and innocence in his virgin forests. The image of American naiveté and simple good
nature was to be further fixed in the European mind by Chateaubriand's
Atala, Natchez, and his *Voyage en Amérique.* America presented a "miraculous picture,"and, Europeans would learn what liberty can do for happiness
and the dignity of man when it is not separated from religious ideas, and
which is at the same time intelligent and holy. Religion was on the side
of democracy in America, while in Europe it served reaction. As Tocqueville
noted, European religion repulsed the very equality which it loved and cursed
liberty as an adversary instead of taking it by the hand to sanctify its efforts.

Europeans tended to overromanticize religious and social freedom in
America, particularly after 1776. If America was in an idyllic state of

nature from the very start, as depicted by Rousseau, how did it then suddenly become the land of social emancipation? How could America wrest its liberty through revolution if it already had it? The habit of romanticizing the Americans was continued in Europe with the rage for the works of James Fenimore Cooper, which showed the resourceful pioneer and the Indian brave on the great frontier.

The image of America which was fixed by Rousseau, Chateaubriand, and Cooper lives on as but one aspect of the many-faceted America we know to exist: wholesome and pure, high-minded, adventurous, and curious about the world of unspoiled nature, but also simple and uniform. Other images of America were to be laid on in successive layers, but this one continues as fresh as it was during the first days when it was blown across the Atlantic. Europeans had become Americans in the New World, a world new with promise but old with the culture they brought with them. Europe and America itself were now aware that while still cousins across the water, America was steering along a different tack and under its own sail. This was confirmed by the American Revolution. However, the Revolution, once effected, did not mean the permanent separation of the New World from the Old.

What had happened to America by 1776? Three and a half million people spread along the Atlantic coast in thirteen autonomous colonies only loosely linked to each other began a guerilla war for independence. An American character had deveoped—however ill-defined—that included the Puritan Yankee, the Southern plantation owner, and the Pennsylvania Quaker. Patrick Henry said at the Continental Congress that one did not feel Virginian, or New Englander, or Marylander, but American.

It is likely that the American Poor Richard wanted a revolution to overthrow an older order and build a heavenly city on its ruins? He saw things in a different light; his lists of grievances always spoke of the novelties being imposed from London, and he wanted a return to the rights he had traditionally enjoyed as an Englishman. Although Rousseau influenced American revolutionary thinking, the American revolutionaries did not use him as an argument for political inspiration. Montesquieu played a greater role in the American Revolution than he did in the French Revolution, which relied more on Rousseau. The tenets of the physiocrats, who loved representing agricultural America as a place where the soil was the single source of wealth, were set aside for the later rationalism of free trade. The American revolutionaries relied on the bedrock of Locke, Blackstone, and Coke, and the revolt was justified in legal terms and legal precedent. This same spirit became fixed in the Constitution with the principle of *certiorari,* which became the legal guarantee of the democratic idea. Of the thirteen original states, eleven adopted new constitutions that were only revisions of their colonial charters, while Connecticut and Rhode Island maintained their old charters without any revision at all. Later states coming into the Union based their constitutions on the earlier ones.

Like loyal Englishmen, Americans blamed the King's ministers for the errors committed, much as the French thought Louis XVI was misguided by corrupt court advisers. The English Parliament was not attacked in the Declaration, and until Tom Paine appeared the sovereignty of the Crown was not very much questioned. Americans were not anti-English but were wounded by the attitude of perfidious Albion. The assembled colonists at Albany in 1754 thought only of fighting the French and Indians as loyal British subjects. Lawyer John Adams defended in court the English leaders of the Boston Massacre, and Jefferson sought conciliation after Saratoga. Thus Burke could support the American Revolution and shudder with horror at the French a few years later. The American revolutionary war cry was a call for return to traditional rights and liberties. It was a revolution with a Puritan refrain, touched by the Enlightenment, but not so much so that Americans had to écraser l'infâme. Feudalism had made European history, in a sense, prehistory for America.

Although the Declaration of Independence does not speak of the traditional rights of British subjects, Americans had been arguing such rights for years. In the Declaration they wanted to make a universal appeal to mankind to find a self-justification, to base their actions on self-evident acts. Jefferson, in writing the Declaration, said that he sought "not to find out new principles or new arguments, never before thought of, not merely to say things which had never been said before, but to place before mankind the common sense of the subject."

The Declaration of Independence reads much like Locke's Second Treatise on Government, the apology for the Revolution of 1688. The Revolution in America was not even utilitarian: in 1776 Bentham was attacking the revered Blackstone, that talmudic judge who had provided the chosen American people with the legal arguments to go marching into the promised land. Had not Blackstone written that "the law of nature is superior in obligation to any other"?

The past had been good to America, and Puritan America with its sense of providential guidance did not scorn it as did a Bentham or a Voltaire. Not only had the past been good, but nature was bountiful and America was the land of milk and honey. What other country celebrates something like Thanksgiving? It is here that Rousseau's credo coincides with American thinking and American tradition in trusting in the goodness of nature and the natural goodness of man. His nature theory also falls in with the sensationalism of Locke's theory of understanding. The search for natural man could help find natural rights and laws best suited for particular men.

Likewise, Puritanism and deism could live side by side philosophically without discomfort. The paradise before the Fall is the same as the deist state of nature, and in the American dream they could both be easily transferred from the past to the future. Both seemed to promise a universal moral order.

Americans could achieve the heavenly city by enlightened progress and constant working toward perfection, a natural society pursuing happiness untainted by the original sin of feudalism. This is one of the taproots of modern American materialist thinking, for twentieth-century materialist technocracy has as its base the eighteenth-century idea of perfectability. If a god, other than deist, is needed to reenforce the argument, the Puritan ethic could be called in to support the spirit of capitalism. Even Tocqueville used the providential and naturalist argument which permitted the Americans to live free and equal. The professor of civics in *Middletown* is told to teach:

> The right to Revolution does not exist in America. We had our revolution 140 years ago, it is not necessary to have any revolution in this country.

and continues:

> No man can be a sound and sterling American who believes that force is necessary to assure the popular will. Americanism . . . emphatically means . . . that we have repudiated old European methods of settling domestic questions, and we have evolved for ourselves machinery by which revolution as a method of changing our life is outgrown, abandoned, outlawed.[5]

Today, as yesterday, Americans idealize virtue and deplore sin; there might be private sin, but there must be public morality. They have high hopes and feel betrayed when perfection is not achieved. They are convinced that with a maximum of goodwill and teamwork a utopia can be found around the corner. Americans believe in the perfectibility of this world through gradual improvement, yet not chiliastic like the Marxists. Americans constantly work in the Augean stables, which is less inspiring but does produce some forward movement.

Another Rousseauean strain entwined in the American character is certainly the General Will, which can as easily be the basis for popular dictatorship as for political democracy, of crushing 99 per cent majorities rolled up in Communist or Fascist countries, as well as Wilsonian plebiscites for self-determination or the "direct" democracy of De Gaulle. When combined with dynamic "Americanism," with the hundred-percenters's outlook, it imposes an overwhelming uniformity and conformity, a threat to valuable dissent and to the yeast of nonconformity which leavens the mass loaf. This is the dangerous dynamite of Rousseau to America and to Europe. Madison said this in the Federalist #51, and was echoed by Tocqueville: "If liberty is ever lost in America, it will be due to the omnipotence of the majority which will have brought the minority into despair," and what he reproached in American democratic government was not its apparent weakness but its inestimable force. "What repulses me the most in America is not the extreme liberty which reigns, but the little guarantee that one finds against tyranny."

In large measure America has a built-in safeguard against the General Will: it is a pluralist and federalist society. Rousseau declared that no particular organization should be allowed in the state. America abounds with clubs, societies, fraternities, pressure groups, unions, associations. Freedom of association is guaranteed by the Constitution. Such a guarantee is still lacking in many European countries, but for this there is a historic reason. "America is the one country in the world where the most use is made of association, and where this powerful means of action is applied to the greatest diversity of ends," said Tocqueville. In the United States, excepting the Know-Nothings, the Ku Klux Klan, and the Birchers, there are no secret organizations of great significance, as in Europe. American Freemasonry has a vastly different character from its European counterpart. The three and half million Masons in America wear their rings and parade their lodge banners, while the one and half million in the rest of the word tend to great secrecy.

In Europe an organization pretends to represent the majority frustrated in the free expression of its rights. A contemporary example was the French rebel organization in Algeria. Despite its ideal, which coincides with the American spirit, there were no *Carbonari* in the United States, and there were few Americans like George Bancroft ready to support the *Carbonari* in Europe. Freedom of association offers a pet cock against revolt; there may be factions but no conspiracies. Tocqueville saw associations in Europe as groups thrown together to take to the battlefields as the only way of impressing their convictions, for minority parties in Europe are so far away from the majority that they seek to conquer and not to convince. In America, however, where opinions differ largely by nuances, association is not dangerous. If associations in the United States pretended, like those in Europe, that they were in the majority, they would try to change the law themselves instead of demanding reform. In Europe they pretend to represent the majority and consequently to legitimize revolution in the triumph of oppressed rights. The French Revolution forbade collective organizations by a law of 22 Germinal, Year XI, which found its way into Articles 414 and 415 of the Penal Code. Syndical organization was not permitted until 1884.

America has a diversity in its associations which affirms apparent uniformity and surface conformity. Whereas the French and English respect the individual as a person, the American is known to a great extent by his associations and seeks his identity through his union, his club, his fraternal order, his professional society. The average American is a "joiner," as Thoreau and Lawrence both noted, but is his identity changed by the association? Who can tell the difference between a Lion, an Elk, and a Moose?

The Americans made a revolution in the name of tradition. "No men," said Lord Acton, "were less revolutionary in spirit than the founders of the American Constitution. They had made a revolution in the name of Magna Carta and the Bill of Rights: they were penetrated by a sense of the dangers incident to a democracy." John Dickinson, an able jurist who spent three years in London's Middle Temple, could say of the Stamp Act, "This is all an innovation, a most dangerous innovation." In his *Letters from a Farmer in Pennsylvania* he put forth the British Whig constitutional argument, particularly that of Pitt. He edited the Articles of Confederation and was in the Constitutional Convention of 1788; he favored political rule only by property owners, yet could not in conscience vote for the Declaration of Independence.

The Constitution that was written went back to the New England Covenants and to the Mayflower Compact, as well as to 1688, by which sovereignty was delegated by the people. It was not like the constitution-writing of the rationalist Europeans nor of the utilitarian Bentham, who in his later years had little packets of constitutions, bills of rights, and basic laws ready to be shipped off at the news of each Latin American revolution. Condorcet was wrong when he wrote that the American Constitution "has not grown, but was planned," and that it "took no weight of centuries but was put together mechanically in a few years." John Adams noted simply on his margin, "Fool! Fool!" Condorcet had a more intuitive eye when he applauded the Declaration of Independence. For him it was not enough that the rights of man

> should be written in the books of the philosophers and in the hearts of virtuous men; it is necessary that ignorant or weak men should read them in the example of a great people. America has given us this example. The act which declared its independence is a simple and sublime exposition of those rights so sacred and so long forgotten.[6]

Herbert Spencer at the close of the nineteenth century made the same mistake about the Constitution when he asserted that the Amricans had a ready-made paper constitution which would take a long time to adjust to the actualities of life. The Constitution is a constant living readjustment around a set of historic guidelines, and becomes itself the instrument for social change.

Anthony Trollope noted on his visit to the United States during the Civil War that the Americans

> refer all their liberties to the old charters which they held from the mother-country. They rebelled, as they themselves would seem to say, and set themselves up as a separate people, not because the mother-country had refused to them by law sufficient liberty and sufficient self-control, but because the mother-country infringed the liberties and powers of self-control which she herself had given.[7]

The Americans had the revolutionary power to change all the laws and set up any utopian theory they wished when English rule was overthrown. Instead, they held to the common law, to the precedents of English courts, and to their earlier charters and constitutions.

The proceedings of the drafting of the Constitution were kept secret, then given to Washington, who handed on the three manuscript volumes to the State Department; they were not published until 1819. Of the sixty-five delegates, only fifty-five signed the final report. With the upper class firmly in power, the Constitution was so conservative a document that it took the Bill of Rights to get it accepted. The mercantilist Hamiltonians and conservative Federalists had won out, at least temporarily, over the West. The Jay Treaty was forced through in spite of much opposition, and the Alien and Sedition Acts helped to hold the conservative Federalists in power.

We should not underestimate the influence of the Enlightenment on the American Revolution, but the Enlightenment was the contemporary and fashionable veneer on the solid oak of Puritanism, Locke, and Montesquieu, even though many of the age-old questions were answered as being "self-evident," "natural," and "self-inherent."

⌒⌒⌒

The Americans did not go back into the forest primeval wearing bear-skins to look for constitutions under logs, as Gierke saw the origin of the German corporation. They turned to classic Athens and Rome, classicism being but another form of traditionalism. They enshrined their Constitution and institutions in new Greek and Roman temples and shrouded their revolutionary heroes in togas. Even those who wanted to go further than the revolution had carried them remained true to pattern; Daniel Shays was not Gracchus Babeuf but rather a homespun Cincinnatus. The American Revolution had its definite limits, unlike the French. The Whiskey Rebellion was firmly put down by the Federalists.

In many ways Tom Paine, whom Theodore Roosevelt was to describe as a "filthy little atheist," belongs more to Europe than to America. America was too commonsensical for him; the "citizen of the world" was better off in the French Revolution where he could play his rationalism and deism to the limit, perfectly in the French spirit of pushing logic to the point where it became illogical. A doctrinaire libertarian and deist, he had come to the colonies at age thirty-seven as a failure and was aided by Ben Franklin who helped him get a job on the *Pennsylvania Magazine*. In France he was a Girondin and was put in prison by the Convention. Paine as a humanitarian idealist had the Voltairean knack of caustic sally and thrust. Much of his *Rights of Man* rings true to American ears today: it contains plans for universal education, abolition of poverty, reform of criminal law, old-age pensions, reduction of armaments, and international peace, all similar to Ben Franklin's typical ideology (the latter included a proposal for an early kind of Marshall Plan for New Zealand and an international "United Party for Virtue"). Tom Paine's last days in the United States after his return from the French Revolution were sad ones.

Jefferson, likewise, showed an American spirit when he wanted to establish an early NATO to combat the menace of the Barbary pirates of Algiers, Tunis, and Tripoli. France agreed, and he then solicited Portugal, Naples, and the two Sicilies, Venice, Denmark, and Sweden to establish a cruising force along the coast to force the pirates from the sea. There was to be a treaty with the Knights of Malta to use a harbor in Sicily. Lafayette was so enthusiastic that he wanted to be commander of the squadron.

Joel Barlow was as spirited as Paine and believed that the collective interest should suppress individual egoism and privilege. He had spent seventeen years in Europe and was a Jacobin during the French Revolution. His "Letter to the National Convention of France" of 1792 was concerned with the expression of the majority and put the people on guard against a faction acting in the name of the people. Barlow finished Volney's *Les ruines, ou méditations sur les révolutions des empires,* which Jefferson had begun to revise and translate, but he thought it then impolitic to acknowledge Jefferson as president. Barlow ended his American diplomatic career when he died near Cracow on a mission to the Russian emperor for the signature of an American treaty of peace and commerce.

After the Peace of Paris of 1763 the French had become rapidly pro-

American. The Declaration of Independence aroused great enthusiasm when news of it arrived in Paris in August, 1776. This culminated in the master-work of the Vergennes-Franklin Treaty of 1778. Vergennes was ready to declare war against England, but the King of Spain would not agree to join France.

Franklin, profiting by this spirit, had made a large cultural impact in Europe. He had visited England in 1757–1762 and in 1764–1775, was already known as a scientist. He achieved a wide reputation as humanist, moralist, economist, and then as a statesman-philosopher. His *Bonhomme Richard* was a sensation. It was recommended as a textbook during the French Revolution and by Dupont de Nemours to Jefferson for American schools. His maxims were compared to Bacon's and La Fontaine's.

Franklin had spent ten of the twenty years preceding the Revolution in England, first trying to get the Penns to agree to a Royal Charter for Pennsylvania, then also as colonial agent for Georgia, New Jersey, and Massachusetts. His negotiations were unfruitful, and he wrote at the end of 1768 "I do not find that I have gained any point, in either country, except that of rendering myself suspected by my impartiality; in England of being too much of the American, and in America of being too much an Englishman." [8] Despite all his efforts to head off the catastrophe, Franklin met with little success in England. He was the friend of Burke and Chatham, of Priestley and Hume, of Adam Smith and Alexander Carlyle. He received honorary doctorates from St. Andrews and Oxford and became a Fellow of the Royal Society of Science. As late as 1774 there was even a thought of forming a ministry of Pitt, Shelbourne, and Franklin to stave off the crisis, but Franklin insisted on an autonomous American Congress in Philadelphia, under the king, which would collaborate with the English Parliament.

In 1767 and 1769 he visited France, where, he said, he was robbed more politely than in England. He met Quesnay and the physiocrats and gave up his mercantilist ideas, which he had gotten largely from William Petty. He maintained his correspondence with French intellectual leaders, and many visited him in London. Franklin returned to America in 1775 with the idea that some kind of federal union of the colonies, Canada, the West Indies, and Ireland under the Crown might still be possible. The Continental Congress debated the idea but it was not voted on. He was named postmaster-general of the colonies, which enabled him to circulate Tom Paine's *Common Sense* through his postal agents. He became at the same time a member of the Committee of Secret Correspondence to gather support for the American cause in England, France, Holland, and Spain.

The Committee had sent Silas Deane, a Connecticut merchant, to France to negotiate a commercial treaty and to win France to the colonists' point of view. While he was able to obtain arms, munitions, and supplies for the Burgoyne campaign and to enlist De Kalb, Lafayette, Steuben, and Pulaski, a greater effort was needed. Franklin and Arthur Lee were directed in 1776 to go to Paris to aid Deane.

When Franklin arrived in Quiberon Bay on the *Reprisal* in 1776 the news quickly spread through France. He had thrown his wig in the ocean and came as the plain American. He *looked* American, whereas other emissaries looked English to the French. The new king and his court were under the sway of the *"économistes"* and the *"philosophes,"* who became well known to Franklin: Vergennes, Turgot, Malesherbes, Maurepas, Mirabeau, and Raynal. The La Rochefoucaulds and the Noailles (one of whom, Adrienne, married Lafayette when she was thirteen and he was sixteen) were won to the American cause.

Franklin remained nine years in France, the simple Quaker in the beaver hat, the unwigged philosopher representing republican virtues, carrying a cane instead of a sword. At the age of eighty he taught his grandson to swim the Seine at Passy, going from bank to bank as he earlier used to swim nude in the Thames. Portraits and medallions of him were everywhere; as he wrote to his daughter,

> The number sold are incredible. These with the pictures, busts and prints (of which copies are spread everywhere), have made your father's face as well known as that of the moon, so that he durst not do anything that would oblige him to run away, as his phiz would discover him wherever he should venture to show it.[9]

No republican, Louis XVI gave the Comtesse Diane de Polignac an elegant chamber pot with Franklin's portrait on the inside bottom. When things were going badly during the American Revolution, Franklin would say "Ca ira, ça ira," and this became a favorite song of the French during their own revolution. Later the King gave him a diamond-encrusted portrait of himself. The American Congress awarded him nothing, not even appointments for his son Temple, nor grandson Bache.

Beyond the personal connections he developed with the court and salons, *philosophes* and physiocrats, Franklin led a constant propaganda for American ideals. He installed a printing press in his house at Passy where he printed his bagatelles and much of his autobiography.

Vergennes had made Deane work through Beaumarchais, who set up a fictitious trading company, Hortalez et Cie. He had obtained one million francs from the King and another million from the Spanish government. Franklin was able to obtain a total of eighteen million francs, plus Spanish contributions, a French army under Lafayette (age nineteen), and a French fleet under de Grasse which consummated the Revolution. It was a prestigious diplomatic effort carried out almost single-handedly, for Arthur Lee was disliked and quarrelsome and Deane spoke no French. As the Vicomte d'Houtetot aptly said: "Though America's destiny lies in his hand, like a true sage he drinks with our band." Lee was recalled, the Spanish court had refused to receive him, and he had gotten no official recognition in Berlin. Deane was replaced by John Adams, but he was disliked by Louis XVI and was sent to Holland. It was inevitabe that Adams would dislike Franklin, but he admitted that Franklin's reputation was "more universal than that of Leibniz or Newton, Frederick or Voltaire; and his character more beloved or esteemed than any or all of them." [10] As a universalist Franklin saw the difference between America and Europe only in a political or economic light. The basic eighteenth-century cultural credos remained the same, and consequently Franklin could carry on alone, enjoying the respect of France and the confidence of his country.

Paris greeted the news of Yorktown with fireworks. Yet what could this mean to Franklin, who earlier had striven so mightily to preserve Crown and colonies? There is the story that Edward Gibbon and Franklin happened to stay at the same inn somewhere between Paris and Nantes and Franklin invited him to his table; Gibbon refused to converse with a "revolted subject." Franklin simply replied that when Gibbon got around to writing the decline and fall of the British Empire that he would be pleased to furnish him with ample material on the subject. Franklin was the combination of Rousseau and Voltaire, the noble savage and the *philosophe,* the apotheosis of the simple New World and the sage of the Old. Undoubtedly American in spirit, he was an international figure, and his rationalism carried the day on both sides of the water. In this case, why should he, like Burke, have disapproved of the revolution in France, even though he had seen only its mildest form before his death in 1790? Perhaps because of older loyalties and former pleasures under the *ancien régime,* but perhaps more because he closed the eighteenth century, while the French Revolution promised to open the different world of the nineteenth. On his death the National Assembly heard Mirabeau's oration and declared a national mourning for three days.

Both Franklin and Washington became demigods to the French, although both had previously actively participated in the loss of French colonies in North America. The French monarchy added to its bankruptcy by financing American republicanism. While John Adams might be annoyed at the French adulation of Franklin, Lafayette could write to Washington that "the spirit of liberty is prevailing in this country at a great rate. Liberal ideas are cantering about from one end of the kingdom to the other," and Jefferson wrote:

> celebrated writers of France and England had already sketched good principles on the subject of government, yet the American Revolution seems to have awakened the thinking part of the French nation in general, from the sleep of despotism in which they were sunk. The officers, too, who had been to America, were mostly young men, less shackled by habit and prejudice, and more ready to assent to the suggestions of common sense, and feeling of common regrets, than others. They came back with new ideas and impressions.[11]

Of the French in general Jefferson reported that their friendship toward America was cordial and widesperad and "that is a kind of security for the friendship of the Ministers, who cannot in any country be uninfluenced by the voice of the people. To this we may add that it is to their interest as well as ours to mutiply the bonds of friendship between us." As the newest member of the diplomatic corps Jefferson was often the last to discuss his affairs wtih Vergennes, but Vergennes was anti-British and Jefferson could report, "I found the government entirely disposed to befriend us and to yield us every indulgence, not absolutely injurious to themselves." Lafayette was a "most valuable auxiliary" to Jefferson and interceded wherever possible. "His zeal is unbounded, and his weight with those in power, great. . . . He has a great deal of sound genius, is well remarked by the king, and rising in popularity. He has nothing against him but the suspicion of republican principles. . . ." [12]

Franklin, Adams, and Jefferson frequented the best salons of Paris, which had become more political than philosophical, and were closely engaged in the intellectual discussions of the day. Sarah Livingston (Mrs. John Jay) was an acknowledged leader of Parisian society in the 1780's. Jefferson established a friendship with the Duc de la Rochefoucauld and with his mother the Duchesse d'Anville, in whose circle moved D'Alembert, Condorcet, Morellet, Mably, Arnauld, Marmontel Turgot and the Baron de Grimm, minister of the duchy of Saxe-Gotha. Morellet submitted his work on the American colonies to Franklin for correction, and Philippe Mazzei's *Recherches historiques et politiques sur les Etats-Unis de l'Amérique septentrionale,* an answer to two works on America by Mably and Raynal, was avidly discussed between Rochefoucauld, Condorcet, and Jefferson. Jefferson also frequented the salons of Madame Geoffrin and Madame Helvetius (to whom Franklin proposed marriage), which were attended by La Harpe, the

Marquis de Chastellux, St. Lambert, Buffon, Madame Necker, Madame de Staël, and the Comtesse de Tessé, aunt of Lafayette and *dame d'honneur* to Marie Antoinette. In his autobiography Jefferson wrote, "I was much acquainted with the leading patriots of the Assembly. Being from a country which had successfully passed through a similar reformation, they were disposed to my acquaintance, and [had] some confidence in me." [13] In August 1789 he wrote to Madison:

> It is impossible to desire better dispositions toward us than prevail in this Assembly, our proceedings have been viewed as a model for them on every occasion; and though, in the heat of debate, even are generally supposed to contradict every authority urged by their opponents, ours has been treated like that of the Bible, open to explanation, but not to question. [14]

During the French Revolution Benjamin Constant wrote, "If things go badly here, I will take refuge in Virginia." Lafayette sent his son to Washington's care during the Terror and Madame de Staël wanted to go to the United States to avoid Bonaparte's tyranny.

The French wanted to establish a closer cultural relation with the new America. Brissot, a friend of Franklin, organized the bourgeois Gallo-American Society in 1787. He visited America and wrote of his experiences there. Jefferson arranged for Houdon to go to America, where he did a life mask and terra-cotta of Washington at Mount Vernon. Jefferson was a frequent visitor to his studio, and Houdon also did a bust of him. David was also a good friend. Quesnay proposed a French Academy of the Arts and Sciences of the United States of America which was to be estabilshed in Richmond, with branches in Baltimore, Philadelphia and New York and with affiliations with European universities. The project was supported by Lavoisier and Condorcet. The French court, the Academy of Beaux Arts, Lafayette, Beaumarchais, Houdon, Malesherbes, La Luzerne, Montalembert, and La Rochefoucauld were enthusiastic, as was Jefferson, who developed some of the scheme afterwards for the University of Virginia. Actual building of the French Academy in America was begun in 1786, but with the coming of the French Revolution support failed, and the building finally served to house the state convention to ratify the Constitution.

Jefferson arrived in this "vaunted scene" of Europe in 1784 at the time when republican America had an unvarnished reputation, when, as Paine later wrote, "the face of America, moral and political, stood fair and high in the world. The lustre of her revoluion extended to every individual; and to be a citizen of America gave a title of respect in Europe."

Franklin had played a more social role than Jefferson, who preferred to study architecture and agriculture. In a quick trip to Italy, Jefferson was highly pleased to pocket some rice to smuggle out for later cultivation and to learn the secret of making macaroni. While his French sympathies were well known, and were later to be used against him, Jefferson held out against American youth coming to Europe to study, unless perhaps to study medicine or modern languages. All else, he felt, was available in America. As for the American student in Europe, we can discern much of his attitude in the following, written in 1785:

> He acquires a fondness for European luxury and dissipation, and a contempt for the simplicity of his own country . . . he forms foreign friendships which will never be useful to him . . . he is led, by the strongest of all the human passions, into a spirit for female intrigue, destructive of his own and others' happiness, or a passion for whores, destructive of his health, and, in both cases, learns to consider fidelity to the marriage bed as an ungentlemanly practice, and inconsistant with happiness; he recollects the voluptuary dress and arts of the European women, and pities and despises the chaste affections and simplicity of those of his own country; he retains, through life, a fond recollection, and a hankering after those places, which were the scenes of his first pleasures and of his first connections; he returns to his own country, a foreigner. . . .[15]

Elsewhere, Jefferson wrote: "Of all the errors which can possibly be committed in the education of youth, that of sending them to Europe is the most fatal. . . ."[16] No American should go to Europe until he was thirty years old.

Jefferson's affection for the French matched his antipathy for the English, although he felt that London was handsomer than Paris, but not as attractive as Philadelphia. He believed that English hostility toward America was greater in 1786 than it was during the Revolution, and he was grateful for the wide ocean which protected America from the "contamination" of its parental stock. He wrote that the English were America's "natural enemies" and the "only nation on earth who wish us ill from the bottom of their souls. And I am satisfied that were our continent to be swallowed up by the ocean, Great Britain would be in a bonfire from one end to the other."

Thus Jefferson, Franklin, and other luminaries of the revolutionary era remained torn between America and Europe, trying to appease both mis-

tresses while maintaining an affection for each, and hoping that each would
stay out of the other's way.

The important lesson of the American Revolution for today is how such
"eggheads" of 1776 produced the necessary philosophy for the Revolution
and gave it a rational formation comprehensible to all people. The intellectual
guiding spirit was framed in the Declaration of Independence and in the
Constitution. After Lafayette returned from America he often said, "When
shall I see myself the Washington of France?" At his home in Paris he had
hung the Declaration of Independence alongside a place for the future
French declaration. He wore his American uniform at military reviews.
Equally important, this spirit was of the ideological moment of the Western
world. The Founding Fathers greatly influenced European thinkers across
the water who had similar spirits and aspirations, for ideas are frequently in
the air at the same time, like apple blossoms appearing all over on the same
spring day. The American example was enthusiastically felt and widely
applauded by Europeans of similar intellectual bent. Those who made the
Revolution of 1776 were in a minority and had the resolution to protest.
They did not follow the crowd but led them, and often the timid did not
want to follow.

The forming of these philosophical principles as a guide for today's
action became lost in Algerism and was seduced by what William James
called the "bitch-goddess" success. Americans now need a new set of
Federalist Papers to redefine their purpose and to show the new way, the
new frontier. Algerism is not sufficient to explain the American success
story. One Alger out of a hundred people automatically implies that there
are ninety-nine other failures. Dr. Pangloss has become an unsatisfactory
counselor. The Federalists were of the intelligentsia and carried out their
role, but beginning with Jacksonian nationalism and the absorbing conquest
of the frontier and industrialization, the political position of the American
intellectual declined until the appearance of Wilson, or perhaps Kennedy,
and is yet to be firmly reestablished.

Americans, then, are pushed and pulled by the force of the Atlantic,
rocked by messianic dreams of *outre-mer* while seeking at other times the
calm haven of isolation. The American character was formed by the immigration of countless nationalities and forged by revolution, and remained

cosmopolitan yet separate. With no real aristocracy, Americans held to the ideal of equality in the race to succeed as embodied in the legal principles of 1776 and the effort to achieve success was constantly to be carried out as a group enterprise.

NOTES

1. There are hundreds of editions of Tocqueville. All citations I have translated are from *De la démocratie en Amérique* (Paris: Charles Gosselin, 1835). The most convenient American edition is *Democracy in America* (Philip Bradley [ed.], 2 vols. [New York: Vintage Books, 1945]). Cf. also Tocqueville's *Journey to America* (J. P. Mayer [ed.], [New Haven: Yale University Press, 1960]).

2. Cited in Alfred O. Aldridge, *Franklin and his French Contemporaries* (New York: New York University Press, 1957), p. 172.

3. Henry Adams, *The Education of Henry Adams* (Boston: Houghton Mifflin Company, 1946), p. 100.

4. Albert Bigelow Paine (ed.), *Mark Twain's Notebook* (New York: Harper & Row, Publishers, 1935), p. 210.

5. Robert S. Lynd and Helen Merrill Lynd, *Middletown* (New York: Harcourt, Brace & World, Inc., 1929), p. 198.

6. *Oeuvres de Condorcet*, VIII, 11. Cited in Carl L. Becker, *The Declaration of Independence* (New York: Harcourt, Brace & World, Inc., 1922), p. 231.

7. Anthony Trollope, *North America,* Donald Smalley and Bradford Allen Booth (eds.) (New York: Alfred A. Knopf, Inc., 1951), pp. 219–20.

8. Benjamin Franklin, Letter of November 28, 1768, *Writings*, V, 182. Cited in R. B. Mowat, *Americans in England* (New York: Houghton Mifflin Company, 1935), p. 35.

9. Aldridge, p. 43.

10. Bernard Fay, *Franklin, the Apostle of Modern Times* (Boston: Little, Brown and Company, 1929), p. 458.

11. Cited in Marie Kimball, *Jefferson: The Scene of Europe, 1784–1789* (New York: Cowaid-McCann, Inc., 1950), p. 79.

12. *Ibid.,* p. 47.

13. *Ibid.,* p. 289.

14. *Ibid.,* p. 292.

15. Thomas Jefferson, Letter to J. Bannister, Jr., October 15, 1785. Cited in Philip Rahv (ed.), *The Discovery of Europe* (Boston: Houghton Mifflin Company, 1947), p. 60.

16. Kimball, p. 256.

⌒ THE ATLANTIC ∽
AND THE FRONTIER

Amerika, du hast es besser
Als unser Kontinent, das Alte
Hast kein verfallene Schloesser
Und keine Basalte.
Dich stoert nicht in Innern
Zu lebendiger Zeit
Unnuetzes Erinnern
Und vergeblicher Streit.

—Goethe

Washington declared in his *Farewell Address* that "Europe has a set of primary interests which to us have none or a very remote relation." Can we believe that with their revolution finished Americans wanted to hoist anchor and cut loose all ties with Europe, to make the American experiment alone and unhindered? Did Americans look only to the mountains and the rolling plains of the expanding West? In 1893 the great Midwest-American historian, Frederick Jackson Turner, maintained that the steady westward movement of the American frontier implied a gradual alienation from Europe, with all its influences, and predicated that a truly American democracy was the result of this westward movement. Europe hindered this development, he also maintained. "American democracy was born of no theorist's dream . . . it was not carried in the *Susan Constant* to Virginia, nor in the *Mayflower* to Plymouth. It came out of the American forest, and it gained strength each time it touched a new frontier." This was like the search of English constitutional historians for the English Constitution in German forests. Turner kept his eyes turned steadfastly west and feared to look at Europe; it was in the West that society was "formed on lines least like Europe. It is here, if anywhere, that American democracy will make a stand against a tendency to adjust to a European type." Thoreau wrote, "westward I go free. I must turn toward Oregon and not toward Europe."

The primeval West was America's Sherwood Forest, its Garden of Eden, but the pioneers also feared the howling wolves, and the howling is still heard today muffled in the American soul. Tallyrand wrote,

Each year, each day, the population makes the most interesting conquests in these wastes. It is a new and curious spectacle to observe the manner in which man takes possession of these empty and immense spaces, which await only his care to become fertile. It is especially piquant for the observer who, leaving one of the principal cities where the social state has reached perfection, traverses successively all degrees of civilization and industry, which steadily declines until he arrives at a formless and rough cabin built of newly cut trees, the debris from which still covers the adjacent ground, which already furnishes subsistence to the master. Such a trip is a sort of practical and living analysis of the origin of peoples and states; one leaves the most complex society to return to the simplest elements. Each day one loses from sight one of those inventions which the multiplication of our needs renders necessary. It seems that one travels backwards in the history of the progress of the human spirit.[1]

America remained the European frontier and its eyes, its hopes, and its commerce were constantly turned toward American shores. It is surprising that American independence was not a greater shock to the English and that the true import of the American experiment was not officially recognized until the North American Act for Canada in 1867. With American independence achieved, Edmund Burke had declared with foresight:

A great revolution has happened—a revolution made, not by chopping and changing a power in any of the existing states, but by the appearance of a new state, of a new species, in a new part of the globe. It has made as great a change in all the relations, and balances, and gravitations of power, as the appearance of a new planet would in the system of the solar world.[2]

The French, through La Rochefoucauld, Crèvecœur, and Tocqueville, had taken an earlier look at the America which had emerged and gave some valuable insights into the kind of America which was developing before their own eyes. They were marvelous interpreters of the American scene to their fellow compatriots. Crèvecœur wrote that a "surprising metamorphosis" was taking place in America; the American "is a new man who acts on new principles, he must therefore entertain new ideas, and form new opinions."

    J. Hector St. John de Crèvecœur, a Norman officer under Montcalm, settled into farming in New York and became a "new man." He was a moderate during the Revolution, was banished, but later was reconciled and became the French consul in New York. His *Letters of an American Farmer*, published in London in 1782, asserted the physiocratic doctrine that the farmer creates wealth that the American farmer by escaping peasant feudalism becomes a useful being to society and the stable element in free political life. "Urged by a variety of motives, here they came. Everything has tended to rejuvenate them: new laws, a new mode of living, a new social system. Here they are become men. In Europe they were so many useless plants. . . . For the first time in his life he counts for something; for hitherto he had been a cipher."

Talleyrand was not only close to the American scene, but he hoped also to restore his fortune in America. He became a good friend of Hamilton, Robert Morris, John Vaughan, General Knox, all engaged in developing American capitalism, land speculation, and industry. Of Hamilton, Talleyrand wrote that he merited the highest esteem and that he had "found the greatest advantage in forming an intimate liaison with him and every day I have reason to felicitate myself on it."

Tocqueville saw in the westward expansion one of the principal forces that held the Union together and which gave American democracy its dynamic force. "The world has never before seen a social phenomenon at all comparable with that presented in the United States. A society spreading over enormous tracts, while still preserving its political continuity, is a new thing." The frontier became a dominating factor: the opening of public lands, Indian wars, claims for grazing, timber, and mineral rights, and eventually railroad expansion, were much in the American saga. As Archibald MacLeish wrote:

> East were the
> Dead kings and the remembered sepulchres
> West was the grass.[3]

The frontier was declared closed by the end of the nineteenth century, but the pioneer spirit continued to conquer—now the new wilderness of the industrial city. Hamlin Garland in *A Son of the Middle Border,* and Willa Cather in *O Pioneers!* and *My Antonia* reflect this frontier spirit as it comes into our own time.

It is true that the tradition of American isolation had in it a certain kind of Hebraic separatism, but, despite the *Farewell Address,* America could not avoid the entangling skeins of Europe. Soon after the signing of the peace, America was again enmeshed in the sideshows of the Napoleonic drama. We must recall that Washington wrote his *Farewell Address* in 1797 when he was viewing the worst excesses of the French Revolution and the spread of revolutionary war all over Europe. He was also aware of the passions that divided American sympathies between England and France.

Jefferson, for example, detested the British and wrote that "of all the nations of earth, they [the British] require to be treated with the utmost hauteur. They require to be kicked into good common manners. . . ." Talleyrand wrote from America that "an entire generation and a new reign will have to pass before the Englishman will believe that the American is his equal. This idea of superiority, entertained by all who surround the throne, is found also in all classes of society." John Adams could write after living in England that

> the delights of France are innumerable. The politeness, the elegance, the softness, the delicacy, are extreme. In short, stern and haughty republican that I am I cannot help loving these people for their earnest desire and assiduity to please.
>
> The cookery and manners of living here, which you know Americans were taught by their former absurd masters to dislike, is more agreeable to me than you can imagine. The manners of the people have an affection in them that is very amiable.[4]

Adams was not as popular in France as Franklin and Jefferson, as he admitted, because he could not speak or understand French, and his wife Abigail, while "agreeably disappointed" in London was "much disappointed in Paris," for it was the dirtiest place she ever saw. As wife of the first American minister to London, Abigail Adams' reaction was strong:

> As to politics, the British continue to publish the most abusive, barefaced falsehoods against America that you can conceive of; yet, glaring as they are, they gain credit here, and they shut their eyes against a friendly and liberal intercourse. Yet their very existence depends upon a friendly union with us.[5]

It was impossible to avoid the European-American entanglement, for the two continents had been too closely woven together to unwind the strand. America could not escape Europe even though it feared its influence. Jefferson loved Europe, particularly France and Italy, but he was afraid of its "contamination," and Adams, who had spent long years as a diplomat in Europe, became a new American nationalist and predicted a great struggle between Europe and America. As the second president, Adams personally favored the Alien and Sedition Acts. No true liberal, he displayed a Puritan authoritarianism that was evident even in his vice-presidency. He wanted a republican oligarchy of the wellborn and wealthy standing between a leveling democracy and a monarchial tyranny. He stood directly against Rousseau and believed that a state of nature led people into factionalism.

The French Revolution and its ultimate excesses disturbed the American conscience as much as it did Burke. Gouverneur Morris, American minister to France, bluntly told the French that they could never succeed in duplicating the American experience. "They want an American constitution without realizing that they have no Americans to uphold it." In his irascible old age Adams wrote of Turgot, Condorcet, and La Rochefoucauld:

> they were as amiable, as learned and as honest men as any in France. But such was their experience in all that relates to free government, so superficial their reading in the science of government, and so obstinate their confidence in their own great characters for science and literature, that I should trust the most ignorant of our town meeting orators to make a constitution sooner than any or all of them.[6]

Before long America was tied up in the Jay Treaty, the XYZ Case involving Talleyrand's efforts to bribe the American commissioners for revision of the commercial clauses of the 1778 Treaty, the purchase of Louisiana, and the War of 1812—a second war of independence, begun by the mercantilist East and finished by the new nationalist West. The peace treaty had no relation to the original causes of the war. Then there was the purchase of Florida. In 1812 the first project to conquer upper Canada was undertaken, to be repeated in 1837. Americans soon had designs on Cuba, Mexico, and Central America. Wanting to stay isolated, it could not, in spite of Clay's "American system" and the Monroe Doctrine (which Lafayette called "the best little bit of paper that God had ever permitted any man to give to the world") and Jacksonian nationalism. Noah Webster proclaimed, "For America in her infancy to adopt the present maxims of the Old World would be to stamp the wrinkle of decrepit age upon the bloom of youth, and to plant the seed of decay in a vigorous constitution." Philip Freneau and Joel Barlow said the same thing. But while Noah Webster had been Americanizing the English language, another American, Lindley Murray, went to England to write an English grammar and reader which predominated in Engilsh schools for over fifty years.

America became the symbol of world revolution, but Americans were not world revolutionaries. Tocqueville wrote in 1832 that America was at that moment the last country of the world to keep in its breast the germs of revolution. Washington was praised by Alfieri and Lessing, celebrated by Coleridge and Byron, and Shelley wrote, "Nay, start not at the word! America!" While the shot may have been heard around the world, there was no missionary zeal among the Americans to export their revolution. The American Revolution produced no Robespierres or Lenins. After the War of 1812 Adams noted in his *History:*

> Rights of Man occupied public thoughts less, and the price of cotton more. . . . Although in 1815 Europe was suffering under a violent reaction against free government, Americans showed little interest and no alarm, compared with their emotion of twenty years before. The War gave a severe shock to the Anglican sympathies of society, and peace seemed to widen the breach between European and American tastes. Interest in Europe languished after Napoleon's overthrow. France ceased to affect American opinion.[7]

America turned inward. Americanism became the antithesis of cosmopolitanism. Frances Trollope noted that "Rousseau, Voltaire, Diderot, etc., were read by the older federals, but now they seem known more as naughty words rather than as great names." [8]

America was still regarded in Europe with distrust and reactionary hatred. In January, 1824, Metternich wrote to the Russian foreign minister, Count Nesselrode:

> These United States of America which we have seen arise and grow, and which during their too short youth already meditated projects which they dared not then avow, have suddenly left a sphere too narrow for their ambition, and have astonished Europe by a new act of revolt, more unprovoked, fully as audacious, and no less dangerous than the former. They have distinctly and clearly announced their intention to set not only power against power, but, to express it more exactly, altar against altar. In their indecent declaration they have cast blame and scorn on the institutions of Europe most worthy of respect, on the principles of its greatest sovereigns, on the whole of those measures which is a sacred duty no less than evident necessity has forced our government to adopt to frustrate plans most criminal. In permitting themselves these unprovoked attacks, in fostering revolutions wherever they show themselves, in regretting those which have failed, in extending a helping hand to those which seem to prosper, they lend new strength to the apostles of sedition, and reanimate the courage of every conspirator. If this flood of evil doctrines and pernicious examples should extend over the whole of America, what would become of our religious and political

institutions, of the moral force of our governments, of that conservative system which has saved Europe from complete dissolution? [9]

Nascent American nationalism wanted to keep the United States pure and free and isolated from Europe. In a Fourth of July oration James Buchanan declared:

Foreign influence has been, in every age, the curse of Republics. Her jaundiced eye sees all things in false colors. The thick atmosphere of prejudice, by which she is forever surrounded, excludes from her sight the light of reason; while she worships the nations which she favors for their very crimes, she curses the enemies of that nation, even for their virtues. . . . We are separated from the nations of Europe by an immense ocean. Why, then, should we injure ourselves by taking part in the ambitious contests of foreign despots and kings?

The intellectual mistrust of Europe was indicated in Emerson's *American Scholar:* "We have listened too long to the courtly muses of Europe."

The American Revolution fixed the European image of the United States for 150 years as the place of refuge, ferment, experiment, and freedom, an image secured by the religious, political, and economic emigration that followed. Barring Switzerland, which did not have a great cultural impact in Europe, America stood for years as the new Roman Republic in the face of the Metternichean reaction and bourgeois monarchies, free of class distinctions and religious persecutions. James Fenimore Cooper, among other Americans, felt the urge to say that America

is rapidly advancing to maturity which must reduce the pretentions of even ancient Rome to supremacy, to a secondary place in the estimation of mankind. A century will unquestionably place the United States of America prominently at the head of civilizations, unless their people throw away their advantages by their own mistakes—the only real danger they have to apprehend.[10]

Americans remained unmoved (except for William Cullen Bryant) by the Greek war of independence which so thrilled Europe. They did not lift a finger during the revolutions of 1830, except for a scattered interest in Poland. Yet the Belgian Constitution was modeled after the American, and, very importantly, initiated the Belgian separation of church and state. In 1830 Bryant became chairman of the American Committee in Paris to aid the Poles in their uprising; Samuel F. B. Morse was a member of the Committee. George Bancroft secretly published Lafayette's speeches in Italy and, encouraged by Byron, joined the Carbonari and attended their outlawed reunions in a forest near Ravenna. Samuel Gridley Howe fought six years for Greek independence and was imprisoned in Germany because of his friendship for the Poles. At this time Tocqueville visited America.

Tocqueville spent less than a year in the United States on a government mission, yet his quick perception was astounding. Like Dickens later (who came primarily for his interest in penal reform), Tocqueville was interested in examining the American effort at democracy and peering into the future of France—after having witnessed the Napoleonic regime as a boy and the Revolution of 1830 as a man. Thus his *Democracy in America* is not a textbook for Americans but a corollary to *The Ancient Regime and the Revolution* for the edification of the French.

The aristocratic Tocqueville had been a magistrate under the Restoration and a deputy in the reactionary chamber of deputies, yet he foresaw for Europe the inevitable course of democratic influence and wished to shape it to finer ends. He was writing at a time when all Europe save Switzerland was under monarchy. With the next phase of historical development, individual liberty had to be preserved in the face of democratic conformity and centralization of power by guidance of the masses by politicians of the intellect. A new political science was needed for a wholly new world, in order to purify its way and teach its true interests against its blind instincts. To this was added the first duty of those who would direct that new society, for if his aristocratic peers would not come out in favor of democracy, the result would be to hand power over to the masses. "My purpose has been to show by the American example, that laws and particularly the customs may permit a democratic people to remain free."

Tocqueville was impressed with the democratic machinery in the United States, but not with those who were running it. Jackson, he held, was a man of violent character and middling capacity and nothing in his career proved that he had the necessary qualities for governing a free people. Tocqueville could not understand why people elected politicians who were more stupid than they, and that men of talent shunned public office. Bryce later noted that neither the legislature nor the administration was at the time confined to competent groups, but "had fallen into the rude hands of little educated men coming from an inferior social class. Brutality and violence began to reign over vast parts of the country." The spoils system had come into full sway, the heroes of the Revolution gone, the Federalists turned out by Jefferson Republicans, who in turn disappeared with the War of 1812, leaving only sectarian and sectional politics based not on principles as much as on material interest and well-being gaining over morality. Tocqueville did not foresee the ultimate regrouping of parties. Yet he felt that America was protected from local tyranny and mob rule by the federal system; while each state was occupied with petty affairs, public spirit and patriotism could be manifested on the national level.

On the whole, Tocqueville came out favorably for American democracy, particularly its laws and institutions, and his analysis of its earlier development shrewdly indicated its later path. The second part of his book on American ideas, habits, and customs he himself admitted had been approached with less ardor, and is consequently less illuminating than other travel books of the period, such as Basil Hall's, or Frances Trollope's. Yet he far overshadows these and others who wrote of America, until the time of Bryce, with his penetrating evaluation of a nascent America. Curiously, his writings on the United States had little effect in France, while they have been of great value to Americans. (Tocqueville continued his political role in France and became minister of foreign affairs, but when he is spoken of now in contemporary French circles he is passed off with a nervous laugh. He concise thinking on the problems of mass society will be examined later.)

By 1848 the Americans and the British cordially detested each other. There was a reaction against Frances Trollope and Dickens, the burning of the *Caroline,* the trial of McLeod, the Oregon Dispute—"Fifty-Four Forty or Fight,"—charges of British meddling in Texas, and the default of America's interest payments, the memories of which were not wholly erased by the Webster-Ashburton treaty of 1842 or the Oregon treaty of 1846. James Fenimore Cooper could write of John Effingham (himself) in *Homeward Bound* that he "was educated under the influence of the British opinion that then weighed (and many of which still weigh) like an incubus on the national interests of America." Cooper continued in his *Journal* that England was "an exceedingly unpleasant country for a stranger, especially an American. It is but a poor compliment to the country of our Forefathers to say we were all glad to get out of it," and Henry Adams could write: "Familiar as the whole tribe of Adamses had been for three long generations with the impenetrable stupidity of the British mind, and weary of the long struggle to teach it its own interests, the fourth generation could still not persuade itself that this new British prejudice was natural. . . . Naturally the Englishman was a coarse animal and liked coarseness."

The revolutions of 1848 saw America disinterested in Europe; the Gold Rush was more preoccupying. It is strange that few Europeans joined in the rush to California, but the glitter had the effect of presenting America as a land of illimitable wealth.

Kossuth's visit to the United States provided little interest after his congressional welcome, and he left with no aid for his native Hungary. Haw thorne, when in Italy, showed no interest in the *Risorgimento,* and Margaret Fuller's efforts in the revolutions of 1948 met with indifference and disaster. Whitman, at least, was moved to write after 1848:

> . . . the frightened monarchs come back
> Each comes in state with his train, hangman, priest, tax-gatherer. . . .
> Yet behind all lowering stealing, lo, a shape,
> Vague as the night, draped interminably, head, front, and form
> in scarlet folds . . .
> Liberty, let others despair of you—I never despair of you.

In *Democratic Vistas* Whitman was later to write, "There is plenty of glamour about the most damnable crimes and hoggish manners, special and general, of the feudal and dynastic world over there, with its *personnel* of lords and queens and courts, so well-dressed and handsome. But the people are ungrammatical, untidy, and their sins gaunt and ill-bred." [11]

The frontier was rude and crude and occupied American interests throughout the nineteenth century. The frontier and its necessary corollary, the railroad, sponsored largely by British capital, wrote a century of history in the United States. The continent was finally spanned in 1869. What was West in Jefferson's time became East in Jackson's and Jackson's West had become the Midwest by 1864. Once the railway lines were laid down, the pioneer could begin to level land and burn trees and plant crops amongst the stumps. The pioneer was a frontier agricultural "miner," a preparer of farms rather than a farmer. It was a rough life, eventually civilized by the advent of women. Frances Trollope noted women's role in civilizing the frontier; she said that the West was one large boarding house with couples living in hotels and women supported only by religion and social bees. Her son Anthony, revisiting the West, later wrote that he had

> eaten in Bedouin tents, and have been ministered to by Turks and Arabs. I have sojourned in the hotels of old Spain and of Spanish America. I have lived in Connaught, and have taken up my quarters with monks of different nations. I have, as it were, been educated to dirt, and taken out my degree in outward abominations. But my education had not reached a point which would enable me to live at my ease in the western States.[12]

Dickens depicted Cairo, Illinois, as the Eden of *Martin Chuzzlewit,* but Anthony Trollope later doubted "whether that author ever visited Cairo in mid-winter, and I am sure he never visited Cairo when Cairo was the seat of the American Army. Had he done so, his love of truth would have forbidden him to presume that even Mark Tapley could have enjoyed himself in such an Eden." [13] In his mother's detested Cincinnati, which Trollope found vastly changed for the better, he wrote of a walk outside of town during which he was

> greeted by a rising flavour in the air, which soon grew into a strong odour, and at last developed itself into a stench that surpassed in offensiveness anything that my nose had hitherto suffered. . . . It was the odour of hogs going up to the Ohio heavens; of hogs in state of transit from hoggish nature to clothes-brushes, saddles, sausages, and lard.[14]

Yet Thackeray, who twice visited the United States in 1852–1853 and 1856, took a milder and more indulgent view of Americans. He loved New York women "lean as greyhounds," and "all dressed like the most stunning French actresses." The Quaker girls in Philadelphia were "airy-looking little beings, with camellia complexions." He took Dickens to task for writing his *American Notes.* "What could Dickens mean by writing that book?" He felt that Dickens should not be taken seriously for his views on America because no one could write of a country without at least five years' experience.

His first voyage was made with James Russell Lowell, who was returning from a year in Italy. Thackeray was going to America to earn enough money to support his separated wife and daughters. Yet in Liverpool he got his first taste of the American press in an article stating that he was just another in that parade of English lecturers who came to criticize and return home with their pockets full.

Thackeray had already decided not to publish his impressions of America; to stir up ill will he thought imprudent. Consequently he was cordially embraced by those who had had a taste of Dickens' commentaries. In Boston he was the guest of Prescott and Ticknor, whose homes were stocked with good wines and good books. With his first American oyster he felt "as if I had swallowed a little baby." Lowell gave a dinner for him at Cambridge which Longfellow described with relish. Thackeray compared Boston to a rich cathedral town in England, grave and decorous, or like Edinburgh with its "donnishness" and Toryism.

In New York he was entertained by George Bancroft and Henry James, Sr., and his lectures were lauded by William Cullen Bryant. Young Henry James was much impressed with him and touchingly remembered him for his avuncular kindness. James, Sr., who wished to talk Swedenborgian philosophy with him, thought that he was an intellectual lightweight, and later told Emerson that Thackeray "could not see beyond his eyes and has no ideas, and merely is a sounding board against which his experiences thump and resound: he is the merest boy." [15] His friend Horace Greeley initiated him into the intricacies of American politics, and Washington Irving complained to him that Dickens was disturbing Anglo-American relations.

He took the same train as Irving to Philadelphia and Washington, and Irving reported that Thackeray seem to be enjoying his American visit exceedingly and that he had gotten pleasurably into American social life. Thackeray arrived in Washington at the time of Franklin Pierce's inauguration. He dined at the White House and was offered dinners by Edward Everett, Secretary of State, Senator Hamilton Fish, and General Winfield Scott the defeated Whig candidate. With Fillmore and Pierce he inspected John Ericsson's new steamboat on the Potomac.

Thackeray thoroughly enjoyed being with Americans:

> You know what a virtue-proud people we English are. We think we have got it all to ourselves. Now, what impresses me here is that I find homes as pure as ours, firesides like ours, domestic virtues as gentle; the English language, though the accent be a little different, with its home-like melody; and the Common Prayer book in your families.

Again, he wrote to a friend:

> There's a rush and activity of life quite astounding, a splendid reckless-ness about money which has in it something admirable too. You get an equality which may shock ever so little at first, but has something hearty and generous in it. There's beautiful affection in this country, immense tenderness, romantic personal enthusiasm, and a general kindliness and servicableness and good nature, which is very pleasant and curious to witness for us folks at home who are mostly ashamed of our best emotions.[16]

He returned to England happy with his American tour, perhaps in part because it was a financially profitable one. Yet the English felt that he over-praised the United States. (He kept his watch set at New York time.) He met Harriet Beecher Stowe, who was being sponsored in England by Lord Shaftesbury. Thackeray was dismayed to find all England reading *Uncle Tom's Cabin,* fearing that it might upset Anglo-American relations again. In London he kept up his American friendship with Lowell, Story, Cranch, and Sturgis.

In 1855 Thackeray left for a second lecture tour in the United States; this time his subject was the four Georges, which titillated American audiences but greatly annoyed the English. His lecture on George I with all his mistresses was rather misplaced, and the London press called his lectures disloyal. At some lectures he made only a net profit of three dollars, but he was glad to be back in Boston with his friends Longfellow and Story. In Richmond and Charlottesville he began to write *The Virginian,* which was eventually published serially in *Harpers* and the *New York Tribune,* as well as in book form. Because American relations with England remained in a bad state, the American press and public were against the book.

While he was in Washington the British minister Crampton was charged with recruiting Americans for the Crimean War, and at a dinner given by Senator Fish, an Anglo-American war was prophesied within three months. Thackeray began to worry about his American railroad shares!

When Thackeray returned to London, relations were still strained. The British minister had been recalled, to Thackeray's disgust: "That kind of humility will never appease your Anti-English over the water or be understood by them." Ticknor, who was at that time in London, said that Thackeray was outraged that the foreign ministry had made a scapegoat of Crampton. Thackeray also became determined not to return to the United States because of his treatment in the American press. His high regard for America lowered visibly because of the journalists: "Those scoundrels managed to offend and insult the most friendly stranger that ever entered your country or quitted it."

Yet he spent the following summer with Motley and later wrote to Longfellow that he planned to revisit America. The coming of the Civil War upset his plans. He had tried to remain neutral between his Northern and Southern friends in the United States, was bothered by the *Trent* incident, and was pleased when Mason and Slidell were freed. To his later regret, he sold his American stocks. Thackeray maintained a cordial relationship with the American Minister Charles Francis Adams and his son Henry, who had arrived at the outbreak of the Civil War, and even spoke for and contributed to the welfare of the Lancashire cotton workers.

In retrospect, Thackeray's influence in the transatlantic relation becomes greater than that of Dickens or Frances Trollope. His coterie of American friends was typical of the international set of American writers and historians such as Irving, Longfellow, Motley, Prescott, and Ticknor. His warm understanding of American *moeurs* put him in an excellent position to interpret the American design to England, even though England was not particularly disposed to follow the pattern. A number of his American friends in

Europe began to reveal more fully the nineteenth-century attitudes which
prevailed between the two continents.

The revolutionary period had produced a number of American diplomats who were equally men of letters: Franklin, Gouverneur Morris, Jefferson, Adams, perhaps, and Joel Barlow. The nineteenth century likewise saw
many American men of letters fixed in Europe by diplomatic posts or international reputation. Washington Irving, Cooper, Hawthorne, Motley, Lowell,
and Howells are typical examples. Their writing, as much or more than their
diplomacy, made a transatlantic bridge between Americans and Europeans,
real interpreters as much in fact as in fiction. Prescott became a member of
the Institute of France and the Royal Academy of Berlin. Motley's *Rise of
the Dutch Republic* was translated and adopted for schools. Longfellow's
Courtship of Miles Standish sold ten thousand copies in England on the first
day of publication.

Washington Irving was a Jamesian type who spent seventeen years in
Europe. Walter Scott was his godfather, Dickens praised his *Sketch Book*,
and Thackeray thought him a consummate man of letters. He had a massive
Puritan reserve (he coined the term "Almighty Dollar"), was the confidant
of women, the perpetual fiancé. He made his first trip to Europe in 1804.
Between Genoa and Sicily his ship was captured by pirates, and he had seen
and admired Nelson's fleet. In Rome, where he met Canova and Mme. de
Staël, he found that "men discover taste and fancy in Italy," and that every
step he took was on "enchanted grounds." He met Washington Allston, who
illustrated his *Knickerbocker,* and thought of taking up painting himself in
Rome. He wanted to study in Paris and London, but the café life in both
places, alas, preempted his time.

After several boring years in the United States, Irving contemplated
going to the war against the Algerian pirates with Stephen Decatur, but he
returned to England in 1815 to work with his brother in a branch of the
family business in Liverpool. It went bankrupt three years later and Irving
had to take up writing seriously. Richard Henry Dana wrote a few years
later that "Mr. Irving is almost the only American who attempted to support
himself by literary labors." The result was the *Sketch Book* which Scott
helped to publish. John Murray had asked him to write for the *Quarterly
Review,* but he refused because the *Quarterly* "has always been so hostile to
my country." In 1821 he journeyed to Paris and wrote new librettos for
Weber's *Freischutz* and *Abu Hassan.* The year 1822 saw the publication of
Bracebridge Hall, a series of essays on English family life which was very

popular and which confirmed his reputation, but which also had little literary merit.

Irving traveled to Germany and France and then in 1826 he was appointed attaché at the American Legation in Madrid, where he was perfectly free to write his history of Columbus. He met Longfellow there. He then became secretary of the Legation in London in 1829. From 1842 to 1845 he was American minister to Spain, the appointment having been urged by Daniel Webster.

Irving's *Sketch Book* had first been published in England in 1820 under the pseudonym of Geoffrey Crayon. Influenced by Goldsmith and Sterne, he recalled Old England, Stratford and the Abbeys and the quaint habits of the English. He described Germany and its folklore in *Tales of a Traveller,* which he thought his best book. It was well received on the Continent, but was disliked in England and America, so much so that Irving considered giving up his literary career. Best of all, he described America in *Rip Van Winkle,* who wakes up to find an old traditional patriarchal America lost replaced by an America bursting with energy and proud of its prosperous and progressive democracy. After seventeen years abroad, Irving returned to the United States to a triumphal welcome as the first American to achieve critical literary acclaim in Europe. He received the gold medal of the Royal Society and an honorary doctorate from Oxford. At a public dinner offered him in New York he denied that he had become less American by staying in Europe so long. He traveled to the western frontier and by his writings he became one of the first image builders of the Far West. Together with Prescott and Ticknor, he made Spanish history popular and his life of Washington was the first popular American history in Europe.

Irving's long European experience had enabled him to see America more clearly. Even from his first tour of Europe he wrote, "My eyes are opened in respect to many things that were hid from me while in America." [17] While his mind was taken up by historical associations and the manners and customs of Europe, while he was "dazzled, astonished, enraptured" by Europe; he refused to be "ensnared." He maintained that his European experiences had only made him a better American, and preferred the "comparative" purity of America to European "profligacy." He wrote five years later, in 1825, that the longer he remained away from America "the greater charm it has in my eyes, and all the coloring that the imagination once gave to distant Europe now gathers about the scene of my native country."

In the 1840's he had struck up a cordial friendship with Dickens, presided over a New York dinner in Dickens' honor, and met with him in Washington and Baltimore. Yet Irving made a strong break with Dickens over the copyright controversy: "after all our extravagant homage to him which he should have been proud of—felt to be a great compliment—pouring abuse on us because we stood in the way of his own selfish interest." The abuse had come out with Dickens' *American Notes*. Like Hawthorne, Irving was strongly opposed to English criticism of America, as he had shown earlier in his *Salmagundi* and the *Sketch Book*.

Aside from his quarrel with Dickens, Irving remained loved on both sides of the Atlantic. Byron said of him, "Irving is a genius, and he has something better than genius—a heart." [18] And as a transatlantic interpreter, Irving put it best when he wrote, "I have wandered through different countries, and witnessed many of the shifting scenes of life." [19]

One of Irving's great friends in Europe was the American painter Washington Allston, who had been a pupil of Benjamin West, had studied in Paris, and then moved on to Florence and Rome. He was an intimate of Coleridge and they had explored the countryside together. Allston did portraits of him and Wordsworth declared one Allston portrait of Coleridge "incomparably the finest likeness," while Coleridge called him a "rare genius," and that next to the Wordsworths he loved and honored him the most. While his Italianate style was to pass out of favor, he, along with Thomas Cole and Vanderlyn and the sculptors Powers and Greenhough, maintained the transatlantic artistic connection. His most famous pupil was Samuel F. B. Morse, whom he taught in London, and who came forward as an outstanding painter before turning his talents to science in the 1830's. James Fenimore Cooper, with decided ideas of his own, tried to tell Allston how to paint when he was copying in the Louvre.

Morse had shrewdly judged the artistic state of the American mind when he made the comparison that art in the United States was made by a lower class of people, while in England it was a constant topic of conversation in the better circles. Allston's faculties dwindled when he returned to bleak Cambridgeport, which made William Wetmore Story and Henry James ever reluctant themselves to return to the United States. James Russell Lowell was told by Story that "Allston starved spiritually in Cambridgeport; fed upon himself. There was nothing congenial without, and he turned all his powers inward and drained his memory dry." Fearful Cambridgeport had stunted and withered him with its scant soil and cold winds.

The Cooper rage in Europe continued. When his fame was established, each new novel was published simultaneously in thirty-four European cities. Cooper, with Washington Irving, was the first American writer to enjoy a European reputation, not only because of his long stay there but also because he portrayed the new American republic of heroes, democratic pioneers, and redskins. "I was in no country of Europe where the name of Cooper was not familiarly known," reported Longfellow, "in some of them he stands almost as the sole representative of our literature." [20] Cooper himself egotistically wrote from France that "the people seem to think it marvelous that an American can write—I do firmly believe that nine-tenths of the French reading world are ignorant that a book was ever made in America, except by Dr. Franklin and M. Cooper, *Américain,* as they call me. You will be surprised to hear that Irving is virtually unknown here, notwithstanding." [21] Balzac called him the "school of study for literary painters." While Irving was popular with the upper class, Cooper struck the fancy of the masses. When Longfellow traveled in Scandinavia he found Cooper's works in peasant cottages and his Indian stories were imitated in France and Germany.

Cooper inherited a comfortable fortune from his father, a Federalist politician, and after marrying into the wealthy and loyalist De Lancey family, built a French chateau, "Angerine," at Scarsdale, where he enjoyed playing the country squire and colonel in the state militia. He was imbued with caste and rank, but at heart was a theoretical liberal; he surprised and confused many by supporting Jackson against the financiers. Cooper lived with his family in Europe from 1826 to 1835, and was named honorary American consul at Lyons.

After his first visit to England, Cooper wrote that "the English gentleman stands at the head of his class in Christendom." His book *England, with Sketches of Society in the Metropolis* was largely disregarded. He was well received in England and became friendly with Godwin, Lord John Russell, and Sir James MacKintosh, among others. On his return to the United States, he found that he had become "fatally cosmopolitan." He wrote to a friend in 1832, "I am not with my own country—the void between us is immense."

At the instigation of Lafayette, to whom he became more closely attached than most second-generation Americans of Lafayette's acquaintance, he published in 1826 *Notions of the Americans,* his first nonfiction, which was purportedly the impressions of an English traveler in the United States and which praised America at the expense of Europe. He was annoyed at the foreign ignorance of the United States and gave a good picture of contemporary American opinion, but it was too partisan to have much effect on the European mind. It was as badly received in Europe as it was in America. His facts and statistics were accurate, but he had an overly utopian conception of the moral and intellectual character of America. Cooper had actually looked at an earlier American democracy with fundamental institutions moral and pure, but which no longer existed in fact. His *Notions* were based on the Federalist Papers, and he could not attempt to compete with Tocqueville. Unlike Tocqueville, Cooper saw nothing of the social and economic discontent which was to usher in Jacksonian democracy, but he did realize that there was a decline in moral standards in many sectors of American society: newspapers, politics, the vulgarians, and the religious zealots.

The first novel which brought him great success was *The Spy*, with an American theme because he disliked the contemporary fashionable British novel. It was an immediate triumph in England and was called the first outstanding American novel. He fell very much under French influence and wrote in Paris that he was "charmed with a gayer and more brilliant society than he coud have known before." He criticized Europe in *The Bravo* on the Venetians, *The Heidenmauer* on the Germans, and *The Headsman* on the Swiss, in an attempt to show the superiority of American democracy to European aristocracy.

Returning to America, he criticized American institutions and customs in his *Letter to His Countrymen*, attacking the President, Congress, and the press, and asserting that he was retiring as a writer of fiction because of the way his work was received by his compatriots. He followed up his invective (in *Homeward Bound* and *Home as Found*) against demagogery and commercialism. Editors and critics alike libeled him for these works, as they did also for his historical integrity in his *History of the Navy of the United States*. Cooper had always wanted to be Secretary of the Navy and his great knowledge of ships would have qualified him for the post. The editors and critics quieted down when he sued for libel and won against Jas. Watson Webb, Horace Greeley, Thurlow Weed, and others. By 1840 he was at odds with almost all aspects of American life.

While Cooper had lived and traveled in Europe for a number of years and was well known in literary and intellectual circles, he strongly defended the newly developing government and institutions of the United States before his European friends. But he condemned Americans for their bad manners, their chauvinism, their contempt for privacy, and their slavish submission to public opinion. He was of an aristocratic bent, believing that the "column of society must have its capital as well as its base," and he lamented that lack of clashing ideas in America. Comparing America with Europe at the time of Jackson's reign, he wrote that other enlightened nations were divided among great opposing principles, while in America everyone was of the same mind, except for a choice between political candidates.

While Cooper's complaint is echoed time and again to the present day, still America's lack of clearly defined political philosophy is found in the absence of a cause for one. The nation was all of the same mind after the Jacksonian revolution, and without opposing principles, the philosophic question did not need to be asked. Old Whiggery's variety and diversity was submerged in a wave of uniformity, the growing tide of "Americanism."

Horatio Greenhough was the artist compliment to Fenimor Cooper, as Allston has been to Washington Irving. Cooper often covered Greenhough's financial difficulties, and he in turn did busts of Cooper and Cooper's friend Lafayette. Greenhough lived twenty-five years in Florence. Emerson, who had met him there, thought his talk more cunning than his chisel, but Landor told Emerson that in America sculpture was flourishing more than in the age of Pericles and, referring to Greenhough and Powers, said, "America is not cast into the shadow of Europe." Greenhough, like Landor, supported Garibaldi and Mazzini, yet he became professor of sculpture at the Grand Ducal Academy in reactionary Florence. Greenhough has become one of the favorites of modern architects for his statement that "form follows function," and he thought that Americans were better off with the style of the clipper ship than reproductions of Greek buildings.

In the forties and fifties Rome was crowded with distinguished Americans. One finds W. W. Story, Ticknor, Motley, Parkman, Bancroft, Charles Eliot Norton, James Russell Lowell, George Inness, Julia Ward Howe and her husband Samuel Gridley Howe, Dorothea L. Dix, and Charles Sumner, who sponsored Thomas Crawford. Crawford married the sister of Julia Ward Howe, became rich and popular, and maintained twelve studios and many stone cutters in the ruins of the Baths of Diocletian. His "Armed Freedom" is on top of the dome of the American capitol. His son, Marion Crawford, carried on the Italian-American tradition as a novelist, spending almost all his life in Italy.

Henry Wadsworth Longfellow, whom Edmund Wilson has described as one of the major interpreters of Europe to America, was a descendent of John and Priscilla Alden, whom he later romanticized. At the daring age of nineteen he became professor of languages at Bowdoin College. He went in 1816 to France, Spain, Germany, and Italy for three years' study. Upon his nomination to a modern language professorship at Harvard ten years later, he made another extensive tour of Germany and Scandinavia for research in Old Nordic. *Outre Mer,* a travel book, resulted from this European visit, as did *Hyperion,* in which he offered his views of European life. His first wife died in Rotterdam in 1835. His second wife, Frances Appleton, was the heroine of *Hyperion.*

Longfellow's knowledge of European literature grew and his circle of European intellectual friends widened. In the spring and summer of 1842 at Marienbad he formed a lifelong friendship with the German revolutionary poet Ferdinand Freiligrath, who was translating American poems. Longfellow visited Dickens and others in England. Another visit in 1868 and 1869 brought him in contact with many artists and scholars, for his works had been quickly translated into all European languages and his reputation firmly established.

Longfellow, in the course of his studies and voyages, had learned French, Spanish, Italian (he translated Dante after his wife had burned to death), German, Swedish, Danish, Dutch, Icelandic, and Finnish. His translation of European authors made him the primary interpreter of continental thought in the middle period of American cultural life, and he spread his friendly mantle over Lowell and Hawthorne.

In spite of *Miles Standish, Hiawatha,* and *Paul Revere,* Longfellow's own image of America grew dim in the 1870's in the same way as Henry Adams was to look at the period, and he wrote:

> Ah, woe is me!
> I hoped to see my country rise to heights
> Of happiness and freedom yet unreached
> By other nations, but the climbing wave
> Pauses, lets go its hold, and slides again
> Back to the common level, with a hoarse
> Death-rattle in its throat. I am too old
> To hope for better days.

Emerson visited Europe three times, but he had a different view of Europe than Longfellow. Of his first visit in 1833, having given up his pulpit in Boston, he wrote, "We came out to Europe to learn what man can, —what is the uppermost which social man has yet done." He was under the influence of Scottish philosophers and the *Edinburgh Review,* yet he managed to meet such a wide group as Macaulay, Thackeray, Dickens, Milnes, Tennyson, Leigh Hunt, Disraeli, Forster, Owen, and Faraday. He said that he would have gone to Germany if Goethe were still living. He was the guest of Harriet Martineau, Wordsworth, Carlyle, and Coleridge. Evidently the sage of Concord had met most of the important intellectuals in England. As he said, he had "crossed sea and land to play bo-peep with celebrated scribes." [22] He established a lifelong relationship with Carlyle, largely through their mutual affinity for the German idealistic philosophers, but he was astonished that Carlyle did not want to read Plato. His visit to Coleridge was a "spectacle rather than a conversation," and Wordsworth was "not prepossessing, and disfigured by green goggles." Wordsworth had a "narrow and very English mind; of one who paid for his rare elevation by general tameness and conformity. Off his own beat, his opinions were of no value." He did not like to travel and this tended to enhance his provincialism, which showed in his 1837 lectures at Harvard, *The American Scholar,* where he pleaded for a strictly American culture. Oliver Wendell Holmes called it "Our intellectual Declaration of Independence."

Emerson's second visit was a lecture tour on *Representative Men* through England and Scotland, in 1847 and 1848. He had already become famous. When Matthew Arnold was an undergraduate in the 1840's at Oxford, Emerson's *Essays* were popular with students and came with "a clear and pure voice, speaking from three thousand miles away." The well-known *English Traits* was one result of his trip; others were warmer friendships with Wordsworth and Dickens, and the forty-year correspondence with Carlyle. He made a final visit in 1872, but his mental powers had begun to decline.

In *English Traits* Emerson maintained that "England is the best of actual nations. It is no ideal framework, it is an old pile built in different ages, with repairs, additions and makeshifts; but you see the poor beast you have got." England, he told Carlyle was an "old and exhausted island," and that the center of the race had shifted to America.

Emerson had weird ideas of race and the effects of climate and region upon nationalities. "A Frenchman may possibly be clean; an Englishman is conscientiously clean." Coal burning in England made the climate milder and made fogs and storms disappear; the Normans invaded England more impure than when they had first gone into Normandy because "they had lost their own language and learned the Romance or barbarous Latin of the Gauls, and had acquired with the language all the vices it had names for." He held that the Norman invasion had drained Sweden and Norway of its best men, and that the Saxons gained the advantage by making the Normans speak their own language and adopt their customs, and which had confirmed English civil liberty. As for the English language, "the male principle is the Saxon, the female, the Latin; and they are combined in every discourse. A good writer, if he has indulged in a Roman roundness, makes haste to chasten and nerve his period by English monosyllables." We learn such things as that "on the English face are combined decision and nerve with the fair complexion, blue eyes and [an] open and florid aspect. Hence the love of truth, hence the sensibility, the fine perception and poetic construction."

Emerson was highly critical of the English intellectuals of his day, for he felt that Plato had been overthrown for pragmatism. Philosophy and letters were mechanical and without inspiration; science was "false by not being poetic." Astronomy was used only to navigate the ships which brought lemons and wine to London. "It was a curious result, in which the civility and the religion of England for a thousand years ends in denying morals and reducing the intellect to a sauce-pan." Where the Germans could generalize and comprehend the English mind, the English could not interpret the German spirit. English thinking stood "in strong contrast with the genius of Germans, those semi-Greeks, who love analogy, and, by means of their height of view, preserve their enthusiasm and think for Europe." While admitting that England was the best of actual nations and London the Rome of today, Emerson woefully concluded that

> no poet dares murmur of beauty out of the precinct of his rhymes. No priest dares hint at a providence which does not respect English utility. The island is a roaring volcano of fate, of material values, of tariffs and law of repression, glutted markets and low prices.

Emerson went to France when the revolutions of 1848 had just begun. He claimed that he found the largest liberty in the civilized world in Paris. All winter he had been admiring the English and disparaging the French, he said, and now he had corrected his prejudices and the French rose in his estimation "many entire degrees." He met Tocqueville. Montaigne was for years his bedside book, and he included him in his *Representative Men*. He had read Bayle, Fénelon, Chateaubriand, and De Staël. He was astonished when visiting Wordsworth that the poet knew Victor Cousin by name only, for all Boston had read him. Later Emerson permitted himself the vices of Balzac, Dumas, and Sand.

He had earlier denounced the French for their lack of moral vigor. On his first visit he did not like Paris, and Notre Dame left him cold. He stayed in his hotel room, except for one occasion, when the Americans in Paris offered a banquet for Lafayette. It gave Emerson the opportunity of shaking hands with "the greatest man that the Old World has given to the New since Columbus."

While he was impressed by Lamartine during the revolutions of 1848, he was horrified by the socialism of Blanqui and Barbès, and Guizot and Thiers counted for little. Emerson believed that French thought was all taken up in the articulation of the language which gave it the appearance of thought. The French were naively satisfied with lucid, coherent, and original formulas which were artificial and contained no ideas. If Emerson was America's great philosopher for the midnineteenth century, it is difficult to ascribe to him anything less than provincialism in his transatlantic intellectual attitude. His transcendentalism was an American permutation of German idealism. His basic apprehension of European life was slight, despite *English Traits* and his literary involvement with several of the best British minds. His predominating influence threw American philosophy into a straitjacket until the 1890's when new European theories began to appear on American shores.

One of Emerson's disciples on the fringe of the transcendentalist movement was Nathaniel Hawthorne, and as a result of his marriage with Sophia Peabody, he had close relations with him, Margaret Fuller, and others associated with their thought. Hawthorne was a college friend of Franklin Pierce: as soon as Pierce was installed in the presidential office, Hawthorne found himself the American consul in Liverpool. The appointment was a valuable one in widening Hawthorne's horizon, even to a better understanding of the American character. "As for my countrymen," he wrote, "I grew better acquainted with many of our national characteristics during those four years than in all my preceding life. . . . my Yankee friends . . . all seemed chiselled in sharper angles than I have ever imagined them to be at home." He spent four years there and much of his *English Notebooks* found its way into *Our Old Home*.

> When our forefathers left the old home, they pulled up many of their roots, but trailed along with them others, which were never snapped asunder by the tug of such a lengthening distance, nor have been torn out of the original soil by the violence of subsequent struggles, nor even severed by the edge of the sword. Even so late as these days, they remain entangled in our heart-strings, and might often have influenced our national cause like the tiller-ropes of a ship. . . .[23]

"An American is not very apt to love the English people," he wrote, "as a whole, or whatever length of acquaintance." Yet he confessed "an unspeakable yearning towards England" and a "singular tenderness" for her institutions. After the War of 1812 he still thought of England as the opponent of America, and having read what Dickens and Frances Trollope thought of the United States, stated that "not an Englishman of them all ever spared America for courtesy's sake or kindness." [24]

"There are some English whom I like—one or two for whom I might almost say, I have an affection," Hawthorne wrote, "but still there is not the same union between us, as if they were Americans. A cold thin medium intervenes between our most intimate approaches. . . . Perhaps, if I were at home, I might feel differently; but in this foreign land, I can never forget the distinction between English and Americans." [25] The British were as outraged at the publication of *Our Old Home* as the Americans were of the criticisms made by Frances Trollope and Dickens. To his publisher Hawthorne wrote in annoyance that the English "do me a great injustice in supposing I hate them, I would as soon hate my own people."

Hawthorne had surprisingly few literary contacts in England, although he met Harriet Martineau with her ear horn and dined with Charles Reade. Longfellow had introduced Henry Arthur Bright to him in the United States and they became good friends in England. He was uninterested in Shakespeare's Stratford, found Southey without color, passion, or warmth, but did enjoy Wordsworth's house and garden. When in London he went often to art galleries, but claimed little understanding, and was unenthusiastic about "modern" art. He was disgusted by the Egyptian and Assyrian collections at the British Museum. Even though he was a friend of Leigh Hunt, whose mother was an American, and of the Americanophile Monckton Milnes, he said that there was "an account to settle" between the two countries for the contemptuous jealousy England had for America. To Hawthorne, all American inventions were superior and all American women were beautiful, yet after four years in England he began to admit that Americans were not people of elegant manners. Of England he could finally say "What a wonderful land! It is our forefather's land; our land; for I will not give up such a precious inheritance." The same attitude is shown by Redclyffe in *Dr. Grimshaw's Secret,* and also by Middleton in *The Ancestral Footstep,* who "felt as if he were the original emigrant who, long resident on a foreign shore, had now returned, with a heart brimful of tenderness, to revisit the scenes of his youth."

Milnes invited Hawthorne and George Ticknor for breakfast with the Brownings and Macaulay. Hawthorne was quite taken by Elizabeth Browning, saying, "She is of that quickly appreciative and responsive order of women, with whom I can talk more freely than with any man," while Robert Browning spoke with appreciation of Hawthorne's books, particularly the *Blithedale Romance.* Hawthorne became better friends with the Brownings in Italy in 1858. In fact the Brownings had quite a number of American friends in Italy, such as Margaret Fuller, William Wetmore Story, and others. Hawthorne described the Brownings and their friends in his Italian journal and gave an excellent insight into their poetic natures.

Herman Melville visited him in 1856. They had long walks and talks together, which was good for Hawthorne, who had become quite restless. He wrote that he was afraid of the vagabond life and feared its effects upon his children. The next summer he jotted in his notebook that he had begun to weary of England and that he needed another clime. Yet he had been in England long enough that to go someplace else seemed a "cold and shivery thing."

Hawthorne went to Paris and then to Italy for two years. While in Rome he sketched out *The Marble Faun,* using his Italian notebooks as a base. Story's *Cleopatra* and *Medea* formed a great part of its description. Of

Rome he said that "no place ever took so strong a hold of my being," and elsewhere wrote of Rome that the intellect found a home there as nowhere else in the world, and "wins the heart to stay with it." He wrote his publisher in 1858, "I had rather be a sojourner in any other country than return to my own. The United States are fit for many excellent purposes, but they are certainly not fit to live in." Yet he returned to Concord in 1860.

In his life of Hawthorne, Henry James realized how rich Europe must have seemed to the Puritan Hawthorne, but also how equally dangerous to his writing. *The Marble Faun* is now virtually unknown and unread. "It takes so many things, as Hawthorne must have felt later in life, when he made the acquaintance of the denser, richer, warmer European spectacle—it takes such an accumulation of suggestion for a novelist." And James wondered that anyone could write an exclusively American novel such as the *Scarlet Letter* or the *House of Seven Gables:* "One might enumerate the items of high civilization, as it exists in other countries, which are absent from the texture of American life, until it should become a wonder to know what was left. No state, in the European sense of the word, and indeed barely a specific national name." [26] Even so, in writing *The Marble Faun,* Hawthorne had "forfeited a precious advantage in ceasing to treat his native soil," and had incurred "that penalty of seeming factitious and unauthoritative which is always the result of an artist's attempt to project himself to an atmosphere in which he has not a transmitted and inherited property." How strange that it was James who would make this criticism! Hawthorne's writings received acclaim in Europe almost as soon as they did in the United States. He was introduced to European readers mainly by a large undertaking of a Leipzig publishing house which between 1854 and 1864 brought out its *Collection of Standard American Authors,* comprising about eighty volumes.

James Russell Lowell was a European resident longer than Hawthorne. That he was a political conservative is amply demonstrated in his *Political Essays.* He felt with Cooper that democracy needed an elite to guide it, but nevertheless he was an ardent champion of the revolutions of 1848 and was delighted when fellow-poet Lamartine assumed direction of the French revolutionary government of 1848. From 1877 to 1880 he was American minister to Madrid and then was minister in London from 1880 to 1885. He was a good friend of Matthew Arnold.

Lowell had made his first trip to Europe in 1851 at the age of thirty-two, taking along with him his wife, two children, a nurse, and a milk goat. After a stay in Italy, they took a guided trip through Europe to England. They returned to America in the autumn of 1852. Lowell was forced to sell land to pay for the trip, and wrote "we shall spend at the rate of about ten acres a year selling our birthright as we go along for messes of European pottage." [27] Still, he had a strong appreciation for European civilization while maintaining his American viewpoint.

In Italy he met the Brownings, who had earlier corresponded with him. Their stay in Rome was marred by the sudden death of their only son. While he liked the "insensible charm" of Rome, which was growing on him, he did not like the English colony into which he was thrown. His critical attitude toward the English continued for some years, as in 1852 when he rushed touristically through London, Oxford, Cambridge, Scotland, and Wales. Apparently on this trip he met only Walter Savage Landor, although on the ship home he had as fellow passengers Thackeray and Arthur Hugh Clough.

When Longfellow decided to retire from the Smith Professorship in Modern Languages, the chair was offered to Lowell. He accepted with the condition that he be permitted to study abroad for a year, with his main objective Germany and the study of German literature. He arrived in France in 1855, spent some time in Paris and Chartres, then went to London, where he saw the Brownings, Thackeray, and Leigh Hunt. His criticism of England had cooled off, for he had made some good English friends, but it was to be exacerbated again with the Civil War, as shown by his plain-talking "Jonathan to John" article. After the Mason and Slidell affair, Lowell displayed his attitude:

> If the result of the present estrangement between the two countries shall be to make us more independent of British twaddle *(Indomite nec dira ferens stipendia Tauro)*, so much the better; but if it is to make us insensible to the value of British opinion in matters where it gives us the judgement of an impartial and cultivated outsider, if we are to shut ourselves out from the advantages of British culture, the loss will be ours, not theirs. Because the door of the old homestead has been once slammed in our faces, shall we in a huff reject all future advances of conciliation, and cut ourselves foolishly off from any share in the humanizing influences of the place, with its ineffable riches of association, its heirloom of immemorial culture, its historic monuments, ours no less than theirs, its noble gallery of ancestral portraits? We have only to succeed, and England will not only respect, but, for the first time, begin to understand us. And let us not, in our justifiable indignation at wanton insult, forget that England is not the England only of snobs who dread the democracy they do not comprehend, but the England of history, of heroes, statesmen, poets, whose names are dear, and their influence as salutary to us as to her.[28]

Lowell returned to America in late summer, 1856, to take up his professorship, remarry, and become the first editor of the *Atlantic Monthly*. He did not return to Europe until 1872.

In 1869 in the *Atlantic Monthly* Lowell showed his true Americanism. In an article entitled "On a Certain Condescension in Foreigners," he wrote:

> Til after the Civil War it never seemed to enter the head of any foreigner, especially any Englishman, that an American had what could be called a country, except as a place to eat, sleep and trade in. Then it seemed to strike them suddenly. "By Jove, you know, fellahs don't fight like that for a shop-till!" No, I rather think not. To Americans America is something more than a promise and an expectation. It has a part and tradition of its own. A descent from men who sacrificed everything and came hither, not to better their fortunes, but to plant their idea in virgin soil, should be a good pedigree. There was never a colony save this that went forth not to seek gold, but God.[29]

In that year he sailed from Boston with his friends Francis Parkman, John Holmes, and Henry Adams, who was his former student, and Adams' bride. Henry James joined them frequently in Europe. In spite of his new friend Leslie Stephen, he maintained his reserved attitude for England and held that it would take a long time for England to give up her patronizing airs toward America, or even to conceal them. While he slowly began to appreciate the English, he was more attracted to France. "I am inclined to be more pleased with Paris . . . than I expected, and may make something of a stay here. . . . They somehow make you feel *welcome,* while the English seem anxious to be rid of you."

Yet in 1875 he returned several times to England, meeting Carlyle, Ruskin, Morris, G. H. Lewes, and his friends the Brownings and Leslie Stephen. He was now well recognized in the English literary world, and Oxford conferred an honorary doctorate on him. He then traveled leisurely for a year through Belgium, Holland, Germany, Switzerland, wintered in Italy, and returned to Paris in the spring with the reflection that "America is too busy, too troubled about many things," and that Europe is the only climate in which society can develop good humour, wit, and the growth of art. "American life boxes us all up in a one-horse *sulky* of absorbing occupation." On his way back to take up teaching again at Harvard, he stopped off in England to receive his second honorary doctorate, this time from Cambridge. Could he perhaps have been mistaken in his attitude toward England? When Lowell next passed through London in 1877 as a minister to Madrid, Henry James met him again and wrote, "It is a great pleasure to talk with Lowell; but he is morbidly Anglophobic." Three years later Lowell was minister to the Court of St. James.

Henry James gave a description of Lowell's early months as minister: "He gets on here, I think, very smoothly and happily; for though he is critical in the gross, he is not in the detail, and takes things with a sort of boyish simpicity." Lowell wrote at the same time, "Yes, I like the people here and always have liked them. The differences between an American of English descent and an Englishman are mostly superficial. . . . I always learn to like people, for it is slow work with me in most cases."

The English seemed to appreciate Lowell's reserve. He became president of the Wordsworth Society and of the Birmingham and Midland Institute. He was proposed as Lord Rector of St. Andrews University, and when, with the election of Cleveland, it was probable that he would have to give up his post, English friends wanted to propose him for a chair of English language and literature at Oxford. But his wife died and he decided to return to the United States. He visited Europe every summer for the next four years. Lowell had sympathetically edited Donne, Keats, Wordsworth, Shelley, and Walton's *Compleat Angler*. His speeches in England, collected in *Democracy, and other Addresses,* cultivated a British respect for American institutions, and his simple manner did not mask his deep culture. At his death he was everywhere mourned as a great American who had interpreted America to Europe and Europe to America in both letters and diplomacy.

Without denying the validity of much of the famous "frontier thesis," the point I would stress is that America remained Europe's frontier as well, that even from the Revolution through Jacksonian nationalism and expansion there was an umbilical cord never severed. America was always tied up with Europe in commerce and investment, in wars and immigration, in the love-hate feuds of writers and artists on both sides who did not fail to invade each other's territory.

NOTES

1. American Historical Association, *Talleyrand in America as a Financial Promoter, 1794–1796,* Hans Huth and Wilma J. Pugh (trans. and eds.), (Washington, D. C.: Government Printing Office, 1942), p. 140.

2. Cited in Halvdan Koht, *The American Spirit in Europe* (Philadelphia: University of Pennsylvania Press, 1949), p. 7.

3. Archibald MacLeish, *America Was Promises* (New York: Duell, Sloan & Pearce, 1939), p. 9.

4. Letters, Nos. 20–21, 51. Cited in Howard Mumford Jones, *America and French Culture, 1750–1848* (Chapel Hill: University of North Carolina Press, 1927), p. 301.

5. Letter to Mrs. Shaw, London, August 15, 1785. Cited in Rahv, p. 49.

6. Cited in Kimball, p. 84.

7. John Adams, *History*, IX, 104 and 221. Cited in Jones, p. 493.

8. Frances Trollope, *Domestic Manners of the Americans*, Donald Smalley (ed.), (New York: Alfred A. Knopf, Inc., 1949), p. 312.

9. Cited in Koht, p. 32.

10. "Introduction to Towns of Manhattan," *The Letters and Journals of James Fenimore Cooper*, James F. Beard (ed.), 4 vols. (Cambridge: Harvard University Press, 1960–1964), p. xxxiii.

11. *Democratic Vistas* (1871). Cited in Oscar Handlin (ed.), *American Principles and Issues* (New York: Holt, Rinehart & Winston, Inc., 1961), pp. 385–86.

12. Anthony Trollope, p. 399.

13. *Ibid.*, p. 402.

14. *Ibid.*, p. 451.

15. *Journals of Ralph Waldo Emerson*, E. W. Emerson and W. E. Forbes (eds.), (London, 1913) VIII, 393.

16. Cited in Lionel Stevenson, *The Showman Vanity Fair* (New York: Charles Scribner's Sons, 1947), pp. 270–72.

17. Cited in Edward C. Wagenknecht, *Washington Irving: Moderation Displayed* (New York: Oxford University Press, 1962), p. 87.

18. *Ibid.*, p. 133.

19. *Ibid.*, p. 179.

20. Cooper, p. xvii.

21. Letter to Mrs. Peter Augustus Jay, March 26, 1827. *Ibid.*, p. 209.

22. Brooks Atkinson (ed), *The Complete Essays and Other Writings of Ralph Waldo Emerson* (New York: Modern Library, 1940), p. 524 *et seq.*

23. Nathaniel Hawthorne, "Consular Experiences." Cited in Rahv, p. 201.

24. Nathaniel Hawthorne, *Our Old Home*. Cited in *English Notebooks*, Randall Stewart (ed.), (New York: Modern Language Association, 1941), p. xxiii.

25. *Ibid.*, p. 270.

26. Van Wyck Brooks, *The Pilgrimage of Henry James* (New York: E. P. Dutton & Co., Inc., 1925), pp. 39–40.

27. Charles Eliot Norton (ed.), *Letters of James Russell Lowell*, 2 vols. (New York: Harper & Row, Publishers, 1894), I, 190.

28. "Mason and Slidell," *Atlantic Monthly* (February, 1862).

29. James Russell Lowell, *My Study Window* (Boston: Houghton Mifflin Company, 1871), pp. 75–76.

ᘡ VIEWS FROM ATLANTIS ᘝ

Dieses ist Amerika!
Dieses ist die neue Welt!
Nicht die heutige, die schon
Europaieret abwelkt.

—Heine

The intellectual men of letters were not the only people to keep Europeans informed of what was going on in the New World. While immigration slowed to a trickle during the war of independence and the Napoleonic wars, it began again after 1815 and increasing waves of "homeless and oppressed," as the Statue of Liberty says, were floated across the Atlantic. Even earlier, Franklin was so deluged in Paris for information about the possibilities of emigration to America that he finally printed a pamphlet in English, French, and later German to answer inquiries for "Information to those who Would Remove to America." [1] Sensible Poor Richard was careful to point out that America was a land of hard work, not a *Pays de Cocagne,* but with diligence all had the possibility of succeeding. Speaking of the immigrants in New York and Philadelphia which he had seen, Tocqueville wrote that "The lower people who inhabit these vast cities form a more dangerous populace than the same in Europe. . . . One encounters in its midst a multitude of Europeans whose misfortune and misconduct push every day into the shores of the New World; these men bring to the United States our worst vices." Anthony Trollope wrote later during the Civil War that Baltimore was "considered to have a strong and perhaps as violent a mob as any city in the Union."

The Irish potato famines of the thirties, the revolutions of 1848, the English, French, and German communitarians, and the pogroms in Polish Russia after 1881 saw more Europeans adding to this massive immigration wave to join in the American experiment. Their letters back home became community property, and public readings were held to discuss the possibilities and dangers of group removal to American shores. In fact, America became better known to Europeans than other neighboring countries of Europe, and the tradition was established, which continues to this day, that

Europeans would recount their travel experiences in America. As American consul, Hawthorne complained that "All exiles for liberty come to me, as if the representative of America were their representative." He had to contend with Hungarians, Poles, Cubans, and French republicans.

An idealized American image was fixed in the European mind. For one hundred and fifty years America was seen as the place of refuge, of ferment, of experiment, and of freedom, a freedom from conscription, onerous taxes, religious persecutions, and political prosecutions. American was a country of cheap land, where the ambitious found equal opportunity with no hereditary overlords. This image remained secure until the twentieth century, when the door closed and the image was shattered into millions of individual personally frustrated pieces. Barring Switzerland (although many Swiss emigrated to America), the United States had stood for five generations as the "New Republic" in the face of Metternichian reaction, bourgeois monarchies, unsuccessful revolutionary upheavals, a new conservatism after 1848, and the unpleasant machinations of *Realpolitik* in the new age of materialism. William Cobbett, who had fled to America to escape his bad debts, wrote from his Long Island farm, "This America, this scene of happiness under a free government, is the beam in the eye, the thorn in the side, the worm in the vitals, of every despot upon the face of the earth." [2] The emigré political idealist looked on America as a last redoubt for the continuing struggle in Europe. Many, such as Karl Schurz and Francis Lieber, became cultural and political leaders on the American scene.

Melville wrote romantically of America:

Settled by the people of all nations, all nations may claim her for his own. You can not spill a drop of American blood without spilling the blood of the whole world. . . . Our blood is as the flood of the Amazon, made up of a thousand noble currents all pouring into one. We are not a nation, so much as a world. . . . Our ancestry is lost in the universal paternity.[3]

Of the millions who migrated to America and fell into the American melting pot, most were fused into the amalgam of American uniformity that is liberal and traditional; there were many, however, who did not fit into the general scheme of American life. It may be useful to view several European philosophies brought across the water by their proponents who refused to amalgamate, and who, instead of wanting to be assimilated, wanted to create new social orders in the freer atmosphere of America. On the fate of the introduction of socialism in America, we shall have more to say. Let us examine the various ideas that have their roots in Rousseau or

Bentham rather than in Locke or Montesquieu, the communitarian utopians.

First of all, we must remember that the social revolutionaries who came to America were different from those who stayed in Europe. It is one thing to stay in Europe and pursue a social struggle on the home front, another to establish a utopia in the New World. It is possible for liberal ideas to be completed in America, if not a utopia, while in Europe the inner and outer struggle goes on between conflicting camps. New ideas are submerged in neglect and nonrecognition by the great central American life-stream or are quite rapidly absorbed like little rivulets into the broad and accommodating American Niagara.

The communitarians and such religious groups as the Rappites had already established successful communities in the United States before the Civil War. There was an essential congruence between the way the communitarians wanted to develop their institutions and the way that Americans looked at the historical evolution of their own society. But where Americans tended to think in terms of Lockeian political freedoms, the utopians tended to think more in terms of social liberties and greater collective economic responsibilities. It is for this reason, among others, that the native Mormon growth removed to the unaccommodating desert flats of Utah, and other religious groups sought isolation from the central current of America. The Utopians looked for a complete reform of society, and even though many have been millenarians they made direct efforts to improve society in their own lifetimes, not to escape but to set an example. They were not revolutionaries, but wanted simply immediate reform without violence, seeking social harmony and voluntary action rather than class warfare. Revolution was too violent for them, but on the other hand governments were too slow with reform. Their model communities, they hoped, would establish a chain reaction to improve man's condition.

On the surface this seems to fit reasonably well into the American scheme of things, but each movement (almost one hundred between 1825 and 1850), despite the best of intentions, ultimately failed. The principle of communitarian socialism was not essentially economic but social, not communism but commonwealth, with individual cooperation in community services and community welfare. There was a subtle interaction between imported ideas and actual conditions encountered for the first time in America. Those who made up the communities were for the most part not Europeans, but were recruited amongst Americans. The European communitarian leaders failed in America largely because theirs was not a response to an American opportunity but an answer to a European threat. Cheap land and individual opportunity, which they hoped would nurture their movements, had the opposite effect: the individual could do better on his own.

The utopian communitarians watched the breakup of their dreams with their own member dissenters dissenting from their previous dissents.

Robert Owen, the successful Scotch manufacturer and industrialist from New Lanark (a worthy recommendation in itself), established in 1824 a colony named New Harmony in Indiana on a thirty-thousand-acre site purchased from another group of communitarians, the German Rappites, whose colony was withering for the logical reason that its members practiced celibacy. Owen believed that only through material equality, an ideal communism, could men find moral and social happiness and well-being. For a time New Harmony prospered and news of its success traveled quickly. It was visited by a number of eminent Americans and Europeans, and Owen was invited to address both houses of Congress before Presidents Monroe and John Quincy Adams. A "Boatload of Knowledge" consisting of some of the best European and American scientists came down from Pittsburgh to visit the colony. Fanny Wright joined them. Then through careless handling, but more because of the antireligious views of Owen and the notions he held about marriage, the community failed. Because of his interest in birth control, the colony attracted twice as many women as men. Ten other Owenite communities were also established, the most notable at Franklin, Haverstraw, and Coxsackie in New York, Yellow Springs and Kendal in Ohio, and Forestville and MacLuria in Indiana. Frances Trollope summed up his movement:

> Mr. Owen is an extraordinary man, and certainly possessed of talent, but he appears to me so utterly benighted in the mists of his own theories that he has quite lost the power of looking through them, so as to get a peep at the world as it really exists around him.[4]

The idealist experiment planted in American soil did not take root, for it strained the Puritan conscience, did not have enough of practicability for the "show me" American, and finally offended the liberal and traditional capitalist position. While Owens' community may seem strangely idealistic and improbable, we may at least note that Owen felt that it was necessary for him to establish his New Harmony in America, where everything could at least be tried. The most he could do in Scotland, which was a lot at the time, was to modernize and rationalize his factories and mills and to ameliorate the housing and social conditions of his workers in a model community.

Similarly, Harriet Martineau, while disliking American spittoons, was very impressed by the various communitarian movements in America. In her *Society in America* she wrote,

Whether any principle to this effect [communitarianism] can be brought to bear upon any large class of society in the old world is at present the most important dispute, perhaps, that is agitating society. It will never now rest till it has been made a matter of experiment.[5]

Although no friend of Harriet Martineau, nor of America for that matter, Frances Trollope was also caught up in the communitarian spirit. Her name became anathema to Americans and is a supposed source in the United States for the term "trollop." Mrs. Trollope was a friend of Fanny Wright, who had visited the United States to expound communitarian living and free love and had published a fulsome book, *Views of Society and Manners in America,* in 1821. Fanny Wright returned to the United States with Lafayette to share in his triumphal tour and met Jefferson and Madison, who encouraged her to establish the Nashoba Community in Tennessee for Negro emancipation. Nashoba, like New Harmony, failed, but not for want of publicity, for it also advocated free love. The director married Fanny Wright's sister, but only to protect the community from civil grievances. Then, in 1829, Fanny bought a church in New York which she renamed the Hall of Science, where free thinking and free love were expounded. The next year found her caught up in the July Revolution in France.

Thus when Frances Trollope sailed for the United States, her image of America was colored by Fanny Wright. She had intended to establish a department store in Cincinnati to recoup the family fortunes, but wound up producing a book, *Domestic Manners of the Americans,* to save her from the bankruptcy of her commercial venture. On her arrival she soon fell in with the New Harmony group, including MacClure, who had established the first American Pestalozzi school in Philadelphia and who had organized for Owen the "Boatload of Knowledge." Her department store in Cincinnati, to be known for years as "Trollope's Folly," was doomed to failure, although its architecture was supposed to present the most refined taste of the day: an Egyptian mosque with gothic battlements and columns, and a rotunda topped by a Turkish crescent. She managed to keep it open for a while by displaying enormous canvases, such as the "Landing of Lafayette at Cincinnati." Yet this failed, she had lost all, her household possessions were seized, and the store served successively as an inn, dancing school, Presbyterian church, theater, mechanics institute, military hospital and a "Physico-Medical Institute" run by a quack doctor.

It is no surprise, then, that Mrs. Trollope was embittered. She was aware that it was easy and insidious to judge the manners and pecularities of others and said that while she did not object to the new or novel, nevertheless "it was impossible not to feel repugnance to many of the novelties that now surround me." She hated the money-grubbing, the spittoons. Yet in her time Cincinnati had a fine arts academy and a theater, a medical school and hospital, circulating libraries, and nine newspapers. Dickens described Cincinnati a few years later:

> a beautiful city; cheerful, thriving, animated. I have not often seen a place that commends itself so favorably to a stranger at the first glance as this does: with its clean houses of red and white, its well-paved roads, and footways of bright tile. . . . Nor does it become less prepossesing on a closer acquaintance. The streets are broad and airy, the shops extremely good, the private residences remarkable for their elegance and neatness.[6]

Mrs. Trollope saw pigs in the street and human brutishness. Women were discriminated against, and their only amusement was to be found in religion and itinerant clergymen.

She was sure that democracy debased the moral and intellectual climate of the country. In her introduction she said that she had endeavored

> to show how greatly the advantage is on the side of those who are governed by the few, instead of the many. The chief object she has had in view is to encourage her countrymen to hold fast by a constitution that ensures all the blessings which flow from established habits and solid principles. If they forgo these, they will incur the fearful risk of breaking up their repose by introducing the jarring tumult and universal degradation which invariably follow the wild scheme of placing all the power of the state in the hands of the populace.

She said that common sense revolted at the "mischievous sophistry" that all men were born free and equal. Of Jefferson's writings she held that "they are a mighty mass of mischief. He wrote with more perspicuity than he thought, and his hot-headed democracy has done a fearful injury to his country." Obviously, the book was taken up with glee by the Tories who were then fighting the Great Reform Bill. It went through four editions in nine months and was immediately reprinted in New York. "Yankee" speech became a fad in London. By the end of 1832 she had earned 1,000 pounds from *Domestic Manners* and from a weak romantic novel, *The Refugee in America*.

Dickens was inclined to agree with her. While praising the frankness and cordiality, the cultivation and refinement, the warmth and enthusiasm of the upper class, he qualified this impression for all Americans. These qualities were "sadly sapped and blighted in their growth among the mass . . . there are influences at work which endanger them still more, and give but little present promise of their healthy restoration," which was a truth he felt ought to be told.

To secure her fortune, Frances Trollope continued to churn out novels and travel sketches of Europe and America. *The Life and Adventures of Jonathan Jefferson, or Scenes on the Mississippi* was violently abolitionist. A satire on American prejudices, *The Barnabys in America,* followed in 1845. In it Mrs. Barnaby is told by an American woman:

> All I want is that you should portrait us out to the world for just what we really are, and that is the finest nation upon the surface of God's whole earth, and as far ahead of civilization in Europe in general, and England in particular, as the summer is before winter in heat.

Frances Trollope was "perfectly certain that I shall be contradicted by one loud shout from Maine to Georgia," and she certainly was. She did draw an unflattering picture of the United States and the Americans, and, because of her experiences, she disliked the Americans in general. "I do not like them. I do not like their principles, I do not like their manners, I do not like their opinions." Yet she liked the country and her American friends who were a "small patrician band," a race apart. Mark Twain in a suppressed passage of *Life on the Mississippi* admitted, "Yet she was merely telling the truth and this indignant nation knew it. She was painting a state of things which did not disappear at once. It lasted to well along in my youth, and I remember it." For better or for worse, she made America known to millions, and as she stated: "at our public schools America (except perhaps as to her geographical position) is hardly better known than Fairyland; and the American character has not been much more deeply studied."

She settled in Florence, and in 1856 at the age of seventy-six produced her thirty-fourth novel. Her marble-terraced villa housed a magnificent library and art collection, and her wide circle of friends included the Brownings and Hiram Powers. Mrs. Trollope had come a long way fom the communitarians and from Cincinnati.

The French contribution to the search for social freedom in establishing communitarianism across the Atlantic was principally inspired by Charles Fourier, a disciple of Rousseau and Comte; his doctrines seemed more palatable to the Americans than Owen's. He himself was strongly against

Owen, as seen in his *Pièges et Charlatanisme des deux sectes de St. Simon et d'Owen.*

Other French socialists had followed Etienne Cabet's *Voyage en Icarie* to establish communities in Texas and Illinois. Somewhat earlier than the Fourierist movement, Etienne Cabet, lawyer and member of the French Chamber, devoted himself to social reform and was a member of the secret Carbonari. He fled to London in 1834 to avoid imprisonment and for five years devoted himself to social research, the result of which was *Voyage en Icarie,* constructed somewhat along the lines of More's *Utopia.* The wide public enthusiasm that greeted his book led him to think of a real utopia, and after consultation with Robert Owen and writing himself a constitution, sent off a preliminary contingent of young men to northeastern Texas as a vanguard for the thousands who were to follow.

This was in February, 1848. Twenty days later revolution broke out in France, and Icarian volunteers formed high hopes of establishing the new order in France itself, leaving the vanguard to fend for itself. Eventually Cabet and some four hundred colonists arrived in New Orleans in 1849 where they were met by the original colonizers. Ideological squabbles soon broke out and the colony was split by factionalism. About one-half followed Cabet to Nauvoo, Illinois, to establish a relatively successful colony, augmented to about five hundred by French emigrants. Factionalism continued, and Cabet was expelled from his own colony in 1856 and died in St. Louis. The original colony failed, and some went to Iowa, where there were other splinterings; others went to California. In 1895 the last remnants were dissolved. The colony of Victor Considérant, a Fourierist, was established in Texas in 1854 under the patronage of J. B. A. Godkin, but it was hardly successful.

Fourier believed that men were naturally good and that in "attractive" industry and "'joyous" labor man could establish a harmonious society. He maintained that private capital was economically wasteful and socially degrading, and that work should be rationally organized by groups of people related in phalanxes. He stressed the dignity of man and the dignity of labor against the drab new industrialism and the cold ferocity of cutthroat competition. It is immediately clear that his arguments were written in the light of a bourgeois monarchy experiencing the pangs of early industrial growth, but this does not fit into the economic and social picture of the United States, which was then undergoing the Jacksonian revolution.

Fourier never visited America and died in 1837 before Albert Brisbane began the movement in the United States. Fourier's influence was catalytic more than anything else, and his followers in France never paid any attention to the Fourierist movement in the United States. Fourierism was, then, not a set of ideas exported by the French, but something imported by the Americans.

Fourierism was hailed by a number of respected and talented Americans during the 1840's. Its chief propagandist, Brisbane, had stumbled on Fourier's writing while studying in Berlin; he went to Paris and induced Fourier to give him private instruction. Returning to America, he introduced Fourierism through his book *Social Destiny of Man* and his columns in Horace Greeley's *Tribune*. With Brisbane were associated Parke Godwin, a reformer and critic, George Ripley, founder of Brook Farm, and Margaret Fuller, a feminist who was onetime editor of *The Dial*.

Margaret Fuller deserves special mention. This warm-hearted and cultivated lady, who had decided to be "bright and ugly," went to Paris at the end of 1846 as a correspondent for Horace Greeley's *Tribune*. She was already known for her book on American literature. She met Lamartine, Béranger, George Sand, and Chopin. In her European travels she also ran across Wordsworth, Coleridge, Carlyle, Tennyson, Manzoni, and the Brownings, whom she introduced to the American public. At Thomas Carlyle's she met Mazzini, who was plotting in London for the Italian Revolution. She fell in love with a follower of Mazzini, the Marquis Ossoli, who was ten years younger than she. Having become pregnant as his mistress, she left the newborn child in an Italian mountain village, married the Marquis, participated with him in the 1848 attack on Rome, and worked in a hospital for the wounded. Margaret Fuller urged America to support the Italian liberation movement. "This cause is *ours* above all others; we ought to show that we feel it to be so." [7] Yet, as we have seen, the Americans were little interested in the revolutions of 1848.

When Mazzini arrived in Rome in 1849 after eighteen years' exile, he went quickly to Margaret Fuller. Soon the French entered Rome, and Mazzini had to escape for another twenty years of exile. When the Revolution was put down, Margaret Fuller went to Florence with the Brownings and William Wetmore Story and finished her book on the Italian Revolution. She was disillusioned by its failure and was determined to return to America. When the Italo-American family was in sight of New York, their vessel was shipwrecked, and she, her husband, and child were drowned.

In the decade after 1840 over forty phalanxes had been established in America, despite the failure of Fourier's own phalanx at Condé-sur-Vire in Normandy. None were completely successful, but perhaps the best known of the failures was Brook Farm, celebrated in Hawthorne's *The Blithedale Romance*. First organized by the transcendalists in 1841, it was converted to

Fourierism between 1843 and 1844. Brook Farm continued to receive experimental thinkers and writers until a general fire finished off the insolvent community in 1847.

The confluence of Fourierist and transcendentalist thought was no accident. Toward the end of his life, Emerson, who had become increasingly interested in social problems, changed his opinion about Fourier. He had thought Fourier too rational, mechanical, and utopian, while he himself was seeking moral and spiritual reform. But he still thought Fourier a genius, whose arithmeticism could advance the human condition:

> Fourier has foreseen everything, except the laws of life. He treats man like a plastic being who can be raised or lowered, stimulated or retarded, polished, condensed or expanded at will. . . . And then the maxim of Fourier is: enjoy yourself. To abstain from pleasure is for him a sin. Fourier was very French. He has committed a gross error in the place of the woman. His concept of marriage rests on prurience and on the absurd superstitions of the French regarding women. He ignores what is serious and highly moral in woman, and how much her nature is chaste, how she follows the rule.[8]

Fourierist thought continued to influence American social criticism. American critics later saw in it an answer to the "dismal science" of the Manchester School and social Darwinism. The very popular *Looking Backward* of Edward Bellamy was strongly Fourierist. European communitarian theories won a hearing in the United States because they represented a careful formulation of inchoate views that had already existed on the American side of the Atlantic. The transit of the communitarian idea was not so much a process of carrying doctrines from Europe to America as of awakening latent ideas and encouraging incipient activity in America.

While English social thinking was represented by Owen, and the French principally by Fourier through communitarian socialism in America, the Germans tended to establish little religious communities that were on the whole more successful. Generally the communities moved *en bloc* from their own country and, for better or worse, hung together in America united by language and religious discipline. Equally important, the Germans were already able farmers who knew how to work the soil, unlike the utopian Owenites or Fourierists who later admitted that socialism was better achieved under urban factory conditions rather than on the farm, which was characteristically individualistic.

Perhaps the earliest German sectarians to come were the Gabadists who established in 1684 a community in Delaware under the leadership of Peter

Sluyter. They denied original sin and the Sabbath, and had peculiar views on marriage. Because others failed to arrive from the mother colony in West Friesland, the Delaware colony faded out after fifteen years, and Sluyter himself became a successful tobacco planter and slave trader.

In 1693 the Pietists set out for America and established a brotherhood near Germantown, which lasted until 1708 or 1709. They were followed by the Dunkards, who estabished a colony in Pennsylvania in 1719. A branch of this colony, Ephrata, continued successfully into the twentieth century. Embued with Christian piety and "liberal," the Moravians and other sects were absorbed into American society and were lost as distinct communities in the American national stream. Under the patronage of Count Zinzendorff, the Moravians had established a community on Lehigh River in 1741 named Bethlehem. It abandoned its communitarian regime after twenty years, but continued to thrive as an American township.

The Harmonists, founded by Johann Georg Rapp, set up in 1843 a five-thousand-acre colony of six hundred persons in Butler County, Pennsylvania. In 1805 they adopted communism, and in 1807 adopted celibacy and renounced tobacco. But because they could cultivate the vine (there were, after all, some compensations!), the whole property was sold and the colony moved to New Harmony in 1814 on the Wabash River in Indiana. Because of malaria and discord with their neighbors, the colony sold out in 1815 to Robert Owen and returned to Pennsylvania to a new town near Pittsburgh, which they called Economy, which was a great financial success largely because of the discovery of oil and coal on their lands.

Those Germans who followed the Moravian and Rappite emigration were also quick to identify themselves with the American pattern. Joseph Bäumeler of Württemberg led a community of three hundred to Zoar in Tuscarawas County in 1817 to practice communism and celibacy, at least until "King" Bäumeler married his housekeeper. Communism was abandoned by the third generation in 1839.

A colony of eight hundred Inspirationists from Germany, Switzerland, and Holland purchased the Seneca Indian reservation near Buffalo in 1842, which they called Ebenezer. It was under the leadership of Christian Metz and the clairvoyant Barbara Teynemann. They found the city of Buffalo five miles away too great a distraction and moved to the Iowa River. When Metz died in 1867, the community numbered 1400 with 26,000 acres of rich land and seven towns. Barbara Heynemann died in 1883, but the community continued successfully, if austerely, with celibacy encouraged, games and music forbidden, and reading for pleasure or information enjoined.

Also, the Swedish Bishop Hill Colony of Devotionalists was established in Illinois. The Mennonites on the James River in South Dakota established the Old Elmspring Community in 1862. The Shakers, an offshoot of the Quakers first founded in England in 1747, began their community at Mount Lebanon, with seventeen other communities to follow, recruited largely from Americans. Another American community was Oneida, which successfully practiced free love and "complex marriages," to the violent consternation of the neighbors.

Utopian communitarianism and religious colonies tended to fade from view in the harsh realities of the Civil War, which preoccupied Americans and Europeans greatly. It is well known that European militarists studied it closely as one of the great lessons bearing on modern warfare and that some of the tactics and strategy developed during the Civil War were used in the Franco-Prussian War. The American Civil War was a war of national unification coinciding in time with the unification of Italy and Germany. New England was, in a sense, the Piedmont and Prussia of the United States. Before the War the United States was about as unified as the North German Confederation. But the parallels end here, for in America there was more bloodshed and Lincoln accomplished his design without foreign intervention, whereas Cavour and Bismarck had to rely on foreign wars to achieve theirs. Many European observers came to see the War in progress; others expressed their interest in its outcome with the pen. From his vantage point in London, Henry Adams described various English points of view, but we shall note his reflections later.

Anthony Trollope presented a vastly different image of America from that recounted by his mother thirty years earlier. In fact, he leaned over backward too far in his praise, for even though a generation had passed and the population had doubled, America was in the throes of an unedifying spectacle of civil war. In planning his *North America,* he wrote that a book on the United States would be "the best means of prophesying, if I may say so, what the world will next be, and what men will next do." For his efforts with *North America* he received £1,250, more than for *Barchester Towers,* which was perhaps the best novel in his popular Barchester series. Naturally, the book was well received in America and sold very well, particularly in the North, which in 1862 wanted foreign friends for its cause. (The English Declaration of Neutrality was a setback.) The book's reception in England was less enthusiastic. Trollope later wrote that it "was not a good book. I can recommend no one to read it now in order that they may be either instructed or amused." But James Bryce thought it was excellent.

In his *Autobiography* Trollope wrote:

My mother had thirty years previously written a very popular, but, as I had thought somewhat unjust book about our cousins over the water. She had seen what was distasteful in the manners of a young people, but had hardly recognized their energy. I had entertained for many years an ambition to follow her footsteps there, and to write another book.[9]

When he visited the United States in 1861, Cincinnati had grown eight times from the twenty thousand since he had left it; it was no longer a frontier city, for the frontier centers were now St. Louis and Chicago. Rude frontier farming had been revolutionized by the McCormick reaper and the binder, and the plains turned into oceans of grain. Still, Trollope preferred the more cultivated East and the society of his friends Hawthorne, Lowell, and Holmes:

> I know no place at which an Englishman may drop down suddenly among a pleasanter circle of acquaintance, or find himself with a more clever set of men, than he can do at Boston. . . . Boston has a right to be proud of what it had done for the world of letters. It is proud; but I have not found that its pride was carried too far.

For him, New York was too wrapped up in the dollar and was too commercial. Washington was an incomplete city: the Washington Monument, for example, remained only one-third done.

In his introduction to *North America* Trollope tells us of his purpose. Writings on the United States which had been most popular in England, he had concentrated mostly on social details which caused laughter in England and anger in America:

> If I could do anything to mitigate the soreness, if I could in any small degree add to the good feeling which should exist between two nations which ought to love each other so well, and which do hang upon each other so constantly, I should think that I had cause to be proud of my work.

Trollope tried to make an objective appraisal, and often his comparisons show real insight. He maintained, for example, that in England there was no level of society, that

> men stand on a long staircase, but the crowd congregates near the bottom, and the lower steps are very broad. In America men stand on a common platform, but the platform is raised above the ground, though it does not approach in height the top of our staircase. If we take the

average altitude in the two countries, we shall find that the American heads are the more elevated of the two.

Some of his dislikes have a familiar ring today. He loathed hotel lounges, and disliked American children who misbehaved and were fed with steak and pickles three times a day. The railroads were uncomfortable, and there was no first class because of a mistaken belief in equality. American women, particularly, made too many claims on their men, who were gentlemen, while the women did not act like ladies. There were ladies' doors, ladies' drawing rooms and salons, ladies' cabins on boats, ladies' windows at the post office. The spirit of chivalry had taken a deeper hold on the men than the women, and Trollope warned: "Let every woman learn this—that chivalry owes her nothing unless she also acknowledge her debt to chivalry. She must acknowledge it and pay it; and then chivalry will not be backward in making good her claims upon it."

He praised American general education, but, in accord with the opinion of many, he thought American newspapers were unreadable and full of vices. He exaggerated when he said that all Americans were intelligent, but perhaps he was close to the mark in noting that

> They are energetic and speculative, conceiving grand ideas, and carrying them out almost with the rapidity of magic. A suspension bridge half a mile long is erected, while in England we should be fastening together a few planks for a foot passage. Progress, mental as well as material, is the demand of the people generally.

Above all, Trollope thought that the United States had finally created its own national literature, which covered all subjects.

> The United States have been by no means barren in the production of literature. The truth is so far from this that their literary triumphs are perhaps those which of all their triumphs are the most honorable to them, and which, considering their position as a young nation, are the most permanently satisfactory.

Nothing showed the settled greatness of America better than the firm establishment of an American literature.

Trollope had seen much in his visit of six months. He made three more trips to America, once to negotiate a post office treaty and then to seek a copyright convention. The latter was unsuccessful and was to continue to plague Anglo-American literary relations for years to come.

There were various European attitudes toward the Civil War, and they were largely formed on the basis of class or political bias. Lancastrian cotton workers were unemployed, yet they supported the North, for Richard Cobden, who had visited the United States in 1854, and John Bright, who had many American friends in England including the Adams family, bolstered their sympathy with ardent support. The North sent wheat and other supplies to Lancaster, and the Manchester unemployed received gifts and funds. John Bright wrote to his fellow Quaker John Greenleaf Whittier:

> With us we are witnessing a great change of opinion, or opinions hitherto silent are being expressed. In every town a great meeting is being held, to discuss the "American question" and the vote is almost everywhere unanimously in favor of the North. The rich and the titled may hate the republic, but the people do not.[10]

In his famous speech a month later at St. James Hall he took the English upper class to task by stating bluntly that "Privilege has shuddered at what might happen if this grand experiment [U. S.] should succeed.

The English conservative viewpoint of a divided America was turgidly summed up by Edward Bulwer-Lytton:

> I believe that such separations will be attended with happy results to the safety of Europe and the development of American civilization. It could have been possible that, as population and wealth increased, all the vast continent of America, with her mighty seaboard and the fleets which her increasing ambition as well as her extending commerce would have formed and armed, could have remained under one form of government . . . why, then, America would have hung over Europe like a gathering and destructive thundercloud.[11]

America's ambitions would be less dangerous to the rest of the world if she remained fragmented. Bulwer-Lytton confessed to John Bigelow, American minister to France at the conclusion of the war,

> Well I must tell you frankly, Mr. Bigelow, I am sorry for it. I had indulged the hope that your country might break up into two or perhaps more fragments. I regard the United States as a menace to the whole civilized world, if you are allowed to go on developing as you have been, undisturbed.[12]

John Stuart Mill took the opposite position, and in his *Autobiography* wrote:

My strongest feelings were engaged in the struggle, which I felt from the beginning, was destined to be a turning point, for good or evil, of the course of human affairs for an indefinite duration. . . . It may be imagined with what feelings I contemplated the rush of nearly the whole upper and middle classes of my country, even those who passed for liberals, into a furious pro-Southern partisanship: the working classes, and some of the literary and scientific men, being almost the sole exceptions of the general frenzy. . . . None of the Continental Liberals committed the same frightful mistake.

England is paying the penalty, in many uncomfortable ways, of the durable resentment which her ruling classes stirred up in the United States by their ostentatious wishes for the ruin of America as a nation: they have reason to be thankful that a few, if only a few, known writers and speakers, standing firmly by the Americans in the time of their greatest difficulty, effected a partial diversion of these bitter feelings, and made Great Britain not altogether odious to the Americans.[13]

Alfred de Vigny advised his American mistress that the Northerners were huns and barbarians and told her to go to Martinique or Jamaica.

Before the Civil War had broken out, Victor Hugo wrote to the London *News* (December 2, 1859) on the trial of John Brown:

At this moment, America attracts the eyes of the whole of Europe. . . . we say to ourselves that this nation is one of the glories of the human race; that like France, like England, like Germany, she is one of the great agents of civilization; that she sometimes even leaves Europe in the rear by the sublime audacity of some of her progressive movements; that she is the Queen of an entire world, and her brow is irradiated with a glorious halo of freedom.[14]

Karl Marx, who was an English correspondent for Horace Greeley's *Tribune,* gave, of course, a particularly strange communist slant to the war. He wrote to Engels in 1862: "The long and short of the business seems to me to be that a war of this kind must be conducted on revolutionary lines, while the Yankees have so far been trying to conduct it constitutionally." Shortly thereafter Marx became quite put out with what he had hoped would be class struggle: "The manner in which the North wages war is only to be expected from a bourgeois republic, where fraud has so long reigned supreme." [15]

The Homestead Act of 1862 tended to encourage European emigration, and immigration officers successfully encouraged the newcomers to enlist in the Union army. As a result, Frémont's Army of the West was composed heavily of Europeans. Colonel Ferri Pisani remarked that it was so full of Germans that "it practically isolated the army from the rest of the population." [16] He feared that Frémont was obviously inclined toward dictatorship —he was "revolutionary" French while Beauregard was "conservative" French—and if he were ever elected president it would indicate a change of mind in the American nation. The English inheritance, "liberal, austere, but egotistic and exclusive," would be submerged and "philosophical and abstract German dogmatism will oppose the practical and positive sense of the English mind. The principle of unity and authority will take over the ground lost by the individualism, at the expense, perhaps, of the material and moral order." [17]

Napoleon III was pro-Southern because two separated American states would not endanger his ideas for a Mexican empire; however, the cotton workers in Paris and Rouen were for the North. When Slidell finally got to Paris in 1862 he was well received, but he was not officially recognized and the South received no material aid from the French.

Not only Germans joined the Union army. The famous General Boulanger, the "Man on Horseback" of France (but then only a captain), sought service in the Union army. The New York 55th Regiment was largely French, and when the Prince de Joinville and his son the Duc de Penthièvre arrived with the Comte de Paris and the Duc de Chartres, they wished to be attached to it, but were assigned to McClellan's staff. Colonel Ferri Pisani wrote that the French emigrants all longed for their motherland: "Of all the immigrants to America, the French are the only ones who cannot forget their tongue, their flag, or the skies of the old country. They die with this memory engraved in their hearts and bequeath it intact to their children." [18]

The Comte de Paris later assembled a widely read *History of the Civil War in America,* some of which is still interesting. He remarked that almost all emigrant soldiers were illiterate, while American troops were all reading newspapers and writing letters home. "It is owing to this general system of education that the New World may be called the country of progress, and that its institutions are founded upon the regular and conscientious practice of universal suffrage." Others noted that the Southerners were more illiterate. Also, Maurice Sand, the son of George Sand, accompanied Prince Napoleon, son of Jerome and cousin of Napoleon III, to observe the Civil War and recounted his experiences in *Six Mille Lieues à Toute Vapeur.*

Prince Napoleon visited Lincoln, but after ten minutes of idle conversation he became bored and took his leave. "What a difference between this sad representative of the great republic and its early founders!" He wrote that Lincoln was a compromise president simply because the people could not agree on a more prominent American: "I fear that the level of human values has fallen considerably. Mr. Lincoln is a worthy enough man, a lawyer from Illinois, and a one-time carpenter, unless I am mistaken. But he's a poor specimen of a President, and they tell me that he is the commonest they have had so far. . . ." [19]

His aide, Colonel Ferri Pisani, repeated the theme: "Since Washington's and Jefferson's time, even since de Tocqueville wrote his famous book, American mores have been deeply altered. . . . the intellectual and moral climate has lowered, particularly in political circles." [20] It was an "unexpected spectacle" to see a weak federal government demonstrate so suddenly the powers of a real dictatorship without, however, changing its nature or passing into other hands. Lincoln's regime was a unified government rather than a confederation of states, and, to Ferri Pisani at least, it was without political principle.

> I suspect them of being rather ignorant of what is called philosophy of history. Without worrying too much about general principles, they run to where the house is burning and throw onto the fire all that they can lay their hand to in order to put it out. . . . They are nothing less than practical administrators. [21]

Prince Napoleon and Ferri Pisani had a high regard for Charles Sumner, with whom the Prince had the closest relation. Sumner knew Tocqueville, and he still maintained personal relationships with a great many French writers and thinkers. Sumner had studied French literature in France and had lived in Europe from 1837 to 1840. "He is an avowed partisan of the French alliance and a warm friend of our legation."

Ferri Pisani related that Lewis Cass, who had been six years in Paris as minister to France, had lost faith in the United States and "sees only misfortune, ruin, and humiliations ahead. In his eyes Washington's work—in which Washington himself did not have complete faith—is in the process of crumbling to pieces." Cass's son was minister to Rome and represented

> rather well the higher social class which de Tocqueville describes as longing for European life and tired of America even before taking roots. Major Lewis Cass is deeply interested in the arts and the things of the mind—activities limited to polite society. All his thoughts are of Italy, where he discovered this type of existence.

Ferri Pisani was surprised that rich Americans did not enjoy luxury, either in their homes, furniture, or at the table, nor did they have an interest or taste in collections, books, paintings. "I have not been able, thus far, to find out what rich Americans do with their money." [22]

Pisani noted with pleasure their reception by the American people: "In a word, they confounded us with their naturalness, patience, and sociability." To a correspondent he wrote that one may wonder why he did not speak of violence, murder, and lynching by a half-savage society in New York. "Well, I must confess . . . that I never saw another city in the world—not excepting Paris—where the *material* order was as perfect as in New York." 23

Yet Pisani felt the Americans were colorless, all dressing the same way and having the same appearance. They were sad without being austere, and uniform without being simple. "If one goes further and listens to the conversation, one is equally struck by the monotonous and simple character of the ideas expressed," which were usually of the price of cotton or corn or political candidates. Even the newspapers had no digressions on art, literature, or science. He wished that America had a class of leisure and intellect:

Perhaps in such a milieu there would develop—naturally or unconsciously—an order of conceptions so far unknown to the American mind, and the absence of which is particularly felt by the foreigner. The easy, irregular, and even anti-democratic but elegant and chivalrous mores of such a group give birth to a current of more elevated, more speculative, less material, and less practical ideas than the ones now feeding America's intellectual and moral climate.24

As things stood, the Americans from one end of the country to the other could be "set into motion by the grossest artifices and the most declamatory eloquence; they can be carried away suddenly and foolishly by all kinds of ideas and persons, without reality or value."

The Italians followed the Civil War closely. In 1861 Lincoln offered Garibaldi a command in the Union army, but Garibaldi wanted the entire command and was in any case still busy unifying Italy. After the defeat of Mazzini's Roman republic he had fled to the United States where he made a small fortune, but he returned to Italy in 1854 and bought the island of Caprera. In 1861 he wrote the American Minister to Belgium that he would be "very happy to be able to serve a country for which I have so much affection, of which I am an adoptive citizen. . . ." Even Polish officers had offered to serve under him if he were to accept a Union command. While recovering from a wound, Garibaldi wrote the next year to the American Minister to Italy that there should be a clear statement on emancipation and that "I think continually of the disastrous war in America, my second country, to which I would gladly be of some use when recovered. I will go thither with my friends; and we will make an appeal to all the democrats of Europe to join us in fighting this Holy battle." Instead of going to America he marched on

Rome in 1862 and was taken prisoner. Garibaldi's ideological colleague Mazzini wrote to an American upon the Northern victory: "You have done more for us in four years than fifty years of teaching, preaching and writing from all your European brothers have been able to do."

The war over, Europe came to realize the vast achievement of Lincoln, not only in preserving national unity but, more importantly, in uniquely projecting the liberal democratic ideal and the greatness inherent in humility, equality, and grandeur in respect for the individual.

⌒⌒

Thus, until our own times, the history of America can be written in the unfolding pages of immigration, of communitarians, utopians, and religious groups hell-bent on heavenly experiments. Then also, the Civil War brought about a fresh wave of immigrants and a keen European interest in American affairs and life.

NOTES

1. A century later the American legation in London wrote to the Department of State: "It is remarkable how ignorant even the educated classes in this country are of the geography, history, and vital statistics of the United States, and how few books can be found here, within the reach of persons intending to emigrate, which will satisfy their reasonable curiosity. . . ."

2. Cited in Allan Nevins, *American Social History as recorded by British Travellers* (New York: Holt, Rinehart & Winston, Inc., 1923), p. 92.

3. Herman Melville, *What Redburn Saw in Launcelott's-Hey*. Cited in Rahv, p. 48.

4. Frances Trollope, p. 153.

5. Harriet Martineau, *Society in America* Seymour Martin Lipset (ed.), (Garden City: Anchor Books, 1962), pp. 176–77.

6. Charles Dickens, *American Notes* (London: Chapman, 1907), p. 160.

7. Letter from Rome, October 18, 1847. Cited in Rahv, p. 179.

8. In Charles Cestre, "Emerson et la France," *Harvard et la France* (Paris: Revue d' Histoire Moderne, 1936), p. 66; translated here by Robert Mead. Also to be found in Emerson's *Lectures and Biographical Sketches* (Boston: Houghton Mifflin Company, 1884), pp. 331–33.

9. Cited in Anthony Trollope, *North America*, p. vii.

10. Cited in Belle B. Sideman and Lillian Friedman, *Europe Looks at the Civil War* (New York: Orion Press, 1960), p. 226.

11. *Ibid.*, p. 93.

12. *Ibid.*, p. 282.

13. *Ibid.*, p. 117–18.

14. *Ibid.*, p. 5.

15. *Ibid.*, pp. 159–60.
16. Camille Ferri Pisani, *Prince Napoléon in America, 1861,* George Joyaux (ed.), (Bloomington: Indiana University Press, 1959), p. 250.
17. *Ibid.*, p. 240.
18. *Ibid.*, p. 149.
19. Cited in Sideman and Friedman, pp. 77–78.
20. Pisani, p. 109.
21. *Ibid.*, pp. 45–46.
22. *Ibid.*, pp. 168–70.
23. *Ibid.*, p. 62.
24. *Ibid.*, p. 61.

⌒ ATLANTIC FOGS ⌒

Ships that pass in the night, and speak
each other in passing,
Only a signal shown and a distant voice
in the darkness;
So on the ocean of life we pass and
speak one another,
Only a look and a voice; then darkness
again and a silence.

—Longfellow

Europe, moving toward its own integration, may draw away from the Atlantic connection into its own fortress. Yet a more viable partnership is at hand, a partnership, that is, of equals. Beyond that, the European sense of cultural superiority over America will be regarded as a self-satisfying myth rather than a hard reality. American scholarship in a number of fields, American science and technology and some of the fine arts, are easily as good as, if not better than, the European. Europe is rapidly learning many things from the United States, more than it likes to admit, and even beyond the so-called Americanization of Europe. Indeed, Europe seems to become more American while America becomes less European and even surprisingly less American as its traditional social values and structures evolve into a different technological collectivity. James Bryce wrote:

> There is a part of the Atlantic where the westward-speeding steam-vessel always expects to encounter fogs. On the fourth or fifth day of the voyage while still in bright sunlight, one sees at a distance a long, low, dark gray line across the bows, and is told that this the first fog banks that have to be traversed. Presently the vessel is upon the cloud, and rushes into its embrace, not knowing what perils of icebergs may be shrouded within its encompassing gloom.
> So America, in her swift onward progress, sees, looming on the horizon and now no longer distant, a time of mists and shadows, wherein dangers may be concealed whose form and magnitude she can scarcely yet conjecture.[1]

All witness that it is hard to avoid being caught up in different intellectual eddies, swirling in whirlpools of particular ideas, going round and round with them, with other new ideas occasionally pulled into the vortex. Cultural movements, constantly being washed up on each Atlantic shore, often get caught in the seines of language barriers or shattered on the reefs of differing cultural moods. The diffusion of ideas, their filtration through another language, or their absorption by another spirit tends to distort the original idea, as happened with the reception of Darwinism in America. When Marx saw how his own son-in-law was developing Marxist socialism in France, he was indignant: "If that is Marxism, then I am not a Marxist!" To see the diffusion and interpretation of one's own ideas is to look at one's reflection in tin. Some language nets block translation and meaning more than others. Twain said that a joke in Chicago was a riddle in Paris. Shakespeare and Shaw, for example, translate badly into French but excellently into German, which is a good reason for their relative standing in each country. Hemingway goes badly in French, although his style has much of its origins in the work of the French realists. It is even extraordinary how an American play loses all its bite and appeal when cast upon a London stage with British accents.

On the other hand, sometimes a creative piece of work can profit by expansion, contraction, or explosion, or can be refined and distilled by another language or cultural situation. The Baudelaire translations of Poe's stories and the Mallarmé renditions of his poems are in many ways superior to the original American. There was a renewal of interest in Melville in France before he was rediscovered in America. D. H. Lawrence wrote on Melville as early as 1923 and republication of Melville's works first began in England.

It is strange that foreigners often admire the wrong writers—from the other country's viewpoint. The French cannot understand the continued popularity abroad of Dumas, Rostand, Maurois, or Romains to the detriment of more important French writers. It was once said that Dumas was France's most valuable foreign asset. France long preferred such American writers as Cooper, Poe, Whitman, Harriet Beecher Stowe, Frank Norris, Upton Sinclair, and Sinclair Lewis, and offered up heavy critical treatises on them. Now Faulkner, Fitzgerald, Hemingway, Dos Passos, and Steinbeck are in the limelight.

At the same time, it is amazing to see the general aversion of nations living side by side and refusing to speak the languages of each other. Emerson said that Coleridge thanked God publicly for keeping him from ever having been able to utter a single sentence in the French language. Can it be that people do not want to communicate even basically? Mark Twain wondered about this in the essay "Some National Stupidities." He held that

The slowness of one section of the world about adopting the valuable ideas of another section of it is a curious thing and unaccountable. This form of stupidity is confined to no community, to no nation; it is universal. The fact is the human race is not only slow about borrowing valuable ideas—it sometimes persists in not borrowing them at all.[2]

The Atlantic cultural flow needs a larger and almost professional class of "interpreters" on both shores, not simply people who will translate words and phrases, but people who can formulate, analyze, and explain and transmit an idea, and in a form which can be understood by our distant cousins. Fortunately such interpreters have existed (such as Bryce and Tocqueville) for interpreting America to Europeans, but as yet there have been few American "generalists" interpreting Europe to Americans, although American expertise in European literature, history, art, and philosophy is acknowledged by all scholarly Europeans. Such indispensable intermediaries exist today, although not in great enough numbers or of enough influence to put the Atlantic dialogue under full sail. T. S. Eliot maintained in 1919 that under the influences of other cultures, "we do not imitate, we are changed; and our work is the work of a changed man; we have not borrowed, we have been quickened and we became bearers of a tradition." [3]

Occasionally our poets, novelists, and scientists enlarge the area of real communication and help in recognition, but they are almost always resisted by the Yahoos and Philistines. Poets, as Keats said, are "God's spies"; it is they who can interpret both the secret and the visible world to us, to point the way and to tell us where we have gone.

In a cosmopolitan age there is no room for parochial ideas or parochial action. Our time is one for stimulating the stream of Atlantic discussion. America and Europe must be intelligently aware of the changes which are taking place in the modern world, changes which may be resisted but not ignored. The two are obliged to make a deep adjustment in mental habits to see what is living or dead in their traditions. "Time," said Marcus Aurelius, "is a sort of river of passing events, and its current is strong: no sooner is a thing brought to sight than it is swept away, and another takes its place."

The impact and acceptance of ideas on both sides of the Atlantic depend on the distance, the time, and the depth of the cultural wave. Boston, Philadelphia, New York, and Charleston at one time were almost as isolated from each other as were London, Paris, Stockholm, and Naples. At the time of the Revolution it took as long to travel overland from Charleston to

Boston as to cross the ocean to Europe, and the journey was no less painful or dangerous. It was safer to send money from Philadelphia to New York via London. Boston, New York, Philadelphia, and Charleston stood rather as cultural outposts of Europe, eagerly awaiting the news and stuffs which each ship could bring.

We smile ironically now at the idea of Phineas Fogg's world tour in eighty days. Seven league boots are out of fashion. In 1927, Europe and the United States were linked by telephone. Now the White House has a private line to 10 Downing Street and a hot line to the Kremlin. Transatlantic commercial air service got underway just before World War II, and now the Atlantic skies are lined with superjets which land passengers in New York almost at the same hour they left Europe. Telstar now transmits direct live television from one Atlantic coast to the other, three thousand miles away.

For early communicaion with England, bags were hung up in coffee houses for letters. By 1657 the New Netherlands regulated the mails, but the colonies had no regular packet service until 1755. Regular coach service was opened for the first time in the colonies in 1766 between Philadelphia and New York, a trip of two days, now made in less than two hours by rail. News of the Boston Tea Party which occurred in December, 1773, did not reach Thomas Jefferson until a month later. As Secretary of State, Jefferson wrote to his American minister in Madrid that he had not heard from him in two years, and expressed the hope that he would have news before the third year was out. Nowadays, presidents can immediately be reached by radio-telephones placed in golf bags, yachts, or automobiles.

A London newspaper claimed a record in announcing Waterloo only four days after the event; news of Napoleon's death reached Europe two months later. By 1810, news to the United States could take from nineteen to twenty-nine days to arrive from Europe, and by 1818, Philadelphia newspapers would arrive a month late in Illinois (which also had extracts from English newspapers of two months before). From the 1830's to the 1840's, the telegraph was applied to news reporting. Polk's inaugural message of 1846 was the first to be transmitted by wire. In 1848 the Associated Press was established for gathering news more quickly. During the American Civil War, Reuters reports were dropped in a can from mail boats off the Irish coast, picked up by Reuters boats, and forwarded from Reuters cableheads in Ireland. The system enabled Reuters to report Lincoln's assassination to the European press two days before other news services. Now the *International Herald Tribune* Paris edition receives copy instantaneously by cable.

Fulton's 1807 steamboat soon saw its sisters on the Clyde, Rhine, and Elbe. Interestingly enough, it was first tried out on the Seine in the summer of 1803 before it made its famous Hudson run to Albany. In 1818 the first steamship crossed the Atlantic in twenty-five days; it was the *Savannah,* with a single-cylinder engine driving paddle wheels that could be unshipped and hoisted aboard when not in use. Moses Rogers then took it to Stockholm and St. Petersburg. The Black Ball Line, owned by the Quaker Isaac Wright, then the richest shipowner in the world, had the fastest sailing clippers and began the first regularly scheduled service in 1818. It consistently made the Liverpool–New York run in fifteen or sixteen days. In 1833 Samuel Cunard's *Royal William* was the first ship to be under steam all the way across the Atantic. The crossing was made in twenty-three days from Quebec to Gravesend. In 1840, after the successful crossing of Cunard's steamship *Britannia,* a dinner celebration of two thousand people was held in Boston, where Longfellow toasted the honored guest, Cunard: "Thus we come to this new age of steamships, each ship will surely be a Pillar of Fire by night, a Pillar of Smoke by day, to guide the future wanderer safely across the broad ocean." [4]

In *The Barnabys in America,* Frances Trollope wrote,

It is an obvious and very agreeable fact, that the social intercourse between the old country and the new, has been rapidly increased, and is still rapidly increasing, in consequence of the great comparative facility with which an excursion across the Atlantic may now be made; and the natural and inevitable result of this has been the formation of many warm and cordial friendships between individuals who were born of the same race, but with this formidable barrier dividing them.

Yet Dickens speaks of the extreme discomfiture he experienced on the ship he took in January, 1842, arriving eighteen days later in Boston. For eighty-six passengers, the mess room served also as the passenger lounge. He had a microscopic cabin with creaking joists and beams, but he claimed that American vessels of the Packet Service were "the finest in the world."

In 1880 it took ships twelve to thirteen days from Le Havre to New York, less than nine days at the end of the century, four and half days on the *Normandie* before World War II, and four on the present *United States.* When after the Civil War both the Federal and state governments set up immigration bureaus, it was possible to go from Stockholm to Chicago for twenty-two dollars. Steam and rail companies advertised an Atlantic crossing from port to port for twelve dollars, including meals.

The element of time is relative not only to the varying speed of the transit of ideas, but also to the state of mind of Atlantic peoples at a particular moment, to their readiness to accept a new trend of thought. Woodrow Wilson wrote in 1890 that our slow world spends its time catching up with the ideas of its best minds, and in almost every generation there are those who embody the projected consciousness of their time. Their thought runs forward into regions where that of the mass will not for many a weary day arrive.

America was no longer isolated from Europe, but a spirit of isolation persisted. It is much the same "spendid isolation" as is frequently seen in England; witness the London newspaper which reported that the fog in the Channel had isolated the Continent. Our barriers now are no longer of a natural or physical sort, but are imposed by man himself: passports, visas, quotas, customs and police lines, exchange controls, political and moral controls by states exacting fealty oaths and depositions.

Ideas are sometimes like a ship sailing against the tide, which seems to make much headway if one looks at the water but does not if we look at the shore. The climate of opinion may not be ready to let a new and suspect idea through the customs gate. Ideas nevertheless are slippery things and have a way of getting smuggled through in spite of public censors and customs watchers, self-appointed or otherwise. Often waves of stormy thought which clash in our cultural channels take a long time before stirring the sandy bottoms, and often much light is filtered out down below.

For example, the layman's idea of science is always behind the times; it reflects earlier scientific thinking. Popular science bears little relation to advanced contemporary science. Just at the time when older and simpler explanations receive general public acceptance, the scientists themselves have come to feel little faith in them or to reject them. Where the layman sees science as based on solid fact with all the right answers tested and proved by the men in white coats, the scientists now see all their work as relative and plural with a number of scientific solutions equally valid or plausible.

We might think, in considering the time element, of the reluctant acceptance of Darwin in the United States, not to be swallowed to any great extent until after the Scopes trial in 1925, years after the publication of the *Origins of the Species*. Three indefatigable Englishmen, all with their own interpretations of what Darwin *really* meant, carried Darwinism to American shores and took from their satchels a packet of ideas wihch was to stir the American conscience deeply: Thomas Huxley, the biologist, Herbert Spencer, the philosopher, and Henry Drummond, the popular lecturer, whose *Natural Law in the Spiritual World* and *The Ascent of Man* were read by millions of Americans. The three spread the scientific gospel of our origins. Americans had thought that this question was conveniently taken care of long ago. How Americans raged against such blasphemy as Darwin's, but when all the tumult and shouting died, they casually wondered what all the noise was about. Darwinism was converted into "social" Darwinism where God and mammon were linked to justify a gilded but hardly golden age.

Huxley and Spencer first started the mental gears of American intellectuals turning on the subject, and the historian John Fiske was among the original converts. He professed to see in Darwinism "a higher view of the working of God and of the nature of man than ever attainable before." Books of such eminent clerics as Henry Ward Beecher's *Evolution and Religion* and Lyman Abbott's *The Theology of an Evolutionist* also preached the doctrine. Their satisfied congregations were pleased to learn that they were the fittest who had survived. Henry Adams wrote that he was a "Darwinist before the letter; a predestined follower of the tide." He reviewed the work of his friend Lyell in the *North American Review,* and admitted that he had like "every curate in English dabbled in geology and hunted for vestiges of Creation."

William Graham Sumner, professor of political economy at Yale, even outdid Spencer and hailed the millionaires as the finest fruit of natural selection. His teaching of rugged individualism and laissez faire economics fitted nicely with the business climate of the time. At Columbia, his theories were equalled by John Bates Clark's. William Lawrence, Episcopalian bishop and proper Bostonian, proclaimed, "In the long run it is only to the man of morality that wealth comes. . . . Godliness is in league with riches. Material prosperity is helping to make the national character sweeter, more joyous, more unselfish, more Christlike." Railroad tycoon George F. Baer said, "The rights of the laboring man will be protected and cared for, not by labor agitation, but by the Christian men to whom God in His infinite wisdom has given control of the property interests of the country." [5] As Mark Twain had pointed out in *The Gilded Age,* presidents were businessmen. The Baptist Philadelphia minister Russell H. Conwell gave his "Acres of Diamonds" speech over six thousand times to enthusiastic audiences. "I say, get rich, get rich! But get money honestly, or it will be a withering curse." Conwell urged that all men and women strive for power, and money is power. There are diamonds in your own backyard if you only knew where to look for them. Conwell himself, of course, became very wealthy in promoting this gospel. In 1891 Andrew Carnegie wrote in the *North American Review* that the rich man was ethical and good and virtuous and stimulated others to become rich. Ten years later he was making over fifteen million dollars a year, without income taxes. The 1880's saw a proliferation of such survival-of-the-fittest books as *Win Who Will, On the Road to Riches, Men Who Have Risen, How to Succeed.* O. S. Marden's *Pushing to the Front* had 250 printings by 1900. Horatio Alger wrote 135 novels, all on rags to riches, which was one of his titles. Others were *Luck and Pluck, Sink or Swim,* and *Bound to Rise,* which gives an idea of their content.

Spencer himself told American businessmen that he thought they had gone too far. He said that work had become too much of a passion with Americans, that while the savage can think only of his present satisfactions the Americans think only of future ones and ignore what the passing of a day can offer. Business used to be disgraceful, but now it had become the honorable substitute for military activity. "Practically, business has been substituted for war as the purpose of existence." There was too much preaching of the gospel of work to the detriment of body and soul. "I should have liked to contend that life is not for learning, nor is life for working, but learning and working are for life."

By 1900 Spencer's books had sold 350,000 copies in the United States, a very high figure for such heavy and boring reading. Perry Miller wrote:

> The popularity of Herbert Spencer in America between the Civil War and the end of the century is a phenomenon that has frequently been described, but remains for all that staggering. Not only village agnostics, but scientists, many theologians, and most captains of industry paid him as great homage as the Revolutionary generation paid to Locke. It be would hardly too much to say that the bulk of American "thought" in this period, measured solely by the bulk of printed paper, was not thought at all, but only a recapitulation of Spencer. When Justice Holmes said, in his memorable dissent of 1906, in Lochner *vs* New York, that "the fourteenth Amendment does not enact Mr. Herbert Spencer's Social Statics," he was not only trying to get back to the original meaning of the amendment, but was blurting out his irritation with the decades in which Spencer had permeated the minds of businessmen and lawyers.[6]

Herbert Spencer's social Darwinism had a missionary appeal to the American public that uncut and undiluted Darwinism lacked. He became known as the "Apostle to the Americans." Evolution meant not only change, but constant "progress," a word on which Americans thought they had a near monopoly. Through the survival of the fittest, evil and immorality would disappear, and the American industrialist could then sit in blissful plush, clipping coupons and seeing no need for social reform. The "natural law" of social Darwinism was invoked to put down the Haymarket riots and to suppress the Pullman and Homestead strikes. Progress was inexorable and inevitable and any attempt to tamper with the machine of evolution by economic and social reform merely hampered the ordinary, natural, and scientific development of society. All could aspire to be millionaires, but, of course, there were some more richly endowed by nature than others. When the Government brought an antitrust suit against Standard Oil in 1907, John D. Rockefeller pointed out that the poor have no cause to despair if they are temperate, thrifty, and honest, and that God appoints people to certain stations in life. Millionaires acted like Borgias and then established libraries, universities, and foundations to prove they were public benefactors, meanwhile keeping Fifth Avenue mansions, country villas and manors, luxurious yachts, and private railroad cars. Even Whitman could see what was happening to American democracy; he wrote that it looked with a "suspicious, ill-satisfied eye upon the very poor and on those out of business; she asks for men and women with occupations, well-off, owners of houses and acres, and with cash in the bank." Incidentally, Bentham's utilitarianism, which had crept in somehow, coincided nicely with social Darwinism in America. Tocqueville earlier realized that the real advantage of American social democracy was not to favor the prosperity of all but to serve the well-being of the greatest number.

Harvard botanist Asa Gray accepted Darwin and attempted to prove that with Darwinism there was a rational design in the universe. By the end of the 1870's, Harvard, Yale, Johns Hopkins, and other universities were teaching Spencer's Darwinism in religion and in the biological and social sciences. While many American scholars accepted Darwin, many others did not, including the famous Harvard naturalist Louis Agassiz, who fulminated against Darwinism until his death in 1875, and the idealist Josiah Royce, who followed the Hegelian argument against Darwin's supposedly aimless workings of natural selection. The argument of the idealists was that while a man might have developed out of a primeval plasma, the conscience or soul of man must have been put in somewhere along the line by divine intervention. This was appealing to the fundamentalists because it methodically defended traditional morality. If social Darwinism came to be accepted in university and business circles, it was constantly fought by fundamentalist churchmen.

The social reformers who could not wait for the millenary evolutionary changes to take place also attacked social Darwinism. Henry George was perhaps the principal reformer of the unrestricted theory. In his *Progress and Poverty,* which went through over a hundred editions in the following quarter-century, he argued that if intelligence is the product of evolution, it should be employed to modify environment and humanize conditions for survival. Natural evolution, he maintained, was wasteful of human talent. By the turn of the century the Muckrakers had begun to attack monopolistic capitalism, exposing trusts and cartels in steel, oil, railroads, real estate, packing houses, and banking. Gustavus Meyer's *History of Great American*

Fortunes appeared in 1910 showing plainly that many were not honestly gained.

It was not until the Scopes trial in 1925 at Dayton, Tennessee, that most people would finally overthrow the archaic ideas propounded by the distinguished orator and fundamentalist William Jennings Bryan, who had given his "Prince of Peace" speech over three thousand times since 1904 defending religion against scientific evolution. At San Francisco, July 4, 1914, he spoke to one hundred thousand people without a loudspeaker. At Dayton, Clarence Darrow reduced him to a shambles and he died shortly thereafter. The case was decided against Scopes. The trial was a conflict between science and theology and since science had brought forth industry, American society was prepared to break the cake of custom and change its religious and moral attitudes. Science had its appeal to the popular mind, as witnessed by the appearance of hundreds of "outlines of science" written in its favor after the manner of H. G. Wells. The Scopes trial did pose some tough moral problems. Was the Bible now simply to be taken as literature? It was no good to say that man could have his God if he could not sustain a belief in him. Here science hedged and referred to the Unknown Absolute, Primal Force, Prime Mover. Science has had a hard time replacing the myths by which men live. As Walter Lippman noted in his *American Inquisitions: A Commentary on Dayton and Chicago,* most men prefer ideas they can count on; better absolute promises than the privilege of speculation.

Thus a new idea came to settle on American shores. It had changed in crossing the Atlantic with Huxley and Spencer and was further altered. "Soon, however, the circle of new ideas is almost completed," as Tocqueville declared, "the experience has taken place, and man is plunged in doubt and universal mistrust," for we are constantly putting new wine into the old bottles of habit and cultural tradition.

It is curious to note the cultural lag here, for if Spencerism was flowering in the United States, it was waning in Europe under the spiritual nationalism of Mazzini, the idealism of T. H. Green, and the socialism of Jaurès. At the end of his life, Spencer himself viewed with alarm the regression of Western society into the imperialism and materialism that he saw at the beginning of the twentieth century. Social Darwinism continued in America under different forms of the "New Imperialist Manifest Destiny" of Theodore Roosevelt, of A. T. Mahan, of Herbert Croly in his *The Promise of American Life,* and rivalries of Anglo-Saxon racism over "backward peoples." The ugly head of racism cropped up again in Southern arguments against racial integration, too often agreed to by the Horatio Algers of the chambers of commerce. The economic side of social Darwinism was finally challenged and aid to rest by the New Deal when Franklin Roosevelt jousted with the "men of ruthless force."

A contemporary example of the slowness with which cultural movements or ideas are spread is the reluctant and mincing acceptance of "classical" American music and painting in Europe as contrasted with the wide acceptance of American architecture and literature. There is little doubt that American composers and painters have much to say and have said much in the last thirty years. They are easily as good, sometimes better, than their contemporary European colleagues, having absorbed European techniques, usually at the source, and producing new creative idioms with a refreshing awareness of dissonance or harmonic style. Europeans forget, or prefer to neglect, the tremendous musical and artistic strides made in the United States between the two world wars and after. The very fact is that Rachmaninoff, Dvorak, Stravinsky, Schoenberg, Bartók, Hindemith, Milhaud, Bloch, and other European composers did much creative work in America, and American composers greatly profited by their presence. The Americans had Mahler and Toscanini and Munch and Koussevitzsky and Mitropolous, and a host of other distinguished European conductors to interpret for them from the podiums of more than a thousand symphony orchestras. Americans themselves sometimes seem unconscious of their great artistic progress.

Nicolas Nabokov said that, as far as music is concerned, the Europeans are

> unaware of the tremendous change that occurred in American culture. While in the Twenties American music or, perhaps more correctly, music written in America was ten years behind European music, both ideologically and technically, today the music written in America is completely in step with European developments. In certain respects composers in the United States are in advance of European composers— however foolish the idea of advance may be in matters of art.[7]

A number of European composers have realized this, and after their solid preparation in Paris or Vienna, stow away to America, where the grime of Morningside Heights, the heat of an Iowa plain or of a California sun seem to have tickled their Euterpean muse. European musical composition has gone into bold experiment as a result of music composed in America.

The New York Philharmonic was founded in 1842, and is forty years older than the Berlin Philharmonic, and outdates the London Symphony and Amsterdam's Concertgebouw, as does the St. Louis Symphony, which was founded in 1885. Tchaikovsky conducted at the opening of Carnegie Hall in New York in 1891, and wrote a "Marche Solennelle" for its inauguration. Gustav Mahler came to the United States in 1907 and was conductor of the New York Philharmonic from 1909 to 1911, when he had a falling out with the ladies of the board. Rachmaninoff first came to the United States in 1909 and returned to stay in 1917 as an exile from Soviet Russia. Stravinsky followed him in 1925 and came and went during the interwar and war period. He became an American citizen in 1945, and only in 1962 returned to Soviet Russia for a series of concerts of his works. Alban Berg was introduced to the United States by Stokowski in 1931. Arnold Schoenberg arrived in 1933 from Paris, where he was a refugee, and joined the music staff of the University of Southern California, then the University of California at Los Angeles. Hindemith came to the United States for the first time in 1937 at the invitation of the Elizabeth Sprague Coolidge Foundation, and shortly thereafter he established himself definitively in the United States. He taught in Zurich after a long professorship at the Yale School of Music, but maintained American citieznship. Martinu and Bartók fled to America at the outbreak of the World War II, the former became an American citizen in 1952, and the latter died in New York in 1945.

It is rare enough to hear American music in Europe, even with the comings and goings of American orchestras and conductors who give but one American "piece" to a program traditionally made up of European and Russian composers. If new music is heard over the national radio networks or played by state-subsidized orchestras, it is the music of their own national composers who are crying to be heard themselves. Europeans will perhaps now listen without too much pain to Copland, Sessions, and Gershwin, but that is about the limit.

Jazz is different, but jazz leads us to the third element in the movement of ideas back and forth across the Atlantic. This penetration in depth of a cultural form into the larger parts of society, and the "shock of recognition," filters down to the last man in Boston, Bologna, or Bergen. Sometimes there is no recognition at all, no penetration into the large consciousness of people. There was, for example, the poor French Breton soldier who emerged from World War I trenches still thinking that he was fighting the English after four years of war.

Jazz went quickly to Europe after World War I. The European interest in primitivism and things African meant a ready acceptance of "The Original Dixieland Jazz Band" which went to England in 1919 and 1921. Sidney Bechet made his first European tour in 1925. The French Colonial Exposition not only confirmed interest in the French colonies but also a general interest in the non-Occidental world: Oriental, Polynesian, and African.

Cocteau in *Le coq et l'arlequin,* Ansermet, and Milhaud wrote seriously on the subject of jazz. In the early days of jazz the important thing was that it was nonwhite and precivilized and consequently might have something to say in a world frustrated by war. It was simplified and naive, yet as complicated as an African mask. It is interesting that when Paul Whitman went to London with his "white" jazz in 1926, he was not well received. The outstanding book on early American jazz is French: Hugues Panassié's *Le jazz hot,* written in 1934 and translated into English in 1936. Interest in Negro art had preceded the War. Vlaminck and Modigliani were attracted by African primitivism, as was Gertrude Stein when she created Melanctha in *Three Lives.*

As with American music, there has been little public recognition in Europe of the vitality and originality of American painting and sculpture; even though, since World War II, the American Government, as well as private groups and museums, have arranged rotating traveling exhibitions of American artists, sometimes with much ballyhoo. Although Europeans have remained cold, the critics often silently frigid, European artists are more than lukewarm, they are often enthusiastic. The whys and wherefores are difficult to explain for art, like science and music, is international in scope if not always in character. It could be that there is an element of snobbish nationalism involved, for Europeans flock to see American collections of European art, which is brought back to be shown on European shores. We are sadly forced back to the earlier day of West, Stuart, Trumbull, and Copley to find a free European acceptance of Americans in a cosmopolitan spirit. How many Europeans today are acquainted with Pollock, Toby, de Koonig, Marin, O'Keefe?

In contrast with American music and painting, American architecture has considerable impact on Europe since the War. During the Depression and the war years, there was little building in Europe and a vast reconstruction was needed. Also important is the fact that many distinguished European architects emigrated to America before the War and found there an ideal ground on which to realize and erect their conceptions, not only because there was money available but also because there was significantly more willingness to experiment. American engineering advances also had much to do with the furthering of the modern "international" style, which had first sprung from the Bauhaus but was literally transferred to the United States by Gropius and colleagues such as Breuer and Neutra.

Probably Harold Laski has found an acceptable reason for Europe's attitude toward American artistic endeavor:

The European refuses to take American Art, in all its forms, at the value he attaches to his own art because he cannot bring himself to accept this blow to his self-esteem. . . . It is still broadly true that interest of Europeans in America is far smaller, both in width and depth, than the American interest in Europe. It is still more true that an American work which criticizes America is likely to arouse more attention, to be received with more satisfaction, than one which is written upon the assumption that American creative talent no longer looks to Europe either for stimulus or standards.[8]

The European discovery of post-World War I American writing provides a clue in this relation, for American realist and naturalist authors express a critical revolt against what they see, and what Europeans think they see, a uniformly-standardized, mass-conforming, material-industrialized American culture. American literature is applauded because its violence and brutality belies the superficially apparent smooth-running, high-speed, fluid-driving, chromed social machine. American literature is generally pessimistic, which coincides with the main attitudes of European thinking. In fact, Europe awoke to American power and culture after World War I largely because the Americans began to criticize themselves. Until the 1890's, Americans unquestionably accepted the European idea of an America with a "colonial" culture not yet come of age; their light was hidden under a bushel. In consequence, few Europeans had seriously diagnosed America before World War I, few American writers were known or studied, and precious little American history was taught. Travel journals provided the basic knowledge of America until Bryce's sympathetic study. Tocqueville had been curiously neglected by the French for almost three quarters of a century even though he was trying to write about the future shape of France as seen in the America of his day.

Once established, for good or bad, an idea settled in the mass mind is almost impossible to change to a new or different one. When an idea has taken hold of the American people, Tocqueville maintained, whether it be right or unreasonable, it is almost impossible to extirpate it. Once formed, public opinion can exercise a stifling tyranny over the minds of men. The consequence is deadly and dangerous for future thought. Myths and codes of a people are the strongest deterrents to new ideas, and creativity must constantly break through strongly entrenched barriers.

The reaction of the intelligentsia against mass culture on both sides of the water has not particularly helped the quality of the enormous amount of predigested cultural pills that we are asked and even demanded by advertisers, cajoled by taste-makers, to take each day. We are constantly assaulted by loudspeakers of commercialization. The revolt of the intellectuals against our contemporary world has had little effect on the great majority of its inhabitants. Rather, the intellectual has become more and more isolated from a world that is not to his liking nor of his making. The world, with its politics and its business, makes its own laws, and the authority of these laws wanes more and more in the private world of the intellect and the spirit.[9] This is the central reason for the schizophrenia we see in the present-day culture. Earlier, James Fenimore Cooper wrote that America was deficient in those things most pertinent to the purposes of the novelist. The American expatriate writers in Paris after World War I did not rescue the country from materialism, as they had fervently hoped. From Cooper on, the American writer has treated the bourgeois American with contempt, but Babbitt has not changed, and the intellectual's isolation has become simply a self-exile to an inner migration. He is a cliff dweller on the mountain of materialism.

The workaday intellectual and the "engaged" writer struggle manfully along, unsung and unloved. They edit newspapers, draft political speeches for their chiefs, and throw themselves into the hurly-burly of party and sectarian activity. Sadly, and more often, they are only contributing to the tactics of their party and not to its strategy, not to the formation of its principles. Too often they become the propagandists, not the originators of policy. Under the Kennedy administration, Harvard moved to Washington like Birnam Wood to Dunsinane and the intellectual world applauded for a thousand days. The engaged writer, like Sartre or Aragon, frequently writes only party journalism and then returns to "real" writing. The Marxists are not really interested in literature, they look only for a vehicle for their own theories.

Nevertheless, the engaged intellectual is about the only drawbridge over the moat between the ivory-towered intellectual castle and the quasi-barren fields beyond. And those in their ivory towers such as Berdyaev, Maritain, Sorokin, Jung, and Eliot remain unread by the politicians and businessmen, or if they are read are not understood. The world of action goes one way, while the world of thought goes another, the two either hostile or indifferent to one another. Einstein's ideas may have affected two cities of Japan and led to the present East-West stalemated relationship, but how many in Europe and America have understood him? Mortimer Adler thinks that America has now found its own way in philosophy, but where America falls behind in comparison with Europe with its older philosophic culture is that the interest

and the participation of the public is absent in the intellectual and political
life of the United States.

᠊᠊᠊᠊᠊᠊

Examining the idea of penetration in depth again, after seeing the easy
absorption of mass media against the difficulties that face the intellectual
heavyweight, we might find that sometimes virtually no penetration at all
occurs. If Darwinism gained over the years a gradual acceptance by the great
mass of people in the United States, Marxism did not. Marxism, which saw
the light of day at the same time as Darwinism, has met with constant American resistance, and indeed this resistance has probably strengthened, except
for the short period in the twenties and early thirties when some Americans
enjoyed playing at being parlor pinks. William Dean Howells summed up an
American attitude when he said that socialism "smells to the average American of petroleum, suggests the red flag, and all manner of sexual novelties,
and an abusive tone about God and religion." [10] Marx never enjoyed any
popular support among the laboring masses in the United States because of
the basic incompatibility between Marxist determinism and a pragmatic,
empirical, and liberal Americanism. The antiseptic moral force of Americanism has resisted ideological changes more than any other country.

Ferri Pisani wrote of meeting General Franz Sigel, a former officer in
the Baden army who had sided with the German Revolution of 1848 and
then emigrated to the United States:

> If one were to meet this striking personality in Germany, one would
> undoubtedly say: "There is the very type of German revolutionary and
> socialist." But in this fortunate American country, one must admit, there
> are neither socialists nor revolutionaries. When one of these terrifying
> doctrines, which shake and ruin our older societies, reaches this country,
> it is absorbed; it melts, evaporates, and disappears with individualism.[11]

Marxism was introduced to the United States by two German immigrants, Joseph Weydemeyer and Freidrich Sorge, both friends of Marx and
Engels. Sorge was leader of the American branch of the First International
and was placed in charge of the First International by Marx when its head-
quarters was transferred to New York in 1872. Engels encouraged Sorge in
his work when he visited the United States in 1888.

Weydemeyer's activities preceded the work of Sorge. (A former Prussian army officer, he emigrated to the United States in 1851 and worked as a
journalist for several German-American newspapers,) during which time he

attempted to sway other German emigrants to socialism. He was a captain in the Union army and ultimately retired as a general to edit a Marxist newspaper in St. Louis until his death in 1866. Despite Weydemeyer's and Sorge's efforts, both Marx and Engels felt that the American socialist movement was not doctrinaire enough, and they sharply criticized the lack of theoretical development.

The Socialist Labor Party, founded in 1877, had a mostly foreign-born membership, many already from a European syndicalist background. In the election of 1892 the party won only twenty-one thousand votes. The party was split by internal doctrinal differences characteristic of all Communist parties then and today, with all the accompanying turbulences of purges, recantations, sanctions, splintering, and revisionism. The founding of the Socialist Party in 1899 by Eugene Debs met with somewhat larger success, but still the American worker shunned Marxism as a "foreign" importation. As a result, union organization developed for the most part apolitically. When he was once asked his philosophy of labor, London-born Samuel Gompers simply replied "More!" which has adequately described labor's position in the United States from that day to this. Under Gomper's leadership the American Federation of Labor resolved in 1908 that it was "partisan to no political party but partisan to a principle" and declared of socialist doctrines that "economically they are unsound; socially they are wrong; industrially they are impossibility." Yet Gompers' "principle" remained largely undefined. The nonacceptance of Marxist philosophy in America stands as one of the best examples of the nonpenetration of some doctrine that is incompatible with basic habits of thinking. In the United States, Marx is interesting only to some professors of social science and philosophy for his economic and historical determinism. Most Americans would agree with Keynes's statement, made in 1926, that socialism is "a dusty survival of a plan to meet the problems of fifty years ago, based on a misunderstanding of what someone said a hundred years ago." It is curious to reflect that Marxist "scientific" socialism has proved just as utopian as the theories of earlier utopian socialists. Even Owen's socialism *did* engender the cooperative movement, whereas the Marxist dictatorship of the proletariat is still a fiction.

The absence of feudalism and of an aristocratic state of mind in America sees its counterpart in the absence of a proletarian working-class conscience. Socialism fought a lost cause, as had a frustrated "aristocracy" in the South, for both lived hopefully on a memory of something that never existed. An agrarian aristocracy could not exist without the peasant or the peasant mentality. America was essentially a country of small farmers who held their land in fee simple, rarely as tenants. An abundance of free land made it impossible to establish a landed-class planter aristocracy except by a slavery binding man forcibly to the land. Peasantry is as alien to the American spirit as is a proletariat: without the one there is not the other. Each worker is a budding capitalist and each farmer a potential "big spread" owner. To abolish millionaires is to abolish one's own hopes. In France there are "have and have not" groups on the Right and the Left hostile to the Government, but if such exist in the United States, they are almost closed out of all serious discussion: one can only successfully argue about politics inside the American system in which everyone has a stake.

The American liberal does not have to fight either feudalism or socialism as does the liberal in Europe, which leads American political thinking to seem simple and plain in contrast with the "deeper" political thought of Europe. Americans did not have to blow up ancient regimes libe those that existed in Russia and France, which have never completed their revolutions. America has had no hereditary aristocracy or priestly caste and, until recently, no bureaucracy. Americans were largely left alone after their revolution and had few dissenters. After the American Tories were shunted out, there was no further dissenting from dissent. There was no reaction, no turning back. Ideological competition became less keen and often more blurred in American political thought and active politics. American political parties did not develop set doctrines or philosophies, but brought up a combination of diverse current ideas from various groups with the hope that the sum total would be successful at the polls.

Matthew Arnold in his *Civilization in the United States,* written and published in 1888, the year of his death, said that

> this play of their institutions suggests . . . the image of a man in a suit of clothes which fits him to perfection, leaving all his movements unimpeded and easy; a suit of clothes loose where it ought to be loose, and sitting close where its sitting close is an advantage; a suit of clothes able, moreover, to adapt itself naturally to the wearer's growth, and to admit of all enlargements as they successively arise.

He thought that the social problem had been solved in America, because there were less profound divisions between rich and poor and less class distinction:

> Comparing the United States with ourselves, I said that while they are in this natural and healthy condition, we, on the contrary, are so little homogeneous, we are living with a system of classes so intense, with institutions and a society so little modern, so unnaturally complicated, that the whole action of our minds is hampered and falsened by it; we

are in consequence wanting in lucidity, we do not see clear or think straight, and the Americans here have much the advantage of us.[12]

Just the same, Arnold noted as an acute and experienced Englishman that "there is no country, calling itself civilized, where one would not rather live than in the United States, except Russia!"

The uniqueness of American thought should be contrasted with Europe's, and going to Europe brings us back to the discovery of America. Europe can better understand itself, likewise, by looking at the American laboratory, where its own reflection is to be seen. C. P. Snow said that the only thing we can learn from history is that no one ever learns anything from history. And this is the crucial time for Americans to suspect their own delusions.

Our interpreters should thrust deeply into the cultural depths and get us out of the shallows of the telephone, telegraph, television, and Comsats. They must penetrate the anthropoid skull of the mass mind with new ideas and attitudes to form a new kind of society, not radically different from our own but on a higher plane with an exalted individualism. The future will not be easy, but unless we clear our eyes, there will not be a recognizable future at all.

NOTES

1. James Bryce, *The American Commonwealth*, 2 vols. (London: Macmillan, 1888), p. 701. Unless otherwise indicated, further references to Bryce may be found in this great classic.

2. Mark Twain, "Some National Stupidities," *Literary Essays* (New York: Harper & Row, Publishers, 1897).

3. T. S. Eliot, "Reflections on Contemporary Poetry," *The Egoist* (July, 1919), p. 59. Cf. also Henri Peyre, *Observations on Life, Literature, and Learning in America* (Carbondale: Southern Illinois University Press, 1961), p. 167.

4. An excellent survey on Atlantic travel is Warren Armstrong, *Atlantic Highway* (New York: The John Day Company, Inc., 1962).

5. Cited in Alfred Kazin, *On Native Grounds* (New York: Harcourt, Brace & World, Inc., 1942), p. 19.

6. Perry Miller, *American Thought: Civil War to World War I* (New York: Holt, Rinehart & Winston, Inc., 1954), p. xxiii.

7. Lewis Galantière (ed.), *America and the Mind of Europe* (London: Hamish Hamilton, 1951), p. 100.

8. Harold Laski, *The American Democracy* (New York: Viking Press, 1948), pp. 727–28.

9. Intellectual trends in this form of thought may be seen in the structuralism of Claude Lévi-Strauss and Herbert Marcuse.

10. Louis Hartz, *The Liberal Tradition* (New York: Harcourt, Brace & World, Inc., 1955), p. 243.

11. Pisani, p. 254.

12. Nevins, pp. 502–503.

✑ TRANSATLANTIC PEOPLE ✑

> *There is a tide in the affairs of men, which*
> *taken at the flood, leads on to fortune.*
>
> —Shakespeare

There is a certain unity in the last of the American Victorians, a unity which vanished in the smoke of World War I. The aristocratic salons and drawing rooms of Howells, Henry James, Henry Adams, and Edith Wharton are period pieces furnished with lapidary transatlantic Americans, the Americans of wealth at home and abroad. They were democratic Americans with distinctly upper-class views, happier in the stratified society of Europe. Clemenceau had an American wife. Kipling married into a wealthy New York and Vermont family and built a $50,000 house near Brattleboro where he lived from 1892 to 1896.

The transatlantic marriage has had a long history and no little social and political impact. In 1799 Frances Cadwalder of Philadelphia married Lord Erskine, and a few years later Maria Bingham ran away to marry the Comte de Tilly. In 1803 Betsy Patterson married Jerome Bonaparte, brother of Napoleon I. Anne Louisa Bingham, sister of Maria and daughter of the wealthy Philadelphia merchant, married Alexander Baring, who, as Lord Ashburton, suitably arranged one of the best Anglo-American treaties with Daniel Webster. Lady Webster, an American of the Tory Vassall family, after her divorce from Sir Godfrey, married Lord Holland and became the leader of an outstanding literary circle. In 1824 the daughter of John Jacob Astor, Elizabeth, married Count Vincent Rumpff, and the three Caton sisters, granddaughters of Charles Carroll, married the Duke of Leeds, Baron Stafford, and the Marquess of Wellesley.

These earlier marriages were primarily colonial in character. New York and Philadelphia had been quite cosmopolitan, but the shift of the capital to Washington, the rise of Jacksonian democracy, and the concentration on the westward-moving frontier broke the European connection. When Louis-Philippe proposed to Miss Abbie Willing, Mrs. William Bingham's sister, the father refused on the ground that Louis-Philippe had nothing to offer her in America, while if he should eventually assume the French throne, his daughter had nothing to offer him. Only the later emergence of the new industrial millionaires, titans of railroad empires and public utilities and captains of finance, restored the connection.

In the third quarter of the century, the frequency of European-American marriages again increased. One reason was that Americans had ceased adhering to primogeniture, whereas entail and primogeniture were practiced in England until 1925. American daughters often inherited as much as the sons. This was an attractive prospect to European nobility, but it also had its appeal to Americans: if a Vanderbilt were to marry an Astor, what could either side offer the other? With no real social or political aristocracy in America, real power has gone with money. Political careers could be unstable, and often represented fronts for the behind-the-scenes maneuvering of wealth. In fact, to be rich was a handicap in politics—until recently. Again, in America the mainstream of society was closed to women, whereas in Europe women played a more interesting and attractive role. In 1905 George Bernard Shaw wrote that American alliances with the British peerage were healthy and well inspired.

From the 1870's on, there was a clutch of European-American marriages. Jennie Jerome, mother of Sir Winston Churchill, married Lord Randolph Churchill. Harold MacMillan had an American mother. Consuelo Iznaga, of a wealthy Cuba-Louisiana-New York family, married Viscount Mandeville, Duke of Manchester; her sister became Lady Lister-Kaye, and her son, the ninth Duke of Manchester, married Helena Zimmerman of Cincinnati. The names roll on: Sir Bache Cunard (Lord Cunard) married Maude Burke; Mrs. Cavendish-Bentinck was American; the Earl of Yarmouth married Alice Cornelia Thaw; the Duke of Rozburg, Miss Mary Goelet; Belle Wilson married the Hon. Sir Michael Herbert (Pembroke), later minister to Washington. Then there was Mary Leiter's marriage to Lord Curzon; she became Vicereine of India. Her sister Margaret Hyde Leiter married Henry Molyneux Paget, Earl of Suffolk and Berkshire; Cornelia Bradley Martin married the Earl of Craven; Virginia Bonynge, Lord Deerhurst; Lilian May, Lord Bagot; Mary Livingstone King, the Marquis of Anglesey; May Travers, Lord Wentworth; and Nancy Langhorne, Lord Astor. The liberal peer, Lord Playfair, had an American wife, frequently visited the United States, and played an important unofficial role in the settling of the Venezuelan dispute. The Duke of Malborough married Consuelo Vanderbilt.

Anthony Trollope described the marriage of an American girl of a rich father to an English nobleman in two novels, *The Duke's Children* and *He Knew He Was Right*, and one of Gertrude Atherton's better novels was

American Wives and English Husbands, published in 1898. *Punch* in 1905 came out with the doggerel:

> Envy of our unrivalled race
> May prompt the alien't vulgar sneer;—
> It is her fortune, not her face
> That captivates the British peer. . . .

In *The Portrait of Dorian Gray,* the American daughter of a dry-goods merchant is to marry an English nobleman. " 'Dry-goods! What are American dry-goods?' asked the Duchess, raising her large hands in wonder, and accentuating the verb. 'American novels,' answered Lord Henry, helping himself to some quail."

Franco-American marriages were almost as frequent as American marriages with British aristocracy. American daughters of wealth were eagerly embraced by European nobility: the Comte de Castellane married Anna Gould, the Prince della Torre e Tasso married Ann Walker. Anna Gould's marriage with Boni de Castellane, already noted, ended in divorce, but she remarried Helie, Duc de Talleyrand, head of the Talleyrand-Périgord family, while Helie's brother, Duc de Valençay, married Helen Morton, daughter of a rich banker and former American vice-president. Duc Dino de Talleyrand-Périgord married Elizabeth Curtis, and there were other Talleyrand-Périgord marriages to Americans. Miss Coudert married the Marquis de Choiseul (Duc de Praslin), and another Duc de Praslin married Elizabeth Forbes. Alice Heine married the Prince of Monaco.

The list goes on interminably to the present day, with even another American princess of Monaco, not to mention marriages with German, Polish, Austrian, Hungarian, and Italian aristocracy. American fortunes constituted an earlier Marshall Plan for European gentility and provided the American industrialist, banker, or businessman with something that he could not gain at home. He could enjoy the chateau and his daughter the title. Where the English had once taken their grand tour to Italy, new American wealth gave the sons of industrial capitalism the opportunity for a grand tour. After 1892, more than 90,000 went each year to Europe, and the number increased to over 286,000 by 1913. Ferrero, the Italian historian, was troubled and asked, "What means the strange and incessant coming and going over the Atlantic; the restless stream from continent to continent, neither of which can apparently exist by itself any longer, nor yet merge itself completely in the other?" [1]

Why did all these American females marry Europeans, while their brothers became new Yankee Macaronis in England and on the Continent? The explanation is simply that the United States had suddenly become a world power with importantly intricate consequences. By 1880 the United States had a greater population than any European country, led in wheat production, and already outdistanced all in territorial size, and further increased by imperial expansion in Hawaii, Samoa, Guam, the Philippines, Puerto Rico, the Panama Canal Zone, and other areas under its tutelage. By the 1890's America had outrun all other countries in capital investments and bank deposits and was the primary producer of coal, iron, and steel. In 1901 Great Britain was the first European nation to seek an American loan. While American investments abroad rose, so did the establishment of American manufacturing. Henry Ford led the way by establishing an assembly plant at Manchester in 1911.

Europe awoke with a start at this new economic challenge across the Atlantic which had heretofore been a market for products, profitable investments, and a convenient dumping ground for surplus population. Thoughtful scholars in every European country began to examine America more closely. Emile Levasseur at the Collège de France began to devote himself almost exclusively to American economic studies. Denis Guibert warned seriously in 1896 in *Le Figaro* that if Bryan were elected, Europe should prepare itself for an Amreican military invasion. In his *Impérialisme américain* Henri Hauser wrote, "One hears nothing spoken of in the press, at meetings, in parliament, except the American peril," while the English journalist W. T. Stead wrote in his *Americanization of the World* that Britain had only two choices: to federate with the United States or to become an English-speaking Belgium. He preferred the former and thought of Americanization as a trend in a general universal cultural development. Conan Doyle wrote from America in 1894: "The center of gravity of race is over here and we have got to readjust ourselves." Edmond Demolins' *A quoi tient la supériorité des Anglo-Saxons?* was widely read in France as an explanation of America. Clemenceau, having married an American, strongly supported the United States in the Spanish-American War. Of the French novels of the time there were Jules Clarétie's *L'Américaine,* Pierre de Coulevain's *Noblesse Américaine,* and Abel Hermant's *Les Transatlantiques,* and then there was Eugène Labiche's play *Les trente millions de Gladiator.*

In his *Expansion of England,* J. R. Seeley wrote in 1883 that the United States was exerting a "strange influence on us by the strange career it runs and the novel experiments it tries," while Bryce ruminated that "America has in some respects anticipated European nations. She is walking before them along paths which they may probably follow." A third distinguished historian, John Richard Green, suggested that the future of the English race would be unfolded on the Hudson and the Mississippi rather than on the Tweed and the Thames.

In his *Notes sur les Etats-Unis* André Tardieu wrote:

> The United States is . . . a world power. . . . When a people have commercial interests everywhere, they are called upon to involve themselves in everything. A nation of ninety million souls, which sells wheat to the universe, coal, iron, and cotton, cannot isolate itself. As Boutmy has written, it has a sense of *puissance oblige*. Its power creates for it a right. The right turns itself into a pretension. The pretension becomes a duty—to pronounce upon all those questions that hitherto have been arranged by agreement only among European powers. These powers themselves, at critical times, turn toward the United States, anxious to know its opinion. . . . The United States intervenes thus in the affairs of the universe. . . . It is seated at the table where the great game is played, and it cannot leave it.[2]

This was the America of the great white fleet, of the Spanish-American War, Algeciras and the Boxer Rebellion, of the Treaty of Portsmouth and the Panama Canal. Let us look at a few transatlantic American literary personalities to savor their felings in the Atlantic cultural relation.

The new American power manifested in the Gilded Age was not accommodating to the American man of letters. He had achieved more personal satisfaction and prestige before the Civil War than after. While there was no book-burning between, say, 1870 and 1910, there was on the other hand nothing to encourage the unorthodox writer, and if he were unorthodox, he could hardly publish. A dull hostility to literary interests often drove our best writers to Europe, where often they were as much *émigrés* to Europe as those who fled to the American shore at the same time. Charles Eliot Norton wrote from Siena in 1870 that while there was an abundance of contemporary thought in England, there was little in America, and Emerson had become as remote from America as Plato, with no one to replace him in "supplying us with the thought itself on which the spiritual growth in the good of the nation mainly depends. Really the *Nation* and the *North American* are almost the only evidences of thought in America, and they drag out a difficult existence in the midst of the barbarian wealth of the richest millions of people in the world."

This provincial isolation was put most strongly by Van Wyck Brooks:

As we can see now, a vast unconscious conspiracy actuated all America against the creative spirit. In an age when every sensitive mind in England was in full revolt against the blind, mechanical, devastating forces of a "progress" that promised nothing but the ultimate collapse of civilization; when all Europe was alive with prophets, aristocratic prophets, proletarian prophets, religious and philosophical and economic and artistic prophets, crying out, in the name of the human spirit, against the obscene advance of capitalistic industrialism . . . in that age America, innocent, ignorant, profoundly untroubled, slept the righteous sleep of its own manifest and peculiar destiny.[3]

Matthew Arnold exemplified the European distrust of the American industrial democracy, which also led John Stuart Mill to revise some of his opinions on democracy. Doubts were raised by Renan and Sainte-Beuve in France about the seemingly inexorable march of American democratic development.

In 1883, the year before he decided to do the routine English lecture tour of America, Matthew Arnold summed up some of his thoughts on the country he was to visit. He knew that the western frontier was raw and crude and not as it had been romanticized. He knew that the spirit of Philistia reigned in the East. And he was aware of the strong fundamentalism in religion. His acquaintance with Howells and Henry James told him that life in America afforded no possibility for a gentleman of culture.

Americans, to him, were simply English provincials across the water; that there should be an "American" literature was unthinkable. The intellectual world in America anxiously awaited the coming of the European sage, attracted by curiosity and repelled by fear of criticism, for Arnold was the great Apostle of Culture, spreading "the best which has been thought and said in the world." Andrew Carnegie met him at the pier in New York, but his first lecture in New York was not a success. The audience could not hear him and walked out in numbers, including General Grant. Andrew Carnegie suggested that he take elocution lessons, which he did.

Whitman, among others, was hostile, perhaps overly so because Arnold had refused to support the case against Whitman's dismissal from the Indian Department because of his publication of *Leaves of Grass*. Whitman said of Arnold, "I accept the world—most of the world—but somehow draw the line somewhere on some of those fellows." What particuarly bothered Whitman was Arnold's attitude toward a native American literature. America, Arnold wrote, cannot have a literature of its own, but has to take account of what other nations and ages have acquired. The American intellect must inevitably come into the movement of European literature. It could remain an independent intellectual power, not a colony of Europe, but without displaying such an eccentric and violent originality. If Arnold missed the meaning of Whitman, he also missed that of Mark Twain. Having met him, Arnold asked, "But is he *never* serious?"

The Boston tour and the New England college towns were more pleasant; in Boston he was in the company of Charles Eliot Norton, the Emerson family, and Oliver Wendell Holmes. In Hartford he saw his friend Howells, who was visiting Mark Twain. To Arnold's astonishment he was fascinated by Twain. Henry Adams and Bancroft entertained him in Washington. He liked the South and had earlier hoped for its secession, not necessarily because he approved of Southern principles, but rather because an independent South might redeem the Northern culture which he disliked, which was lacking in distinction and beauty, was restless, mobile and with an unending rootlessness. Tocqueville earlier expressed the same reaction in writing, "Restlessness of character seems to me to be one of the distinctive traits of this people. . . . So he enters the great lottery of human fate with the assurance of a gambler who only risks his winnings."

Nevertheless, Arnold enjoyed his fatiguing trip. He returned to England with six thousand dollars and with his daughter engaged to an American, and in due time he was happy to have an American granddaughter. A quick return visit to America was made in 1886, but his health suffered with the climate and he was glad to return home. He died shortly after delivering an address at the unveiling of a window in St. Margaret's Church, Westminster, which was donated by an American.

William Dean Howells had assumed the mantle of Lowell and consequently became the midwestern spokesman for the Boston Brahmins. He was a friend of Mark Twain and Henry James. He was awarded the consulate in Venice for having written a biography of Lincoln for the 1860 campaign. In Venice he avoided the passions of the Civil War, and led a dilettante life in conjugal harmony writing *Venetian Life* and *Italian Journeys* as a detached observer and with a bourgeois view. With his lack of enthusiasm for the Civil War, he wrote that he would prefer to add to American literature than sweep Confederate cruisers from the Adriatic. He learned German in order to read Heine and also studied Icelandic. He edited the plays and memoirs of Goldoni, and enjoyed the Venetian canals in a gondola with Motley, American minister to Austria, who was then writing his *History of the United Netherlands*. He finally returned to America because, as he confessed, he feared a deleterious moral decline if he stayed longer in Europe, and had "seen enough of uncountreyed Americans in Europe." Yet in *My Literary Passions* he stated that living in Venice had changed the whole course of his literary life and had made him a realist. The books which followed his Italian writing continued to contrast Americans and Europeans in Victorian optic with Venetian scenes: *A Foregone Conclusion, The Lady of the Aroostook,* and *A Fearful Responsibility. Indian Summer* recalls Howells' stay in Italy. The Italian novels all contrast a dying civilization's effect on young Americans.

Perhaps his best novel, admired by Taine, was *The Rise of Silas Lapham,* the mixing of the self-made, rude millionaire with the Boston blue-bloods, or Alger among the Puritans. Howells has Mr. Gorey say that Europe is dangerous for the Bostonians:

> We are constantly going away, and coming back with our convictions shaken to their foundations. One man goes to England, and returns with the conception of a grander social life; another comes from Germany with the notion of a more searching intellectual activity; a fellow just back from Paris has the absurdest idea of art and literature. . . . It ought to be stopped—it ought, really. The Bostonian who leaves Boston ought to be condemned to perpetual exile.[4]

The French naturalists were looked on by Howells with little enthusiasm, and he wrote of the "rather brutish pursuit of a woman by a man which seems to be the chief end of the French novelist." He told John Hay that Zola's *Nana* was bad art because it arose from bad French morality. Yet Zola achieved fame from Dreyfus, while Howells' opinions on Haymarket were ignored. James was more sympathetic to the French in general, as Howells was to the Italians.

Howells' angle of vision changed from observations of the restricted society around him, and after 1887 he became interested in social problems, standing against economic injustices as a conscientious Brahmin and publicly protesting the condemnation of the pretended anarchists of Haymarket. This was his best period, signaled by his quitting Boston and *The Atlantic* for New York where he became editor of *Harper's Magazine.* He refused the chair of Longfellow and Lowell at Harvard.

Howells had set the stage for Henry James's transatlantic novels. Although the two were friends for over fifty years (one of James's last pieces of writing was on Howells), Howells thought that James had made a mistake in concentrating on the transatlantic relation. Yet Howells himself strongly felt the European attraction. He went back in 1882 for a year and produced *Tuscan Cities* and *A Little Swiss Sojourn,* in which he wrote: "I am perpetually interested in the life of a foreign community, which is yet so kindred in ideas and principles to ours." He made seven more trips to Europe: He had become not only the Dean of American Letters, but an international figure. Oxford conferred on him the Doctor of Letters degree in 1904. His trips provided grist for American writing, such as *Modern Italian Poets, Roman Holidays, London Films,* and *Certain Delightful English Towns.*

He was always attracted and repelled by the Italian atmosphere. In *Indian Summer* he wrote that "It's well that tourists come to Italy so ignorant, and keep so. Otherwise they couldn't live to get home again; the past would crush them." In "Louis Leban's Conversion" we feel the tug between the Old World and the New. While the *campanili* peal, the air fills with incense, and solemn devotions are chanted all around him, he hears the "passionate voices of the people that sang in the virgin heart of the forest." And again,

> Yesterday, while I moved with the languid crowd on the Riva,
> Musing with idle eyes on the wide lagoons and the islands,
> And on the dim-seen seaward glimmering sails in the distance,
> Where azure haze, like a vision of Indian-Summer,
> Haunted the dreamy sky of the soft Venetian December—
> While I moved unwilled in the mellow warmth of the weather,
> Breathing air that was full of Old World sadness and beauty,
> Into my thought came the story of free, wild life in Ohio,
> When the land was new, and yet by the Beautiful River
> Dwelt the pioneers and Indian hunters and boatmen.

Howells saw nothing wrong with American writers living and working abroad, in spite of his feelings for James. "As matters stand, I think we may reasonably ask whether the Americans 'most prominent in cultivated European opinion,' the Americans who 'habitually live out of America,' are not less exiles than advance agents of the expansion now advertising itself to the world." American literature, he felt, was "independent even of our independence," and that "literary absenteeism, it seems to me is not particularly an American vice or an American virtue. It is an expression and a proof of the modern sense which enlarges one's country to the bounds of civilization." [5] Howells wrote to Henry James that they were both in exile from America, but for him it was

> the most grotesquely illogical thing under the sun; and I suppose I love America less because it won't let me love it more. I should hardly like to trust pen and ink with all the audacity of my social ideas; but after fifty years of optimism content with "civilization" and its ability to come out all right in the end, I now abhor it, and feel that it is coming out all wrong in the end, unless it bases itself anew on a real equality.[6]

The best example to illustrate Howells' Atlantic thinking may be represented by Henry James, who brought transatlantic writing to its peak.

Henry James remains a true American whose Puritan judgments always prevail over his aesthetic ideas. He is the perfectly passionate pilgrim, educated by his wealthy family in Geneva and Bonn and surrounded by millionaires and *literati* at the family home in New York and Newport, where Washington Irving and Emerson were often guests. His father had wanted to protect him from America's cultural crudeness, and the idea of Europe was inculcated in him as the land of taste, honor, and civilization. His early European experience fixed a lifetime attitude: Europe was elegance and beauty, varied and individual. "It's a complex fate being an American, and one of the responsibilities it entails is fighting against a superstitious valuation of Europe." [7] Years later he wrote that "I was somehow in Europe, since everything about me had been 'brought over' " to his life in the United States, and he wondered whether America had an identity of its own instead of being just a noisy chaos made up of ugly boys he didn't want to play with. Remorsefully, he felt that the great American tradition had been ruined by trade and that he himself might sink in the American commercial quicksands or go under in the social swim of Newport.

The Newport scene that so frustrated the talents of James was described by Henry Adams, returned from seven years in London:

> He went to Newport and tried to be fashionable, but even in the simple life of 1868 he failed as a fashion. All the style he had learned so painfully in London was worse than useless in America where every standard was different. . . . Society seemed founded on the law that all was for the best New Yorkers in the best of Newports, and that all young people were rich if they could waltz. It was a new version of the Ant and the Grasshopper.[8]

James left his law studies at Harvard to write for the *Atlantic* and the *Nation*. He went to Rome ("At last—for the first time—I live!"), Florence, and Venice where he began *Watch and Ward* and *Roderick Hudson*. England was a "good married matron" when compared to the Italian "beautiful dishevelled nymph." In Florence he was condescending toward his compatriots:

> Their ignorance—their stingy, defiant, grudging attitudes toward everything European—their perpetual reference of all things to some Ameri-

can standard of precedent which exists only in their own unscrupulous wind-bags . . . these things glare at you hideously. . . . It's the absolute and incredible lack of *culture* that strikes you in common travelling Americans.[9]

James makes them sound like Twain's *Innocents Abroad*. Those were not the Brahmins who went to Europe before the Civil War, but a new kind of tourist herded from city to city, groups of wide-eyed peeping toms unashamedly denuding Europe with their vulgar gaze.

His brother William, who was with him in Florence, tried to get him to return home, but wrote back to the family that Henry could not do literary production at home, and that "his temperament is so exclusively artistic that the vacuous, simple atmosphere of America ends by tiring him to death." Henry himself was in a quandary and wrote to Howells, "What is the meaning of this destiny of desolate exile—this dreary necessity of having month after month to do without our friends for the sake of this arrogant old Europe which so little befriends us?" He then settled in Paris, perhaps for good, but at least to learn his craft from the French writers. There his writing took form under the influence of Flaubert, Zola, and Daudet, and the development of his psychological novels began. For him, words and gestures and all exterior attitudes were but the symbols of an inner conscience. He was writing counter to the current of realism and the naturalism which followed. Fortunately he gained more recognition as people came to realize that the two schools had come to the end of their road. James was a critic of *moeurs* and had no illusions about the society he depicted, a society always concerned with money even while trying to play money down.

He was well received by Flaubert and Turgenev, although they found his writing pallid. He often met the Goncourts, Zola, Daudet, and De Maupassant. Like himself, they were all seeking precision, clear observation, and lucidity of style, but James did not like their naturalism, which, as Van Wyck Brooks says, "dissected the human organism with the obscene cruelty of medical students." But he had learned their techniques: unity of tone from Flaubert, the actual in different shadings from Flaubert, and the analysis of small groups of characters from Turgenev. Still, he could not get along with them for "fifty reasons"; as he wrote Howells, he could not "like their wares." The good Puritan, he wanted to do "respectable" writing. Where they used the microscope he wanted to use opera glasses.

James wrote to his brother William of the French,

I have done with 'em forever and am turning English all over. I desire only to feed on English life and the contact of English minds—I wish greatly I knew some. Easy and smooth-flowing as life is in Paris, I would throw it over tomorrow for an even very small chance to plant myself for a while in England. If I had but a single good friend in London I would go thither.[10]

Actually, he had already been introduced by the Nortons to Leslie Stephen, Ruskin, William Morris, and to Dickens' unmarried daughter. He had visited Rossetti's studio and met George Eliot. He went back to London in 1870, where he gloried in meeting the aristocracy, as well as Swinburne, Browning, Kinglake, Huxley, Spencer, Darwin, George Otto Trevelyan, Anthony Trollope, and J. A. Symonds. Lord Houghton invited him to dinner with Tennyson and Gladstone. He luxuriated at Mentmore, the country house given by Baron Meyer de Rothschild to his daughter Lady Rosebery, admiring all the Veronese on the walls and the Golden Thrones of the Doges of Venice. He resolved to make a successful career among those of "atrocious good fortune." Lord Rosebery, whom James described as the "favorite of the Gods," knew America well and claimed that the really happy life was in New England "living like Longfellow."

James also went to the American painter Millet's house in Worcestershire, where there were also Abbey and Sargent, the English critic Edmond Gosse who lectured successfully in America, and the English painters Alfred Parsons and Fred Barnard. Yet he gained few intimates or close friends, and always felt himself the stranger in England; still he felt that he was more cosmopolitan than the average cultured Briton. From 1876 on, he lived there. A year after his arrival he wrote to Grace Norton, "I feel more at home in London than anywhere else in the world." He made only two subsequent visits to the United States. In 1915 he became a British citizen, unhappy that America had not stepped in to defend Western civilized democracy.

His American compatriots were indisposed to him and were annoyed that he wrote of cosmopolitan circles rather than of definitely American subjects. One college textbook on American literature said, "It is doubtful that Henry James really belongs in American literature, for he criticizes America and admires Europe." Parrington was against him and Van Wyck Brooks regretted his pilgrimage to England. H. G. Wells compared his novels to a brilliantly lit but empty church where there was placed on the high altar, with much intensity, a dead cat, an egg shell, and a piece of string. James was more than that. He was an American conscious of the pull of two continents toward each other and depicted the personal relation between Europe and America. He was not interested in the social problems of the day, but neither was Hawthorne earlier or his contemporary Henry Adams. The personages in his novels do not *have* to earn a living, as the characters in realist novels must.

Almost all his novels contrast the difference between Americans and Europeans and fall into three stages: 1875–1901, the Americans in Europe or at home; 1885–1901, the British; 1901–1916, the Americans on the Continent. This last stage, the search for the figure in the carpet, is not the best artistically. In *Roderick Hudson,* one of his first novels, which was begun in Florence, he shows the pure American seduced by wicked Europe which prevents him from completing his work. The theme is hardly novel in American letters. A wealthy benefactor sends a talented young sculptor to Italy who quickly gets rid of his Puritan and provincial fiancé for an amoral cosmopolitan woman whose influence kills his talents and finally kills him. The violation of the code meant disaster, as it did with Hawthorne. The Puritan theme is repeated in *Daisy Miller* where the virtuous young woman flirts with an Italian in the Colosseum at night, again violates the code, and as retribution consequently has malaria and loses her reputation and her life. It was his first real success, and was published in 1878 through the efforts of the friendly Leslie Stephen in *The Cornhill Magazine.*

James shows more maturity in setting off the contradictions between the two ethics, American and European, in *The American.* With Paris and Saint-Germain as the setting, James discusses the differing attitudes and approaches between an excellent American of the West and a young aristocratic widow. Christopher Newman is the traveling American businessman, a passionate pilgrim who wants to rejuvenate Europe and efficiently admire its cathedrals. The rupture is complete, for Claire de Cintré is not permitted by her mother and brother to marry the American. The novel was not warmly received in France. The Anglo-Saxon coldness was unappreciated, along with his rarified atmosphere and his unreal descriptions of French salon society. To this day in France, James has been respected as an important writer, but read by few. Proust knew him my name only, and Gide said he could not read him. Perhaps it is because France has its own psychological-analytical novelists who seem less remote and devious. Nor is the genteel tradition he represented (as well as Wharton, Glasgow, Cather, Porter, his female successors) much appreciated, although all are translated.

James returned to the American scene with *Washington Square* and *The Bostonians.* He felt that New Yorkers and particularly the Bostonians had declined from their golden age and had become fatuously faded. A young genius (himself) could no longer fit into this society, for one should not deviate from an established pattern or be conspicuous with one's talent. In these two novels it is clear that James believed he understood America, his America. As he wrote to his brother William, "I know what I am about, and I have always had my eyes on my native land." His instincts and standards remained American, but he always tried to find traces of Europe when he wrote of America.

He wrote to his publisher that *The Bostonians* was "an attempt to show that I *can* write an American story. . . . A very *American* tale, a tale very characteristic of our social conditions." It was a complete failure with the American public; James believed his American reputation to be ruined, so he turned to the English reader with another international story. It was over twenty years before he looked at the United States again in *The American Scene,* which was composed mostly of travel notes for an American novel, never finished. America had become too large for him to grasp and he had been away too long. He returned to the European theme with *The Portrait of a Lady,* his best novel, which he had begun in Florence. Isabel Archer, spiritual and transcendental, instead of marrying an English lord marries an aesthetic Anglo-Italian. Because of her Puritan code, she must then accept with elegant stoicism the shock that her best friend becomes her husband's mistress.

English moral standards came to stand above American or Continental ones. When James transferred to London, he remarked that it was more substantial to live upon than the "romance of Italy." He wrote in 1888, "I am getting to know English life better than American and to understand the English character, or at least the mind, as well as if I had invented it." In *The Tragic Muse* he first attacked a purely English subject on a large scale.

Concerning the conflict between Anglo-Saxon and Latin cultures, James tends to be less critical in two later novels. The continued antagonism between two civilizations is again the theme of *The Ambassadors* in which an American goes to Paris to rescue an American boy from the arms of a French girl. Arriving as the spokesman for American morality, he himself gradually cedes to the charm of the Old World and does not reprove the romance. *The Golden Bowl* is the reverse: an Italian prince representing elegant European society is set before two moral codes, and finally accepts the Puritan virtues—which somehow he is able to humanize.

His later novels are the result of his unsuccessful playwriting, where all the drama is in the situation, surrounded by things, and where all character is deliberately suppressed for the figure in the carpet. There is no life, or no real life, in his later writing. Colorless narrators walk round and round unimaginable episodes as if winding thread on a spool. His writing became, as H. G. Wells said, something like a hippopotamus resolved on picking up a pea, or, as another critic, Litell, said of James's *In the Cage,* it was like watching Henry James watching through a knothole somebody who was watching somebody else through a knothole.

James kept wondering whether he should return to America and how his writing might have developed had he not lived in England. His brother William had constantly urged him to return. He made his second and last return in 1910 and went to New York, Newport, Boston, Philadelphia, Richmond, Florida, and California. He had been away too long to readjust; he was repelled, outraged, and disillusioned; he hurried back to England, homesick for his house and garden in Rye. His feeling was summed up in his story *The Jolly Corner:* Spencer Brydon returns to the New York brownstone house he left twenty-five years before and wanders from room to room wondering what would have happened to him had he stayed. Finally in the hall of his old house he encounters his alter ego, who drops his hands and reveals a face of horror. Did James feel that this would have been his fate had he stayed?

William Dean Howells' last piece of writing was devoted to a retrospective essay on James's published correspondence in which he sympathetically touches on the author's self-sought European exile, for he was a companion spirit in his personal affection for Europe.

> James was less a sufferer in Europe than in America. He was better in Paris than in Boston, where he was always suffering and when his brief French sojourn became his English life of forty years it was, not mainly, because he was better in England, but it was more largely so. The climate was kinder to him than ours, and the life was kinder than his native life, and his native land. In fact, America was never kind to James. It was rude and harsh, unworthily and stupidly so, as we must more and more own, if we would be true to ourselves. We ought to be ashamed of our part in this. . . .[11]

As he gradually became disenchanted with Europe, James switched his romanticism for Europe to a romanticism for America and began to feel that perhaps New England society, circumscribed by Puritanism, clean and white-washed, was after all better than beautiful but decadent Europe. A transatlantic American, James admitted the moral fiber of the United States and its virtues, but what he saw as the sterility of American art he felt was the result of no refinement itself in the United States. His Americans travel in first-class luxury through an unreal world, or at least a world far removed from politics and production. He himself preferred mundane salons to literary coteries and enjoyed being the confidant of women, young and old. While his novels generally have European settings, his plots deal with Americans and from his foreign vantage point what he essentially created were psychological delineations of his compatriots, showing the moral cracks

and strains of the American upper class. He developed the individual consciousness against herd instincts, set off the individual mind and nature
against society. His earlier novels are all concerned with intellectual tyranny
and the shackling of individual expression. In America the individual is
pushed, shoved, manipulated, repressed, exploited, and reproved, and all his
characters have to escape to Europe usually without knowing why. James has
Roderick Hudson, say, "It's a wretched business, this virtual quarrel of ours
with our own country, this everlasting impatience that so many of us feel to
get out of it. Can there be no struggle then, and is one's only safety in
flight?" 12

James himself was like Roderick Hudson, the artist-hero hungry for
culture. Though America may have been artistically infertile, it had hope
and promise—Europe was growing old and was coming to its end. James
died in the second year of World War I. He had dreamed of creating an
international spirit, an international community of intelligence. He had
wished that no one would know whether he were an English or an American
writer. He had hoped for an "eventual and sublime entente between persons
of education" to overcome contemporary international struggles and future
dangers and difficulties.

Henry James and Mark Twain form an interesting contrast in their
transatlantic careers. They could hardly be friends and their only link was
the friendship which Howells bore for both of them. James said that Twain
could only appeal to rudimentary minds. Authorship for James was an art;
for Twain it was a trade. Twain had made over a dozen trips abroad, and
once lived nine years in Europe. While he was feted by royalty and literary
luminaries, his lectures eagerly attended, and his fame preceding him everywhere he went, he could not, like James, fit into or understand the European
pattern. He never chose a European subject and always used Europe, the
Old World going back even to the Middle Ages, as a backdrop for the
practical and ingenious Yankee. His *Tom Sawyer Abroad,* which does not
include Europe at all, is a weak piece of writing when compared to the real
Tom Sawyer at home. After Mrs. Trollope, Dickens, and so many European
writers who came to the United States to describe its foibles, Twain was
received with glee when he took Europe apart in *Innocents Abroad, The
Prince and the Pauper, A Tramp Abroad,* and *A Connecticut Yankee.*
England was shocked by the bad taste of *A Connecticut Yankee,* while
America reveled in this twisting of the lion's tail of nobility and tradition
subjugated to modern advertising and practical know-how. Twain had earlier

developed a great number of notes on England, but he was afraid to endanger his popularity, or, as he said, to "offend those who had taken him into their hearts and homes." The *Connecticut Yankee* was written largely in a pique after Matthew Arnold's American visit. Twain wrote to his English publisher that the book was not composed for Americans, but for the English! "So many Englishmen have done their sincerest to teach us something for our betterment that it seems to me high time that some of us should substantially recognize the good intent by trying to pry up the English nation to a little higher level of manhood in turn." [13]

Huck and Tom are known to every schoolboy in Europe. Where the King and the Duke represent a decayed Europe, impostors posturing, Colonel Grangerford represents the noble ideal of paterfamilias. Twain's talent for vaunting American "innocence" coupled with American practical ingenuity, and for flaunting European decadence, was a sure combination for success in the new mood of an ebullient America. Twain became a spokesman for America, and was even suggested for the presidency. He traveled with consular dispensation and called himself the "Ambassador-at-large of the United States." He treasured his honorary doctorate and liked the company of the famous and the noble; he also liked the company of the hoi polloi, and for their enjoyment—and his own—poked fun at the famous and the noble. He dined at the Kaiser's right hand and applauded the German Empire, and in his hotel room wrote against monarchy. Kipling had called him "great and godlike," and Shaw declared that America had only produced Poe and Twain as geniuses; Shaw told Twain that he was persuaded that future historians of America would find his work as indispensable as the French historian the political tracts of Voltaire.

It is often possible to get a better insight into a writer, particularly with transatlantic ties, by looking at his dislikes and prejudices than those proclivities which are adopted and absorbed. While professing to admire democracy, Twain reveled in nobility (as did Emerson) and privately wrote in praise of aristocracy while outwardly criticizing it. "I am a democrat only on principle, but by instinct—nobody is that," he declared in his notebook, and "essentially, nobilities are foolishness, but if I were a citizen where they prevail I would do my best to get a title, for the consideraton it furnishes— that is what we want." [14] Berlin to him was a "luminous center of intelligence. . . . I don't believe there is anything in the whole earth that you can't learn in Berlin except the German language." [15] He admired modern Prussian Germany and its militarism, and could not accept republican France. He wrote that the Frenchman was the "most ridiculous creature in the world" and that his own "only race prejudice was against the French." He did not like Flaubert or other French writers, but his earliest romantic attraction was to Jeanne d'Arc. Still, in his first view of France in *Innocents Abroad,* he wrote, "What a bewitching land it is! What a garden! . . . I have observed that Frenchmen abroad seldom wholly give up the idea of going back to France some time or other. I am not surprised at it now." He was essentially indifferent to European writers and the European intellectual scene, and could sometimes be hostile, as in his "What Paul Bourget Thinks of Us."

Twain joins with Henry James, Henry Adams, and, strangely, even Howells (who had taken up social questions in America), in the complete absence of curiosity in the tremendous upheavals which Europe was experiencing in the later industrial revolution. His attempt to describe the political situation in "Stirring Times in Austria" provides no idea of what was actually happening in the *Reichsrath,* just as Henry Adams' visit to investigate coal mining winds up with only a description of high society in Manchester.

Twain mocked foreign languages, and particularly enjoyed inserting long-winded German phraseology in his works. To him foreign languages were ludicrous because they avoided plain English. Twain even mocked "English" English: "There is no such thing as Queen's English. The property had gone into the hands of a joint stock company and we own the bulk of the shares." [16] Howells, who was his most intimate friend and who maintained the American faith while understanding other nationalities, wrote that Twain was the "national spirit as seen with our own eyes." Yet despite his European popularity as a lecturer, writer, and humorist, the feeling still lingers of the American huckster carpetbagging around Europe. Twain maintained that "Europe has lived a life of hypocrisy for ages." [17]

Twain knew his Europe, if not the whole Europe, and said that going abroad did the American good, made a better man of him. "It rubs out a multitude of his old unworthy biases and prejudices," and, as he wrote elsewhere, "the gentle reader will never, never know what a consummate ass he can become until he goes abroad." Yet for all his European experience, Twain remained the man of the American West.

⌣⌣⌣

Stephen Crane is another American writer involved in the transatlantic cultural relation. Although he was to die at the age of twenty-eight he left behind enough superlative writing to place him close to the front ranks of late nineteenth-century American authors. With Frank Harris, he was one of the first to take up the naturalist style of Flaubert and Zola. His *Red Badge of Courage,* which was a bestseller in England before it was fully recognized in America, was for a time more popular than the works of

Kipling, Zola, or Tolstoy. It is much like *La Débacle,* as his *Maggie* resembles *L'Assomoir.*

After a charge of dissipation he fled America for England in 1897, writing to his brother William: "There seem so many of them in America who want to kill, bury and forget me purely out of unkindness and envy— And my unworthiness if you choose." The American public has been indifferent to *Maggie,* virtually unknown until 1930, but it brought him the friendship and encouragement of Howells. He was already suffering from tuberculosis when he rented a large manor house which was filled with uninvited guests who made large inroads on his precarious income. But the literary great also came to him: Joseph Conrad, the neighbor for whom he had a "warm and endless friendship," and Henry James also a neighbor, who watched him slowly wither away. Crane was probably the model for the journalist in James' *Wings of the Dove.* In 1900 H. G. Wells wrote in the *North American Review* the first sympathetic critique of Crane.

His health led him to take a melancholy view of his last years spent in England. In 1897 he wrote:

> Now that I have reached the goal I suppose I ought to be contented; but I am not. I was happier in the old days when I was always dreaming of the thing I have now attained. I am disappointed with success, and I am tired of abuse. Over here, happily, they don't treat you as if you were a dog, but give everyone an honest measure of praise or blame. There are no disgusting personalities.

Unlike James, he was not particularly interested in English society, but, he said, "Englishmen aren't shocked as easily as we are. You can have an idea in England without being sent to court for it." Conrad saw him off for Badenweiller in the Black Forest, hoping for a cure, but he died shortly thereafter, a regretted child prodigy.

A Welsh-born American and Puritan-hater, Frank Harris was another American writer to strengthen European-American literary ties. He studied at the University of Kansas and then at Göttingen. While in England he so impressed old Carlyle with his lively accounts of America that the sage wrote to Froude, "I expect more considerable things from Frank Harris than anyone I have met since Emerson." In England Harris wrote for the *Spectator* and *Fortnightly.* He returned to the United States to write *The Bomb* on the Haymarket affair, and again during the War in 1916 after a conviction of contempt of court and a short sentence in Brixton. That year he published his second volume of *Oscar Wilde: His Life and Confessions* in the United States because it was not acceptable in England. In spite of his English residence, he disliked the English and in 1898 had attempted to provoke war between England and America. He was a Germanophile, admired Bismarck, but thought little of the Kaiser. In 1922 he settled on the Riviera and spent the rest of his life there.

Other transatlantic writers developed American interest in the new European writing. Vance Thompson, in his not very critical *French Portraits,* introduced the younger French authors. James Gibbon Huneker crusaded for all modern European culture to be carried across to the "Modern Babylon" of America. Huneker ran away to Paris in 1876, and returned to the United States ready to teach Americans all about European writers—Ibsen, Shaw, Sudermann, Hauptmann, Huysmans, Stendhal, Anatole France, Maeterlinck—in his *Promenades of an Impressionist.* Huneker himself was most taken by the writings of the Goncourts, Huysmans, De Gourmont ("my dear friend and master"), Barrès, and Nietzsche. Huneker's *Painted Veils* was another typical transatlantic novel of this misunderstood American writer and critic, the idealistic son of a wealthy father who drinks himself to death.

As a transatlantic interpreter Oscar Cargill described Huneker:

> If not a critic, James Gibbon Huneker remains the merchant prince of all the importers of European ideas at the turn of the century. Never cordial towards the Russians, whose pessimism and moral depth oppressed him, and overcautious in regard to Americans (Whistler, Whitman, and Poe are all whom he chose to praise), he selected almost unerringly people of real importance to discuss. He was, above anything else, a gifted connaisseur.[18]

Another American writer who immersed himself in pre-World War I Europe and interpreted it to the United States in *Impressions of Europe 1913–14* was Randolph Bourne. The Continent was ready to plunge itself into a holocaust, but he was blinded by Old World charms and wrote that he felt "the sense in these countries of the most advanced civilization, yet without sophistication, a luminous modern intelligence that selected and controlled and did not allow itself to be overwhelmed by the chaos of the twentieth-century possibility." [19]

Bourne had gone to Europe after his graduation from Columbia in 1913. While his antipathy to England was intense, he was completely charmed by France. "Why do we not have more in America of the incomparable superiority of French civilization to the English?" he asked.

> Our loyalty to the latter is an enormous mistake. . . . Paris is a great spiritual relief after London . . . Paris, democratic, artistic, social, sen-

suous, beautiful, represents almost the complete reversal of everything English. . . . The irony and vivacity of the French intellectuals delight me; their total absence in England made it seem the most alien of all the countries I have seen.

Even though he admitted that he had been exceptionally well treated in England, he wrote after ten days in Paris that he had "pulled down the curtain on England with a resolve" and that England had made him ready to renounce Anglo-Saxon civilization. He began to feel the same way toward his own compatriots in Paris:

The Americans here are still a great trial to me. They unanimously denounce the French temperament and all its ways, and none of them seem to see the intellectual and literary side that I admire so much. They are all concerned with the horrible immorality, and the contrast with the purity and beauty of the American home. I can never discover why so many of them live permanently among people whose faithlessness they abhor, whose political corruption they shudder at, whose abused femininity they shudder over, whose inefficiency enrages them, and whose literature they would sooner think of burning than reading.[20]

To Randolph Bourne, Americans abroad were like the early Christians in the Roman Empire—in the world, but not of the world.

Despite his intense admiration for the French and his interpretation of France to America, Bourne was fiercely against American entrance into the War, and he poured out a stream of pacifist pamphlets, posthumously collected as *Untimely Essays*. He died in the famous influenza epidemic of 1918.

There was no dearth of American artists working in Europe side by side with their American compatriots and European colleagues before World War I. Like the novelist Julian Green, Mary Cassatt is considered by the French to be one of their own and by the Americans to be slightly suspect. She was, in fact, wholly American and wholly French in spirit. Born in Allegheny, Pennsylvania, she had no financial worries, for her elder brother was president of the Pennsylvania Railroad. As a youngster she had spent five years in Paris, and went again in 1868 when she decided to become an artist. After study in Italy, Spain, and Belgium, she returned to Paris in 1874. She became the single female pupil and friend of Degas, who normally avoided women, and was accepted into the Impressionist circle. She exhibited between 1879 and 1886 with Manet and Courbet and was admired by Renoir and Puvis de Chavannes. She held her first individual exhibition in 1893 at Durand-Ruel. Because of her wealth, she moved as easily in the social world as in the world of art, a condition which was not always made possible by the fortunes of her good friend James Abbott McNeill Whistler.

Whistler is mostly known to Americans because of his mother's portrait framed in a postage stamp, embodiment of "momism" in mauve-violet. The portrait is actually in gray and black, a finely balanced study of color contrasts and form, largely under a soft Japanese consciousness of order. It was refused in 1872 by the Royal Academy, but by the time it was bought by the French Government in 1891 for the Louvre, it was hailed as a masterpiece and Whistler was proclaimed a genius. His career was difficult largely because of his antagonism to the pre-Raphaelites.

Whistler's turbulent life was often too much for the Americans and barely supportable by the English, while his off-and-on residence in France made it difficult for him to become a permanent member of any one art circle. He gained one farthing in his lawsuit against Ruskin, who partly for this reason gave up his Slade professorship at Oxford a year later. It was a scandalous lawsuit that presaged the art-for-art's-sake movement of Oscar Wilde and Aubrey Beardsley. Whistler himself was left bankrupt. He had to turn to lecturing for D'Oyly Carte at Prince's Hall and attacked critics with his *Gentle Art of Making Enemies.* His attack on Oscar Wilde was typical; he described Wilde's lectures on American experience as banal, and he said that Wilde was "picking plums from our platters for the puddings which he peddles in the provinces." Henry James disliked the canvases of Whistler which he saw at the Grovesnor Gallery, preferring Burne-Jones, and his animosity was shared by Mrs. Henry Adams. English critics were also hostile to his "Nocturnes," and to the idea of labeling a picture a symphony or a harmony. "Under the same roof with Mr. Whistlers' strange productions," one critic wrote, "is the collection of animal paintings done by various artists for the proprietors of the *Graphic,* and very refreshing it is to turn into this agreeably lighted room and rest on a comfortable settee while looking at *Mother Hubbard's Dog* or the sweet little pussy cats in *The Happy Family.*"

Whistler spent six youthful years in St. Petersburg while his father was engineering railway construction from St. Petersburg to Moscow. There he learned French and studied at the Academy of Fine Arts. After a short stay in England, where he had been sent in fear that his health would be damaged by another Russian winter, the family returned to America in 1849 after the death of General Whistler. Whistler was dismissed from West Point for failing a chemistry examination. "Had silicon been a gas, I should have been a major general," he later said. He worked a while on etchings for the Coast and Geodetic Survey and then in 1855, after reading Henry Murger's "Scènes de la Vie de Bohème," he decided to go to Paris. Working in the atelier of Gleyre, he enlivened the bohemian life by amusing grisettes and can-can dancers. He became the friend of George Du Maurier, who had been born in Paris, and of Thackeray, who had come over to see the International Exhibition.

His works were not selling well in Paris, so he went to London with his friends Fantin-Latour and Legros. His portrait of old Carlyle is of this period. He fell into the good company of Swinburne, Meredith, Rossetti, and Burne-Jones. His painting which had been refused by the Salon (although his *Little White Girl* was a success at the Salon des Refusés) was accepted by the Royal Academy. He introduced Japanese screens, paintings, prints, and porcelains to England and incorporated an Oriental style in his own art, that is, often misty, yet with a strong sense of line and form and not unlike the chromatic "filmy" tone music of Debussy.

Another transatlantic American artist raised like Whistler in a European spirit was John Singer Sargent, his Chelsea neighbor. Sargent was born in Florence to Bostonian parents, and educated in Italy, France, and Germany. Sargent moved in the glittering international set of the Edwardian age, painting American heiresses who were wives of British peers and Central-European Jews who had become British financiers. He did a portrait of Henry James which had been subscribed to by three hundred English friends. He traveled everywhere, and his valet had his valise always ready for immediate departure. He painted ceilings in the Luxembourg Palace with Carolus Duran, and lived mainly in Paris until his return to London in 1884, when his *Mme Gautreau* created a scandal at the Salon. Yet he continued to exhibit regularly in Paris. Highly respected, he became a member of the Royal Academy. Eventually the Tate Gallery established its Sargent Room.

Two other American artists working in the European scene deserve at least passing mention, for little attention has been accorded them lately: Frank Millet and Edwin Austin Abbey. Millet was a Harvard graduate and a correspondent for the New York *Herald* and two London newspapers during the Russo-Turkish War. In 1878 he served on the International Art Jury of the Paris Exhibition and won medals for his oils at the Paris Salon of 1889. He was the secretary of the organizers of the American Academy in Rome. He went down with the *Titanic,* a symbolic loss to the bridging of the arts between Europe and America. His friend Abbey, who was much under the influence of Millet and Rosetti in his painting, had first gone to England in 1878 to illustrate English life for *Harper's,* much in the earlier spirit of Irving. After a visit to Paris with Millet and a new American sojourn, he bought a house in the Cotswalds in 1890, and later another in

London, and lived for twenty years in England entertaining such English acquaintances as William Morris and Robert Browning. He knew John Hay well when he was minister to London and maintained a long correspondence with him when Hay became Secretary of State. Abbey became a member of the Royal Academy and did a number of panels in the House of Lords, yet he continued to think of himself as very much the American artist. He said himself in 1880 that he was sure that in ten years American art would be on an equal footing with any other country's. Abbey and Sargent united with Puvis de Chavannes in doing the murals for the Boston Public Library, which had been modeled after the Bibliothèque Sainte-Geneviève.

If Henry James had hope for the future of America and saw the cultural attraction and infection of Americans by aging Europe, Henry Adams tried to reconstruct his world within the pretext of an education which he claimed had deformed him. In despair he turned away from the disintegrating influence, as he saw it, of the multiplicity of industrial America, the centrifugal force of the dynamo, to the unity he saw in thirteenth-century France. From the highpoint of medieval France, the world was slowly degenerating, slowly running down. History was not progress, and in his *Education of Henry Adams* he observed that America's decline could be seen from Washington to Grant, and then following: "One might search the whole list of Congress, judiciary, and executive during the twenty-five years of 1870 to 1895 and find little but damaged reputations. The period was barren in purpose and barren in result." Adams became a stranger in his own country, hating the politicians and businessmen who ran it, yet admitting that "he must accept the regime." In 1880 he wrote a satirical novel, *Democracy*, which described the political corruption of Washington. He still felt this way fifteen years later. Our ancestors had steadily declined and virtually reached rock bottom. Religion and art were lost. Only the most useful practical qualities were retained and there was only a "dull instinct recalling dead associations. So we get Boston."

To the destructive violence of modern industrial civilization described in his *Education,* Adams apposed the spiritual vitality and unity of the Middle Ages in *Mont St. Michel and Chartres,* which was not intended as art criticism although he was interested in architecture. A friend of his, the architect Ralph Adams Cram, persuaded him to publish this monumental and enduring study. Adams contrasted the warlike eleventh century, represented by the Archangel Michael, to the peaceful twelfth century of the Virgin

Mary, as seen through three great queens: Eleanor of Aquitaine, Blanche of Castile, and Mary of Champagne. Adams' curiosity was aroused by the force of woman in society, where her sex was life-giving strength, where the venus-virgin force influenced history. In the *Education* and *Mont St. Michel and Chartres* he explored the difference between French and American women: "The Woman had once been supreme; in France she still seemed potent, not merely as sentiment, but as force. Why was she unknown in America?" Then he answered his own question: because of the Puritan tradition, woman was considered shameful in America: "Anyone brought up among the Puritans knew that sex was a sin. In any previous age sex was strength." Adams believed that the venus-virgin could never exist in America, for it had been replaced by the dynamo, the former producing great art and literature and the later science and technology.

It took Adams a lifetime to discover what he was looking for, and his tormented and hesitating thought finally found liberation when he realized what the French tradition meant. He did not discover France itself until much later in life, but then he was able to bring a mature and deliberative reflection to bear on his philosophy of history. After many detours, the descendant of Puritans, the son of Boston Unitarianism, and the sceptic finally concluded that one of the essential forces of progress was the sentiment which in the Middle Ages built the marvels crowned by the Archangel Saint Michael and the cathedral of Chartres crowned by the Virgin Mary, queen of men.

Adams' previous neglect of France is interesting. Boston was against the Second Empire. Charles Francis Adams, his father, detested Paris. Henry wrote that he himself "felt no love for Europe, which, as he and all the world agreed, unfitted Americans for America." Harvard, which he entered in 1854, was dominated by German methods and scholarship. He was a student of James Russell Lowell, who admired the German Romantics. The spirit of Emerson, Carlyle, Matthew Arnold, (even of Renan), was Germanic. It was therefore natural that Adams should continue his studies in Berlin. There he felt the exhilaration of Europe and wrote to his brother Charles upon arrival,

> Here in Europe, away from home, from care and ambition and the fretting of monotony, I must say that I often feel as I often used to feel in College, as if the whole thing didn't pay, and if I were my own master, it would need more inducements than the law can offer, to drag me out of Europe these ten years yet. I have always had an inclination for the Epicurean philosophy, and here in Europe I might gratify it until I was gorged.[21]

He continued to say prophetically that there was one pleasure that until then had not entered his calculations—art.

Adams concluded his Berlin studies and wrote later that "although he insisted that his faith in German thought and literature was exalted, he failed to approach German thought, and he shed never a tear of emotion over the pages of Goethe and Schiller." Adams realized that the Berlin he saw in 1860 was not the Germany of Goethe, but one of brutal discipline and rote, that the "German government did not encourage reasoning." He was glad to flee to Italy after his second winter, writing that he had "floundered in a mere mess of misunderstanding." "He loved, or thought he loved the people, but the Germany he loved was the eighteenth century which the Germans were ashamed of, and were destroying as fast as they could. Of the Germany to come he knew nothing." [22] Like Carlyle and Lowell, he preferred the eccentric and disunited Germany, but it was all being changed by coal and railways.

When Adams went to Italy to visit his married sister, he wrote that she was "like all good Americans and English, hotly Italian." "She not only adored Italy, but she cordially disliked Germany in all its varieties. She saw no gain in helping her brother to be Germanized, and she wanted him much to be civilized." Adams finally "locked the German door with a long breath of relief." He loved Rome, but felt that it was the "worst spot on earth to teach nineteenth century youth what to do with a twentieth century world." There, he said, "no sand-blast of science had yet skimmed off the epidermis of history, thought and feeling." He bore dispatches to Garibaldi who was in Palermo and with whom he had dinner.

Adams passed through France on his way to London and decided that he did not like the "esprit français." Instead of giving a long list of those things about France that displeased him, he pronounced a general condemnation. "He squandered two or three months on Paris. From the first he had avoided Paris and had wanted no French influence in his education. He disapproved of France in the lump." He disapproved of the French mind and "the whole, once, for all, and shut them figuratively out of his life. France was not serious, and he was not serious in going there."

Then followed seven years in London as secretary to his father during the Civil War, where he worked on swaying London opinion to the Northern cause. England tended to regard the Civil War from an economic and political point of view rather than an ideological one, at least until the Emancipation Proclamation. The New Englander Adams viewed it as a civil war between Puritans and Cavaliers. Adams worked hard to establish his social position, but he had little contact with the English literary world; he did meet Swinburne and J. S. Mill, and later Jowett, Stubbs, and Maine. Adams wrote in the *Education* that after the Civil War was over, he could only breathe the atmosphere of English thought and method and that, although he was acquiring English attitudes, he "at heart felt more hostile to them than ever"—even while England became more and more amusing to him. He was afraid of becoming un-American; yet, after his appointment to the Harvard faculty, he returned to England in 1870 and was able to confess of his visit, "He loved it all—everything—had always loved it." He was to return for his honeymoon in 1872 and again in 1879 for historical research. He later said that "London had become his vice," and that

> his heart was wrenched by the act of parting. . . . He had become English to the point of sharing their petty social divisions, their dislikes and prejudices against each other; he took England no longer with the awe of American youth, but with the habit of an old and rather worn suit of clothes.

His early attitudes toward France and the French were as difficult to understand as his early attitudes toward England. After a visit to his friend Richardson, who was studying architecture in Paris, he wrote of Paris as an "infernal city" and a "God-forsaken hole." It is surprising that Richardson, an architect, did not give Adams a clue. Adams had read Ruskin and Viollet-le-Duc, and had evidently learned nothing from seeing Notre Dame de Paris and Amiens. During the Franco-Prussian War he hoped that both France and Prussia would be defeated, and a decade later, he was still against Paris, against the brutal realism of the new literature, and against the overly complicated art nouveau. Still another decade later, in 1891, he declared that after reading Maupassant he learned why he disliked the French: of all the people he knew (and he had spent two years in Polynesia and the Far East) the French were the most depraved. All was unhealthy in Paris: literature, theater, art, public and private morality, even cooking. He wrote from Paris in 1891 that "if I abhor the French more in one genre than another, and find their fatuity more out of place in any other part of the world than in that where I happen to be, my abomination of them is greatest when they try to escape from themselves, and especially when they become oriental." Shades of Whistler!

It is surprising that Adams did not know France until 1895, in spite of his natural curiosity, his historical interests and his penchant for studying habits and customs. He had been there several times before, but with closed eyes. Then in 1895 with Henry Cabot Lodge he went to see Norman churches for the first time. From this visit Adams realized that his training in German methods made him forget what the Germans forget. Until then he had had a horror of being an antiquary, and the Rhine castles, German cathedrals, the Middle Ages still seen in the Rome of 1860, Winchester, Salisbury, Canterbury, and Westminster had little effect. Now, upon seeing the Norman churches, Adams could write, "In spite of all, France has just the same more to offer than any country I know," and he returned to Washington with "a new sense of history."

From 1895 to 1914 Adams went each year to Chartres, Mont St. Michel, Caen, Coutances, or another French cathedral. "After thirty-five years of postponed intentions, I worshipped at last before the splendor of the great glass gods," Adams wrote, and confessed to Brooks Adams in 1895, "Of all these familiar haunts the one that moved me most with a sense of personal identity with myself, was Coutances." [23] He had experienced what his teacher Lowell had said while standing before Chartres, that he was the "son of an age which lectures and which doesn't create." He could now develop his theme that there were two forces which directed mankind, the medieval spirit which led to creative unity and the modern drive which led to destructive multiplicity. It is true that at one point he took up Comte's positivism in trying to develop a philosophy of history, but then he got lost in Darwinian evolution and wasted several years working on Lyell trying to find a historical evolutionary synthesis. Now he began to explain the enigma of the split between the Middle Ages and a Chaplinesque "Modern Times." Since Gibbon, he said, history-writing was a scandalous spectacle a hundred years behind the experimental sciences, and less suggestive than Scott or Dumas. Now he had found the key in the French twelfth century.

In 1900 Adams took an apartment near the Trocadero and went almost every day to the Exhibition of 1900. There he found his idea of the dynamo which governed modern society. The new scientific and technical discoveries, far from showing the unity of nature, increased its shattering centrifugal forces. He went with St. Gaudens to Amiens and remembered there what he had recognized in the Norman churches in 1895. It was the immaterial force of faith which created the unity he sought. Thomism was the most complete expression of the linking of spirit with unity, and the French were the most faithful followers of this tradition. The French twelfth century was a complex hierarchical society with a subtle theology, a fragile edifice which, like their cathedrals, was sustained by the unity of faith.

Adams was a thinking person who was more at home in another country and who opposed men of action like Teddy Roosevelt. Adams tried to open the window on the problems of the spirit while Teddy Roosevelt was more adapted to "facts and figures," to technology and political force. Adams saw

that he was useless bric-a-brac in the new society, which was concerned only
with the development of a continent which had no place for the thinker:

> On the new scale of power, merely to make the continent habitable for
> civilized people would require an immediate outlay that would have
> bankrupted the world. As yet, no portion of the world except a few
> narrow stretches of Western Europe had been tolerably provided with
> the essentials of comfort and convenience; to fit out an entire continent
> with roads and the decencies of life would exhaust the credit of the
> entire planet.[24]

Henry Adams was much less in the American vein than Theodore
Roosevelt, who stood for deeds before words, speaking softly but carrying a
big stick. In *The Strenuous Life* (1899) Roosevelt wrote: "Let us therefore
boldly face the life of strife, resolute to do our duty well and manfully;
resolute to uphold righteousness; resolute to be both honest and brave, to
serve high ideals, *yet to use practical methods.*" Adams had high ideals, so
sky-high that they were heavenly, but it is certain that he would not use
Roosevelt's practical methods to achieve his ideal. Few would argue that
Teddy Roosevelt was as profound as Adams. The British Ambassador Cecil
Spring-Rice wrote, "you must always remember that the President is about
six," while the elder La Follette said, "Theodore Roosevelt is the ablest
living interpreter of what I would call the superficial public sentiment of a
given time, and he is spontaneous in his response to it." Alfred Kazin quotes
one of Roosevelt's profundities: "We are neither for the rich man as such
nor for the poor man as such; we are for the upright man, poor or rich," and
Kazin concluded that it took twenty years for American critical intelligence
to mull this over and to realize that he had said nothing at all.[25] The Adams-
Roosevelt dichotomy would be interesting to explore as typical of the deep
division between American thought and action, idealism and reality, histori-
cism and contemporaneity in the American vein. But let us pass on to a
charming transatlantic lady whose career successfully bridged the two Atlantic
cultures.

Edith Wharton, a member of the New York "Four Hundred," followed
in the pattern of Henry James, her mentor. Having divorced a neurasthenic
husband, she established herself in Paris after 1907, and wrote of the rigid
conventions of a society, whose exterior elegance was supported by money
rather than real culture. Her indebtedness to James is great, and one marvels

that she was able to continue the Jamesian tradition without wearing out her public welcome. In 1925 in *The Writing of Fiction,* she studies her own literary techniques along with James' and other writers.' In her autobiography, *A Backward Glance,* James fills as much space as she does.

In turn, James was worried about the effect of expatriation on her writing. He wrote, "she *must* be tethered in native pastures, even if it reduces her to a backyard in New York," and added that this was the essence of his own wisdom and experience. To Edith Wharton herself he admonished, "Your only drawback is not having the homeliness and the inevitability and the happy limitation of the affluent poverty of a country of your own." [26]

In describing the Americans at home and abroad in a Jamesian manner, she became a Parisian silhouette more and more imbued with French culture; her guide along this path was Paul Bourget. In 1909 she even wrote a short story in French, "Les Metteurs en Scène." In *French Ways and Their Meanings* she showed her love for French taste and artistic integrity. Most of her books are autobiographical, having much finesse but lacking in general ideas. She also spoke Italian perfectly and knew the eighteenth century of Goldoni and Guardi well. Her first novel, *The Valley of Decision,* centered on Italy; other Italian works followed: *Italian Villas and their Gardens* and *Italian Backgrounds.* In Italy she became a friend of Bernard Berenson and traveled with him to Weimar and Berlin. She violently disapproved of the German vulgarity which she found evident in their way of life, in their political forms and practices, and in their architecture. She wished to save the French from a Gothic invasion that would have been as bad as the invasion of her New York society by the brash Midwest.

Like Dorothy Canfield, she did Red Cross work during the War, a war which both considered noble, just, and purposeful. Gertrude Stein felt the same way and drove for the American Fund for French Wounded. The red blood of Americans on French soil served glory, civilization, art, and religion against crude militarism. Along with Henry James, Edith Warton was indignant over America's slow entrance into the War, which she expressed in *Fighting France* and *The Marne.*

Although Edith Warthon's reputation was largely recognized after 1920, she did her best work before World War I. Except for the *Age of Innocence* her postwar novels are uninteresting and weak. Where James was able to do fine-figured and complex writing on the European-American social relation, Edith Wharton kept to her genteel New York–Fifth Avenue society of leisured good conversation with the "right people." She wrote of the impolite invasion of that society by the *nouveaux riches* and the parvenus, bankers and industrialists, and the eventual breakdown of the old order. Her museum-like society characters are exquisitely hard, all nicely arranged like colorful butterflies pinned down on cotton under a shiny glass cover. This society vanished with the coming of the great catastrophe which weakened all interest in anemones and bygones.

In 1914, America still held the image of Lafayette, but it was more sentimental than active. The domestic scene in America on the eve of the War left much to be desired by those aware of the importance of the transatlantic connection. Bryan was a pacifist and isolationist, making paid lecture tours as Secretary of State. From that august figure came the astonishing judgment in a 1913 speech that "conditions promising world peace were never more favorable than now, and in saying that, I have special reference to those wars that might occur between great powers."

When Woodrow Wilson was inaugurated in 1913, he came into the White House as the first Democrat since Cleveland, and his New Freedom was widely hailed by youth, intellectuals, tired progressives, and liberals. Where Teddy Roosevelt was strong on foreign policy and Taft continued his dollar diplomacy, Wilson hoped to concentrate on domestic reform and regulation. Before his inauguration he remarked, "It would be the irony of fate if my administration had to deal chiefly with foreign affairs." This is not to say that Wilson personally or emotionally was dissociated from Europe. His travels in Europe, the joys of bicycling through England and Scotland, his research and teaching, indicated his private interests. Yet Theodore Roosevelt wrote to his friend Senator Lodge that Wilson "is a ridiculous creature in international matters."

Wilson distrusted his isolationist Secretary of State from Nebraska, relying more and more upon Colonel House, and Bryan distrusted his own Department of State. Wilson was mortified when Charles W. Eliot, President of Harvard, refused the ambassadorship to the Court of St. James because of Bryan, and when Walter Hines Page was prevailed upon to take the post he was soon to write Colonel House that Bryan's handling of the State Department was worse than unfortunate. The American Ambassador to Berlin James W. Girard spent the year before the outbreak of the War looking for embassy quarters which would be suitable to him.

In March, 1913, Bryan publicly congratulated the Irish upon their achievement of the Home Rule Bill, calling it "the virtual end of hereditary rule." The British were furious, the English press called him a "mountebank," and the German press chimed in to call him a "clown." He bumbled along. He endeared himself to the Washington diplomatic colony by serving grape juice at his first state dinner.

Not only had he badly handled the question of Japanese immigration to California and the Six-Power Loan to the Chinese Republic, but he also tangled with Great Britain on the Panama Canal tolls and the Mexican War, and it took the secret diplomacy of House and Sir Edward Grey to rearrange the situation. Meanwhile, the Balkan stew simmered on.

The United States in 1913 was woefully unprepared diplomatically and militarily for any great European war. The landbound Secretary of the Navy Joseph Daniels had asked Congress for a modest increase of two battleships, but the House of Representatives, following Churchill's proposal, announced its own naval holiday by a vote of 317 to 11. Bryan thought America should set the Europeans an example by unilateral disarmament. American active land forces then stood at 35,000, while Germany had 700,000 and France 550,000. In the *Independent,* Andrew Carnegie wrote "The Baseless Fear of War," in which he asked: "Has there ever been danger of war between Germany and ourselves, members of the same Teutonic race? Never has it been imagined. . . . All nations are our friends and we are the friends of all."

At the close of 1914 the American Association for International Conciliation congratulated the Kaiser for "the maintenance of twenty-five years of unbroken peace between Germany and the other nations of the world," signed by Nicholas Murray Butler, Andrew Carnegie, and the presidents of U.S. Steel, the American Historical Association, the National Educational Association, the American Bankers Association, the American Bar Association, and the National Academy of Science. Soon they would be calling sauerkraut "liberty cabbage" and banning Bach, Beethoven, Brahms, and Wagner, and kicking little dachshunds.

America did not understand the issues clearly and did not foresee, nor want to see, an involvement in the European crisis. When Mark Sullivan decribed the "Wilson Tango" as "One step forward, two steps backward; hesitate!" he was also describing a general American attitude that remained indecisive until the sinking of the *Lusitania.*

In 1914, Wilson not only declared neutrality but asked Americans to think neutrally and reserve their judgment until after the War. In 1919 he himself realized that Americans should not have been idle spectators, and that he had not understood all in 1914. Was Tocqueville right when he declared that the greatest privilege of the Americans was not necessarily to be more enlightened than others, but to have the faculty of making errors which could be repaired? America was "for" international conciliation and "for" world peace, but wanted no commitments or responsibilities—without which effective American leadership in the world arena was made impossible.

America's participation in the War was a strange one. America was not an ally but an "associated power," and somewhat detached from the renewed old quarrel between France and Germany. Even so, America's late entry was decisive; the Allies were about down. England had six weeks' reserves and no more French could be called up. When the French were about to collapse in March and April of 1918, William E. Dodd noted in his diary letter that "no real obligation to the United States was recognized, nor have I ever heard a single Frenchman admit that Woodrow Wilson saved France, though all Germans say: 'Wilson defeated us, the treacherous Wilson.' " 27

Edith Wharton was not a direct participant in the War and saw it from a maternal point of view. The war generation saw the War as dirty mud and blood, stupid and absurdly nonpurposeful. She turned her *Trips to the Front* into a war novel, *A Son at the Front,* published in 1924. It was as unworthy of her talent as it was unreal when compared with Hemingway's *Farewell to Arms,* Cummings' *Enormous Room,* or Dos Passos' *One Man's Initiation.*

Like Edith Wharton, Willa Cather looked at the War as a nonparticipant, and produced a similarly weak novel, *One of Ours,* in which the boy from Nebraska typifies all that Nebraska lacks, and in the incredibly short time he is in France learns all about art and culture and then dies nobly and meaningfully—he gives his life for an idea. The two women writers learned that they were describing the War in outdated terms; terms and words which once had meaning were now rendered meaningless. They described the American scene better: Wharton's *The Age of Innocence* recreated prewar values and won a Pulitzer Prize, and there was much merit in Willa Cather's study of American immigrants, *My Antonia.*

World War I had brought American Victorian-Edwardian writing to an end and had closed the doors of the fashionable salons. A new evaluation of writing began to take place, beginning with Eliot and Pound in their search for a newer expression. Wharton herself realized that her style had become dated and wrote less and less. The twentieth century, Henry Adams notwithstanding, did not begin at 1900, but after the War. One era was brought to a close, and a new one, which had little relation to it and constantly denied it, was born—either on the Marne or in Paris, but surely in France. The world of James and Proust had vanished. The search for new identities and new meaning in art and the human situation began. The War had been a departure from the rules, and the postwar world tried to set up new rules.

Willa Cather recoiled from the new era: "The world broke in two in 1922 or thereabouts." The comfortable house of Mrs. Fields on Charles Street had been replaced by a garage, an automotive vulgarity had replaced the intimacy of the drawing room and an elegant dining table over which good conversation had been made livelier by good food and good wines, and where all had looked forward with confidence to the growth of their country in the finer amenities of life.

Science had now provided us with ingenious toys which distracted man from the important problems of life, but traditionalist Willa Cather felt that since these problems were insoluble, one should at least be grateful for the distraction. She was not, however, enthusiastic about the social novel of industrialized society: "Are the banking system and the Stock Exchange worth being written about at all?" she asked in "The Novel Démeublé."

The product of a raw childhood in Virginia and Nebraska and a few years' teaching in Pittsburgh, she made her first pilgrimage to Europe in 1902. As isolated as Nebraska may have seemed, it was a Nebraska filled with Europeans. There were so many that as a young girl Willa Cather would spend Sundays attending services conducted in French, Norwegian, or Danish. One could pass an entire day without hearing a word of English.

She was already well read in several literatures, including Greek and Latin, and had made a cult of Flaubert. Nevertheless, Europe was a revelation to her and made a deep impression. Her likes and dislikes were quickly recorded, and remained with her. England was curiously strange, France mystically beautiful, and Germany crudely barbarian. She was shocked by the untidy dress of English men and women. Even though the English considered toothbrushes only for members of the royal family, she still thought the English "thoroughly engaging and attractive." France she loved most of all, and on her first approach to the French coast she heard among the passengers "a babble of voices, in which I could only distinguish the word 'France' uttered over and over again with a fire and fervor that was itself a panegyric." For her, everything French was grace and beauty, white towns wrapped in pale pink mists with purple shadows, urchins whose cries were "musical," porter's "smooth, clear voices," the children all happy and pretty, and flowers everywhere. "People know how to live in this country." [28]

For Americans with sensibility and talent, France was a refuge from a flat, colorless America. The cultural hero of *One of Ours* is David Gerhardt, the gifted violinist who speaks French and German well. As a sign of the breaking up of culture by the War, his violin is smashed to pieces—a Stradavarius, of course: "A man like Gerhardt, for instance, had always lived in a more or less rose-colored world; he belonged over there, really." [29] The War had destroyed what was supposed to be permanent in art, cathedrals, and statues.

In Claude, Willa Cather shows much of her own feeling for France and her long expatriation. He dies giving America more credit than it deserves, and thinking France the best possible country; echoing Hemingway, he could not go home again after the emotion of France.

Like Henry James and Edith Wharton, Willa Cather was indignant at America's slow entry into the War: "He had been due in France since the first battle of the Marne; he had followed false leads and lost precious time and seen misery enough, but he was on the right road at last, and nothing could stop him." Others were to make the same reproach and final happy resolution for America's final entry into the Second World War, but Willa Cather was not willing to put off the shame. She had the delicate but resolute Melle de Courcy saying, " 'We,—we were taught from the childhood that someday the Germans would come, we grew up under that threat. But you were so safe, with all your wheat and corn. Nothing could touch you, nothing!' Claude dropped his eyes. 'Yes,' he muttered, blushing, 'shame could. It pretty nearly did. We are pretty late.' "

George Santayana, another philosopher-writer like James, Eliot, and Pound, personified the transatlantic cultural bridge. He thought the United States was like the stars—he preferred to admire them from afar. His American roots were not as deep as James', yet he remained American. He preferred Europe for his philosophic thought, yet always wrote in English, and declared that it was the only language suitable for his expression. His expatriation, if we can call it that, for he was a true transatlantic being, and his life in England and Italy significantly parallel the expatriation of Eliot and Pound.

Santayana was brought to the United States by his American mother when he was nine and later he was educated at Harvard. He went to Berlin for two years' study and returned for a Harvard Ph.D. After studies at King's College, Cambridge, he taught philosophy at Harvard and was Hyde Lecturer at the Sorbonne. In 1911 he resigned his professorship at Harvard to live in Europe. His *Character and Opinion in the United States* and *Soliloquies in England* indicated an eventual estrangement from the American scene. A greater sign of alienation was *The Last Puritan,* probably modeled after Butler's *The Way of All Flesh.* Puritan Oliver Alden, wealthy and virtuous, meets his death in World War I, and for the best it is implied. Like his father Peter, he was bewildered and unhappy. But unlike his father, who lived it up on his yacht in Europe, he had a "moral nature burdened and overstrung, and a critical faculty fearless but helplessly subjective—isn't that the tragedy of your ultimate Puritan?"

T. S. Eliot in some ways resembles Santayana in the transatlantic pathway in that he straddled both sides of the Atlantic but left his homeland for good. He began the search for a modern language to express modern man's sentiments. He couldn't find it in modern English writing, and pushed further and further back until he settled on the Elizabetheans, particularly Donne. His real formation for handling language was explicitly French, and he even wrote a poem in half-French.

After Harvard, where he had studied with Santayana and the humanist Irving Babbitt, he studied philosophy and French literature at the Sorbonne and followed Bergson's courses at the Collège de France. After teaching philosophy at Harvard, he went on a scholarship in 1914 to Marburg, but with the outbreak of the War he moved to Merton College, Oxford. He then taught a multitude of subjects, including swimming, in English grammar schools and worked in Lloyds Bank, somewhat happier, because he disliked teaching. He had tried to join the United States Navy, but was refused. Eliot began writing, and in 1917 he published "Prufrock," reflecting the styles of Laforgue and Corbière. In 1922 appeared "The Waste Land" which won a prize from *The Dial*. This led him to the editorship of *The Criterion* for the next seventeen years. In 1925 he quit Lloyds, where he had become chief of the Foreign Information Bureau, and joined Faber & Faber. Two years later he became a British subject. During 1932–1933 he returned to lecture in America.

Conservative and Catholic Eliot sought a renewed classicism and pronounced the sovereignty of the intellect. He turned to the French to find expression for his rebuilding of English writing. He discovered Jules Laforgue and rediscovered Baudelaire, saying later that without Baudelaire he believed he never could have learned to write. In 1940 Eliot said, "The kind of poetry that I needed to teach me the use of my own voice did not exist in English at all; it was only to be found in French." [30] "The Waste Land," dedicated to Pound, showed the postwar malaise in new and modern language, the idea of the plague which touches everything, which was to be repeated by Camus. William Carlos Williams said that "The Waste Land" "wiped out our world as if an atom bomb had been dropped on it. . . . Our work staggered to a halt under the blast of Eliot's genius. . . . Our brave sallies into the unknown were turned to dust." [31]

Eliot's criticism was influenced by Julian Benda, Georges Sorel, and Maurras, to whom he dedicated a little book on Dante in 1929. Through the *Action Française* he learned about Maritain, but after his "Sacred Wood," Eliot filled a void in the English criticism which had been vacant since Matthew Arnold.

Like Pound, Eliot became more and more conservative and antidemocratic and attacked the individual *arrivisme* found in democratic society, which Henry Adams had been doing earlier. In the spirit of classicism, he saw that what America needed was a Montaigne; what was provided was an Emerson. He wrote in 1924,

> There is a form of literary culture which shrinks from direct contact with a great work of art. . . . This aversion for the work of art, this preference for the derivative, the marginal, is an aspect of the modern democracy of culture. We say democracy advisedly: that meanness of spirit, that egotism of motive, that incapacity for surrender or allegiance to something outside of oneself, which is a frequent symptom of the soul of man under democracy.[32]

Eliot was saying the same things that Cooper castigated years before. Steadfast Dodge in *Homeward Bound* is made to assert,

> we can have few originals in our part of the country, you know. . . . For to say the true, it is rather unpopular to differ from the neighborhood, in this or any other respect. Yes sir, the people will rule, and ought to rule. . . . I do not know that any man has a right to be peculiar in a free country. It is aristocratic, and has an air of thinking one man is better than another.[33]

In *The Idea of a Christian Society,* Eliot called for a clerisy, a select body of intellectuals to put a new spirit into the people and to influence politicians, an impossible thing for a non-Catholic nonaristocratic America.

When one thinks of Santayana and Eliot, another transatlantic figure may be recalled. Ezra Pound went to Europe as an Idaho boy of twenty-three for his Ph.D. thesis on Lope de Vega, visiting Spain, Provence, and Italy. His first poems, *A Lume Spento,* were published in Venice. In 1908 he published "Personae" and "Exultations" in London. T. E. Hulme and Ford Madox Hueffer then influenced him toward the French decadents. From 1912 he spent eight years in London, and launched imagism to replace the symbolism—with a London coterie including Amy Lowell, cigar smoking sister of the president of Harvard, and H. D., American wife of the poet Richard Aldington. He spent four years in Paris from 1920 to 1924, where he was the first to recognize Joyce and to encourage Wyndham Lewis and George Antheil. He lived at Rapallo until the close of World War II, when he was brought back for a long interment in an American mental asylum, despite the protests of the literary world. He was the complete expatriate, the passionate pilgrim, as he wrote in "L'Homme moyen sensuel,"

> Tis of my country that I would endite
> In hope to set some misconceptions right.

Radway of the poem has been educated by "lecturers and secret lechers" who corrupted his soul with their "stale infection." In America, man had become only a "social function," and the artist had to go abroad for recognition, away from business ethics.

> For as Ben Franklin said with such urbanity:
> "Nothing will pay thee, friend, like Christianity"

which

> 'Twas as a business asset *pure an' simple*.[34]

Pound was a great influence on postwar writing. He helped Eliot cut and revise his "Waste Land" and helped Hemingway with his style. After "Pavannes and Divisions" and "Hugh Selwyn Mauberly," he began his Cantos, the first published in 1925. He wrote of the War's futility, and his own "half-savage country, out of date"; Mauberly was "out of key with his time," when "the age demanded an image of its own accelerated grimace." Those who had served during the War

> walked eye-deep in hell
> believing in old men's lies, then unbelieving
> came home, home to a lie,
> home to many deceits,
> home to old lies and new infamy;
> usury age-old and age-thick
> and liars in public places.
>
> .   .   .   .
>
> There died a myriad
> and of the best, among them
> for an old bitch gone in the teeth,
> for a botched civilization.

But the poet is not a social thinker out to remake the world:

> The glow of porcelain
> brought no reforming sense
> to his perception
> of the social inconsequences.
>
> .   .   .   .
>
> He made no immediate application
> of this to the relation of the state
> to the individual . . .[35]

There was little point in walking eye-deep in hell for a botched civilization. The War was verdigris, dead stinking horses, and gangrene, and there were no heroics such as Cather, Wharton, and Canfield saw, religious, clean, and white.

Pound and Eliot and MacLeish and Tate tried to give new meanings to words, words that had become nullified or distorted by propaganda or ridiculous slogans mouthed by politicians. Pound was unpopular in London, stood against Wyndham Lewis and the vorticists, and took no interest in the War. Discouraged by the death of many friends during the War and breaking with the London imagists, Pound quit London for Paris. He had said earlier that Americans should not change their allegiance from London to Paris, but he, like Eliot, was more and more coming under the influence of French writing. In February, 1918, he did a long article on French poetry in the *Little Review* and another on French literature in *The Dial*. He wrote in the *Fortnightly Review* (December, 1915), "Paris is the laboratory of ideas. It is there that poisons can be tested and new modes of sanity be discovered. It is there that the antiseptic conditions of the laboratory exist. That is the function of Paris."

And so, with transatlantic marriages, the interlocking of burgeoning American capitalism and of industry with Europe, the comings and goings of American writers and artists to Europe (mostly goings), the Atlantic dialogue was carried through the Gilded Age into World War I, and from there to a new era strangely alien to the older generation.

NOTES

1. Cited in Richard H. Heindel, *The American Impact on Great Britain, 1898–1914* (Philadelphia: University of Pennsylvania Press, 1940), p. 42.

2. André Tardieu, *Notes sur les Etats-Unis* (Paris: Calmann-Lévy, 1908), pp. 267–68.

3. Van Wyck Brooks, *The Ordeal of Mark Twain* (New York: E. P. Dutton & Co., Inc., 1933), p. 74.

4. William Dean Howells, *The Rise of Silas Lapham* (Boston: Houghton Mifflin Company, 1937), p. 66.

5. William Dean Howells, *Literature and Life* (New York and London: Harper & Row, Publishers, 1902), p. 203.

6. Cited in Kazin, p. 5.

7. Cited in Brooks, *The Pilgrimage of Henry James*, p. 25.

8. Henry Adams, p. 5.

9. Letter to his mother from Florence, 1869. Cited in Henry Seidel Canby, *Turn West, Turn East: Mark Twain and Henry James* (Boston: Houghton Mifflin Company, 1951), p. 80.

10. Cited in Brooks, *The Pilgrimage of Henry James*, p. 66.

11. Cited in Kazin, p. 49.

12. Cited in Brooks, *The Pilgrimage of Henry James*, p. 48.

13. Cited in Brooks, *The Ordeal of Mark Twain*, p. 222.

14. Paine, *Mark Twain's Notebook*, p. 367.

15. *Ibid.*, p. 219.

16. *Ibid.*, p. 327.

17. *Ibid.*, p. 217.

18. Oscar Cargill, *Intellectual America: Ideas on the March* (New York: The Macmillan Company, 1941), p. 483.

19. Cited in Kazin, p. 184.

20. Letter to Alyse Gregory, Paris, April 20, 1914. Cited in Rahv, pp. 461–62.

21. *Letters of Henry Adams (1858–1891)*, Worthington Chauncy Ford (ed.), (London: Constable and Company, 1930), p. 5.

22. Adams, *The Education of Henry Adams*, pp. 78 ff.

23. Letter to Elizabeth Cameron, August 29, 1895. Letter to Brooks Adams, September 8, 1895. Cited in Rahv, p. 367.

24. Adams, *The Education of Henry Adams*, p. 239.

25. Kazin, pp. 102–103.

26. Cited in Brooks, *The Pilgrimage of Henry James*, p. 160.

27. William E. Dodd, December 3, 1935, *Diary*, (New York: Harcourt, Brace & World, Inc., 1941), p. 283.

28. *Willa Cather in Europe; her own story of the first journey*, George N. Kates (ed.), (New York: Alfred A. Knopf, Inc., 1956), Pp. 94, 135.

29. Willa Cather, *One of Ours* (New York: Alfred A. Knopf, Inc., 1953), p. 375.

30. "The Poetry of W. B. Yeats," *Purpose*, 1940. Cited in Peyre, p. 167.

31. Cited in Van Wyck Brooks, *From the Shadow of the Mountain* (New York: E. P. Dutton & Co., Inc., 1961), p. 78.

32. T. S. Eliot, "A Commentary," *Criterion* (April, 1924), p. 235.

33. James Fenimore Cooper, *Homeward Bound* (New York: G. P. Putman's Sons, 1896), p. 95.

34. Ezra L. Pound, *Personae* (New York: New Directions, pp. 238, 246.

35. *Ibid.*, pp. 190–91.

⌁ EBB TIDE ⌁

> *America is God's crucible, the great melting-pot where all the races of Europe are melting and reforming. . . . The real American has not yet arrived. He is only in the crucible. I tell you— he will be the fusion of all races, perhaps the coming Superman.*
>
> —Zangwill

Once two million American troops were safely back on their own shores following the first major contact with Europe, and with an idealism chastened by the European holocaust, America decided to retreat from all European imbroglios, to look inward and avoid any further complicated entanglements. The Great War had killed between ten and thirteen million and left seventy million maimed. The United States had lost one hundred thousand, but the European toll was staggering: one and one-half million French, two million Germans, one and three-quarter million Russians, one million British, and one-half million Italian troops lost their lives, plus others from influenza, typhus, and cholera. America no longer wanted to sing "Over There" and the yellow press forgot about Belgian babies. The results of the War made people think that they had been deceived, that it had all been a bad joke. America wanted to withdraw from Europe and return to its original innocence. Wilson's evangelic missionary fervor had mounted during the first American crusade in Europe. He said: "I hope and believe that I am, in gress on January 22, 1917, he proclaimed: "I hope and believe that I am, in effect, speaking for liberals and friends of humanity in every nation and of every program of liberty. I would fain believe that I am speaking for the silent mass of mankind everywhere. . . ." [1]

But having crusaded to make the world safe for democracy, America refused to see it through and to sign the Versailles treaties. Versailles disintegrated into a shambles, a race for territories and reparations. Lloyd George asked his secretary whether Britain was giving away Upper or Lower Silesia. The American delegates did not seem to know where Austria proper was and some thought unredeemed Italy was on the Lower East Side of New

York. The Chinese delegate thought the Cameroons were some part of Scotland. Reparations were made possible by loans from New York banks so that the Allies could pay off American war debts. Americans refused to join the League, because it was too full of foreigners. The League was destined to become powerless without even the moral support of the new world power which America represented. Wilson showed moral grandeur, but his idealism had been remolded by national groups seeking his support, and his policy of self-determination backfired into a mockery of his idealistic principles.

The Wilsonian concept of peace without victory was quietly but firmly laid aside at the conference table by the European powers. Colonel House had seen this when he left Paris in 1919 with conflicting emotions:

> We had to deal with a situation pregnant with difficulties and one which could be met only by an unselfish and idealistic spirit, which was almost wholly absent and which was too much to expect of men come together at such a time and for such a purpose. And yet I wish we had taken the other road, even if it were less smooth, both now and afterward, than the one we took. We would at least have gone in the right direction and if those who follow us had made it impossible to go the full length of the journey planned, the responsibility would have rested with them and not with us.[2]

Keynes's *Economic Consequences of the Peace* indicated how viable economic relations of regional groups had been scorned in the shout for territorial claims. It had been Europe's war and the settlement was European. There is no doubt that American military and economic aid turned the tide, for France had drawn on its last reserves and English resources were strained to the limit, but the treaty-making was almost wholly in the tradition of nineteenth-century European statecraft. As the Wilsonian ideal became more and more unrealizable, Wilson became more unreal and more rigidly stubborn. Allen Tate wrote later:

> Proud Wilson yielded ground
> to franc and pound,
> made pilgrimage
> in the wake of Henry James,[3]

and Harry Elmer Barnes affirmed that Wilson had "produced more cynics than any other figure in modern history." Eventually almost all the new postwar democracies created by Versailles foundered and fell under Fascism from within or without because the political formulas envisaged ignored economic and social conditions. Even French democracy finally tottered into a corporate state as a result of two decades of political and social attrition and a humiliating defeat in 1940.

America's rejection of the League spelled the eventual defeat of the League itself. With the United States in the League, full hope might have been permitted; without it, it proved a tragic farce.

With all faith in man shaken, America had come out of the War, as Fitzgerald said, to find that all gods were dead. After the failure of Versailles, Americans retired to their tents, opening flaps from time to time to call out disinterested advice. The American withdrawal into noble isolation exerted no effect on any cause.

Wilsonian idealism was dead, the Fourteen Points discredited, the hopes for a better world were lost somewhere along the Marne and could not quite be refound. Clemenceau thought that Wilson needed four more points than God to save the world. Wilson, who had been joyously acclaimed by Europe in 1919, lost much of his prestige, and his politics, depending on the country involved, were looked on as naive, misleading, or even underhanded. The United States, as Philip Wylie wrote in his *Generation of Vipers,* sat "like a benign Dutch uncle at the peace table and hand[ed] out Sunday School rules and diplomas to the infuriated peoples of Europe." [4] The American Puritans had set the bar so high that nobody could vault over it; consequently all crawled underneath.

Still, the participation of American troops in the War had opened European eyes to American idealism, an idealism which had not until then been seen. Before, America was a country which had profited by neutrality through traffic in munitions and arms supplies. Soon after 1920, however, the European Left which had sponsored American ideals in Europe felt they had been betrayed, and that their defense of America had been false. European liberals could not defend an America which had become conservative and reactionary. The European Left came to distrust the America which it had applauded since 1776, and the European Right now generally supported American policies until the advent of Roosevelt's New Deal, when the Left began to show again a sympathetic interest in the United States. The American immigration bars, which had gone up at the same time as the Russian Revolution began, had a great effect on the left wing in Europe. Even though there was virtually no immigration to Russia (or more likely *because* there was no effectively large emigration), the Soviet Union now offered a new ideological orientation to set against the United States. America promised to make you rich, while Russia promised to make you equal.

After the War, the American liberal ship of the first twenty years of the century had gone down with its colorful characters, such as Lincoln Steffens, Ida M. Tarbell, and other muckrakers, leaving only Upton Sinclair and Robert LaFollette, Sr., with the *Nation* and the *New Republic,* on an isolated raft in a sea of mammon. Progressivism had become politically inadequate, for it could not anticipate or explain the historic postwar changes in political, social, or national attitudes. The War had failed to fulfill the promises of its liberal leaders: the only hope was seen in Dewey's *Reconstruction in Philosophy* and in James Harvey Robinson's *The Mind of the Making.* Wilson's first inaugural now had a bitter ring: "Men's hearts wait upon us; men's lives hang in the balance; men's hopes call upon us to say what we will do. Who shall live up to that great trust? Who dare fail to try?" They had tried, but American liberal doctrinaires had become too preoccupied with outward mechanical forms, as Lord Bryce had earlier warned.

Moral indignation with the War's results gave rise only to unconstructive criticism and the liberals resigned themselves to the triumphant business, bad taste, and an unbuttoned lack of restraint which characterized the twenties. Whisky "just off the boat" was elegantly served in teacups, and many a bathtub was rendered antiseptic with homemade gin. The corner druggist achieved a new social standing.

The Americans wanted to return to "normalcy," another way of saying that Americans wanted to wrap themselves in the Stars and Stripes and retreat into traditionalist isolationism, prophylactic and disinfected. Warren G. Harding put the slogan in 1920: "Stabilize America first, prosper America first, think of America first, exalt America first," an attitude which may be said to have prevailed generally until the political conversion of the great Republican leader, Arthur Vandenberg. Woe to those who did not follow the lead of the American Legion in their 100 per cent Americanism, or of other well-meaning hundred-percenters, up to and including the America First Committee. The American community wanted to be hebraic and separate. Herbert Hoover pronounced for rugged individualism and stated that at the end of the War "we were challenged with a peacetime choice between the American system of rugged individualism and the Europe philosophy of diametrically opposed doctrines, doctrines of paternalism and state socialism. The acceptance of these ideas would have meant the destruction of self-government through the centralization of government." [5] Today's America portrays a different aspect, and while the welfare state is accepted in transformed American terms, and while undoubtedly there has been government centralization, self-government has not been destroyed.

Should there sadly have been unearthed some stray anarchists or socialists, deportation was in order. An Act of Congress of October 16, 1918, provided for the deportation of anarchists of any kind, where previously a distinction was made between the bomb-throwing "destructive revolutionists" and the philosophical anarchists. Several hundreds were shipped off on the S.S. "Buford" in 1919, un-Americans who were in effect told to take their Old World ideologies back to the Old World. The charter of the German-American League was revoked in Congress, German names of towns and streets were changed as rapidly as biographical place names change in Soviet Russia. America had looked at death in Europe and turned its face.

Harding said in 1920 that he did not want to "menace the health of the Republic in old world contagion" and that "one cannot be half-American and half-European or half something else," disliking what he called hyphenated Americans (even if three years later he broke down and let British sailors march in a Fourth of July parade).

Before that, five pitiful socialist members of the New York legislature were expelled, and Attorney General Palmer began the earlier McCarthy fight. The watchwords were "expel the troublemakers and make sure that no new ones entered; America must be preserved intact for red-blooded Americans, even if one had to use Pinkerton men." Virtually overnight the immigration gates were slammed shut and the portcullis raised, breaking the image of America as the only land which welcomed the homeless and the oppressed, the land where man could start the new life.

America should not forget the fundamental role played by immigrants in its historic development, those whose tears and sweat built an entirely unparalleled civilization in less than two hundred years. One of the grievances cited in the Declaration of Independence was that England *hampered* immigration. Franklin wrote to an English friend in 1784,

> You do wrong to discourage the emigration of Englishman to America. In my piece on population, I have proved, I think, that emigration does not diminish but multiplies a nation. . . . Why should you be against acquiring by this fair means a repossession of it [America], and leave it to be taken by foreigners of all nations and languages, who by their numbers may drown and stifle the English. . . . It is a fact, that the Irish emigrants and their children are now in possession of the government of Pennsylvania, by their majority in the Assembly, as well as of a great part of the territory; and I remember well the first ship that brought any of them over.[6]

Dickens noted in 1842 that it would have been hard to keep the model republic going without the Irish doing the digging work, the domestic work, and the driving across the continent.

All emigrants were essentially pioneers. They were pioneers when they left home as a result of some crisis or deep dissatisfaction; they were pioneers in crossing the Atlantic under great hardships; they were pioneers in adjusting themselves to a new and alien civilization; they were pioneers in helping to build that civilization.

The sufferings and persecutions of the Old World were transformed in the New into the American code of optimism and of human and spiritual energy. Franklin D. Roosevelt reminded all Americans of this when he addressed the corseted and corsaged Daughters of the American Revolution as "Fellow Immigrants!" The vast influx of Europeans did not simply mean more noses to be counted and more souls to be assimilated; there was also an immigration of professionals and skilled artisans, from the simple potter or glasscutter of the eighteenth century to the composer or nuclear physicist of the twentieth. The New England textile industry was founded in 1789 by Samuel Slater, who left Derbyshire to establish a textile-spinning factory in Rhode Island with the machinery plans carried in his head.

America has always been a polyglot cultural pluralism, but that did not lessen the fear that the dominant German-Anglo-Saxon cultural strain would be submerged. American xenophobia has deep roots. Cotton Mather wrote his dismay at the coming of the Scotch-Irish Presbyterians in his diary on August 7, 1718: "But what shall be done for the great number of people that are transporting themselves thither from ye North of Ireland," while John Winthrop in the same year moaned, "I wish their coming so over do not prove fatal in the End." In 1797 an American Congressman rose to declare with conviction that while immigration was a good thing before the country was fully populated, the United States had now reached maturity and the gates should now be closed. Fear of European immigration continued with the Alien Acts of 1798, which extended the period of probation to fourteen years before a foreigner could be naturalized. Jeffersonians later reduced the period of waiting to five years. The Loco-Focos and the Know-Nothing movement of the 1850's were aimed primarily at the Catholic Church; the American Protective Association, also anti-Catholic, was another strong native movement against foreign immigration. James Fenimore Cooper wrote to give an earlier idea of immigration, "Depend on it, so far from there being a desire to receive rich rogues in America from other countries, there is a growing indisposition to receive emigrants at all: for their number is getting to be inconvenient to the native population." [7] Lyman Beecher in *Plea for the West* (June, 1835) was sure that the millenium would arrive in America, but not when "foreign immigrants whose accumulative tide is rolling in upon us, are, through the medium of their religion and priesthood, as entirely accessible to the control of the potentates of Europe as if they were an army of soldiers." Samuel F. B. Morse expressed the same attitude in his *Brutus, or a Foreign Conspiracy against the United States.*

New York State, which quite naturally had borne the brunt of immigration, tried to relieve some of the misery and to control disease; but in 1875 the Supreme Court decided that it was unconstitutional for a state to regulate immigration.[8] Selective immigration was initiated in 1882 when the Congress inaugurated a head tax on every immigrant and excluded convicts, lunatics, idiots, and those likely to become a public charge. Three years later contract labor was excluded. In 1891, polygamists and those with loathsome or contagious diseases were excluded. In the elections of 1892, the Republicans called for more stringent laws for the "restriction of criminal, pauper, and contract immigration," while the Democrats urged "all legislative efforts to prevent the United States from being used as a dumping ground for the known criminals and professional paupers of Europe." In 1896, Senator Lodge introduced a bill for the famous literacy test, which passed both houses but was vetoed by Cleveland. Finally, in 1903, the first comprehensive immigration law was passed, based on the findings of the Industrial Commission set up five years earlier. Anarchists and prostitutes were added to the blacklist and the administrative machinery was perfected.

H. G. Wells was not backward in coming forward with his opinion. In 1906 he wrote in his *The Future of America,* "I doubt very much if America is going to assimilate all that she is taking in now; much more do I doubt that she will assimilate the still greater inflow of the coming years. . . . I believe that if things go on as they are going, the great mass of them will remain a very low lower class—will remain largely illiterate industrialized peasants." [9] Many Americans were prepared to acknowledge the prophesies of the expert on the future; his opinions were profit without honor.

In 1907 a new law set up an immigration commission to control the activities of the transportation companies and minutely defined those people restricted and excluded from immigration. In 1917 the literacy restriction was finally imposed over Wilson's veto, who had said that it was "not a test of character, of quality, or of personal fitness, but would operate in most cases merely as a penalty for lack of opportunity in the country from which the alien seeking admission came." The Immigration Act of 1918 contained the first mention of "advocating the overthrow of the government," and two years later Congress gave the Attorney General of the United States the power of deportation for membership or affiliation with an organization, a clause which established the principle of guilt by association.

There had, of course, always been a fundamental antipathy to the benighted immigrant with his strange language, often his religion, his weird habits, and, more important, his willingness to work for less, whether as a Chinese on the Union Pacific Railroad or a Pole in a Pennsylvania coal mine. The union worker could wave the flag as much as the American capitalist, for organized labor stood against immigrant contract labor and always felt menaced by the possibility that immigrant labor could be brought in to break a strike.

The immigration figures gave the Americans cause to pause. President Truman's Commission on Immigration estimated that forty million people had come to America since the time of the *Mayflower*. In any analysis, the fact is that the American population was showing a greater rate of increase than that of immigration and that by and large the American immigrants, or at least their children, were readily absorbed in an expanding America. Indeed, the first-generation American was at pains to become more "American" than the American, *plus royalist que le roi,* and—perhaps to the detriment of American culture—quickly sloughed off his original language, customs, and former cultural trappings. It is curious that the great hordes of immigrants had little effect on American cultural thought, surely less than the few Greeks who fled to Italy from Byzantium in 1453. The fact is simply that few were cultural leaders before they came, and those who rose to eminence were to be found largely in the American grain of business, scientific technology, and invention. There has been no American Joseph Conrad. The genius of artists imported has normally had a prior establishment abroad and American influence on their work has had little effect.

Bryce noted at the peak period of immigration,

> This peculiar gift which the Republic possesses, of quickly dissolving and assimilating the foreign bodies that are poured into her, imparting to them her own qualities of orderliness, good sense, self-restraint, a willingness to bow to the will of the majority, [which] is mainly due to the all-pervading tone of opinion, which the new-comer . . . breathed in daily till it insensibly transmutes him.

Archibald MacLeish wrote,

> She's a tough land under the corn mister:
> She has changed the bone in the cheeks of many races;
> She has winced the eyes of the soft Slavs with her sun on them:
> She has tried the fat from the round rumps of Italians:
> Even the voice of the English has gone dry
> And hard on the tongue and alive in the throat speaking:

She's a tough land under the oak-trees mister:
It may be she can change the word in the book
As she changes the bone of a man's head in his children:
It may be that the earth and the men remain . . .[10]

Below are some figures which illustrate the increasing waves of
Europeans coming to America, an immigration unequalled in the history
of any peoples and greater than the barbarian invasions of Europe.

Years	Immigration
1790–1820	250,000
1831	23,000
1837	78,000
1839	52,000
1865	250,000
1868	326,000
1873	460,000
Total of 1870's	2,812,191
Total of 1880's	5,246,613

By 1905 over 1,000,000 a year were coming to the United States until World
War I. During the year ending June 30, 1921, over 800,000 arrived.

Problems of assimilation became greater as the pattern of immigration
shifted from the British Isles and northern Europe to southern Europe, the
Balkans, and Russia, introducing more Catholics, Orthodox, and Jews into
a predominantly Puritan Protestant America. Americans saw a threat to
catholicize America and feared that Jews would gain absolute control of the
money market. It is perhaps worthwhile to remember that there are as many
Irish in America as in Ireland and certainly more Jews than in Israel, one-
half as many Norwegians, and one-quatrer as many Swedes as in their home-
lands. The north Midwest is a greater new Scandinavia than Gustavus
Adolphus and Oxenstierna had ever planned for Delaware. Let us note in
the order of their importance the countries that furnished the most immigrants from 1820 to 1943 as noted in the following table.

Henry Pratt Fairchild's *The Melting Pot Mistake* provided a pseudo-
scientific-scholarly argument for restriction. His bias is evident today, as is
his racism, but it was not so recognized at the time. Samuel P. Orth's
Our Foreigners, in the famous "Chronicles of America" series was along
the same lines. For example, for the Finns, "Drink has been their curse"
and "the glittering generalities of Marxian socialism seem particularly allur-
ing to them." The Pole is clannish, has no "desire to fuse socially," prefers

Countries	Immigration	Maximum Attained in
Germany	6,028,337	1882
Italy	4,719,825	1907
Ireland	4,592,525	1851
Great Britain	4,264,728	1888
Austria-Hungary	4,144,366	1907
Russia	3,343,480	1913
Canada	3,037,561	1924
Scandinavia	2,359,049	1882

"his saloon and is unresponsible to his American environment." The Ukranians spend free time in the saloon and "learn nothing of American ways." The Slovaks prefer to "keep aloof from things American and only too often prefer to live in squalor and ignorance." The Slovenes get the worst marks: 'The brutality with which they treat their women, their disregard for sanitary measures, and their love for strong drink are evidences of the survivance of medievalism in the midst of modern life." Their fecundity is "amazing"—but the author credits the Irish, German, Chinese, and all others with the same human trait, so that one is left unamazed. Apparently the Lithuanians have only one "national vice," which is drinking: "They measure the social success of every wedding, christening, picnic, and jollification by its salvage of empty beer kegs." (One is led to wonder if Mr. Orth ever went to a truly American cocktail party and witnessed its debris.) As for the Jews, "They cannot forget that Karl Marx was a Jew: and one wonders how many Trotzkys and Lenins are being bred in the stagnant air of their reeking ghettos." They "push with characteristic zeal and persistence into every open door of this liberal land." Of the Italians, "thousand of these swarthy criminals have found refuge in the dark alleys of our cities." Finally, "if Americans are to hold back this 'racial infiltration,' it will take more than an association of old families, determined on keeping the ancient homes in their own hands, to check this transformation." Immigrants have "rooted out the decencies and comforts" of real Americans and have "supplanted them with the promiscuity, the filth, and the low economic standards of the medieval peasant," and "no mental contagion of democracy reaches them." Such reflections, hardly gratified as thoughts, had a wide influence in America in the twenties; there was little affection for the European "furriner."

The immigrant was often badly demoralized, it is true, by the incompatability of his old social codes with the forced assumption of new American ones. Mutual aid societies, lodges, national associations, and settlements in little Romes, Naples, Warsaws, and ghettos in New York, Chicago, and other urban centers helped protect him from a too rapid Americanization. The public school, for both adults and youngsters, was the main bridge to participation in American life when the immigrant became an "Allrightnik," as the Jews said. City politicians and ward bosses, corrupt as they were, often aided with a basket of food or coal, or five dollars on voting day when the immigrant could show his gratitude. The ill effects of slum immigrant voting on city politics were evident with the rise of political machines, frequently allied with crime for profit, waxing fat on pubic franchises and contracts. When Lord Bryce said that American city government was "the one conspicuous failure of the United States," he was confirming Jefferson's apprehension when he wrote to Madison in 1787, "I think our governments will remain virtuous as long as they are chiefly agricultural," but when the American people "get piled up on one another as in Europe, they will become corrupt, as in Europe."

After World War I, New York City contained only one-fifth American-born stock. It was the largest Italian city in the world, and the largest Jewish city, containing one and one-half million Jews, or more than one-tenth of all world Jewry. "Manhattan is a city of aliens," wrote Hamlin Garland, "who know little and care less for American traditions. After a lecture trip in the interior I return each time to New York as to a foreign seaport." [11] Between 1880 and 1914, one-third of the Jews of Eastern Europe came to the United States, mostly settling in the Lower East Side of New York. They wrote a great epic in the garment industry and set a new style in labor relations. Boston had become overwhelmingly Irish. A Harvard professor told G. K. Chesterton, "We have solved the Irish problem; we have an entirely independent Irish government."

It is true that many immigrants had no intention of becoming citizens and resisted Americanization, hoping only to reap enough money to return to their native land and live well. Many did return, often in old age to be buried alongside their families, but more stayed and earned enough to pay the passage of relatives to join them in America.

In response to American opinion, Congress acted quickly. The Mendelian doctrine of heredity and Gobineau's philosophy that races could not be assimilated were applied; the assumption was generally maintained, but difficult to prove, that America was White, Anglo-Saxon, and Protestant. The 1921 Immigration Act set up quotas and limited immigration to three per cent of nationals already in America according to the 1910 census. This meant that only 350,000 people could enter the United States and that the largest number would come from the British Isles and northern Europe. In 1924 a new act was passed to limit immigration to 150,000 and two per cent of the national quotas according to the census of 1890, still further reducing the number from southern and central Europe. England tried to restrict emigration by subsidies to the unemployed. Italy acidly protested American restrictions in the hope of relieving overpopulation. The 1924 act was generally regarded as an affront to friendly nations.

In 1929 the National Origins Act stabilized immigration at 150,000 according to the 1920 census of national origins as the basis for assessment. This meant effectively that four-fifths of the immigration would originate from northern and western Europe. It is interesting to note that war-torn France received more than 1.5 million emigrants from Poland, Italy, Belgium, Switzerland, Russia, Austria, and Hungary between 1920 and 1928. Among these were many intellectuals who fled to Paris unable to stand Communism or Fascism, or the confines of smaller capitals like Vienna or Budapest or Belgrade, which were isolated from the cultural swim.

The President's Commission on Immigration and Naturalization asserted in 1952 that, without controls, immigration rose in times of prosperity and declined during depressions. It is possible to conjecture that the drop in immigration in the thirties following the restricted immigration of the twenties actually encouraged the Depression by stopping an expanding market. In any case, between 1931 and 1936 there were 240,000 more aliens who left the United States than were admitted.

To carry the immigration story to the present day, the 1940 Alien Registration Act prohibited teaching or advocating the overthrow of the Government by force or violence, the first time since the 1798 Alien and Selection Acts that there was a peacetime sedition statute. The 1950 Internal Security Act barred, even for a short stay, Communists, anarchists, members of any totalitarian party, or any person who would attempt to overthrow or lead others to overthrow the American Government by violence. Consuls were instructed to bar any who might menace the public interest, prosperity, or security of the United States. The McCarran-Walter Act in 1952 continued in this spirit and further restricted immigration by forcing political restrictions on would-be immigrants and stiffened the immigration requirements. President Truman vetoed this bill, objecting to the "outdated national origins quota system" as unworthy of American tradition and ideals, and in violation of the great doctrine of the Declaration of Independence that all men were created equal, but it was carried nevertheless.

According to the census of 1940, 10 per cent of the American white population was born abroad, and 19 per cent of those born in the United States were born of at least one foreign parent. Thus 29 per cent of the population is more or less of foreign origin. If grandparents were included in this 1940 census, we would easily see that more than half of the American population is closely tied to European origins, although the restrictive quotas since Warld War I sharply changed the picture for the present and future generations. Sinclair Lewis described his typically American St. Cloud, Minnesota, as "a town with a French name, founded by the Swedes, administered by the Irish, even though the population is half-German, and with a Polish mayor, even though the Poles are a small minority."

Closing immigration was not enough to satisfy the chauvinist appetite. Red-baiters found it necessary to impose Alger nationalism to achieve uniformity and conformity. Hysteria mounted against the "Dagoes" and the "Hunkies," the "Chinks" and the "Japs," against the dangerous "radicals" and "leftists." It was astonishing to see the national preoccupation, led by Palmer, with the Red Scare, when there was not the slightest likelihood that a socialist revolution could be achieved in America, either from within or from without. When G. K. Chesterton visited America he was asked if he were in favor of overthrowing the Government of the United States by force. He replied, "I would prefer to answer that question at the end of my tour and not at the beginning."

The American conscience is still bothered by the trial of the anarchists Nicola Sacco and Bartolomeo Vanzetti, convicted of a double murder in South Braintree, Massachusetts, in 1920, and who went to the electric chair seven years later. Felix Frankfurter wrote in 1927 in his *The Case of Sacco and Vanzetti:*

> By systematic exploitation of the defendants' alien blood, their imperfect knowledge of English, their unpopular social views, and their opposition to war, the District Attorney invoked against them a riot of political passion and patriotic sentiments; and the trial judge connived at—one had almost written, co-operated in—the process.[12]

Harvey O'Higgins wrote in Mencken's *Mercury* (March, 1929) that the fear of Bolshevism was a "popular mania that has had no equal in America since the early Puritan went wild about witchcraft and saw a torturable witch in every old woman who had lost her teeth," and that the current fear was a psychic fear of failure, the sin of the American business world. Sacco and Vanzetti were finally executed at midnight, August 22, 1927. There were riots and parades in Boston and New York, and in foreign capitals. The reaction among American intellectuals was deep. Upton Sinclair wrote *Boston;* Edna St. Vincent Millay, Malcolm Cowley, and others

wrote about it; more than any other event it influenced the writing of Dos
Passos' *U.S.A.*

America had turned from Wilsonian liberalism to a blatant and conservative nationalism, a Puritan Algerism with strident tones of Volstead.
The lion's tail was again twisted with joy, and King George was threatened
that he would be punched in the nose if he came to Chicago. Economic
isolation had been put into practice with the Fordney-McCumber tariff in
1922, which put the highest duties yet known on imported goods. Unscrupulous Europe refused to pay its war debts—they had borrowed the
money, hadn't they? as the Puritan Calvin Coolidge said. The wave of
prosperity was a sign of America's Algeresque success, therefore morally
righteous for the society of the elect. "The business of America is business,"
Coolidge said in another thought-provoking adage. It is only later that we
learn that the Great Gatsby is also bootlegging. The Moose, the Elks, and
the Lions were advancing American civilization, and the Rotary gearing
the American machine-made culture. The conspicuous consumption that
Veblen saw lacked that vibrant and driving moral force in the American
conscience. Puritanism had become the ally of Algerism and there was no
balm in Gilead.

Walter Lippman and Lewis Mumford began to combat the generally
accepted idea that American opulence meant American grandeur, success,
power, or greatness; that pleasure meant real happiness; or that a celebrity
was a hero. They were to be followed by John Kenneth Galbraith and
Adlai Stevenson, who have shown that affluence is not a prerequisite to happiness or stability. It became almost un-American to assert this. The pursuit
of happiness became the pursuit of "welfare," not an individual thing but
public, governmental, and essentially impersonal. One hundred years earlier,
Tocqueville had had the perspicacity to see that the American "is accustomed to regard his prosperity as his own work. Thus he sees in public
wealth his very own, and he works for the good of the state, not only by
duty or pride, but I would almost dare to say, by his own cupidity." Was
Teapot Dome to be the standard? The Americans, said Tocqueville, "find
wealth almost everywhere, but not happiness. With them the desire for
well-being has become a disquieting and ardent passion which increases in
satisfying it." We can leave this thought for later discussion, but it might
be useful to see what Bryce said of this American characteristic, which was
to be the mystique of John F. Kennedy:

The enormous force of public opinion is a danger to the people themselves, as well as their leaders. It no longer makes them tyrannical. But it fills them with an undue confidence in their wisdom, their virtue, and their freedom. It may be thought that a nation which uses freedom can hardly have too much freedom; yet even such a nation may be too much inclined to think freedom an absolute and all-sufficient good, to seek truth only in the voice of the majority, to mistake prosperity for greatness. Such a nation, seeing nothing but its own triumph, and hearing nothing but its own praises, seems to need a succession of men like the prophets of Israel to rouse the people out of their self-complacency, to refresh their moral ideals, to remind than that life is more than meat, and the body more than raiment, and that to whom much is given of them shall much also be required.

One of the first voices raised in protest and with the essentially negative cultural criticism of the twenties (as contrasted with the helpful constructive criticism of the thirties) was that of Harold Stearns. He asked in *America and the Young Intellectual:* "Where is a young man, just out of college, to find the necessary contact with the national culture?" After rejecting business, politics, reform, art, music, and literature, he groans, "here my hand falters, the picture is too pathetic. Even if he ignores these activities, and wants only to live a gracious and amiable and civilized life for himself, has he a chance in a hundred?" [13] In 1922 Stearns edited the volume *Civilization in the United States,* to which Mencken, Brooks, Nathan, and others contributed. They all came to the dire conclusion that there was no such civilization, and almost all laid the fault on the doorstep of Alger-Puritanism. James Huneker, like Mencken, wanted to forget the nineteenth century and "our demigods of plaster and plush, Emerson, Poe, Longfellow, Hawthorne, Lowell, Walt Whitman, the biggest group of self-illuded bores that ever existed." [14]

It was not the seventeenth-century Puritan that the postwar critics attacked, for after all he did have his moral code and deliberately built his society around it. It was the Puritanism of the late nineteenth century, and after that was arraigned, that self-seeking, self-satisfied commercial Puritanism which Mencken and Van Wyck Brooks saw, and which Parrington wanted to replace with the Jeffersonian tradition. William Carlos Williams did make a blanket condemnation of three hundred years of Puritanism and was against all the arrogant, bigoted Puritans in *In the American Grain* who were not fit to build the great new world which was at their disposition: "The Pilgrims, they, the seed, instead of growing, looked back at the world and damning its perfections praised a zero in themselves." [15] Randolph Bourne's famous essay, "The Puritan's Will to Power," and Mencken's

A Book of Prefaces had begun the campaign against the new Puritanism. For the moral security of the middle masses, Puritanism had been raised as the dictator of taste and decency. Virtue is publicly announced and vice privately committed as Pound's Radway in *L'Homme moyen sensuel* joins an organization for the suppression of sin and enjoys sin secretly. The joyless Puritan had not learned to laugh and live. Freud, who had lectured in the United States, should have become a naturalized American the way he was eagerly embraced, for American Puritan repression had become a national neurosis. If analysis on the couch did not relieve the Americans of their "problems," there was always the good French professor Emile Coué, whose lectures were highly popular in America, and whose *Self-Mastery Through Conscious Autosuggestion* was long a bestseller. Significantly, Eleanor H. Porter's prewar *Pollyanna* kept up a good sale.

The roaring twenties wanted none of the prewar imperatives. There was a repeal of reticence and an unbuttoned emancipation. Even in the Depression of the thirties, which was a moral depression as well as an economic one, there was a quest for unprohibited, relative morality. The twenties stood for unrepressed, "natural," "healthy" emotion, for Puritan oppression had dammed up emotion in unrelieved tensions and everyone wanted to revolt like Huck or Tom. Fitzgerald rightly called the thirties the "Great Hangover," and like all hangovers it had moral shakes and trembles as well.

In the fate of the Algerism of the twenties, where the individual disappeared more and more into the crowd and lost his personality in the midst of communal obscurity, creative activity seemed destined largely to be relegated to the "Ash Can" school of painting and social realism in writing. Many writers and artists, however, beat a strategic retreat to the Left Bank in Paris where they were able to establish an exhilarating and racy climate for creative production and where there was more breathing space for independent spirits. They regretted, with Tocqueville, that in America "all minds come together, some in rising, some in lowering." America was just too homogenized and pasteurized for the new and lost generation, just as Tocqueville had noticed that in spite of the great distance, Maine and Georgia were more alike than Normandy and Brittany, which are separated only by a little river. Ezra Pound's search for precision and perfection in writing set the keynote in detesting the teaching of mediocrity as a virtue in America. In *Exile's Return,* Malcolm Cowley wrote that his group of literary and artistic exiles after 1921 came to Europe "to recover the good life and the traditions of art, to free themselves from organized stupidity, to win their deserved place in the hierarchy of the intellect." [16]

The moral imbalance of America was pointed out by Van Wyck Brooks in *America's Coming of Age,* published in 1915, but more adapted to the postwar scene. After all, America had been coming of age longer than it seemed decent to remember. But American writers continued their "groping" to grasp the "real" America. Brooks saw a bifurcation in American culture: the impractical idealism of Emerson set alongside an opportunistic Puritanism, which had become a philosophy with Franklin, and, passing through the nineteenth-century humorists, permeated the atmosphere of the contemporary business world. Emerson, however noble, was able neither to convince nor to become acceptable to contemporary America. Others, like Mencken, Waldo Frank, Harold Stearns, and Upton Sinclair, took up the cry against the postwar world of Mah-Jong, flagpole sitting, psychoanalysis, crossword puzzles, and marathon dances.

Mencken in *Men Versus the Man,* a debate on socialism, had already attacked the American *Herdenmoral,* where the mob was inert and moved ahead only when dragged or driven. It clung to delusions with an appalling pertinacity:

> The Anglo-Saxon of the great herd is, in many important respects, the least civilized of men and the least capable of civilization. His political ideas are crude and shallow. He is almost wholly devoid of aesthetic feeling; he does not even make folklore or walk in the wood. The most elementary facts about the visible universe alarm him, and incite him to put them down.[17]

Mencken's interest in German thinking and writing is curious. He and Sinclair Lewis often exchanged letters in barbarized German-American, and Cargill has noted that "when, in the international intellectual exchange, the mark was worth virtually nothing, Mencken imported whole cargoes of German ideas, which he dispensed, like Woolworth, with Yankee sales talk." [18] Any attempt to raise the mob only lowers the first-class man. Even though his proselytizing for German culture and his Teutonism was suspect after World War I, Mencken continued to Americanize Nietzsche in his *Notes on Democracy.* The inefficient and fraudulent American democrat, "incapable of realizing the true meaning of liberty, ignoring the true merits of the elite . . . tries his best to interfere with the liberties of exceptional men." He did not condemn the middle class for making money, but for turning the making of it into a religion and a morality, the "Gospel of Service" and the "business ethic." He detested the Philistine who cemented the alliance of the church with business.

A bestseller of the time was Bruce Barton's *The Man Nobody Knows.* Jesus was the first real business organizer who had welded twelve obscure men into a great company organization. Jesus had followed "every one of the principles of modern salesmanship," and his parables were powerful advertisements. To prove his argument, he even cites "Know ye not that I must be about my father's *business?*" Barton was to become a partner in one of Madison Avenue's largest advertising and public relations firms.

Of all the writers of the twenties, those who stayed in the United States and the American expatriates abroad, the one who best hit the tempo of the middle-class American spirit was Sinclair Lewis. Although largely shunned by his colleagues—particularly by what he called the "Parisian bunch"—and in spite of a frightful inferiority complex and numerous personal problems involving his own adjustment to American society, Lewis set the keynote for the twenties as Steinbeck was to do for the thirties. His realism in *Main Street* was the first to appear since Frank Norris and Dreiser's suppressed *Sister Carrie. Main Street* was an immediate financial success, although not wholly a critical one. The jury for the Pulitzer Prize of 1921 voted for it, but was overruled by the trustees of Columbia University, who awarded the prize to Edith Wharton for *The Age of Innocence.* The 1922 Pulitzer Prize was given to Booth Tarkington for *Alice Adams,* rumored to be his answer to *Main Street.* When Lewis was finally awarded the Pulitzer Prize in 1926 for *Arrowsmith,* he had his revenge by refusing to accept, as he refused membership in the American Academy of Arts and Letters by stating that juries and amateur censorship produces "safe, polite, obedient, and sterile" writers. Lewis limned the average American so truly that he could only laugh at himself and go along with the joke, and much to his own surprise, for he thought he was being a rebel against small-town bigotry, narrowness, and prejudices. He found himself liked, honored, and loved! "Red" Lewis was embraced and slapped on the back as "one of the boys" in the smoking car. Lewis found he really liked George F. Babbitt as much as the other Babbitts did.

Although he lived and traveled widely in Europe (including a visit to Moscow while courting his future wife, columnist Dorothy Thompson) and died a miserably pathetic death alone in Rome, he remained the son of the Midwest, not cosmopolitan enough for the American *literati* of Montparnasse. He wandered about Europe like *Dodsworth,* lonely and confused, pulled here and there by a culture-mongering wife. The Europeans in Lewis' novels are all portrayed as intellectuals several notches above his plodding, good-hearted Americans; Max Gottlieb in *Arrowsmith* and Bruno

Zechlin in *Elmer Gantry* are European humanists who suffer, misunderstood, in the American wilderness. Lewis has the German Professor Braut say:

America wants to turn us into Good Fellows, all provided with the very best automobiles—and no private place to which we can go in them. When I think of America I always remember a man who made me go out to a golf club and undress in a locker room, where quite uninvited men came up and made little funny jokes about Germany and about my being a professor! [19]

In general, Lewis was against the "Francomania" of the "Parisian bunch," to which he also accused Edith Wharton of belonging, although he greatly admired her and, surprisingly, dedicated *Babbitt* to her.

In May, 1921, Sinclair Lewis sailed in first-class style to England; his earlier trip fourteen years before had been on a cattle boat. He settled into a sixteenth-century house in Kent and eventually met almost everyone in the English literary world: G. B. Shaw, Galsworthy, Rebecca West, Rose Macaulay, Norman Angell, Laski, Beaverbrook, Keynes, Virginia Woolf, Osbert Sitwell, Frank Swinnerton, Jonathan Cape, Lytton Strachey, Arnold Bennett, Hugh Walpole, and H. G. Wells, after whom he named his son. But he was no happier than he had been in Sauk Center, Duluth, or New York. Lewis told an American reporter, "the farther I get from America the more I want to write about my country. It's surprising how love of your native land seizes you. . . . I want to go back to the United States and live there." [20]

Instead he went to Paris with Harold Stearns, who had just finished editing *Civilization of the United States,* and the two led a wild life there with Lewis Galantière. There was a quiet friendly lunch at Edith Wharton's Pavillon Colombe at St. Brice-sous-Forêt, a cold meeting with Joyce, whom he called the "great white boar," and an equally cold encounter with Edna St. Vincent Millay. He shocked André Siegfried, who had come to talk with him at his hotel, by appearing disguised as G. B. Shaw. Ignored by the expatriate writers, he sought friendship with the journalists at Harry's Bar.

Lewis then moved to Italy, which he loved, to try to finish *Babbitt,* which he had begun in England. In Rome, he fell in with Blaise Cendrars, who wanted to translate *Main Street* and who remained a staunch Lewis admirer. In the summer of 1922 he went to the United States with *Babbitt* under his arm, as Mark Schorer said in his outstanding biography of Lewis, "one more exile's return, leaving behind him the unsatisfactory elsewhere, returning to the inadequate nowhere." [21]

In 1923 Lewis went back to France, where he wrote *Arrowsmith,* spent some time in England, then took a walking trip in Switzerland, back to Paris, then southern France, and Italy. During this time he decided to write a novel of Americans in Europe and came out with *Dodsworth,* which was the last kind of Jamesian novel to prove that life was better in Europe than America, with Sam the well-meaning but bumbling American businessman and his wife Fran, a culture-monger who knew the price of everything and the value of nothing. Dodsworth asks: "But why are the Americans here? OK, a few of 'em to get social credit for it, back home, or to sell machinery, but most of 'em, bless 'em, come here as meekly as school-boys, to admire, to learn!" [22]

After a couple of years in America, where he wrote *Elmer Gantry,* the biting satire on preachers, Lewis was back in Europe in 1927 living in Venice, taking trips in Alsace, Basle, and the Black Forest, and then to Berlin where he met Dorothy Thompson, followed her to Moscow, married her, and returned to the United States in 1928.

In keeping with the changing times, Lewis began shifting his interest to social problems. He had long toyed with the idea of a labor novel, with Debs as his Christ-figure, and had taken numerous notes, employed a special secretary, and conducted many interviews. The novel never appeared. He also became interested in the Negro problem, which eventually appeared as *Kingsblood Royal.* In 1931 he brought out *Ann Vickers,* a novel on women's rights, sexual emancipation, and reform.

The next year he was back in Italy and England with his wife Dorothy, who was at home in Europe (like Fran Dodsworth) as much as Lewis and Sam Dodsworth were not. As the War approached, Lewis became more and more an isolationist, and even though he supported Roosevelt, he remained an "America Firster" to the last. In 1941 he was arguing that "pure culture" should go on in spite of and oblivious to the coming war which was carrying America rapidly downstream into deeper and more roiled seas.

In 1948 and 1949, he was back again in Europe with a villa in Florence. He was trying, in spite of alcoholism, to do a new novel, *World So Wide,* which was to deal with the American colony in Florence, "especially with an American who is lured from the sensible security of money-making into the sick-sweet perils of scholarship," [23] as he wrote his London publisher.

Mark Schorer summed up the attitude of the novelist's relation to Europe: "To Lewis, the diagnostician of America, Europe had always been a necessary point of reference, even as it had always been an irritant to him, from his first novel to his last. . . . There is in these novels an undercurrent of fear, fear of Europe itself." [24] In *Dodsworth* and *World So Wide* there is the fear of corruption by staying too long, of renouncing the American heritage by accepting a vitiating alien tradition. Yet, strangely, it is the

"Europeanized" women in his novels who communicate these intellectual and spiritual values, and his European characters themselves are cosmopolitan philosophers contrasted with the homespun American of Gopher Prairie.

While Coué was having the same great success in American middle-class circles that Samuel Smiles had held in an earlier American age, Gertrude Stein held court in the rue de Fleurus. She wrote in *Paris, France* that American writers went to Paris because they could not write at home, where they could only be dentists, which was to be practical: "Writers have to have two countries, the one where they belong, and the one in which they live really. The second one is romantic, it is separate from themselves, it is not real but it is really there." [25] The writer has to be an individual, but America had invented the "characteristic thing of the twentieth century," the production of things in a series, all alike, and quantities of them, what Pound was to call "Fordization."

Gertrude Stein was born in 1874 at Allegheny, Pennsylvania, the daughter of a wealthy businessman. At six months of age she was taken to live in Vienna and then Paris, and she knew German and French before she was reading in English. After living in Oakland, California, she studied at Radcliffe under William James, from whom she absorbed the Bergsonian concept of time and who had recognized the profound qualities in his brilliant student. After three years of medical studies at Johns Hopkins, she had had enough, and did not bother to take her diploma. She had spent each summer in Europe during her Radcliffe and Hopkins studies, settled in 1903 with her brother in London, and finally chose Paris for the rest of her life. "America is my country and Paris is my home town," she declared. "France let you alone, and it was not what it gave you, but what it didn't take away from you which was important." [26] She became friendly with all the literary and artistic avant-garde: Picasso, Matisse, Braque, Rousseau, Juan Gris, Max Jacob, Derain, the Ducans, Apollinaire, Eric Satie. Her *Tender Buttons* was an attempt at cubism in words—no narrative, no external references, it depended on words alone. During World War I she was a chauffeur for the American Fund for French Wounded.

Her reputation grew. She published her lectures, *Composition as Explanation* at Oxford and Cambridge in 1926 and returned to America in 1933 to do a series of lectures, which were not successful, and published the *Autobiography of Alice B. Toklas,* a success. She passed the Second World War living simply in a little village in the Ain, and after the liberation published *Wars I Have Seen*. World War II had not been a "nice war," not like 1914 when everyone knew what to do and think, when everybody was a hero. World War II, she thought, saw everybody sacrificed and imprisoned and was finished only because it was inevitable that it would end. She died in 1946, a person who influenced others rather than herself, creating much of great value. She implicity criticized the false diamonds of American civilization and was a revolutionary for humanity and liberty in letters and art.

Gertrude Stein was but one important American in Paris. The names of others who flocked there is incredible, in fact almost all the important post-war writers except Faulkner—Hemingway, William Carlos Williams, Sinclair Lewis, John Dos Passos, Ezra Pound (who had quit London and had brought Joyce up from Trieste), E. E. Cummings, Thornton Wilder, Sherwood Anderson (who had suddenly walked out of the presidency of a paint business to write), Katherine Anne Porter, Archibald MacLeish, Allen Tate, Glenway Wescott, Henry Miller, Lincoln Steffens, Malcolm Cowley, Edna St. Vincent Millay, Scott Fitzgerald, Hart Crane—a brilliant group of writers churning out solid writing with a great burning intensity. James T. Farrell and his wife almost starved in Paris until Putnam got him into print. John Gunther directed the Paris office of the *Chicago Daily News* and Elliott Paul represented the *Chicago Tribune*. During the prosperous years between 1924 and 1930, the Department of Commerce noted an increase of over one hundred per cent in tourist travel to Europe, largely stimulated by the inauguration of the "tourist-third" class in 1923. Students, writers, and teachers flocked to Europe.

The expatriate American writers were working to make American writing come of age, and the best of them were quite unlike the expatriate in *The Sun Also Rises:* "You're an expatriate. You've lost touch with the soil. You get precious. Fake European standards have ruined you. You drink yourself to death. You become obsessed with sex. You spend all your time talking, not working. You are expatriate, see? You hang around cafés." [27] This was the general American impression of them, created also by Fitzgerald's characters, who were wealthy joy-seekers commuting between Paris and the Riviera on one long binge, but Glenway Westcott's autobiography *Fear and Trembling* discusses the truer meaning of their expatriation of the twenties. In *A Story Teller's Story,* Sherwood Anderson summed up the excitement of going to Europe as something tremendous: "It was infinitely more important than, let us say, getting married. . . . Such and such a one had been to Europe three times. He was consulted upon all occasions, was allowed to sit on the platform at political meetings, might even claim the privilege of carrying a cane." [28]

Almost all of the American writers gathered at one time or another in the bookshop of Sylvia Beach, "Shakespeare and Company," where they were able to meet Georges Duhamel, Luc Durtain, André Gide, Louis Gillet, Jacques de Lacretelle, André Maurois, Paul Morand, Jean Paulhan, Jules Romains, Jean Schlumberger, Paul Valéry, Raymond Queneau, Bernard Fay, François Mauriac, André Chamson, and Claude Farrère. As Schlumberger wrote of the bookshop, "A foyer of intellectual exchange has been formed here and we can appreciate its radiation." Hemingway "liberated" Sylvia Beach at the same time that he liberated the Ritz Bar in 1944. One French writer having a wide effect on the expatriate writers was Rémy de Gourmont, who had an American mistress, Natalie Barney, to whom he wrote *Lettres à l'Amazone* and *Lettres Intimes à l'Amazone*. Ezra Pound translated de Gourmont's *Philosophy of Love*. When all is analyzed, however, American expatriate intellectuals were more interested in themselves, their own positions, and their personal relation to America. They lived among themselves and had less contact with French cultural life than their predecessors, such as Henry Adams, Edith Wharton, Sargent, Whistler, or Mary Cassatt, or, even earlier, Cooper, Greenhough, and LaFarge.

The postwar writers in Paris took a vastly different view of the War than did Edith Wharton, Willa Cather, Dorothy Canfield, and even Gertrude Stein, with her "nice war." Their boots and puttees had been in the mud and filth, and they saw little reason for personal engagement in the International Follies of 1914 and 1918. Malcolm Cowley's *Exile Return* offers a vivid picture of his life as an ambulance driver and then as an expatriate writer in Paris during the twenties. Dos Passos, who joined the French ambulance service after graduation from Harvard in 1916, published his first novel, *One Man's Initiation,* in England in 1920. It was much like *One of Ours,* in that the young hero is an architect-poet who hates war because it doesn't provide him enough time to admire his gothic cathedrals. But there the comparison ends. Two citations are enough to get across Dos Passos' point of view: "Oh, the lies, the lies, the lies, the lies that life is smothered in! We must strike once more for freedom, for the sake of the dignity of man." [29] Dos Passos' real war novel, *Three Soldiers,* is full of brutal realism and was more popular than *One Man's Initiation*. Again, however, the real hero is the musician from New York who deserts to write a great orchestral poem, and when he is captured by the police to be taken away, his sheets of music blow away. Dos Passos brought out the maddening incongruity of war:

You mean that the soldiers in the trenches are all further from the people at home than from each other, no matter what side they are on?

The little doctor nodded.
God, it's so stupid! Why can't we go over and talk to them? [30]

E. E. Cummings, after graduating from Harvard, served in the Norton-Harjes Ambulance Corps, which had been subsidized by a Morgan partner, until he was arrested in 1917 and held over four months in a vile detention camp at La Ferté Macé on suspicion of "treasonable correspondence." Amid all the degradation of his camp, *The Enormous Room*, he found men "cursed with the talent of thinking" just when "great governments . . . demanded of their people the exact antithesis of thinking." All slogans were meaningless, reality meant personal disaster in an unreal world of surrealist movement. He continued as a private in the American infantry after his release. After a later visit to Russia, he described the Soviet Union in *Eimi* as an even more enormous room.

Archibald MacLeish quit a successful law practice in 1923 to go to Paris. He wrote in his World War I *Hamlet of A. MacLeish* (after the Laforgue *Hamlet*):

> The Marne side. Raining. I am cold with fear.
> My bowels tremble. I go on. McHenry
> Hands me his overcoat and dies. We dig the
> Guns out sweating. I am very brave:
> Magnificent. I vomit in my mask.[31]

This was not a war of glory, and those who followed were to be so much more unpleasant that one could not even poetize about them like Rupert Brooke. During uneasy peace and unwholesome wars, governments pursued the individual, destroying the nooks of creative life.

Ernest Hemingway enlisted in the Italian ambulance service, and was seriously wounded by a shell burst on the northern Italian front in July, 1918. Like Nick Adams, he suffered the "unreasonable wound," wanted out of the War, having paid and made his "separate peace." Everybody loses, nobody wins. Wounds received were personally suffered and were not contributions to a cause, and individual death was not simply a statistic, as in Randall Jarrell's poem *Losses*, "our casualties were low." In *A Farewell to Arms*, the retreat from Caporetto becomes disorderly, and then unreasonable, for Lt. Henry when Italians kill Italians. Henry renounces his personal responsibility and flees with Catherine to neutral Switzerland, which is coldly unreal and infertile, and where, with Catherine's death, he suffers another wound, where death in childbirth symbolizes the shock and helpless anger at the sterility and barrenness of life. Mussolini suppressed both the book and the film in Italy.

Sterility is also apparent in *The Sun Also Rises* when Jake says, "I got hurt in the war." "Oh, that dirty war." [32] Faulkner's *Soldier's Pay* of the same year employs the same symbolism as Hemingway's, only the hero Lt. Mahon is faceless, his face being torn away in an airplane crash. It was not until 1940 with *For Whom The Bell Tolls* that Robert Jordan defends the cause that Lt. Henry deserted; Jordan has a cause and is prepared to die for it. Hemingway's only novel with an American setting was *To Have and To Have Not,* but actually all his settings and characters are universal and deal with absolutes. Hemingway finally reaches the universal man pitted against nature in 1952 with *The Old Man and the Sea,* who makes his separate fight, separate death, and separate peace, just as Robert Jordan does. His carefully chiseled prose may be imitated by succeeding French and American writers, but never with the same success.

Hemingway learned much from Pound, Sherwood Anderson, and Gertrude Stein. Stein called him her best student, but he broke with her after editing her *The Making of Americans* in 1925 for the *Transatlantic Review.* He claimed later that he had helped her to success. In any case, when he came to Paris to perfect his writing (which then consisted of journalism) to learn economy and simplicity of expression he was closer to Stein's *Composition as Explanation* and far away from Edith Wharton's *The Writing of Fiction.* His *Torrents of Spring* confirmed the break with Stein, but when all is said, he probably got as much style from Eliot and the King James Bible as from Stein.

Two transatlantic writers, Waldo Frank and Ludwig Lewisohn, deserve special mention for their interpretation of Europe to America and the United States to Europeans. Frank had had private schooling in Switzerland and a brilliant record at Yale. In 1913 he spent a year in Europe and during World War I had registered as a conscientious objector. At the request of an official French mission to the United States, he wrote *Our America* to give some understanding of the highways and byways of American thought and culture. He portrayed American thinking as moving westward across the continent for two centuries and then turning back east to a new contact with European ideas. The clash of eastern and western American thinking produced a "neurosis" and an "organic weakness." This pattern was followed by his *The Rediscovery of America* in which he urged America to define its intellectual needs and set up some "method for achieving specific controls within us."

The brilliant Ludwig Lewisohn had many difficulties with his American career. He had difficulty in securing a university post because he was a Jew and Comstock had suppressed his novel. *The Spirit of Modern German Literature,* an excellent interpretation to Americans of modern German thought, appeared in 1916 at a bad moment in German-American relations. He was investigated and obliged to resign from Ohio State University. As a sort of purge, he published *The Poets of Modern France* in 1918. He joined the staff of *The Nation* for several years and then, like so many others, saw expatriation in Europe as the solution. Lewisohn deserted his Christian wife and in 1924 went to Europe with the "Thelma" of his own religion, described in his *Mid-Channel.* He remained in Europe until the Depression and became an ardent Zionist. His last book to interest Europeans and Americans was *Expression in America,* published in 1952, which examined contemporary American literature and its background.

Little reviews in English sprang up like flames on the banks of the Seine, burning brightly and then sputtering out: *Transition, This Quarter, Broom, Secession, Transatlantic Review, Little Review.* They published much new scintillating material and served to get young authors introduced. The Olympia Press and Harry Crosby's Black Sun Press turned out material that could not be published in America, such as the work of Henry Miller. Sylvia Beach published Joyce. There were not only American writers in Paris, but also composers and artists who had made the spindrift pilgrimage. Isadora Duncan promulgated modern dance. George Gershwin could symbolize the liberating influence in his "American in Paris." He himself had come under the influence of Ravel and could see what Milhaud and Messiean were doing. Other American composers arrived: Aaron Copland, George Antheil, Walter Piston, Virgil Thomson, and those who grouped around Nadia Boulanger. The artists in the long run were not perhaps as distinguished as the writers and composers. The more notable were Man Ray, who stayed, and Alexander Calder, who finally settled in France.

The sensitive American writer and artist had fled from the conformism which he felt in America during the twenties, but even though Babbitt's values were not his, he could not shake them off or replace them with another set. His Americanness remained in his Puritan conscience, reflecting a certain sadness and regret, a personality split with heart and mind torn between America and Europe. America was home, but culture was in Europe for the expatriates. MacLeish's "Memory Green" gives an impression of the nostalgia felt by the American expatriate as he kicks the leaves along a Paris quay and yearns through tears for the American Indian summer. This regret was not a novelty of the postwar generation; it was evident in Henry Adams and Henry James, as it was in Cooper and Hawthorne before them. Americans escaped to the land of Duhamel, but it is doubtful if they escaped from his *Scènes de la Vie Future*—poor Duhamel, who could not pardon America because of the thermometer forced into his mouth by the immigration doctor on his first arrival. Midwesterners could not escape America and wrote of it in Paris with sentiment and longing, however unwilling they were to return to the sluggish tedium. We see this most in Glenway Westcott's *The Grandmothers, Goodbye Wisconsin,* and in the Midwest orthodoxy of *Apple of the Eye.* As Hemingway said in *A Farewell to Arms,* "you could not go back," you couldn't go home again, even though you were homesick, for things were not the same. Dos Passos also summed up the spirit in *Manhattan Transfer:* "It's all the same, in France you are paid badly and live well; here you are paid well and live badly." [33] "All during the 1920's," Malcolm Cowley wrote in *Exile's Return:*

> We had come three thousand miles in search of Europe and had found America, in a vision half-remembered, half-falsified and romanced. Should we ever return to our own far country?

> many, and perhaps most, of the serious American writers felt like strangers in their own land. They were deeply attached to it, no matter what pretence they made of being indifferent and cosmopolitan, but they felt obscurely that it had rejected them. [34]

The Paris of the twenties still held a nostalgia for deported American writers. It was a time of unleashed spirits. Henry Miller included "Vive la France" in his *Air-Conditioned Nightmare,* and said:

> When I look back on it now, it seems as though I had packed a thousand years into that brief decade which ended with the war. . . . I remember that I felt a great peace then, a peace such as I had never known in my own country. I looked at my wife and she had become a different person. Even the birds looked different. [35]

In their general retreat from Puritan Algerism, what the expatriate writers admired most was the French *attitude* toward art, not simply French art. The cultural pull of France for Americans is interesting in comparison with Germany and England. American travelers in 1929 spent over $137,143,000 in France, compared with $44,676,000 in Germany, and $40,590,000 in England. Can this mean that France had over three times as much as Germany or England to say to Americans?

The life and art patterns of Rimbaud and Baudelaire were interpreted by the imagists Pound and Eliot. Eliot in his *Baudelaire* says of him:

the possibility of damnation is so immense a relief in a world of electoral reform, plebiscites, sex reform and dress reform, that damnation
itself is an immediate form of salvation—of salvation from the ennui of
modern life, because it at least gives some significance to living.[36]

Scott Fitzgerald reflected the same sentiment when he wrote that the
Lost Generation found "all gods dead, all wars fought, all faiths in man
shaken." The Lost Generation was all dressed up with no place to go, spiritually speaking. It was a reaction against the "Old Gang," as the prewar
writers were called, and a reaction against the system of values inherent in
modern industrial society. Their Bohemia was a utopian wish, where the
artist had an immense self-confidence and a distrust of the wisdom of others
and elders, where he withdrew alone from the very society which supported
him into the unreal world of art.

The American expatriates, in spite of all fulminations, failed to rescue
America from materialism. America read what they had to say and continued
on its own way, a way different from Europe's, which churned in its own
cultural and political crises. Like Cooper's Effingham a hundred years earlier,
"You have been dreaming abroad while your country has retrograded in all
that is respectable and good, a century in a dozen years." [37]

Yet Europe became fascinated with the new rough-and-tumble American
writers, who, like Hollywood, encouraged the cult of violence. Europe no
longer viewed America through the looking glass of Cooper and Twain,
Hawthorne and Howells, and Dos Passos, and an enormous amount of Sinclair Lewis. European movements of decadence and primitivism returned in
changed garb from America to intrigue the European mind. Sartre wrote:

The greatest literary development in France between 1929 and 1939 was
the discovery of Faulkner, Dos Passos, Hemingway, Caldwell, Steinbeck. . . . To the writers of my generation, the publication of "The
42nd Parallel," "Light in August," "Farewell to Arms" effected a revolution similar to the one produced fifteen years earlier in Europe by the
"Ulysses" of Joyce.[38]

Blaise Cendrars and Philippe Soupault also thought that the Americans
would put a new vitality into European writing. Sartre looked into American
writing seeking "something quite different from its crudities and violence,"
and Malraux picked up the same theme in saying, "To my mind the essential
characteristic of contemporary American writing is that it is the only literature whose creators are not intellectuals. . . . They are obsessed with funda-

mental man. . . . The great problem of this literature is now to intellectualize itself without losing its direct approach." [39]

The Depression further increased America's isolation from Europe. President Hoover stated in his inaugural address that the problem of poverty had been solved in the United States. Eight months later, millions were unemployed, only one-third of industrial production was engaged, thousands upon thousands were bankrupt, one-quarter to one-third of the population was on public relief, banks were closed, and farmers' mortgages were foreclosed. The last *Time* issue before the crash announced the forthcoming publication of a new magazine called *Fortune,* which could hardly have been more ironic. The boom had fallen with a crash, and America drifted under the sagging windless sail of a depression. Then Hoover assured the Americans that prosperity was just around the corner, but no one could find out which intersection he meant. America passed from riches to rags.

Even with the election of Roosevelt and the resuscitation of liberal hopes, America occupied itself largely with home affairs and used home solutions to cure its ills. The Depression itself was looked upon as being European-inspired, because of its failure to pay twenty-two billion dollars of war debts and the failure of European bankers to keep *their* house in order. Since 1920 the war debt question has empoisoned the relations of France and Britain with the United States, and the Hoover moratorium in 1931 was looked on as the bad ending of a bad story. The Johnson Law prohibited American loans to any European government which had defaulted on payments. America cut loose from the rest of the world when it went off the gold standard, a most symbolic gesture, and decided to go alone in seeking national economic recovery. We should remember, however, that England set the lead when it went off gold in September, 1931. The French held on until Blum's Popular Front. Roosevelt devalued the dollar by forty per cent. America was determined to contract out of the world situation.

From 1930 to 1934, the number of American visitors to Europe fell by one-half, and during depression years more people fled America than entered it, an effect of earlier immigration laws and the breakdown of the happy picture America had presented before. Franklin Roosevelt, in a speech to the Commonwealth Club in 1932, was obliged to state, "We are not able to invite the immigration from Europe to share our endless plenty. We are now providing a drab living for our own people." Instead of the milk and honey of the American dream, one saw bread lines, apple sellers, police savagery, and Pinkerton men. *Babbitt,* the representative of the twenties, was replaced by *The Grapes of Wrath* of the thirties. Americans had read all the how-to-do-it books, and all the success stories, but obviously the Depression could not be explained by people's failure to read the right success books or develop the correct virtues. The Depression was as much a moral crisis as it was economic, and more deeply felt in America than in Europe. Depression literature was depressing, and it was not particularly lifted by Roosevelt's dictum that the only thing Americans had to fear was fear itself. The literature of the thirties was committed but unhappy. There was Sherwood Anderson's *Puzzled America,* Edmund Wilson's *The American Jitters,* Theodore Dreiser's *Tragic America,* Caldwell's *Some American People,* as well as the Lynds' searching *Middletown in Transition.* Americans read Pearl S. Buck's *The Good Earth* in order to learn that they were better off than the Chinese peasant. Sales of the *Confessions* of St. Augustine soared, perhaps with the hope that a new City of God would show itself.

The year 1929 opened as a financial panic which continued into World War II as a social crisis for American life itself. Americans could no longer flatter themselves before Europeans with their success story. There was a loss of confidence, a new searching for the whys and wherefores in the midst of despair and failure. MacLeish's *New Found Land* gives a sufficient idea, supported by his enormous "Frescoes for Mr. Rockefeller's City," rediscovering his native health. Conventional values were reexamined historically and sociologically, and documented more with the hope of buttressing them than casting them out. Even Gertrude Stein and T. S. Eliot returned to the American scene. Gertrude Stein said that the thirties were not realistic because things were no longer real. Other American expatriates could no longer count on their dollar transfers to Amexco, rue Scribe. Gertrude Stein, perhaps unsure of herself, perhaps also to excuse her absence, announced on her return, "So much has happened since I left. Americans are really beginning to use their minds, more now than at any time since the Civil War." We may wonder if Americans used their minds more during the Civil War than after, and also whether that held true for the thirties. Fitzgerald's last novel, *Tender is the Night,* was the swan song of the expatriates—jaded and disillusioned Americans on the Riviera, older but not wiser and no more mature.

America wanted to remain aloof from Europe and its problems and even more so with the rise of fascism and communism, which were regarded with aversion as "European" ideologies, bookish medicine for sick nations plagued with age-old social and national controversies. The continuing isolation was reflected in the three neutrality acts from 1935 to 1937, the attitude toward Ethiopia and Spain, and the growth of the America First Committee. Even such a first-rate liberal as Sinclair Lewis, who had spent years in Europe, and whose wife, Dorothy Thompson, was an outstanding internationalist and interventionist (perhaps because of that) remained an isolationist throughout the period and up to Pearl Harbor.

America saw its own type of fascist lunatic fringe, but it was unlike European fascism, which called for hierarchy and authoritarianism; indeed, it lacked any formal order. The native brand were all totally "Americanists." Huey Long was right in saying that fascism would only come to America by denying that it was fascism. Long himself was used as a model for American fascism in Robert Penn Warren's *All the King's Men*. The movement, whatever form it might take, would not be known as Fascism, still less as Nazism. It would be given some native American slogan, such as Efficiency and Freedom or the American Cleanup, and it would still go under the rubric of the American Way of Life. Today, one of the extreme right-wing groups calls itself the "Minute Men," after the vigilant revolutionary heroes of 1776. Lawrence Dennis was the only outright American fascist, and Mosely and Maurras were vastly different in outlook from Dies, Hearst, Huey Long, Father Coughlin, and Gerald L. K. Smith.

The picture was well painted in a badly written novel by Sinclair Lewis, *It Can't Happen Here,* published in 1935. It became another bestseller and was turned into a film, which was banned in spite of a postcard campaign and union protests. Strangely enough, it was translated into German, *Das ist bei uns nicht möglich,* and, obviously, was also banned. The only thing that the American extreme Right had in common was an "anti" attitude, be it anti-communist, anti-Europe, anti-Jew, anti-Catholic, or simply anti-Roosevelt. Roosevelt himself was able to cut them all to size by the masterly sublimation of "Americanism" himself, and the Hudson river patroon could envelop "my friends" in a refined American social mysticism. The Fair Deal of Truman paled in comparison to the inspired national enthusiasm for the New Deal, for Roosevelt had led a mass movement greater than that of Jackson.

We might wonder where the political or social philosophy is in the New Deal, born out of the suffering of the Depression and narrowly averting a revolution, surely the most soul-shaking national episode since the Civil War, surely topping World War I in its effects on the whole population. But just as no social or political philosophy came out of the Civil War, except the negative one that nullification did not exist, and just as Wilsonian idealism came to naught in World War I, there was no New Deal philosophy as such. It was only a continuation of the American liberal tradition transmorgified. Roosevelt himself was pragmatic in the best American manner and solved "problems" without the need for theory. Even the supposed influence of Keynes is overrated, and Roosevelt hardly understood him during his visit to the White House. The Tennessee Valley Authority was regarded as an "experiment," not an effort to introduce insidiously foreign socialism on American shores. Roosevelt, when asked outright about his social philosophy, was somewhat mystified, and replied simply that he was a "Christian and a Democrat." Earlier Cleveland had similarly defended his tariff policy by stating that it was "a condition, not a theory which confronts us." Thus the United States cannot be understood by anyone who hopes to see a strict logic in its action, or in the attitudes and reactions of its people. That rationality which Europe thinks America possesses does not exist.

As the thirties wore on, American intellectuals turned their eyes away from Europe, whose democracies and culture were being challenged by the rising tide of fascism and communism. The former literary and artistic expatriates in Paris were now regarded as having run out on America, instead of staying to fight the good fight. MacLeish, himself an expatriate, in his fourth section of *Landscapes for Mr. Rockefeller's City* entitled "Oil Painting of the Artist as an Artist," sharply criticized the expatriate. He was soon to give up poetry almost altogether to enter the political fray against fascism, first as Assistant Secretary of State, then as Librarian of Congress. In 1940 he published *The Irresponsibles,* a critique of intellectual leaders. As John Gould Fletcher wrote from England,

> To call a thing "European" now fails to ring a bell in American breasts. . . . The list of great European writers seems steadily to grow less. . . . I think Europe is tired out and one cannot expect more from England, France and Italy than they have done. Nobody here sounds new deeps. Of course Europe is a great continent and it will go on emitting sparks . . . but with diminishing lustre.[40]

The postwar American exiles of the twenties now had a different attitude. They discovered that European intellectuals were just as frustrated as they were.

Under the influence of the WPA Federal Act Project, patriotic, historic, and nationalistic murals began to decorate schools, post offices, courthouses, and libraries executed by such artists as Ben Shahn, Thomas Hart Benton, Charles Burchfield, Edward Hopper, Rockwell Kent, John Sloan, Charles Sheeler, and Grant Wood.

The only American novelist of stature who spent any time in Nazi Germany was Thomas Wolfe, whose preference for violent emotionalism over reason, anti-Semitism, anti-Negro, mystic sensualism was widely popular in that anti-intellectual milieu. He enjoyed spending his German royalties there, but he was not a Nazi, although he verged on it with *Of Time and the River*. The Third Reich "was a plague of the spirit—invisible, but unmistakable as death." He maintained faith in America. "I believe that we are lost here in America, but I believe that we shall be found, . . . I think that the true discovery of America is before us. I think the true fulfillment of our spirit, of our people, of our mighty and immortal land, is yet to come." Yet his last novel, *You Can't Go Home Again* revealed his own tormented spirit in trying to maintain that faith.

A different case was Ezra Pound, whose authoritarianism led him further and further away from the American ethos to embrace fascism and finally to be condemned as a traitor by his country. From his retreat at Rapallo he wrote *Jefferson and Mussolini,* in which he urged Americans to revere Mussolini because Jefferson had so much in common with the Italian dictator. In Italy he had no financial difficulties, for he had always had an independent income from the United States, but when America entered the War, his funds were cut off and he earned a meager living by broadcasting for the Italian Radio.

Hemingway, who had gone into a temporary eclipse, took an active interest in the Spanish Civil War. He gave money for ambulances, and with Dos Passos and MacLeish formed Contemporary Historians, Inc. to film *The Spanish Earth* portraying the loyalist cause. Hemingway went to Spain to write the story and translate the dialogue, and was also a correspondent for the North American Newspaper Alliance. Out of his experience came the magnificent *For Whom the Bell Tolls,* with Maria as the symbol of a raped Spain.

Americans looked inward, and like Van Wyck Brooks, became interested in the American past and its worthies. The historical novels of the thirties mostly tended to show that the Americans had withstood greater crises and had managed to come out all right, and even though many old values had gone with the wind, they buttressed American pride against the radical writings of the depression years. Even the social writings of Steinbeck, Dos Passos, and Steffens saw a flicker of hope for the future. With Europe succumbing to fascism, the United States became the stronghold of Western culture. John Dos Passos sought roots to the past to steady himself in the changing situation. *The Ground We Stand On* affirmed, "In times of change and danger when there is a quicksand of fear under men's reasoning a sense of continuity with generations gone before can stretch like a lifetime across the scary present." [41] His writings best illustrated the passage from the damnation of the twenties to the social suffering of the thirties. Stephen Vincent Benét went deep into American folklore, Kenneth Roberts into the American Revolution, and Margaret Mitchell into the Civil War. Van Wyck Brooks, who in the twenties had found Twain and Henry James alienated by American business culture, now turned to American ancestral worship in *The*

Flowering of New England, New England Indian Summer, and the *Life of Emerson.* Brooks later wrote in *From the Shadow of the Mountain* of his thinking in the thirties, "Certainly the lack of a tradition was not responsible for all our ills, but did it not partly explain the abortive careers of so many of our writers, and I dare say also of many of our artists?" [42] He felt that America seemed unable to do as Europe: to project its past into the present and into the future. But European writing of the thirties, he said, was exhausted and America stepped in to fill the vacuum. Some critics turned to the classical formation of Paul More and Irving Babbitt's New Humanism. After thirteen years in Europe, Harold Stearns came out with *America, A Reappraisal,* and Edmund Wilson wrote *Europe Without Baedeker,* both critically disillusioned with the Old World. The thirties also saw Parrington's great *Main Currents of American Thought.*

With the Depression, America had again been cut loose from Europe, but the migration of European intellectuals to the United States meant essentially that the European past and future were put in American hands for temporary safekeeping. European intellectuals on American shores imposed a new sense of responsibility and ironically forced the restudy of America's own culture. There was a sense of pride in maintaining the torch that was falling from Europe's grasp.

If the Americans became expatriates in the twenties, then Europeans fled to the United States in the thirties in an opposite movement. Over 400,000 Germans emigrated in the decade of the thirties, and Italian emigration greatly increased after 1938. European scholars and intellectuals, labor leaders and bankers, artists and writers, politicians and poets, harried and hurried out of Europe by totalitarianism, were cast up on American shores. As the cultural level in Germany, Italy, and Austria declined, America's rose. To the great benefit of America came the wandering scholars in exile whose flourishing brilliance was stimulated by the American scene. American committees proliferated in their efforts to bring intellectuals to America, away from persecution and mental restraints. Refugee scientists, Jewish scholars, German, Austrian, and Italian sociologists, psychologists, philosophers, and economists, and Italian political thinkers fled across the Atlantic like Greeks fleeing Constantinople. They were stimulated not only by the free American world, but by American scholarship itself. They raised anew the question of the relation of Western-world humanism to American culture. Even an incomplete list of émigrés is impressive: Thomas Mann, Franz Werfel, Einstein, Einaudi, Stefan Zweig, Borgese, Salvemini, Bruening, Halvden Koht,

Fermi, Gropius, Dufy, Saarinen, Neutra, Breuer, Marc Chadourne, Wilfredo Pareto, Salvador Dali, Igor Stravinsky, Alban Berg, Pevsner, de Koonig, Feininger, Paul Hindemith, Kurt Weill, Schoenberg, Grosz, Chagall, Léger, Lipschitz, Max Ernst, Toscanini, Paderewski, Saint-John Perse, Maritain, and Maurois. The intellectual flotsam and jetsam were important not only for American cultural activity at the time but also for the later return of many to Europe, their ideas modified and expanded by American experiences and influences.

What a paradox that the American went to Europe in the twenties and early thirties for his cultural liberation, while the European came later to America for his! Perhaps there is a difference to be found with the European cultural émigrés. By and large their creative effort was in art and science rather than in letters. Even when Thomas Mann began writing in America, his novels remained Gothic German novels, untouched by Americanism. Feuchtwanger went into almost complete isolation in Los Angeles. Brecht settled in Los Angeles in 1941 and was on the periphery of the movie colony until 1947. In that year he was subpoened by the House Un-American Activities Committee, and his testimony was so bewilderingly casuistic that the Committee dismissed him with thanks as an exemplary cooperative witness; he left immediately for Europe and wound up in East Berlin. In general the European writer seemed to remain at home in what was termed an "inner migration," going underground rather than being uprooted to come to America. But art, like science, transcended boundaries and lept oceans with greater ease. If nuclear physics was embraced with American wartime fervor, European architecture found ground ready for building in America. European architects, together with Frank Lloyd Wright, made America the leading architectural country. Architecture, more than painting, easily took hold in the best American spirit, for it was practical, useful, modern, constructive.

The intellectual refugee is as old as history, for the scholar is the conscience of society, and society does not like to have moral needles stuck in its body politic. Banishment from Athens, the only center of civilization, meant intellectual death, for politics and culture were then identical. In Hellenistic and Roman times, an exiled scholar could go from one city to another. Ovid was banished by Augustus to the Black Sea. With the rise of a universal Christian culture, scholars could wander from one university to another, one language to another; Dante, expelled from Florence, went to Verona, Bologna, Paris, Oxford, and Cologne, albeit unhappily; Marsilius of Padua, exiled from Paris, did fruitful service with Louis of Bavaria, writing *Defensor Pacis* for him; Hugo Grotius, escaping in 1621 from Maurice of Orange, lived ten years in Paris, where he wrote *De jure belli ac Pacis*. When the Roman Church and the newly created Protestant churches put religion into politics, or the growing of national monarchies integrated national political designs with culture, the results were sometimes unfortunate: Galileo, Bruno, Cardan, Servetus.

The modern political refugee scholar is the result of the type of thinking embodied in Rousseau's last chapter in the *Contrat Social* on civic religion as necessary for a community spirit. Rousseau would expel those who violate this civic religion, or execute those who pretend to practice it but violate it. Exactly this was done by Robespierre's Reign of Terror, and fascism and communism continue the practice. It must be frankly admitted that there are those in America and Europe who would like to see some greater control over man's mind; such people have always existed. Authoritarians are no longer content to attack man's body; they must also control his thought. It is not surprising that virually no creative thought (outside of science, perhaps) existed under Hitler and Mussolini, for creative thought must be free. Fascism produced the worst kind of cultural degradation, and was capable only of making propaganda. Croce was not persecuted, but was effectively silenced in isolation. Pasternak, forced also into intellectual isolation, is vividly tragic. The same had happened with Eisenstein and countless others who might have gone on creating, but could not. Again, the American State Department is no better judge of art or writing than is the American Legion. It is better to leave a culture to find itself in anarchy than to have a predetermined official line. The Constitution of the United States in its infinite wisdom did not provide for an official national educational system, safeguarding to the individual states the culture of the young.

The openness of American society and its universities made the integration of the European refugee scholars relatively simple, and many chose to remain in their adopted country after the War. Those who returned to Europe brought back new views, were "stretched" by America. They brought back a desire to liberalize and make more flexible their European educational systems, though it is perhaps too difficult to judge the result of the great changes in the democratization of the gymnasia, lycées, and universities. American literature and history were given a vastly increased place in the syllabi and curricula, and, very importantly, an increased scholarly use of the pragmatic approach to learning began to take place. In intellectual circles, as well as others, such as business, English is now at least as important on the Continent as German or French, and this can hardly be attributed alone to a closer relation of England to the Continent, but rather to the American influence.

It is again difficult to point directly to the contributions of the refugee intellectuals in America, but some generalizations may be permitted. Since the earliest settlements, European culture had been grafted onto American stock, and, naturalized, flourished on the new soil. Many deeply rooted European traditions could not be transplanted, and for good reasons, but there continued to be much cross-fertilization. For example, German thinking is by and large theoretical and historical and thus made a large splash on American nineteenth-century philosophical idealists. They are now a bit outdated by the logical positivists and others such as the mathematical and linguistic analytical philosophers. Now the classically French critical spirit, always doubting, always questioning, gains stronger footholds. Of the influence of European science, music, and architecture we have spoken elsewhere.

America has always borrowed its culture from Europe, while Europe remains the most creative of all continents. There is nothing wrong with borrowing culture. The Greeks borrowed from the Cretans, the Romans from the Greeks, the Middle Ages from Rome, the French, English, and German Renaissance from the Italian and from each other *und so weiter*. The important thing in the assimilation of another culture is that something be added in the process of cultural transformation. American culture, borrowed and transformed, is hardly as bad as some of its envious European carpers and native critics would have it; certainly the refugee scholar on American shores is obliged to admit this as much as he is obliged to admit that he had to flee a Europe which his own culture created. Let us simply note that there have been very few Americans who have had to flee their country for intellectual or political reasons.

Harold Laski described somewhat lengthily what happens to the American adaptation of European culture:

Whatever the volume of the baggage imported from Europe in the settling of America—and no doubt it was very large—once unloaded, it began immediately to undergo significant changes; it became, in fact, American. . . . When all is said that can be said of American indebtedness to European, and especially English, civilization, the debt is less than the contribution brought by America itself to the product involved in the mixture of the European and, indeed, oriental heritage with the American environment. For we must regard the culture of the United States not as the provincial expression on the circumference of civilization of something that can be grasped only at its center. We must rather regard it as an effort, often groping and uncertain, after a civilization of its own; in the course of which it borrows, sometimes with glad acknowledgement and sometimes with unhappy shame, from the achievements of the older world. . . . So that whatever is taken or received from the Old World becomes different as it is adapted to its new home. It is obvious that American furniture of the eighteenth century was greatly influences by the careful perusal of Thomas Chippendale designs; but it is not less obvious that the result is not Chippendale furniture. There can be little doubt that Paul Revere owes much to the great French tradition in silverware design, the art, for instance, of Paul Lamerie, but there can be little doubt, also, that he mixed with that tradition something of his own, and that this was American character.[43]

European culture, having passed through the American intellectual mill, becomes of renewed value to the European. Although not all changes may be for the best, the very fact that an idea has been tested in a different laboratory makes it worth looking at anew. American thinkers are able to look at European cultural crosscurrents with an objective eye and, from a distance, are often better able to see the woods from the trees, while Europeans often get caught up in the daily conflict of ideas and opposing philosophies.

With the disillusionment of the liberals, the breakdown of Wilsonian ideology and the triumph of conservative isolationism in America, the intellectual writers and artists had to regroup on the Left Bank to work in a freer atmosphere, homesick as they were and yearning for a better America. They got the depression. They came home. They became "engaged" writers and artists out of both necessity and desire. They sought new roots in the American past for security in an uncertain world and were joined by a huge emigration of European intellectuals fleeing Nazism and fascism. Despite all the dangers, America seemed after all a better place in which to live.

NOTES

1. "Universal Covenant" address to Congress, January 22, 1917.

2. Edward E. House, *Intimate Papers*, June 29, 1919 (Boston: Houghton Mifflin Company, 1928), pp. 487–89.

3. Allen Tate, "Ode to Our Young Pro-Consuls of the Air," *Poems, 1922–1947* (New York: Charles Scribner's Sons, 1948), p. 97.

4. Philip Wylie, *Generation of Vipers*, new ed. (New York: Holt, Rinehart and Winston, Inc., 1955), p. 4.

5. *The New York Times*, October 23, 1928. Cf. also Handlin, p. 229.

6. Letter to William Strahan, August 19, 1784. Cited in Rahv, p. 30.

7. Cooper, *Homeward Bound*, p. 477.

8. Lincoln had witnessed the value of the foreign immigrants' loyalty to the Union and in a message to Congress in December 8, 1863, called immigration a "source of national wealth and strength" and urged a Federal system for the

encouragement of immigration. A law was passed, but was soon repealed; it was the only instance when the Government directly encouraged immigration, except for occasional grant-in-aid to groups—Scioto, for example, or Cuban refugees.

9. H. G. Wells, *The Future of America: A Search after Realities* (New York: Harper & Row, Publishers, 1906), pp. 142–43.

10. Archibald MacLeish, *The Collected Poems of Archibald MacLeish* (Boston: Houghton Mifflin Company, 1962), p. 87.

11. Cited in Alan Valentine, *1913: America Between Two Worlds* (New York: The Macmillan Company, 1962), p. 113.

12. Felix Frankfurter, *The Case of Sacco and Vanzetti* (Boston: Little, Brown and Company, 1927), p. 59.

13. Cited in Kazin, p. 197.

14. Brooks, *From the Shadow of the Mountain,* p. 62.

15. William Carlos Williams, *In the American Grain* (New York: Albert & Charles Boni, 1925), p. 65.

16. Malcolm Cowley, *Exile's Return* (New York: The Viking Press, 1959), p. 81.

17. Kazin, p. 202.

18. Cargill, p. 493.

19. Sinclair Lewis, *Dodsworth* (New York: Modern Library, 1947), p. 250.

20. Cited in Mark Schorer, *Sinclair Lewis: An American Life* (New York: McGraw-Hill, Inc., 1961), pp. 310–11.

21. *Ibid.,* p. 332.

22. Lewis, *Dodsworth,* p. 252.

23. Cited in Schorer, p. 797.

24. Schorer, p. 797.

25. Gertrude Stein, *Paris, France* (London: B. T. Batsford, 1940), p. 2.

26. Gertrude Stein, "An American and France," *What are Masterpieces* (Los Angeles: Gertrude Stein, 1940), pp. 61–70.

27. Ernest Hemingway, *The Sun Also Rises* (New York: Charles Scribner's Sons, 1962), p. 115.

28. Sherwood Anderson, *A Story Teller's Story* (New York: B. W. Huebsch, 1924), pp. 391–92.

29. John Dos Passos, *One Man's Initiation* (London: George Allen & Unwin Ltd., 1920), p. 120.

30. *Ibid.,* p. 34.

31. Archibald MacLeish, *Poems, 1924–33* (Boston: Houghton Mifflin Company, 1933), p. 31.

32. Hemingway, p. 17.

33. John Dos Passos, *Manhattan Transfer* (Boston: Houghton Mifflin Company, 1953), p. 36.

34. Cowley, pp. 83, 214–15.

35. Henry Miller, "Vive la France," *Air-Conditioned Nightmare* (New York: New Directions, 1945), pp. 65–67.

36. T. S. Eliot, *Selected Essays* (New York: Harcourt, Brace & World, Inc., 1950) pp. 378–79.

37. Cooper, *Homeward Bound,* p. 223.

38. Cited in Peyre, p. 101.

39. André Malraux, *Horizons,* January, 1945. Cited in Peyre, p. 97.

40. Brooks, *From the Shadow of the Mountain,* p. 57.

41. John Dos Passos, *The Ground We Stand On* (New York: Harcourt, Brace & Wolrd, Iñc., 1941), p. 3.

42. Brooks, *From the Shadow of the Mountain,* p. 67.

43. Laski, p. 397.

ᴄᴀ MIDCHANNEL ᴇᴏ

O'er the glad waters of the dark-blue sea,
Our thoughts as boundless, and our souls as free,
Far as the breeze can bear, the billows foam,
Survey our empire, and behold our home!

—Byron

Our European-American cultural chain is strong, but we have to take the rust off the links. American and European cultural vitality must be refined and tempered in the intellectual forges on both sides of the water. Europe cannot neutralize itself from America, nor can America ignore the fact that much of its cultural content is European. It is impossible to think that Europe could become a no-man's-land, a cultural vacuum between two superpowers. Paul Valéry worried in 1940 that Europe might become a little peninsula of the Asian continent and hoped that it would remain a primary intellectual center after the War. American intellectual power stations cannot go long unobserved by Europeans without the danger of an intellectual blackout. André Siegfried is not too optimistic: "The gulf separating the American and the European civilizations is rapidly widening; the New World has lost all sense of reality of contact with Greco-Roman culture, and, if it remains fundamentally Christian, it is in the Jewish rather than the Greek sense, following the testimony of the Bible rather than critical argument." [1]

Americans seem to go from alarm to alarm, from one crisis to another, thinking that somehow the way has been lost or betrayed, and consequently to look to the past for comfort. Robert M. Hutchins and Mortimer Adler, glossators, seek the way in the "Great Ideas" and the *Encyclopedia Britannica*. Statesmen look for guidance in their predecessors. Truman read Thucydides and Plutarch, as both Thucydides and Plutarch wrote history to influence the statesmen of their time. Civil War literature abounds, along with the morals of the American frontier story. Americans look to the old signs and guideposts to put them back on the track. A half-century ago Americans thought that they were marching in a bright light and creating the "New Life." Now they wonder and are confused, and the light grows dim. Americans have passed uncertainly through the New Deal, the Fair

Deal, the New Frontier, and are now concerned with the future of the Great Society.

After the ebb tide of the twenties and thirties, America began to come back to Europe in fits and starts. In spite of popular approval of the earlier neutrality acts, in 1939 Congress lifted the embargo on arms on the basis of cash and carry in foreign bottoms. American ships were forbidden in the territorial waters of the belligerents. The fall of France was a moral shock to the United States, as the painfully slow entry of the United States into World War I had been to France. It was discomfiting to think that the wine of 1789 was to be replaced by Vichy water. Now it seemed that the Americans were once again too late, and bundles for Britain were not enough. The bundles had to be bigger and harder and eventually brought over by men in uniform. In September, 1940, Roosevelt put through the destroyers-for-bases deal.

While on one hand Roosevelt, like Wilson, was assuring Americans that he would never lead the United States into war; on the other hand he was, unlike Wilson, better preparing the country for war. He introduced peacetime conscription, and factories were converted for arms production. Greenland was occupied, the convoy system was established with American naval escort, and merchant vessels were armed. America was almost at war when its Navy received orders to "shoot on sight" at submarines or other vessels threatening convoy operations. The Atlantic Charter, vague as it was, was proclaimed before America's entry into the War and set the goals in the same way as the Fourteen Points.

Senator Vandenberg, internationally recognized spokesman for isolationism and strong conservative candidate for the 1940 Republican presidential nomination, recorded his reaction to the passage of the Lend-Lease Bill (March 8, 1941) and showed his shift into bipartisan foreign policy as America inched into war:

> If America "cracks up" you can put your finger on this precise moment when the crime was committed. It was at this moment that the Senate passed the so-called Loan-Lease Bill. . . . We have torn up 150 years of American foreign policy. We have tossed Washington's Farewell Address into the discard! We have thrown ourselves squarely into the power politics and the power wars of Europe, Asia, and Africa. We have taken the first step upon a course from which we can never hereafter retreat. . . . Our fate is *now* inseverably linked with that of Europe, Asia, and Africa. We have deliberately chosen to "sit in" on the most gigantic speculation since time began.[2]

Vandenberg echoed many an American's uneasy feelings about the departure from isolation and a gradual entrance into another world war. After all, the United States had watched Europe running downhill: the failure of the League, the virtually unchallenged rise of dictatorship, the efforts of Baldwin and Chamberlain, Daladier, and Laval to isolate and protect their two countries, even at the expense of others, which were being gobbled up. Was Europe, was the transatlantic connection, worth America's fighting for?

From the vantage point of time, we can look back to see that World War II had a psychological complexion vastly different from that of World War I, and not only because it was a more complex war strategically. Some former allies had changed sides, as former enemies were to become allies, and former allies to become enemies shortly after World War II. It was a changing of world power structures and balances. State-sponsored ideologies surely played a stronger role in the Second World War than in the First, which had been primarily a European quarrel winding up with Europe's settling the affair. In the Second World War, the stakes were as much outside Europe as in, and the settlement depended and still depends on two extra-European superpowers.

Charles de Gaulle was later to write that the American people had long been inclined to isolate themselves from overseas affairs and to mistrust Europe, which was always torn apart by battles and revolutions. Now a sort of messianism raised up the American spirit and turned it toward vast designs. The United States, admiring its own resources, felt that its dynamism no longer found a large enough career in America itself. Wanting to aid those who where unfortunate or subjugated in the world, the Americans through Roosevelt tried in every way possible to do their part in the world conflict. "But once America made war," de Gaulle continued, "Roosevelt meant that the peace would be an American peace and that it belonged to himself to dictate its organization and that the states swept by the trial be subjected to his judgment." [3]

This is not the place to go into American wartime diplomacy, except to note that it was characteristically American in that it had short-range immediate goals and that the future would eventually take care of itself. Roosevelt's confidence that he could "handle Joe" was a bad piece of political naiveté for an experienced politician. In fact, now that the hurly-burly of Yalta and Teheran has died down, it seems that Roosevelt "gave" no more than that which the Soviet Union could easily "take." In 1815, Castlereagh reported to London from the Congress of Vienna that there was little he could do about Poland since Russian troops were already in occupation. It is interesting to see that the occupation frontiers as finally fixed followed closely the same classic lines of the Europe of Charlemagne.

The American effort was massive and decisive and confirmed America as a world power, if there had been any doubts before. As America's strength increased beyond previous imagination, Europe's relatively waned. The specter of another world power, Soviet Russia, loomed over Europe. The Atlantic tie, once more forged in war, was to be more strongly bound by America's return to European shores in the presence of tens of thousands of young GI's.

But World War II was not a nice little war, as Gertrude Stein had described World War I. It was not a war that Edith Wharton or Willa Cather could have written about, and it would have heavily taxed the post-World-War-I writers such as Cummings, Hemingway, and Dos Passos. No really great literature came out of the Second World War, at least none comparable to Remarque's *All Quiet on the Western Front,* the novels of Rolland, Barbusse, Romains, the poems of Rupert Brooke or Siegfried Sassoon, the protests of Russell and Shaw, or the American Lost-Generation writers. The Second World War primarily produced works of journalism or fictionalized contemporary history. There was little literary protest at genocide, human life was no longer a thing to be talked about, and Brecht, Koestler, and Camus make painful reading. Out of World War II people felt only a sense of general guilt, but not at all personal. With the coming of the atomic era, all began to realize that a decisive victory could only be won in another life in another world. Indeed, we are now so accustomed to the idea of the end of the world that it is sometimes difficult to believe that it will not happen.

The songs of World War I had something durable about them: "Madelon," "Tipperary," "Over There," "Mademoiselle from Armentières." World War II produced only one great song, "Lili Marlene," which expressed humane values and was sung by both sides, and perhaps another, virtually unknown to the Americans and the English, "The Song of the Partisans," which is immensely stirring. Others were only fatuous and falsely sentimental: "God Bless America," "Praise the Lord and Pass the Ammunition," "White Cliffs of Dover," "When the Lights Go on Again All Over the World." Outside of the documentaries, most of the really good films of World War II started at least a decade afterwards, time enough to forget the old horrors and indulge in new ones. With World War II, everyone spoke of the "end of the war," seldom of victory. Edmund Wilson's *Europe Without Baedeker* recorded the immediate postwar disillusionment:

How empty, how sickish, how senseless, everything suddenly seems the moment the war is over! We are left flat with the impoverished and humiliating life that the drive against the enemy kept our minds off. Where our efforts have all gone toward destruction, we have been able to build nothing at home to fall back on amidst our own ruin.[4]

One could not even get plunder or empire from the ruined enemies, only more harassing duties. As a result, except for Poland and East Germany and the Baltic countries, European boundaries returned essentially to those of 1919.

Europe and America in a real sense were isolated by the results of the War. Having fought loyally together, the one found itself in ruins to be rebuilt and virtually bankrupt, the other dangerously prosperous with a bursting wartime industry to be converted to peacetime uses. D. W. Brogan did some plain speaking:

Many Europeans do not regard the United States with unalloyed enthusiasm. Their respect for America's power is, let us admit it, tinged with envy and criticism. Because of certain extravagancies and follies in American life—and because America has not taken the trouble to explain the real sources of its strength to Europeans—they are apt to say that luck is the reason for America's present position [1948]. It is therefore important for both Americans and Europeans to understand that the key to America's power lies in qualities which derive from the political and social soil of the United States. . . rather than material power as such.[5]

Postwar American diplomacy was also to be tried and tested as America's military strength had been tried, and its makeshift efforts underwent many strains under new pressures and new responsibilities. On August 14, 1945, the end of the War, there were eleven million Americans in uniform; a year later there were one million.

The War concluded, Truman, unlike Wilson, brought Republicans to San Francisco. The American commitment to a new internal order was marked by the conversion of Senator Arthur Vandenberg, the ranking Republican of the Senate Foreign Relations Committee. This distinguished isolationist Senator from Michigan had voted against the repeal of the Neutrality Acts, the Draft Act, the Draft Extension Act, and Lend-Lease. With great courage, reversing his lifetime conviction of America's role in the world, he addressed the Senate in early 1945: "I do not believe that any nation hereafter can immunize itself by its own exclusive action. . . . I want maximum cooperation. . . . I want a new dignity and a new authority for international law. I think American self-interest requires it." [6]

Truman entrusted the Japanese peace treaty to the Republican Dulles and let Republicans assist in the formation of the Paris peace treaties and NATO. American diplomacy went into a new, more mature phase. Open diplomacy was discarded except for the press-agentry of summit conferences.

America resorted to time-tested international dealing: secret diplomacy, alliances, spheres of influence, and balance of power. Wilson's Fourteen Points seemed strangely obsolescent: "open covenants openly arrived at," abolition of all "leagues and alliances," and of the "great game, now forever discredited, of the balance of power." Roosevelt and Hull had tried to keep up the Wilsonian ideology. Roosevelt proclaimed that Yalta was designed as the end of systems of unilateral action, exclusive alliances, and balance of power which had always failed in the past. Cordell Hull explained to Congress that with the United Nations Charter there would no longer be any need for spheres of influence, alliances, blocs, balances of power, or any instruments where in the past, nations had attempted to guarantee their national security and interests. This all changed. In that year of 1946, Winston Churchill crossed the Atlantic to warn Americans in a speech at Fulton, Missouri that an Iron Curtain had fallen in Europe from Stettin to Trieste and that a fresh mobilization of Atlantic energies was needed.

Acheson became the new Castlereagh and Dulles a new Metternich. Eisenhower set a new note which stood against the traditional American optimism, yet was closer to the complex realities of today's international situation by declaring: "Remember that in these vast problems that affect the lives of every one of us there is no thought that you can cut out the knots. You must untie them slowly and laboriously." 7 The normal American frontier spirit would have been to take an ax to them.

Americans began to learn that there are some problems that cannot be solved but which must take care of themselves in their own tedious way. Perhaps the frightening cathartic administered with brinkmanship, agonizing reappraisals, massive retaliation, and unleashing armies and rolling back curtains sobered Americans to the dangers of veering too wildly one way or the other. Americans began to understand that the international society is morally and institutionally imperfect, that even the loftiest ends will fall short of ideal standards, that in international relations it is often necessary to compromise with perfection. From containment and liberation, America moved to coexistence.

President Kennedy educated the public in the same way as General Eisenhower did, untying and unraveling knots, and insisted that there cannot be a purely American solution; otherwise the United States would be acting like the Soviet Union, using the strong hand rather than the guiding hand. Problems had to be faced that did not lend themselves to easy, quick, or permanent solutions, and the fact that the United States was neither omnipotent nor omniscient had to be recognized. There is no American solution for every world problem.

The complicated situation in Germany was the first major problem to be tackled by the Allies, and evidently it has not yet been solved. After World War I, the occupation of Germany took place only in the Rhineland and a few areas in central and eastern Europe, with a legitimate German government functioning. After World War II, there was a complete occupation with no central government. The old provinces were realigned into economic regions, which proved to be good sense, and Prussia disappeared completely, its former capital sticking out like a white thumbtack on the Red map of East Germany.

The effort of denazification was a dismal farce: while the little fish were caught and tried at Nuremberg, many big fish slipped away. The mockery of denazification was limned in the bestseller *Die Frageboden* by Ernst von Salomon, which showed the futility of trying to answer long questionnaires wrapped in red tape.

The occupation of Germany gave a good example of the American effort to "democratize," to "reeducate" other peoples in American ideals. A massive effort through rearranging German university programs, introducing "American studies," and American cultural centers, may have had some impact. The American High Commissioner in Germany, John J. McCloy, summed up his impressions of the American attempt to change the German character:

> Naturally American ideas have had some effects, but sometimes I suspect we have mostly convinced our friends and left our enemies untouched. People who have a natural bent for our way of doing things were eager to learn. The others admired a few American traits, our efficiency, our machines, our financial capacity, perhaps, and seldom bothered to go to the source of our power, which is liberty. Some Germans follow our leadership only because we have defeated them. Has our experiment been successful? I wish I could say yes. I don't know. It will take years to know. It will depend on how history will develop in the next few decades, whether our kind of Germans will be able to keep the leadership of their country and whether the rest of the world will find it convenient to go on admiring our ideals.[8]

What kind of example did American troops set? After all, American troops, civilians in uniform, were about as "average Americans" as one could find. American troops abroad tended to isolate themselves in military ghettos, using American food and drink imported from the United States, PX's, private service clubs, and separate housing facilities. It was, let us concede, their right to live as Americans, or as they pleased. Yet the occasional sorties out of antiseptic camps frequently gave rise to such questions as whether the water or the milk was safe to drink (although Europeans did not seem harmed by them) which leads to the supposition that Americans thought of themselves as a separate race of men from another world. Even English-speaking England has had a hard time understanding *this* American accent.

Arnold Toynbee called the PX a lodestone to the American exile and an offense to the native of the country, setting up a caste barrier and losing much goodwill. The American is living in a closed circuit as far as cultural communication is concerned, guarded by a high wire fence and military police, and the indispensable PX card. One has seen American cars drawn up in large parking lots next to the PX, the beauty shop, bowling alleys, baseball and football fields, liquor stores, and snack bars, where the military community was completely self-sufficient. If Napoleon's *Grande Armée* marched on its stomach, the American Army marched on its PX. Servicemen and their dependents depended on this life without ever meeting people in their host country. An American wife in Rome was asked to bring a macaroni and cheese casserole to a church supper and desperately refused, saying, "but the PX is closed!"

Without doubt, our Atlantic ties were greatly increased since World War II, at least officially, with the Marshall Plan, NATO, and constant American support of the Council of Europe, and the European Trade Organization, later the OEDC. Once again, Americans were asked to come over to Macedonia and help. After World War I, Herbert Hoover's American efforts in Belgium and later in other countries had brought a largesse of American wheat, blankets, medicines, clothes, coal, and cotton. This aid had helped countries avoid falling into civil war and revolution as had Russia, Hungary, and Germany. UNRRA imitated this orginal effort and served the same purpose.

The background of the Marshall Plan for direct economic assistance was Lend-Lease, the $3,750,000 loan to Britain, and the Greek-Turkish Aid Bill. A clear warning of Europe's dilemma was given by Churchill at Albert Hall in May, 1947: "What is Europe now? It is a rubble heap, a charnel house, a breeding ground of pestilence and hate." The following month Secretary of State George Marshall addressed the graduating class at Harvard University and called upon Europe to unite its efforts at recovery and to designate its needs. Eastern Europe and Russia as well were included as a calculated risk. Ernest Bevin and Georges Bidault set immediately to work, and less than a month after the Harvard speech, European statesmen, as well as Molotov and the eastern Europeans, had gathered in Paris.

Led by Vandenberg, the Republican Congress (the Truman "do-nothing 80th"), passed the European Recovery Program 69 to 17 in the Senate, and with House approval it became law on April 2, 1948. It was made more urgent by the Czech Revolution of February, 1948, the Greek Revolution, the Berlin blockade in March, 1948, and the critical Italian elections of April, 1948.

The Marshall Plan was to continue only until 1952, by which time fourteen billion dollars had been spent. Under different names similar heavy financial and technical aid continued. Over a hundred billion dollars have been spent since the War in ninety-seven countries for economic and technical aid. Americans might justly ask themselves how much the Marshall Plan (outside its counterpart Fulbright program) and NATO have really maintained the spiritual and cultural alliance necessary to our contemporary situation. Too often these programs have been looked on as international health projects. While ultimately designed to strengthen the cultural and spiritual tie, the idea somehow gets lost in military, economic, and political officialdom. We find both American and European prejudice against economic and political cooperation: the American who wants his tax dollar spent for public improvement at home, or not spent, or better, wants not to be taxed at all; the European who accepts with a shrug the cost of playing war games on Europe's plains and can neither sympathize with us nor understand the silver dollars that went into new hydroelectric plants or port facilities. At best, Europeans have the vague feeling that the money came from some hidden slush fund and that it was necessary somehow for America to spend in order to avoid its own economic collapse. Europeans, like Asaph, thought of Americans that God has been truly good to them.

> They speak softly,
> Even to such as are of a clear heart
> But as for me my feet were almost gone; my steps had well nigh slipped
> For I was envious at the foolish, when I saw the prosperity
>   of the wicked. . . .
> They are not in trouble as other men, neither are they plagued
>   like other men.
> Therefore pride compasseth them about as a chain, violence covereth
>   them as a garment.
> Their eyes stand out with fatness: they have more than heart could wish.
> Who prosper in the world: they increase in riches.
> Surely thou didst set them in slippery places . . .
> How are they brought into desolation as in a moment. . . .
> —*Psalm 73*

Actually, the Marshall Plan cost the individual taxpayer $120.00 per year, plus the inflation which resulted. A poll made in 1947 indicated that

57 per cent of the British felt that the United States wanted a say in running Britain's affairs through the Marshall Plan. In France, 47 per cent felt that the Marshall Plan was developed out of a need for foreign markets to avoid a depression, 15 per cent, that it was a way to intervene in the internal affairs of Europe, and only 18 per cent that it was a sincere desire to aid in European recovery. Europe would not see the humanitarian side of the Marshall Plan, for such an action had never before been tried on such a large international scale. At the same time, many Americans would have been delighted never to have to come to the rescue again.

Both sides forget the effort made. The famous Friendship Train which went from one coast of America to another collecting spontaneous offerings of anonymous American citizens has been forgotten. The activities of CARE are virtually ignored. It is a mistake to underestimate or malign American generosity and goodwill, for the Ameircan does not like to be deceived or to be taken for a "sucker."

Santayana affirmed:

> If it is given to me to look into the depths of a man's heart, and I did not find goodwill at the bottom, I should say without any hesitation, you are not an American. But as the American is an individualist his goodwill is not officious. His instinct is to think well of everybody, and to wish everybody well, but in a spirit of rough comradeship, expecting every man to stand on his own legs and to be helpful in his turn. When he has given his neighbor a chance he thinks he has done enough for him; but he thinks it an absolute duty to do that.[9]

General Marshall's commencement speech at Harvard can be read in that context.

While the New World rightly and successfully stepped in to redress the economic balance of the Old, it was still not enough to avoid the Russian bear who had already begun to put his paw into the electoral honey urns of a dissatisfied Europe. The long road back from military demobilization began in April, 1949, with the signing of the North Atlantic Treaty in Washington. Now Americans are told that they must persevere, that their defenses must be ever stronger, and they wonder as they watch the callow-khakied youth striding on the Champs Elysées, Piccadilly, or Kurfurstendam, or the streets of Vietnam, how they defend America compared with the tough unshaven GI's in their jeeps. Did the United States act like imperialists in the economic and political recovery of Europe, as the Communists allege? Did Americans follow the traditional divide-and-conquer role of the imperialists? America sought a new and virtually unknown unity for Europe, a Europe with increased economic and political strength.

When Americans take an overall look at their European-American economic and military situation since World War II, they can justly say that they have done well. After having stumbled badly and lost most of central Europe to Russia's grip during and immediately after the War at least they have held on to what was left and strengthened it. The Red banners have now become faded in Europe and the industrial and technical kickoff has been a great success. Whether they shall "roll back the curtain" (curtains should be raised, or parted) remains to be seen.

The Marshall Plan showed the advantages of economic cooperation, but the mounting cold war shifted its emphasis to more military support within the NATO framework. With the opening of the Korean War in June, 1950, the United States began to foresee the need for German rearmament, which worried France and some other European countries. The French argued for a unified army under a European Defense Community, a treaty for which was signed in Paris in May, 1952. However, the French Assembly refused to ratify the treaty in August, 1954, and as a substitute the Brussels Pact was revised into the Western European Union to allay French fears of German miltarism, adding Britain and Germany as signatories and creating an inner circle for NATO. The year 1953 marked a definite change in the international climate. European economics were rapidly expanding (the number of automobiles more than doubled in the fifties, not including scooters) and reconstruction was almost completed. The Russians exploded the hydrogen bomb, the Korean War ended in stalemate, Stalin died, and Eisenhower became the first military president since Grant. Russia and the United States began peaceful coexistence through a balance of terror.

With Dulles as the shield of the republic and McCarthyism rampant on a bar sinister of hate and mistrust of things and persons, Europe began to pull away from America, feeling its own oats instead of American ones. From 1953 on there was a European trend toward conservatism and a weakening of the Left. The opening of the Suez crisis in November, 1956, indicated another break away from America. Then when de Gaulle became president in November, 1958, he began actively to cement Franco-German entente and to create a separate nuclear striking force. The decade of the fifties saw the creation of the Coal and Steel Community (1951), Euratom (1958), and the Common Market (1959). The early sixties witnessed efforts at the integration of the Outer Seven within the Common Market and a closer economic integration with the United States in a wide liberal trade area. In spite of setbacks, this integration will probably be completed. With America's economic and military situation reasonably relieved Americans should not doubt that sooner or later they may expect a closer political integration, the first two leading naturally to the third.

Where, however, is America's cultural and intellectual contact? "In spite of the contacts, the differences between Europe and America are increasing; America is more American than it was some years ago, when it could be considered as a daughter of the old European continent who had not yet attained her majority," said André Siegfried.[10] Kafka's *Amerika* concluded that the America of the future would travel a different road from Europe. Despite the foreshortening of time and space and the conquest of leagues of ocean barriers, one may justly wonder if Siegfried and Kafka are right. For a long time Americans have had a relatively solid knowledge of the political, economic, and military relation between Europe and America. What they do not know are the qualities of various national tempers and characteristics, which are the traditional grains running through social life in international relations. Europeans and American myths and symbols, often but not always indicators of national temper, are used for different ends and purposes—and in a different context—when carried across the Atlantic. This is neither startling nor new, as Tocqueville noted, but it is too often ignored by scholars and other interpreters on both sides of the water.

Despite the efforts of American official information services (or perhaps in spite of), Americans still suffer from too many *malentendus,* sometimes petty and irritating, sometimes important and irritating. Their cultural telegrams get garbled by official lines of communication. The effect of the European information services in the United States is hardly felt and realized, and the American information services in Europe, while composed of earnestly dedicated people with the best intentions (as those Europeans in the States), produce mediocre results and are hamstrung by a parsimonious Congress at home. Services are restricted or closed down in Europe because there is no danger of a revolution or a Communist takeover as elsewhere, and the lines of communication are thinned out. The American Information Service, once McCarthy-soiled, is timorous of parochial criticism and unable to make clear the American "message," if the message is to communicate beyond platitudes and moral preaching.

Worst of all for the long run, official information services present the "favorable image" to dazzle the unsuspecting foreigner, but the foreigner is neither dumb or blind and knows perfectly well the black spots as well as the bright ones. What is given in official handouts will be balanced against his own newspapers and reviews. The official image, moreover, tends to tell people what Americans think of themselves, rather than what might be interesting or useful to the minds and feelings of others. For example, the pat illustrations, written or pictured—"biggest," "highest," "most powerful," "fastest," "cleanest," "strongest"—make no difference to those who prefer "most cultured," "best tasting," "most discreet," "most agreeable," or "most soothing." Moreover, information offices can, like chameleons, turn into censorship offices simply by gilding or gliding over the facts, even gelding them.

It is a pity that the argument has turned for the most part on communism versus capitalism, for the idea of classic capitalism is abhorrent to many and nobody is ready to die for capitalism in Europe, Africa, Asia, or even America. The point is that America has transcended capitalism, reforming it into a new economic humanism which is just beginning and which may take a century for full development. The hopes of Europeans and others can be aroused by an idea of the final outcome of this development. Some European intellectuals have grasped this, but certainly the mass of Europeans do not have the slightest idea. Communism has likewise changed in historical development; the mask it wears now shows a different complexion.

America should boost its candlepower to brighten its picture; it could also make an effort to understand Europe, at least in general outlines. Europeans complain that Americans do not understand their mentality or their problems and are ignorant of their history. It is silly to confuse Switzerland with Sweden, Geneva with Genoa, to think all Swiss are watchmakers and yodelers, all French are perfumed lovers, and all Scots penny pinchers. But then, Europeans likewise tend to think of Americans as rich and oversexed, and confuse Idaho with Ohio.

The American Algeresque success story is represented simply as a success, success as the opposite of failure, and therefore empirically right, right in itself morally and psychologically. Americans should not lose sight of the fact that many noble causes have been noble failures and are also worth respect. Americans point with pride to their unique and successful experience and are hurt when others are either unimpressed or fail to imitate—"the sincerest form of flattery." The "bitch-goddess" success is not sufficient in itself to carry the moral message.

Sherwood Anderson wrote in *Windy McPherson's Son* that Sam was rich and succeeded materially, but failed spiritually. Americans seem to think that all the world is Midwestern and bourgeois at heart, thinking basically the same and wanting basically the same. This is partially true and wholly false. It is ridiculous to think that communism could be checked by distributing Sears Roebuck catalogs in all the troubled areas of the world.

"You are advancing in the night, bearing torches toward which mankind would be glad to turn," says Maritain, "but you leave them enveloped in the fog of a merely experimental approach and a mere practical conceptualization, with no universal ideas to communicate. For lack of an adequate ideology, your lights cannot be seen." [11] The American beacon does shine brightly, but more brightly for some than for others.

On July 4, 1962, in an impressive speech at Independence Hall, Philadelphia, President Kennedy recalled the uniting of the thirteen American colonies in liberty as a model for a new declaration of interdependence between Europe and the United States. Stating that since World War II American policy had been to encourage a strong and united Europe, the United States would welcome the New Europe as a partner in a true Atlantic community. Without trying to foresee a final political structure, for a united Europe cannot be built overnight, he said, "the greatest works of our nation's founders lay not in documents and declarations, but in creative, determined action. The building of the new house of Europe has followed the same practical purposeful course. Building the Atlantic partnership now will not be easily or cheaply finished." In a declaration of American policy, President Kennedy stated:

> I will say here and now, on this day of Independence, that the United States will be ready for a declaration of interdependence, that we will be prepared to discuss with a united Europe the ways and means of forming a concrete Atlantic partnership, a mutually beneficial partnership between the new union emerging in Europe and the old American union founded here 175 years ago.

It should be noted that he spoke of a partnership, not a confederation. Paraphrasing the Preamble to the American Constitution, President Kennedy noted the necessity for a strong Atlantic community, for the United States cannot alone establish justice throughout the world, assure its tranquility, provide for its common defense, or secure the blessings of liberty to ourselves and to prosperity. "But joined with other free nations, we can do all this and more," in aiding the underdeveloped countries, expanding trade and commerce, and establishing world law. The Atlantic partnership would not be a "rich man's club," would not look inward or be restrictive, but would look outward and would serve as a nucleus for all free nations. Kennedy added that he was not thinking of a "grand design" with all goals decided on and new institutions already on the drawing boards.

London, Bonn, Rome, and other European capitals except Paris enthusiastically supported the speech. *Il Messaggero* termed it "historic," and the London *Times* editorialized that it was "an imaginative idea, typical of his sense of style and history. . . . There are those in Europe who feel a need to escape from dependence upon the United States. To them President Kennedy was saying that America would not try to crab the scheme but would seek a genuine partnership, based on growing responsibility."

After more than two decades of effort toward European and Atlantic community, it remains to be seen whether an inward-looking "little Europe" of the six nations or a larger, stronger, outward-looking Europe of at least thirteen nations will prevail. To the critics of the "Atlantic Colossus" (with Europe only a satellite of the United States), common sense would indicate that the more European countries thrown into the balance of European community, the more weight could be brought to countervail the fears of American predominance.

From a purely economic point of view, a narrower and limited Europe is predicated on the economic situation of today with markets largely absorbed. If we consider a constant rate of European economic expansion at the prevailing five or six per cent of the gross national product, we shall easily see that the future of the European community must be outward-looking, seeking new markets in a wider free-trade area, including the United States and members of the British Commonwealth, Latin America, and the emerging countries of Asia and Africa. American economists have not been afraid to say that such a large step forward is entirely possible, and the vistas of a cornucopia of world peace and plenty can be envisaged.

America's coming back to Europe *en masse* for the second time in World War II had upset the balance of power. The Marshall Plan and NATO, both American inspired, tried to restore an equilibrium, but the balance passed outside of Europe during the cold war to Russia and America. John F. Kennedy's thoughts on interdependence might usefully be reviewed today.

NOTES

1. André Siegfried, *America at Mid-Century* (New York: Harcourt, Brace & World, Inc., 1955), pp. 45–46.

2. Arthur H. Vandenberg, Jr. (ed.), *The Private Papers of Senator Vandenberg* (Boston: Houghton Mifflin Company, 1952), pp. 9, 11.

3. Charles de Gaulle, *Mémoires de Guerre. L'Unité: 1942–1944* (Paris: Librairie Plon, 1956), p. 80.

4. Edmund Wilson, *Europe Without Baedeker* (New York: Noonday Press, 1966), p. 178.

5. *The New York Times,* November 14, 1948.

6. Vandenberg, p. 30.

7. Cited in Luigi Barzini, Jr., *Americans Are Alone in the World* (New York: Random House, Inc., 1953), p. 201.

8. *Ibid.,* pp. 117–18.

9. George Santayana, *Character and Opinion in the United States* (New York: Doubleday & Company, Inc., 1956), p. 97.

10. Siegfried, p. v.

11. Jacques Maritain, *Reflections on America* (New York: Charles Scribner's Sons, 1958), p. 116.

⌒ THE ATLANTIC CURRENT ⌒

Thy way is in the sea,
and thy path in the great waters,
and thy footsteps are not known.

—Psalm 77

American cultural and intellectual prestige might be upgraded in Europe, perhaps more by Europeans themselves than by Americans. The European problem in the true understanding of America is to have enough elasticity of mind to be able to embrace all the inherent contradictions of the American cultural pattern. Many wonder if there is actually an American cultural pattern. Many wonder if there is actually an American civilization or if American culture is simply an extension of the European. It is both at the same time. The Greeks asked the same of Rome. Cato scourged the Romans for becoming Hellenized instead of keeping simple, Roman, republican virtues, much as some Americans scorn their other compatriots for being "un-American." An Englishman can live a lifetime in Venice or Rapallo without being less English. An American preferring to live in London or Paris for six months or longer becomes un-American, an expatriate—both negative, both unvirtuous.

France suffers an Athenian complex self-consciously aware of its intellectual preeminence. The French are assured of their intellectualism by the generations of scholars and artists who have flocked to Paris seeking creative liberation. Paris has its Parnassians, its Olympia, Odéon, Latin Quarter, and academies. In France the intellectual is the leader who may only incidentally be in politics. The French are rightly annoyed when they are judged by their kitchens, bathrooms, and nude revues, when they would prefer to be judged by their artistic and literary refinement. The French enjoy their Art of Living. The Americans have their Way of Life.

England suffered a psychological shock when it realized that it no longer had to assume the white man's burden, that the "burden" was wanting to move along under the steam of its own assumptions. For a cruel time after the Second World War, Britain not only was no longer the world's banker, but gave every aspect of being one of the world's paupers. *Pax Britannica* was being replaced by a *Pax Americana,* and there was no place for two Romes. If Paris were the new Athens, London had been the new Rome, with White-hall architecture there to prove it. Gone are Britain's Gibbons and Kiplings, its legions and viceroys. The colonial administrator is no longer the hard-shell representative of the Crown, but the underpaid technician advising local authority, no twentieth-century Warren Hastings.

Britain regards the American as the young nephew who developed a successful business enterprise abroad and married a woman of mixed nation-ality and uncertain social background, not sure whether she was an Irish maid, a Polish seamstress, or a German farmer's daughter. Just the same, the boy has English blood in his veins! The English question whether the American Way of Life can be attributed to superior virtue or simply better luck in being able to exploit a vast virgin continent. Since their revolution, Americans have always questioned Britain's moral superiority. Americans have always criticized Britain's colonialism, Britain's British color line, its Albion diplomacy of divide and rule, or maintaining a balance of power. Having now turned over the wheel, the British now enjoy being backseat drivers. The British relished even the American difficulties assumed in the Near East: Greece, Turkey, Palestine, Egypt, Lebanon, Syria and finally Suez. The French relish the American Vietnam predicament.

Despite official floods of books, films, lectures, concerts, exhibits, and press handouts, Europe continues its own way much as before, while the real American impact is being made by the novelists, the soldiers, Holly-wood, tourists with cameras and tired feet and Kleenex. But is this cultural impact the true one? Proust, Gide, and Sartre no more represent a real pic-ture of French life than do Caldwell, Steinbeck, and Faulkner the American one. Is the European image of America formed by the tourist who demands ham and eggs, hot dogs, and apple-pie art? Jules Monnerot rightly sees that intercultural communication is a two-way street:

> I am very much afraid that although the Frenchman feels that the American should by all means supplement his sketchy knowledge of Europe, he does not think that he on his part should do the same in regard to America. He does not understand that the specifically French and the specifically American problems are inner problems belonging to the same level of a culture the main characteristic of which is pre-cisely its diversity.[1]

Allowing for the population increase, more than five times as many Americans travel abroad today as a century ago. We can only guess what the

American tourist brought with him as cultural baggage to barter in the European cultural fair. We can only wonder what the American with rolls of camera film brings past Ambrose lightship: Chanel No. 5, a cuckoo clock, a litho from a bookstall along the Seine? The picture of libidinous American undergraduate girls in moccasins and tartans bunched together in little coveys for protection against the wicked ways of evil Europe should not be elaborated, nor should chaste ears hear what Europeans say of them. At least their presence is a healthy sign, at least they are learning and seeing something, and at least they are being seen. Tourism can, however, backfire. Emerson wrote in his journal in 1848, "the facile American sheds his puritanism when he leaves Cape Cod, runs into all English and French vices with great zest," and doesn't stand for "any known thought or thing, which is very distasteful."

There is a wide difference between the traveler and the tourist; the former has practically vanished and the latter is omnipresent. Adam Smith's *Wealth of Nations* speaks of the valued English custom of sending youngsters to the Continent who return home "much improved." Hamlet quit Denmark to study abroad and got a good piece of travel advice from Polonius: "To thine own self be true." Christina of Sweden lived in Paris and died in Rome; Peter the Great modernized Russia as a result of his European travels; Arthur Young trotted all over France with the single-minded purpose of studying agriculture and roads, and was oblivious to the revolution breaking out all around him. As for the Adams family, Henry Adams wrote that all the success, he, his father, and grandfather achieved "was chiefly due to the field that Europe gave them." Yet his great-grandmother Abigail, otherwise intelligent, could write from London: "Do you know that European birds have not half the melody of ours? Nor is their fruit half so sweet, nor their flowers half so fragrant, nor their manners half so pure, nor their people half so virtuous; but keep this to yourself, or I shall be thought more than half deficient in understanding and taste." [2]

"Sight-seeing" entered the dictionary in 1847; the first continental Cook's tour was made in 1856, to be followed by trips to the United States and the Holy Land. American Express grew out of Wells Fargo; in 1895 it established its first European office, and it now has offices throughout the world. Travel agents have changed the style of traveling. Then, the old-fashioned traveler set his own pace and itinerary, used to employ a courier to precede him, and arrived to spend several weeks or months, studying architecture and galleries by use of the Baedeker and literary travel guides. He was armed with letters of introduction to local society, and was frequently well enough versed in at least one foreign language to enjoy its company. Now, the tourist buys a package tour of things someone else tells him he must see (Louvre, 25 min.; meet at main entrance for Versailles, 1 hr.; lunch, 20 min.). It is really the tourist who is "packaged" and neatly "personally conducted" with fifty other identical packages well wrapped with camera strings, airline kits, and binocular cords, all prepared for the "rewarding experience." There is no contact allowed with the "natives," for one might be "taken in," which does not mean what it should mean, that is, received hospitably; contact is only with the native guide, the multilingual hotel clerk, and the ticket collector. Four times as many people travel by air than by sea or land, and the tourist is again encapsulated from seascape or landscape; he arrives without the impression of having gone anywhere, and this impression is fortified by booking into identical grand hotels, making an immediate beeline into the bosom of Amexco, and running into countless compatriots, the "folks back home." No letters of introduction, only the green passport guaranteeing protection against chicaneries of foreign officials and civilians.

For "local color" the travel agent has arranged that the tourists see pre-fabricated folk-dancing in original native costumes, a "typical" Parisian or Roman nightclub with an international revue and an international clientele. It is little wonder that tourism, as contrasted with travel, has little effect on one's thinking or feeling. The tourist returns home with some strange mementos for the mantel and a box of photographic slides to test his memory of where he has been when showing them to the neighbors so unfortunate as to have only done the "all-inclusive" Easter trip to Washington, D. C., and who are waiting in impatient boredom to show *their* slides.

Cultural contacts can have disastrous effects, and it is not at all certain that international understanding can be brought about by cultural exchange, tourism, and other kinds of confrontation between peoples. It is not enough to know each other in order to like each other. Henry Adams said that if one wanted to meet and study the true American he should see him in Europe:

> Bored, patient, helpless; pathetically dependent on his wife and daughter, indulgent to excess; mostly a modest, decent, valuable citizen; the American was to be met at every railway station in Europe carefully explaining to every listener that the happiest day of his life would be the day he should land on the pier at New York. He was ashamed to be amused; his mind no longer answered to the stimulus of variety; he could not face a new thought. All his immense strength, his intense nervous energy, his keen analytic perceptions, were oriented in one direction, and he could not change it.[3]

But Arnold Bennett in *Your United States* praised the zeal of the American tourist shopkeeper from Milwaukee in the Uffizi as the most passionate pilgrim. Would the shopkeeper from Huddersfield or Amiens be there? It is more likely that he would be on a beach at Scarborough or Trouville, and if he went to Lucerne he would rank little lower than Columbus.

There is here a paradox in cultural communication. Often men seem to be more social at a distance. Direct contact can sometimes be unpleasant and is often a chief worry of diplomats over repeated face-to-face summit meetings of world leaders. Often the lapse of time between expression and reception, as in letter writing, can have the effect of making thought or an idea more possible. The rapid discoveries of the telegraph, telephone, wireless telegraph, wireless telephone, and radio-television may have a contrary effect for real communication, the contact and exchange of ideas, because reflective thought and reaction is not quick enough for the medium of communication. The result is a system of codes, something unintelligible, or the meaningless dashing of a note: "Having wonderful time, wish you were here."

International exchange of persons can have much the same effect as tourism: quick contact and little understanding. Washington Irving remarked in his *Sketchbook* how little he trusted the Englishman's impressions of America while he implictly believed all that Englishmen wrote about Tibet. Dickens noted on his visit to the United States about the same time that the English visitor in America displayed an 'insolent conceit and cool assumption of authority, quite monstrous to behold." The American tourist's attitude toward Europe may be as distorted. Cooper in his *Homeward Bound* wrote of Mr. Steadfast Dodge, the quick-traveling American tourist in Europe, that he "enjoyed a great advantage in his mode of travelling; for by entering a town in the evening, and quitting it only in the morning, he had a whole night to look about him." [4] Tocqueville wrote earlier that "an American leaves his country with a heart swollen with pride; on arriving in Europe he at once finds that we are not so engrossed by the United States and the great people which inhabits them as he had supposed, and this begins to annoy him."

Tourism and traveling have been advocated for their educational value and their promotion of good relations between peoples. Tourism can also be one of the most deadly engines for international prejudice. "The more nations help each other and the better they know each other, the more they hate each other," wrote Rémy de Gourmont.[5] Former German soldiers took great and unthinking delight in showing off their former residences in Holland or Norway to their new little *hausfrauen,* all to the great annoyance of the Dutch and Norwegian householders. The American dowager at Southampton's customs house firmly refused to join the line marked "Alien,"

just as the Englishman on a Rhine cruise overhearing the guide speak of
"foreigners," corrected him saying, "It's *you* who are the foreigners." Mark
Twain concluded on the return of the *Innocents Abroad:*

> We always took care to make it understood that we were American-
> Americans! When we found that a good many foreigners had hardly
> ever heard of America, and that a good many more knew it only as a
> barbarous province away off somewhere, that had lately been at war
> with somebody, we pitied the ignorance of the Old World, but abated
> no jot of our importance.

Instead of the rapid two-week grand tour arranged to the last minute
by Cook's, we should spend some time in a country trying to understand it,
and helping it to understand us. The American novelist Gertrude Atherton
was seeking local atmosphere in the town of Haworth, but sadly related:
"I never got inside the parsonage. The incumbent had been so exasperated
by tourists that he had conceived an unpriestly hatred of all Americans, and
vowed that not another should cross his threshold." [6] G. K. Chesterton in
his *What I Saw in America* began by saying that travel narrows the mind
and that one can better imagine a country in an armchair through books.
In 1792, Joel Barlow wrote a letter to the people of Piedmont saying that
even though he did not know them, and would probably never see their
country, nevertheless "I love you, and cherish the ties which ought to be
mutual between us," as fellow creatures.

A French lawyer thought American Negroes were kept on reservations
and were not permitted to learn English. It was hard to clear his confusion
with Indian land reservation policy. An American Air Force officer was asked
to Sunday lunch after church services by the local vicar, but his digestion
was upset when the vicar's wife asked, "I say, Lieutenant, do you have
chu*rr*ches in America too?" Edmund Wilson met an Englishman who had
been in America who thought that Vermont was a town in Florida, and
tells of an Oxford Don who thought Whitman a great South American
writer. There was a legend current that the long legs of American women
were the result of the prevalence of Negro blood. Wilson concluded:

> Thus an American of English stock, coming to England at a time
> when we are supposed working in close alliance, finds himself estranged
> from the English more than ever before. . . . We take a friendly
> interest in England, and we remember the past without rancor; we
> cannot understand to what lengths they go in order not to know
> about us.[7]

Cross-cultural communication becomes more perverse than ever. The Senate Committee on Foreign Relations reported in 1948 that "with all the good will in the world, the United States, unless trusted by ordinary people of Europe, cannot help them in their perplexity. They must first know and understand us then they will believe us," and went on to speak of the "false picture already existing in the mind of the average European."

Many more antennae must be kept out to capture each other's ideas and moods. Good feeling toward others does not automatically mean good understanding. Sometimes it seems that nations have a better idea of what their adversaries are up to than what their allies and friends are doing, usually because more trouble is taken to study and calculate their chessmate mores, motives, and machinations. Certainly more Japanese was learned in the United States during the War than at any other time.

On the balance, most would hold that the discovery of new worlds through travel renews men's minds. Descartes maintained, "Travelling is almost like conversing with men of other centuries." In any case, it stretches our imagination and makes us think more objectively, even to the point of bringing home disturbing new ideas.

"Don't lead the American to speak of Europe," said Tocqueville; "he will ordinarily show too great a presumption and a stupid enough pride." Trollope wrote that he did not know that the American as an individual was more "thin-skinned than an Englishman, but as the representative of a nation it may almost be said that he has no skin at all. Any touch comes at once upon the net-work of his nerves and puts in operation all his organs of feeling with the violence of a blow." [8] If the American is to meet and understand Europe, he must not be a first-class passenger insulated by travel agents and English-speaking personnel in first-class hotels. Let him learn the mysteries of the geyser, the *turque,* the *bidet,* the *vasistas.* Let him try the bouillabaisse, or the bubble and squeak, and then, if likes, leave it to the indigenous. In *A Tramp Abroad,* Mark Twain said that between fools and guidebooks it was possible to acquire enough ignorance in a day to last him for a year.

Travel must certainly somehow increase understanding between Europe and America, even if it is only rubbing shoulders. Many American eyes have been opened by the technical and agricultural advances of Europe, and many a European has been healthily enlarged by the vastness and complexity of the length and breadth of America. If he thought that America was irretrievably uniform and standardized, he might soon realize that about the only thing the Texan and the New Englander might have in common is a Coca-Cola bottle or a Chevrolet in the garage. He may find Southern-fried chicken in the North and Boston baked beans in the South, but it is unlikely that either tasted the same. "Travel is fatal to prejudice, and narrowminded- ness, and many of our people need it sorely on these accounts," wrote Mark Twain in *Europe and Elsewhere;* "Broad, wholesome, charitable views of men and things cannot be acquired by vegetating in one little corner of the earth all one's lifetime."

If the three-quarters of a million Americans who flood Europe each year do not have some cultural impact we should be surprised. Over 600,000 foreigners, not including those from Mexico and Canada, visit the United States each year. General Eisenhower designated each American tourist as an unofficial ambassador (roving emissary would have been better), and if the cultural exchange rate on the intellectual bourses of Europe may not be to the American's satisfaction, his own intellectual currency has not suffered any drastic devaluation.

Americans have rapidly become more cosmopolitan and have cultivated a taste which is not only for vintage wines. They may ask, walking a gang- plank in Bangkok, "What in the world are we doing here?" and then spend the rest of the afternoon in a Buddhist temple trying to find the answer to the question. For a European to have an American visa, he must swear before the American flag that he does not practice polygamy (it used to read bigamy) or harlotry, is not a dope addict or an alcoholic, does not belong to a subversive organization or plan to overthrow, singlehandedly, the govern- ment of the United States. Antiseptic and disinfected, he walks proudly out of the consul's office carrying an enormous sealed visa-packet in finger-print- stained hands. Recently, tourist visa requirements have been vastly reduced, and the Department of State said that 80 per cent of all tourist visas can now be issued in thirty minutes. But the government of the United States still spends less on tourist promotion than the government of the Bahamas. The main visitors to America have been government officials, businessmen with expense accounts, teachers, and students. The "Visit America Year" was an admitted flop. Once in America the Europeans feel estranged: no one wants to exchange his "foreign" money for "real" money. A French couple wishing to exchange francs in the Midwest were jailed for trying to pass phony currency.

What of the "Americanization" of Europe, of the penetration of mate- rialism and so-called low- and middle-brow culture since the War? Two elements have greatly speeded the process: mass media and the new con- sumer wealth in Europe, which brings in its train a materialist attitude and accommodates a mass-culture pattern. Europe becomes more and more like America, but America is getting less and less like Europe.

Edmund Wilson observed the American impact in England immediately after the close of the War, when Britain seemed to have become "rather neurotic" about Americans. At a time when Britain was crammed with U. S. soldiers and sailors, American slang and chewing gum were quickly picked up, particularly by the petit-bourgeois.

> Certainly this new lower middle class, which may be destined to absorb the others, supplies an eager and growing market for the worst—in movies, radio and journalism—that the United States has to send them. Our Hollywood stars are already their stars, our best-sellers their best-sellers. To an American, these signs of Americanization seem mostly stale and depressing. The British feed themselves on our banality without catching our excitement and gusto. Many of them now chew gum.[9]

To every thinking person's distress, it is only too often that in the rubbing of one culture against another the superficial material and decorative elements are most quickly taken up: beads and whiskey, the naked African in the top hat. Outer trappings and symbols are more quickly and easily acquired than deep cultural values.

Jazz, Coke, slot machines, Gable, and Monroe are omnipresent. But so are Loren and Lollobrigida! As Raymond Aron puts it,

> Suffice to say that European branches of your advertising firms, the European circulation of your mass-produced magazines, the taste acquired by millions of Europeans for your comics, your movies, your capsule-culture journalism and crime stories have quite sincerely frightened the European intelligentsia and have been taken by them as a threat to serious thinking and disinterested art. When they see the tin can replacing home cooking, Coca-Cola substituted for the noblest product of the soil (I mean, of course, wine), the taste-destroying refrigerator threatening the extinction of the earthen cellar, they grow properly alarmed.[10]

Perhaps Maritain can best answer his own compatriot:

> It is too easy for certain high brow Europeans with large bank accounts and delicious wines in their cellars to make fun of all the gadgets, bathtubs, refrigerators, dishwashers, washing machines, kitchen appliances, vacuum cleaners and so on, which everybody, so to speak—that is a very great number of the people on slender resources, the majority of the nation—enjoy here. The same Europeans hasten to buy the

gadgets in question as soon as they can. These gadgets serve, in actual fact, to make material life less overwhelming for common humanity, and to emancipate the human being from the servitude of matter in the midst of the chores of everyday life.[11]

Trollope had already noted a hundred years ago that "the great glory of the Americans is in their wondrous contrivances, in their patent remedies for the usually troublous operations of life," and was impressed by the elevator, steam heat (which he hated), and cold running water, soda-water bottles, Pullman sleeping cars, a ticket system for luggage, and the fact that nearly everyone carried watches.

The English expert of America, Sir Denis Brogan, said, "the ineluctable fact [is] that in the United States is to be seen the model modern progressive society—fluid, comparatively classless, technically enterprising, materially rewarding—that all the free world envies, copies, admires, and fears. *Odi et amo* is the reaction of all the old European societies to the sight of this dominant child." [12] The European wants to preserve what he cherished in his old culture, and while he is prepared to accept much of what is good in the newer American culture, he wants to filter out other influences regarded as evil or corrupting to the older civilization.

Standardizatioin and uniformity are often misunderstood. It is true that the materialist race for acquisition of things tends to drive out or overshadow the important nonmaterial aesthetic and intellectual interests which have constantly to be shored up, bolstered, and reenforced as they are always being ground down by mass media and materialism. It is too true that Americans are more concerned with things which are interest-bearing rather than with things interesting in themselves. However, dangers of standardization have been overrated because the same criterion which has been applied to machines is applied to human beings, and even more overstressed by those who look upon uniformity itself as bad and variety as good. Uniformity and variety are polar characteristics, neither in itself good or bad, and neither of which should be eliminated from the conduct of life. Standardization plays the same part in our social economy that habit plays in the human organism. Habit pushes below the human consciousness the recurrent elements of daily experience and frees the attention for the newer creative, unexpected, and personal experience.

We must obviously have some rational stability between desire and demand for the material product of our machine civilization. A harem may be necessary to the vanity of a sheik, but what sheik is well enough endowed to satisfy the needs of a harem? A plethora of material goods has no essential relation to what we seek in the good life of a civilized culture in a natural environment, which is neither machine-made nor the product of an assembly line.

America is no more responsible for mass culture than it is for capitalism, as Europeans often pretend. A simple look at mass cultures existing in the dictatorships of Communism and Fascism shows this. Boring Soviet realism and the *kitsch* of the Nazi are more insupportable than anything produced by television or Hollywood. The real cause is modern technology, and mass culture becomes universal as technological progress becomes universal. Europe often regards mass culture as the only culture in America; in reality it is more the relative importance that it assumes in American life that is open to criticism. The problem is one of the interpenetration of mass and high-brow culture where there is no clear hierarchy of intellectual values.

The American-European transit of mass culture quickens with each decade. The thirties saw the expansion of the film, of radio, and of aviation. Sound films were introduced in 1929, thirty years after the first silent film. With the passing of the great days of the early twenties, of the classic films of producers like Griffith, von Stroheim, and Eisenstein, the film industry became more and more the demon of mass media, churning out tasteless sex unsentimentally instead of being a taste-maker, a leader in cultural progress. Cecil B. DeMille set the mode with *Male and Female,* patterned after *The Admirable Crichton,* and others followed, such as *Flaming Youth, The Bedroom Window, Forbidden Fruit,* and *Passion Flame,* depicting people getting in and out of baths and beds, taking off and putting on clothes.

In 1930, eighty-five million Americans went to the cinema each week. American films were exported all over the world, creating a stronger and more different image of America than any other cultural medium. Today more than half of Hollywood's revenues come from the export of more than a thousand films produced each year. The majority of films shown in Europe are American, and more people abroad see American films than Americans do. The American Motion Picture Export Association tries with some success to present the better American films, and will even lend a hand to the State Department when a particular film might be useful. This was the case with the showing of *Ninotchka* during the Italian elections of 1948. There was also a one-hour show from Hollywood to raise funds for Italian orphans.

Films may not be as bad as they formerly were, but they are not as good either. The old films seem pathetically funny today since Hollywood glamorized vulgarity in their celluloid jungle. The Hays Office established the code of ethics for cinema-makers to live within rather than by. Breastlines and the length of a kiss were calculated with fine precision. The film and the cinema house itself set a standard of decor, glorified *art moderne* of swirling, bulbous, grandiose sham, keeping Grand Rapids busy shaming the interiors of millions of homes in imitating imitation Hollywood luxury. The style of Ravel and Debussy, debased, wonderfully suited the tremolo of the theater organ and the filmstrip. A whole world of nonmusic was "composed" to titillate but not be heard, to emote but without emotion itself. It was the apotheosis of "background" music, of music to do things by, of washing dishes or going to bed, not to "sleep or to dream." Distracted sensibilities were massaged with spasmodic gaiety.

If music suffers, so does book-writing. Many an author is ready for the insane asylum after "collaborating" in chopping up and manipulating his text into "script." Some commercially minded authors write with an eye peeled for prospective movie rights, rather than for publication and the critical esteem of their books. Others more honestly simply write books for direct translation into film. The upshot of it all comes out in the upside-down, inside-out publicity release: "You have seen the film, now read the book." Thus, we suppose, many people have been unexpectedly led to read the Bible according to King James rather than Cecil B. DeMille. A new paperback industry has sprung up of writing books out of popular films.

More than the press or the radio, the film projects and forms national stereotypes. Europe is only slowly beginning to realize that the Hollywood picture of America is deliberately distorted and that it is not simply heightened realism. Chicago is not necessarily the land of the sawed-off shotgun, the South composed of belles, Blacks, and barefeet, or the West of badlands, bawds, and badmen. Also, the strange formation in American minds of national stereotypes of Europeans has not easily been passed over: Monty Woolley bearded, English as "By Jove"; Charles Boyer, the Gallic lover with that ineffable accent; Rudolph Valentino, the swarthy Italian (although the turban confused the picture a bit); von Stroheim, the steely-eyed, head-shaven Junker officer; Greta Garbo, the cold unapproachable Swede from the North. Every European country is represented by a star, including Ireland and Spain. These stereotypes become fixed, and once fired are hard to change; to change them quickly requires a mass brainwashing.

In some ways it is now a happy thing that the film has met its challenge in television, for the film-makers are obliged to get back to making films of some artistic merit. Soon after the War, the Italian and the French showed the way with their realistic films, as did the Swedes; even the value of light English comedy was seen by Hollywood through such producer-actors as Alec Guinness and Tony Richardson. Rossellini and De Sica in Italy brought a new realism to the films by shooting outdoors instead of in studios, and by using amateur actors (because they had little film and little capital). Ingmar Bergman combined poetry and mysticism with stark realism, and French producer-directors such as Cluzot and Renoir intertwined pathos, gaiety, and sadness into their new films. David Susskind, writer and movie-TV producer, knowledgeably said that there was a new wave among movie-makers abroad, but that in America there was only a tired old ripple. It was impossible to make great films in the United States in the foreign manner, with taste, imagination, daring, fidelity to human truth. Foreign films do not exaggerate, are not extravagantly ugly or sweet; they are creative rather than merely artistic in a technical sense. Hollywood's standing in Europe (and in America) has never been so low. It is true that Hollywood is conducted as a business and not as a social trust, but European critics no longer write subtle essays on Hollywood producers or artists such as Chaplin. Hollywood's relation to European thought and culture is a curious thing, for few Americans or Europeans stop to think that probably a healthy (if not unhealthy) majority of the top stars and producers are of European origins. Independent American producers now are breaking the stranglehold of the mogul-run corporations and the star system. Europe saw the Hollywood dilemma earlier cut the Gordian knot, and adopted and refined the technique. Now television needs an overhaul.

The tin can and the TV dinner are already in Europe, and the European intellectual must learn to live with them just as his American *confrères* must learn. Neither can be like a William Morris trying to turn the clock back, bowling on the green, and doing folk dances around a maypole. Sadly, this happened to the once-cosmopolitan Vienna, now become a provincial city of zither and *heuriger,* no longer the great intellectual center of Stefan Zweig, Musil, Karl Kraus, Freud, Egon Friedell, Hoffmansthal, and Max Reinhardt.

Romanticism cannot be an alternative to industrial civilization. It must complement it. Romanticism should be the essential ingredient to humanize machine civilization and mass society. A great danger is the intellectual's retreat from society, a withdrawal into a schizophrenic *fichisme,* deliberately making himself difficult to understand and obscuring his thinking in "word-ology" or scientific jargon, a mysticism designed for the select few. There is much of this in Gertrude Stein, some in Eliot, almost all of the German and American sociologists, in abstract expressionism, and in much modern music. It is an effort to mystify or rarify culture to keep it alive in the midst of popular confusion and violence. Art for art's sake becomes abstract, secret, pure, absolute, and nonobjective. High culture is frequently difficult for many to accept simply because it reflects and reiterates the conflicts and problems of the contemporary scene, while people wish to escape from it. Mass culture offers the soothing, easy way out.

Instead of resorting to abstract or secret intellectualism, another reaction is to fall back into classicism, academicism, Alexandrianism. Professors find security in teaching accepted themes by rote: it is easier. Schools and colleges capsulize teaching into safe catchphrases, presliced and predigested for easy student consumption. Students get "credit" for regular absorption. Genuine cultural or aesthetic experience is too difficult in the face of mass culture.

Mass culture engenders an avant-garde culture, the setting up of intellectual bohemias on Left Banks or in Greenwich Villages. Bohemias emerged at the same time as the new scientific industrial technology, at the same time as mass culture. Murger's *Bohême* shows how necessary it is for the intellectual bohemian to live off bourgeois capital. It is an error to think that creative people work best when hungry and unhappy.

For better or for worse, and with much courage and suffering, the "engaged" intellectual is still to be seen in the marketplace. If there is a Barth, there is a Tillich, if a Heidegger, a Russell or a Sartre, even though their messages may seem confused and their thought misinterpreted. Their problem is that no art, ethic, or knowledge can withstand vulgarization. The writer for newspapers and mass-circulation magazines becomes as alienated from his work, rewritten and rearranged, as the industrial worker from his handiwork.

The intellectual malaise we see today should not incite despair but rather the hope that something creative will be produced out of the cultural flux. Gallons of tears were shed over *Werther*, but Goethe's was a great cultural epoch. Tocqueville wrote:

> [it] sometimes happens in the life of people that in a moment ancient customs and habits are destroyed and belief shattered. When reason is incomplete, political rights badly assured or restrained, men regard their country only in a doubtful light, and do not find themselves either in land, which has become in their eyes inanimate, or in their elders whom they look on as a yoke. They doubt religion and law, neither made by them nor in the legislator. They fear and mistrust the legislator. They can see nowhere, under one light or another, and they retire into a narrow and unreasonable egoism. They flee into prejudice without recognizing the empire of reason and they [are] stopped in the middle of confusion and misery.

Are not Tocqueville's thoughts a perfect description of French existentialists, the American beatniks, and the Angry Young Men in England? He continues, "In this century, where the destinies of the Christian world seem in suspense, some hurry to attack democracy like a powerful enemy, even though it continues to grow; others adore it like a new God coming from nowhere; but neither the one nor the other know but imperfetly the object of their hate or their desire, they fight in the shadows and hit wildly." These notes seem so contemporary, so close to our present situation that one wonders why a historical school of Tocqueville has not been established in the United States or Europe as with the Whig interpretation of history.

The facile but sterilizing charms of mass media with all its oversimplifications impose a terrifying totalitarianism, with millions "reading" *Reader's Digest* in many languages (twelve million in English alone), millions watching the same television program, or millions forming a single outlook on the world through a single weekly magazine. These powerful cultural agents operate against diversity and paralyze true individuality. Our democratic cultures on both sides of the Atlantic tend to become as homogenized as the French girl wearing an American girdle and the *Américaine* blithely perfuming herself with "My Sin." Mass public opinion is a constant danger to private thought.

American social discipline is applied to the world of ideas. André Siegfried writes,

> Thus the average American has a supreme belief in education, [while] more mature nations have realized that there are things which cannot be learned. The American has not had to be convinced, for it pleases him to think that industrial methods can be applied to the dissemination of thought [,] he appreciates canned science, science presented in the form of pills, simple ideas, prepared by the experts in an easily digestible form. This has given rise to a certain measure of intellectual laziness, further encouraged by motion pictures, radio, and television. The expert has thus become dangerously authoritative; critical facilities have diminished and are less easily exercised in a community whose organization on all sides swamp the individual.[13]

Tocqueville, as ever, shrewdly saw the danger of public reaction to private opinion, and he echoes Siegfried:

> Thought is an invisible and almost untouchable power which can be greater than all tyrannies. . . . I do not know of any country where there reigns, in general, less independence of mind and of real freedom of discussion than in America. . . . In America the majority traces a formidable circle around thought. Within those limits the writer is free, but woe be to him if he tries to step out of them! Not that he has to fear an auto-da-fé, but he becomes the butt of every sort of disgust and of daily persecutions.

He attacked the heavy weight of mass opinion: "The majority lives, then, in a perpetual adoration of itself[;] only foreigners or experience can put certain truths into American ears. If America does not have any great writers we don't have to look very far for the reason: no literary spirit can exist without a mental liberty, and there is no free spirit in America," and he adds that one can already see the bad effect on the national character of the Americans. This, of course, is an exaggeration, even considering the period in which he wrote, though it does point out the present danger. When Fenimore Cooper was in Europe, he felt this American characteristic strongly; "Europeans maintain that, in things, *innocent in themselves,* but which are closely connected with the independence of action and tastes of men, the American is less his own master than the inhabitant of this part of the world; and this is the fact I, for one, feel it necessary to concede to them."

John Adams thought that there were too many things to be accomplished by the young nation and believed that the writing of literature should be postponed for a generation or so. Martin Chuzzlewit is told in 1842, a decade after Tocqueville,

> I believe no satirist could breathe this air. If another Juvenal or Swift could rise up among us tomorrow, he would be hunted down. If you have any knowledge of our literature, and can give the name of any man American born and bred, who has anatomized our follies as a people, and not as this or that party; and has escaped the foulest and the most brutal slander, the most inveterate hatred and intolerant pursuit; it will be a strange name in my ears, believe me. In some cases I could name to you, where a native writer has ventured in the most harmless and good-humored illustrations of our vices and defects, it has been found necessary to announce, that in a second edition the passage has been expunged, or altered, or explained away, or patched into praise.

Even now George Santayana affirmed:

> what maintains [American] temperament and makes it national is social contagion or pressure—something immensely strong in democracies. The luckless American who is born a conservative, or who is drawn to poetic subtlety, pious retreats, or gay passions, nevertheless has the categorical excellence of work, growth, enterprise, reform, and prosperity dinned into his ears: every door is open in this direction and shut in the other; so that he either folds up his heart and withers in a corner—in remote paces you sometimes find such a solitary gaunt idealist—or else he flies to Oxford or Florence or Montmartre to save his soul—or perhaps not to save it.[14]

The danger of American democracy is that it always endeavors to expand a majority into unanimity; thus the constant drive to uniformity and consolidation. People are gregarious in their thinking and prefer social ideological agreement, just as cows all face the same direction while grazing on the hill.

The American collective spirit shows greater social rigidity as it becomes more and more crystallized, almost in the German corporate manner. This helps to explain the difficult absorption of minority groups in the United States. To succeed, racial and religious minorities must conform to the majority wish, blotting out as far as possible all differences. The Greek orthodox constantly proves his "Americanism," there is the "white" Negro, and Catholic Notre Dame University produced its "All-Americans" through the leadership of a Swede.

American sensitivities and sensibilities should not be too injured by European criticism of mass culture, which Europe also faces, but should understand the nature of this criticism in order to elevate mass culture and form it, and not suffer the high brow to descend to the lower or middle brow. Will people always turn to the poor or mediocre in mass culture? Perhaps much intellectual criticism reflects a snob attitude as reprehensible as mass man's antiintellectualism. How much do we really know of the social effect of radio and television? There has been much discussion, but very little of it is enlightening. It seems to have changed the social situation less than the invention of the automobile. Is television responsible for violence, crime, and sex, or the increase of any of these, any more than the rumble seat? It is as hard to prove as it is to deny.

The American standard of living is indisputably high, but have Americans questioned themselves if their standard of life is not going down? Intellectual activity is often regarded as useless time wasting, and even at times as disloyal. American intellectuals do not hang together; they tend to disorganization. Adlai Stevenson quipped, "Eggheads of the world, Unite; you have nothing to lose but your yolks!" Gilbert Seldes thought that the intellectuals could make a bargain with mass media to raise the level of mass culture. Dwight MacDonald fears a sellout if this is done, that *kitsch* takes out of high culture all its strategems and themes for its own purpose and throws away many inherent essentials—a parasitic tapeworm inside real culture. It is a grim view indeed of the cultural future if mass media are unchangeable and are incapable of reform.

T. S. Eliot and Ortega y Gasset would like to see an intellectual aristocratic control restored. The problem there is that the modern intelligentsia only partially corresponds to the old cultural elite. According to Ortega y Gasset, mass man no longer respects the values of the cultural elite, but sets up his own commonplace values. Low-level mass culture tends to block out all distinctions of class, and the old cultural barriers cannot be rebuilt. The cultural audience has been transformed by mass media. A century ago there was an elite audience with relatively high standards: few were literate, few bought books, few attended the theater or a symphony, and few traveled to urban centers. With the spread of literacy, more people read, but they understand less and are unable to assimilate critically. While the taste of the mass has been raised, the elite has been swallowed up and the intellectual standard lowered. The artist and the intellectual now work for the mass. The electrification of the arts has dimmed the cultural lights. There are few distinct cultural groups left, and even distinctions between age groups are blocked out. Adults are offered childish programs and children become prematurely adult. We even have baby talk in popular songs. Forty million comic books are sold each month in America, for about $100 million a year, or roughly four times the amount spent on public libraries. Some seventy million people read the comic strips in newspapers.

Popular culture has to be upgraded by intellectual leaders in all sectors to infuse the new culture with new values. Certain hopeful signs have been seen. There is, for example, educational television. There was the program "Omnibus," which was not accomplished without massive injections of money from Bell Telephone and the Ford Foundation. The Sloan Foundation financed "American Inventory." "Invitation to Learning" was known in broadcasting circles as the "Hour of Silence": unfortunately, when the cultural content of mass media is boosted, people listening simply turn off or switch the dial. Mass media canalizes existing attitudes rather than trying to create new ones. Interest is preserved rather than created. Radio-TV frequently degenerate into a mere time killer, hardly entertaining, hardly a cultural informer. The radio-TV waves will not advance human purposes if they are given over to gossip of scandal and the misdeeds of thugs, keyhole journalism, and fishbowl publicity. Americans need the three-minute break for the advertising of four-way pain killers for acid indigestion and headaches to give that "deep penetrating relief" from programs. Real cultural entertainment is not a narcotic, but stimulates and enlivens, makes us think and feel real emotions rather than emoting. Let us not deny the good in broadcasting. Television is the widow's window on the world. Almost every major city has a "good music" station, which leads the recording industry to cut a variety of music composed from the year One to only yesterday, and in a staggering quantity unimaginable only a few years ago.

Nor is it a question of the comparison of the quality of American versus European radio, or of nationalized versus independently owned radio-TV The BBC did not start its Third Programme until 1946, and continental programming has been based on the English pattern. Independent television in England now proves strong competition for the BBC, as does Radio-Luxembourg for the French and Belgian radio. (Incidentally, England now has more TV sets than bathtubs, but what sociological conclusion can be drawn from this?) The National Broadcasting Company gave Toscanini an orchestra with which to continue his great work, his personal orchestra until the very end of his life. The Metropolitan Opera has been broadcast for years, thanks to an oil company. Fifteen million people listen to it every Saturday afternoon. The National Broadcasting Company showed an hour and a half of the Sadler's Wells representation of Tchaikovsky's *Sleeping Beauty,* and the same company spent over a half-million dollars to televise Laurence Olivier's *Richard III* for three hours. According to *Trendex,* over fifty million persons saw a part of it, and half that number saw all of it.

Americans have invested over $25 billion in television sets and services, and today they are in 50 million homes and more than 1.5 million in public places. Advertisers spend more than $1.5 billion on television, surely an indication of great profit to industry in general, but particularly to television as a self-generator. Favorite programs at a prime listening hour easily attract 12 million people. Statistics involving people can bore, but think of the more than 6 million Jews exterminated as a "final solution," that is to say, 6 million individuals. The 50-megaton bomb of the Russians will rack up the same calculable numbers, which where before the twentieth century we would have been called *in*caculable. American television is now dominated by "ratings" of programs, and the competition is fierce between different networks. Happily, the advertisers have less to say over programming and the networks are trying to resume control. Newton N. Minow, former chairman of the American Federal Communications Commission, called television a "vast wasteland."

Television, it was thought, would be a great impetus to education, and universities are struggling to introduce closed-circuit programmed instruction. Foundations have done their best, but unfortunately the pattern was set too early, and besieged by too many compromises. The public may be interested in a popular program, but do they ask if it is in the public interest? We have worldwide television. What shall be done with it? Shall we show the cowboy films and the tear-jerkers? Half of the human race is still illiterate. Will television continue to cater to illiteracy or open another vista? What will the Western producers (Eastern as well) say to these people? International surveys have shown what one would already suspect: time spent listening to radio and TV is in inverse proportion to the amount of education a person has had. The same could be assumed for the relation of magazine-reading to book-reading.

Turn, however, to the mass-circulated magazines. *Life,* to take one instance, produced an excellent series on Western culture, great religions, paintings and architecture, even original writings of T. S. Eliot and Hemingway. The late *Saturday Evening Post* did an excellent series, "Adventures of the Mind," with outstanding contributors. Mass culture and its progenitor materialism are not bad in themselves, only in the manner of their production and reception. This is neither uniquely American nor uniquely European. Radio, television, magazines, properly handled and creatively used, can enlarge our learning capacities and refocus our cultural interest.

Nevertheless radio-TV and the phonograph tend to discourage active participation. Simply put, it is easier to twist a dial or put on a record than sing a song or play the piano. Unable to carry a tune, we take a transistor radio on the picnic. Listening to a panel-discussion program implies that others are doing the thinking and talking. Mass culture is effortless. The passive ease of radio-TV lets somebody else do all the work. Dime magazines provide us with armchair yachtsmen and hunters, gardeners and private detectives. The best way not to watch a particularly offensive TV program is to have the energy to get up and to turn it off. Mass culture provides amusement, while art gives pleasure through disturbance. Norman Rockwell is easier to understand than Matisse because he puts everything in to see: the ham-and-eggs art that Harry Truman likes and the socialist realism of the USSR. Art lives on the threshold of action, the catharsis of Aristotle's individual fulfillment. Schopenhauer said that music was the "world once more."

It was Hitler at the Nuremberg rallies who first realized the power to be wielded through the loudspeaker. Mass media can make the public conform to the economic and social status quo. There is no need now to use physical force to control; there is the hidden persuader which forces the unconditional surrender of the critical faculties. Khrushchev could assign his adversaries to minor posts, that is, oblivion, without having to liquidate them, and then justify his action through control of all mass media.

Moreover, people are not organized in masses, they are disorganized. The hidden persuader in the hands of the politician lines up the molecules, not individual persons. McCarthy knew how to use the press. Happily, it was also the harsh glare of television lights and the exposure of the press that brought him down, once one had the simple sense (courage?) to do it.

Certainly Franklin Roosevelt was able to exert a sort of direct democracy with the famous fireside chats. Mass society voted Roosevelt into power at the same time it voted Hitler into power. Their careers with their publics were curiously intertwined, and both disappeared from the world scene at the same time. A parallel study of how they led their collective societies by means of mass media might be very fruitful.

General de Gaulle holds regular television addresses as a way of by-passing the representatives of the people to reach the people themselves, just as railroads in the nineteenth century made such a direct democracy possible for Louis Napoleon on whistle-stop tours. Direct mass communication leads to mass reaction, in no way qualified as mass thinking. Thinking is a matter for the individual; individual thinking demands reflection, and reflection demands time, which the mass media deny by their rapidity of communication.

Strangely, our traditional freedoms of speech and press are limited by mass media. Newspaper and radio editors can blue-pencil a serious article because it does not have "news value," and an announcer can "sell" us on the false merits of soap that washes whiter or a toothpaste that stops bad breath. The United States has come a long way from 1925 when Secretary of Commerce Hoover said that the public would never allow "so great a possibility for service to be drowned in advertising chatter." Business sponsors mass communications, and is naturally concerned with profit-making and not alienating certain public sectors.

Mass media can also work in a different way. Freedom of speech has little meaning to those who do not have effective access to the principal means of collecting and disseminating information. The best the average citizen can do is to write an angry protest letter to the editor and usually the letter is concluded in such terms of frustration that others are not willing to read it. The individual can be heard in a town meeting, but the chief instruments of propaganda are not open to the average citizen. The "little" citizen can hardly afford to buy radio time, nor can he buy the *Washington Post* as Eugene Meyer did, or the Chicago *Sun* as Marshall Field did, to get his ideas across.

Forms of information are overcharged and swamped with too much information of a dubious sort. It is almost impossible to keep abreast with all the tintinnabulation of newspapers, magazines, radio-TV in order to play the important roles of forming our own ideas and usefully contributing to public opinion and thought. It simply cannot all be assimilated. Around seven thousand magazines are published today in the United States. At the turn of the century no magazine had a circulation of a million; now there are fifty with a circulation of over a million. *Life* and *McCall's* sell over six million copies, and *Reader's Digest* sells more than double that.

The mass media usher us into the Age of Consent. The mass audience becomes passively receptive, its critical outlook numbed in order to "buy" the product, whether it be soap or politician. The public must be amused, cajoled, excited, kept in a good mood. The public must be provided relief from the humdrum monotony of nine-to-five work, without making it unbearable to return to work. Whole sectors of the individual's personality are blocked out by mass communication; the intimate and warm life of private perception and private feelings are submerged. The public frontier of man's existence is expanded and his own private world narrowed.

Harold Laski takes a relatively optimistic long view of mass media:

> There is something in the psychological climate of America which resists any ultimate regimentation of behaviour or opinion. Something always escapes the net which is thrown about the people. . . . The enjoyment of dissent almost equals the enjoyment of conformity. It is aided by the restless zest for change which infects at some time almost all Americans.[15]

It is possible to break out of the propagandist's circles.

The beginnings of mass culture are to be found in Europe in Wagner, Eugène Sue, G. A. Henty, Offenbach, De Maupassant, and Victorian Gothic. The first bestseller was Abbé Prévost's *Manon Lescaut,* and if we look over the list of best sellers since World War I, we can see how few have stood the test of time, where other dark horses have persisted. Emma Bovary was perhaps the first to fall into the trap of mass culture. Influenced by too much "choice" fiction she found after all her emotional experiences that she was no calmer or more satisfied. The artificial impersonality of mass culture lowers the human relation, and the reaction to cultural emptiness is seen in violence, speed, sexuality.

Intellectual critics of mass culture often blame modern mass media because they think that art and life were synonymous in another age. Art was less important to the mass of people in the eighteenth or nineteenth century than it is today. In Plato's *Phaedrus* it was argued that the new arrival of writing would be bad for culture because it substituted reminiscence for thought and mechanical learning for discourse. Writing could lead to scholasticism and grammarians and glossators, and memorizing led to medieval academicism and encyclopedism. The invention of printing with movable type revolutionized two thousand years of manuscript culture and became the first of the mass media.

Only in the twentieth century has there been an immixture of popular folk culture with the culture of the elite. The mass culture of today tries to unite the two and produces a corruption of both in a formless middle-brow culture. Folk art and high-elite culture were separate; now high culture competes with mass culture and is constantly and parasitically raided by it to satisfy its voracious appetite. Either the cream of high culture is skimmed off the top, making the whole less valuable for further intellectual development, or the milk is condensed and the original creative flavor is lost. Dwight MacDonald has said that the screen between mass and high culture is so open that it is porous. Mass culture pervades everything because it is standardized and easily produced and exported everywhere. Mass culture is sicklied o'er with a pale cast of thought.

Our senses are battered and bruised by the constant stimulation of mass media. We become culturally hungrier as we are given less intellectual nourishment, faring on a cultural celluloid-thin diet. Mass media offer a snack bar for instant opinion precanned, low-calory capsule ideas vitamin enriched, already answered, and predigested. High culture invites after-dinner conversation and reflection.

A person can receive more stimuli than he can reasonably absorb. The new techniques of communication tear down all barriers, and there is nothing left to screen the individual from the penetrating eye of the TV, the chatter of the radio, or the jangle of the unwanted telephone call. A doctor can make you wait hours in his office before seeing you personally, but you can always telephone him; in fact, doctors are always "on call." The gain in rapid communication cancels itself out. As Bertrand Russell has shown, each improvement in traveling increases the distance over which we are obliged to move. Where we used to walk to the office in a half-hour, now we spend at least a half-hour in our car or on a subway, which is less healthy to say the least. The freedom from exertion gained through the development of mechanical services leads to the same physical paralysis as the mental paralysis arising from looking at television. Automobile riding constipates.

In *The Riddle of America,* Gugliemo Ferrero asked if the worship of materialism was not the greatest threat to Western culture and civilization since the Tartars and the Huns. If materialism be the desire for wealth and ease, it is in the nature of every man living or dead, not more American and less European. Europe is crammed with chateaux, schlosses, and palazzi, which are in turn crammed with works of art accumulated, plundered, and hoarded over the centuries. As Charles Dickens observed in his *American Notes,* "The golden calf they worship at Boston is a pigmy compared with the giant effigies set up in other parts of that vast counting-house which lies beyond the Atlantic; and the almighty dollar sinks into something comparatively insignificant, amidst a whole Pantheon of better gods."

Lewis Mumford has described the mania for having several television sets, radios, telephones, hi-fi's in the home. He shows that this is nothing new, but the expression of the materialist "country-house" culture to which the Renaissance gave rise, the best early descriptions of which were given by Boccaccio, Rabelais, and Marguerite of Navarre. It is the unproductive and uncreative drive for the acquisition of "things."

Yet Dickens said, "It would be well, there can be no doubt, for the American people as a whole, if they loved the Real less, and the Ideal somewhat more," [16] and wanted to see more lightness and gaiety; to him the American had a "dull and gloomy character." Americans pursue happiness doggedly but happiness is not necessarily pleasure, nor is pleasure necessarily real joy. Without this realization, Americans often give the impression of being sad and restlessly impatient. Europeans do with less and have related their lives with greater happiness and peace of mind. This is more easily felt than described, particularly when different material essences or characteristics are compared, for it is easier to portray an idea than a sentiment.

If Americans are "materialists," then England is a "nation of shopkeepers," and neither can compare with the thriftiness of the French peasant and bourgeois classes. Tocqueville said that the first of all social distinctions in America is money, but added that the preeminence of wealth in a society was less fatal for equality than the prejudices of birth and profession, for wealth was in the reach of all. Still, the ostentation of wealth was offensive to him:

> It is paraded in America much more impudently than with us; talent, merit, which in France decidedly outweigh it when the two are in competition, are here obliged to give place to it. . . . In France, intellectual pleasures and gifts of the mind have always been held in high esteem. In America, in absence of all material and external distinctions, wealth appeared as the natural test to measure man's merit. Besides, the Americans are a people with very little feeling for the pleasures of the mind.

In every worthwhile culture art should be made for life, and not the other way around as the aesthetes would have it. The problem for art and culture in an industrial democracy is that it has to be spread wide and deep and not kept under glass cases in private drawing rooms. A lively culture for today cannot avoid the marketplace; indeed it belongs there, where ideas may be freely hawked with other goods in the hurly-burly. It is a truism that great cultures and great artists depend upon business: for example, commercial Athens, the bankers of the Renaissance, the imperial plundering of Victorian England. Economy, efficiency, and invention are not the exclusive province of business or industry, but are the basic norms for art itself.

There is no necessary conflict between the arts and business. What American or European scholar or artist has not benefited directly or indirectly from such businessmen as Rockefeller, Ford, Carnegie, Harkness, or Guggenheim? Great universities have been founded on oil, tobacco, and railroads. Industrial democracy is bound to produce mass culture and materialism, and it is bound to develop in Europe as it has in America. "For, in the first place," as Maritain has said, "they are in no way specifically American, exactly the same symptoms, in relation to similar sociological or psychological areas leap to the eye everywhere (especially in Europe) where the industrial regime prevails and its congenial ideological forces are prevalent. . . ." [17]

How obvious it is that our Atlantic cultural relation is based completely on trade for its sustenance, but the businessman and the intellectual ignore this basic fact and tend to go their separate ways. It has already been indicated that wealth is necessary to the creation and continuance of any culture, whether it be supplied by the medieval church, Renaissance princes, national kings, landed aristocrats and bourgeois city dwellers or financial or industrial capitalists. Atlantic trade links up and binds the cultural ties and provides the reservoir of capital and communications necessary to the continuing strength of the cultural relation. Business directly or indirectly pays the professor, the artist, and the writer, and it would be well for the former to recognize its greater responsibility to the latter, as well as for the intellectual to give more than grudging acknowledgment to the businessman who supports him. In the long run, art for art's sake does not succeed when divorced from society, nor can the businessman "get down to business" only. Great philanthropists earlier recognized this and great corporations on both sides of the water are now devoting more and more of their profits to the business of culture, not only under the spur of corporate tax deductions, but also acknowledging that aside from good public relations, it actually helps business. *All* the profits from Denmark's two greatest breweries are channeled into two great foundations, the one sponsoring scientific research, and the other artistic, social, and cultural endeavors. The two largest foundations in England and America stem from the automobile industry. Oil and steel, the basis of modern industrial society, have been responsible for at least two great American foundations.

With the exception of the monastery, which produced an essentially static and priestly culture, and the troubador-jongleur culture of knightly castles, cities have been historically responsible for our cultural life. Cities are the home of the bourgeois trader and businessman, and the trade routes between cities, whether by land or by water, have also traditionally been the trade routes of culture. We owe our alphabet to Phonecian merchants traversing the Mediterranean, and our system of numeric symbols to Arab traders.

It is easy to trace the spread of the Renaissance from the northern Italian commercial cities by trade routes into southern Germany, France, and the Low Countries, and finally into Jacobean and Elizabethan England. Europe's creation of commercially profitable empires in the New World led Western civilization there. Had it not been so, Londoners and Parisians would be even more astonished at Americans than they are today, for the American tourist at Picadilly or on the Champs Elysées would most likely be wearing feathers, buckskin, and beads, and his wampum would be worth about as much as the cultural baggage he brought with him.

Atlantic culture moves along with trade. Columbus was leading a scientific expedition, but he and his sponsors were hardheaded and business-like in seeking primarily the wealth of the Indies by an easier, cheaper route, less hazardous than those subject to Venetian and Arab monopolies and depredations. His was as much a business venture as a scientific adventure. The Bible and *Pilgrim's Progress* went along in the Conestoga wagons, open-ing new trade routes through the wilderness of the Western frontier, along which also rode the itinerant preacher and teacher, dancing master and lim-nist. With the trappings of Western culture went also its techniques, carried by emigrant thinkers, potters, glassmakers, architects. Expanding trade was commercially and technically beneficial on both sides of the Atlantic cause-way. Cotton, for example. The cotton culture of the Southern plantations could hardly have met the challenge of the spinning jennies without the subsequent American invention of the cotton gin, and both eventually en-abled Britain to put calico on the backs of countless Hindus. The British-American connection in the cotton trade was more than a soulless commercial operation. Sons of wealthy plantation owners were frequently educated in England, and younger sons of English cotton brokers were often assigned to American agents for training.

Other commercial, industrial, trading, and labor relations across the Atlantic could easily be enumerated. The warp and woof of Lombard and Wall Streets have been woven into a tight fabric which cannot be cut along strictly national lines, just as the academic world, as it is aptly called, is a real, forceful, and living community of scholars with mutual Atlantic inter-ests. Business and cultural prosperity, intertwined, affect us all on both sides of the Atlantic.

Business might take a new look at its cultural spawn and define its relation to contemporary cultural output, in particular the ends it seeks to cultivate. For over a hundred years, but even more vitally in the present switch from industrial to technological revolution, everybody has complained that business and "art" are out of balance, the one trying to denigrate the other, the first as crass and the second as effete, the one usefully necessary, the other unpractical and asocial. Businessmen who have considered their lasting contribution to society have realized that their machines wear out, their automobiles go out of style; in short, they plan for obsolescence, knowing that their wares are temporary and are bound to be replaced with something better, improved, or at least different, because of the competition to meet the consumer's changing wants and desires. Their "research and development" branches are constantly occupied with this. Does business continue the same train of thought to its conclusion, namely, seeking out that contribution which can be made to society which *is* permanent? The answer is simply that art is long and life is short.

A classic never dies: few people wonder or need to know anything about Homer the man, nor is it important that perhaps Shakespeare did not write his plays after all. The business world has begun to feel its longer-reaching role and the importance of helping shape the society of the future. Not only are corporations sending their junior executives back to schools for advanced training, but they are establishing their own schools and research institutes, sometimes even on campuses in order to utilize university facilities. Other business organizations help provide educational opportunities for children of employees. Some companies provide in-service training of employees by transfer to subsidiary companies abroad for certain periods, and for employees of subsidiary companies to come in exchange to the home office. One worldwide corporation has even set up an institute for its clients to attend in order to learn the maximum potentialities of its product. Many organizations have achieved prestige and renown by investing more heavily than would be absolutely necessary to house their companies in exciting new buildings designed by outstanding architects, that, aside from creating obvious goodwill, contibute lastingly and importantly to the cultural and aesthetic life of a city.

All these things help to extend the cultural effect of business. It does not necessarily create culture itself. Business can be more aware of the indirect contribution it may make to culture. Sometimes business does create aesthetic art forms, particularly in the wide fields of industrial design and industrial architecture; more often it can contribute effectively to artistic activity. Many corporations buy painters' and sculptors' works for their offices; others maintain a continuing program in publicity and advertising of presenting works of art, and occasionally we even see bits of poetry. Radio-TV, in itself "big" business, provides a medium for drama and music. Yet large corporations have a heavy responsibility in this field for providing the best cultural offerings possible, avoiding the merely popular, the vulgar, and the violent. It is by no means proved that cheap soap operas sell any more soap than would ordinarily be bought, nor that grand opera might sell less.

Business sponsorship of culture should not be entered on the red side of the ledger. It is an asset. American operations are allowed tax deductions up to five per cent for cultural contributions, but, up to now, only one per cent has been claimed. European governments do not permit such deductions at all. One prominent American manufacturer has sponsored so much French culture in America that he has earned international recognition, is known as the number one friend of France, and has been made Grand Officer of the Legion of Honor. Needless to say, his sales are not hurt. Where medieval guilds once sponsored the morality plays, the modern corporation underwrites theater productions, symphonies, and art shows. Businessmen make up the majority on boards of directors of colleges and universities, museums and symphonies. Their roles as trustees of our cultural institutions should be fulfilled by transcending their everyday point of view. Trustees often think of museums, symphonies, and universities as business enterprises, which they are to some extent, but their more important functions and purposes are far removed from production, profit, and payrolls. They deal, or are supposed to deal, with the fundamental intangibles in preserving and extending our various cultures, while business deals with tangible immediates. Both have their roles in our lives, the one nourishing our minds, the other our bodies.

Too often trustees look for museum curators or college presidents who have the same qualities they like to see in themselves: business acumen, administrative ability, charm, money-raising prowess, the solid citizen of club, church, and chamber of commerce. It is a happy occasion indeed to find a curator or college administrator who is also scholarly humanist able to lead and inspire his research specialists and professors, informed of and able to cope with their more special problems. Businessmen-trustees *cum* civic leaders are enormously conservative and would no more gamble on controversial art or thought than a bank president would take a long shot on a loan to launch a new invention. Our cultural centers thrive on controversy and the clash of minds; radical professors, boisterous students full of life and latent energies, controversial, thought-provoking books in libraries, all provide that necessary stimulus to new and creative work; yet, these three elements are most feared by trustees. They must play the safe side to avoid publicity and to have the comforting pat of public approval. Thus a winning football team for alma mater is more warmly regarded than a piece of brilliant research, and the coach is rewarded with three times the salary of the professor. We can be pleased that much is done by business for culture, but we can also regret that much that is done is done without business understanding exactly what it is doing for culture. This is particularly so for our transatlantic cultural exchange.

The largest corporations are almost all transatlantic corporations with offices and heavy investments abroad, with top management working in many European languages. Yet only a handful of these corporations appears interested enough to establish transatlantic educational and cultural programs, while others work only on a national basis. The businessman is international-minded only when he is doing business. When business is concluded, he snaps his briefcase closed and heads for home. It might be worthwhile for him to examine with his Atlantic partner what can be collectively done for our Atlantic culture, for there are any number of things which could be done individually or collectively to fit each corporate purse.

The traveller has become the tourist. Cultural diversity and private thought are swamped in a morass of mass media. High culture is raided by mass culture in both America and Europe. Businesses, foundations, universities may help to encourage a diversity of high culture within the unity of the Atlantic world.

NOTES

1. James Burnham (ed.), *What Europe Thinks of America* (New York: The John Day Company, Inc., 1953), p. 6.

2. Letter to Mrs. Shaw, November 21, 1786. Cited in Rahv, p. 52.

3. Adams, *The Education of Henry Adams,* pp. 297–98.

4. Cooper, *Homeward Bound,* p. 447.

5. Cited in Peyre, p. 168.

6. Cited in Heindel, p. 44.

7. Edmund Wilson, p. 30.

8. Anthony Trollope, p. 507.

9. Edmund Wilson, p. 17.

10. Galentière, pp. 24–25.

11. Maritain, p. 90.

12. Franz M. Joseph (ed.), *As Others See Us: The United States through Foreign Eyes* (Princeton: Princeton University Press, 1959), p. 24.

13. Siegfried, p. 116.

14. Santayana, p. 96.

15. Laski, pp. 622–23.

16. Dickens, pp. 245–46.

17. Maritain, p. 32.

ᴄᴀ HIGH TIDE ʙᴏ

Truly there is a tide in the affairs of men,
but there is no gulf stream setting forever in one
direction.

—J. R. Lowell

The questions that Americans and Europeans should pose together are not ones of power politics, production, or publicity, but deep moral and intellectual questions. Rather than the publicist and the politician shouting shibboleths, we need the poet and the philosopher to meditate and measure, to give us some idea of how far we have come and the general direction of our path to the future.

Maritain sees a wholly new America emerging, going beyond and transcending industrial capitalism, and bypassing socialism, where a pragmatic, vital, completely unsystematic pressure is imposed by the American people on the structure of modern industrial civilization, transforming from within the internal dynamism and the historical tendencies of industrial society. Similarly, André Siegfried saw an American civilization distinguishing itself more and more from traditional European civilization, and, being preeminent, making the whole world feel it.

Our contemporary civilization of the West is surely new; perhaps it is like America itself. Europe may look on it as the transition to a new and different epoch—a new Hellenistic age? a new renaissance? a new technological industrial revolution?—in any case, hardly tranquil times, but times of change and readjustment.

Public order is frequently disturbed; there is a search for new moral values, more relevant to our times, times where worried conservatives take to book-burnings and purges, roasting Brunos, making Galileos recant, Luddites breaking machines, unions resisting automation, and scientists and professors taking loyalty oaths. Out of it all we may expect to see a vastly different society than that envisaged by Huxley, Orwell, or Waugh, whose fantasies were, after all, based on the spectacle of the breakdown of the old order rather than on the genesis of the new. We are challenged to shape the Brave New World, rather than be idle spectators to the haphazard Topsy-like growth of an order which may not be to our taste, liking, or spirit. America and Europe together can provide that vital spark to enflame a bright new system.

If we can keep our European and American cultural patterns well sorted out, with lines as distinctly traced as possible, we can hope for an expanding and healthy interaction which can sharpen and illuminate new ideas on both Atlantic shores. A constant cultural push-pull between America and Europe can provide the useful stimulation of both within our Hellenistic-type civilization. This challenge and response will give us the vigor to bring about a new cultural renaissance based on a modern and progressive technological democracy.

The Italian writer Piovene wrote in *What Europe Thinks of America,*

> America is endowed with the elements of an original civilization, which must not only enrich but transform us. Because these elements have not yet all been revealed and brought to fulfillment, we can ourselves help them to flower. . . . Union with American civilization should give Europe a breath of air and a feeling of roominess which it does not possess today. . . . And this is a hope for Europe, when intelligent energy abounds but is imprisoned in an accumulation of the irrational.[1]

America and Europe, needing each other, should continue to differ and be different from each other. In one small area, European culture presents an immense variety in contrast to the monolithic culture of the Continental Unites States. The American genius has established an amazing technocracy; American inventiveness is good at gadgeteering, absorbing, tinkering with, and improving new and fundamental ideas. Over half the Nobel Prizes in original science have gone to Americans since the War and there has been a gratifying number of Nobel Prizes in literature as well, plus thirteen Nobel Prizes for peace. Europe has customarily shown itself as the generating plant of basic ideas and philosophies and of reflecting on the consequence of human and social beliefs once launched. Europeans continue to exemplify the widest variety of differences in ideas and are the most avid in exploring the ultimate reaches of experience, in achieving the maximum of self-awareness, and then accepting or rejecting what they find.

Bryce compared Europe with America in this way:

> Life in America is in most ways pleasanter, easier, simpler than in Europe; it floats on a sense of happiness like that of a radiant summer morning. But life in one of the great European centres is capable of an intensity, a richness blended of many elements, which has not yet

been reached in America. There are more problems in Europe calling for a solution; there are more passions in the struggles that rage round them; the past more frequently kindles the present in a glow of imaginative light. In whichever country of Europe one dwells, one feels that the other countries are near, that the fortunes of their peoples are bound up with the fortunes of one's own, that ideas are shooting to and fro between them.

If the heart of Europe stops beating, all the universities, libraries, and galleries in America could not replace that kind of creativity which is European.

Europeans are frightened themselves that they may lose this specific creativity or that it will be stifled by American culture. This is surely the major source of friction and irritation between America and Europe and produces the sometimes ferociously inimical attitude of Europeans that makes an active and effective working partnership so difficult at times. Together, America and Europe can make a dynamic team and can show the world that we are not some dying or practically extinct cultural volcanoes, an Atlantis sinking into the sea of time. Many of the cultural differences between Europe and America are valuable ones and should at all costs be preserved, if only as differences; others can be mutually acquired and thus disappear as differences, while still others which are ridiculously obsolete should be consigned to the junk heap forthwith.

The conditions for collective work and research in America are great, and great results have been achieved in those domains of knowledge where one scholar cannot possibly absorb all the "data" necessary. Teams of scholars and batteries of computing machines have advanced some fields of knowledge so rapidly that the humanist philosopher is terrified by the problem of interpreting. As the Queen told Alice, you have to run just to keep up. Under these conditions, says André Siegfried,

> The critical spirit, individual by nature, diminishes in importance in relation to the practice of collective output; culture as such, with all that it means of the personal, tends to be eclipsed by technique and by the prestige of gadgets. A civilization more and more directed toward the realization of the collective type follows, in which the individual, acting alone, thinking alone, is reduced to impuissance: the mass-man takes over from the anarchic individual. . . .[2]

Inasmuch as it is the businessman who keeps the wheel turning in America, the scholar emulates him with office hours, telephones, appointments, all aimed at efficiency, haste, and productivity, whereas leisure is the most important requirement for the maturing of ideas. The young scholar literally needs to "fool around," and some are lucky with Guggenheims and Fulbrights, but generally the young Ph.D. is forced into the race for literary production to assure academic advancement, at the same time shouldering what is offensively called a "teaching load." The wrenching of young doctoral candidates through their studies is perhaps good, but they then need time to learn through leisure rather than the frenetic productivity required to climb academic hills. The scholar's duty is to suggest new ideas and imaginative solutions to our fagged brains, dulled by the narcotic of unceasing toil. In 1884, James Russell Lowell was defending the necessity of a leisure class to preserve culture in a democracy. Poor Lowell would be astounded to see the pressures built up now. The nine-to-five straitjacket of business and university life can restrict individual intellectual freedom as much as bell and book in a monastery. We might recall that "leisure" comes from the Greek word meaning "school." The contemplative mind had always been associated with a suspicion of aristocratic intentions which run counter to America democratic pretensions. Americans prefer as idols Franklin or Jackson, Eli Whitney or S. F. B. Morse, Edison or Bell, Grant, Theodore Roosevelt or Ford rather than Jefferson and Madison, Hawthorne and Melville, J. R. Lowell and Henry Adams, Wilson and Adlai Stevenson.

Perhaps the creative individual is better off in Europe, where he can do his long, lonely work with obstinate tenacity, not knowing whether the result will be worth the trouble. Such an intellectual isolation is not particularly welcome in the American community of academic bonhomie. There is the moral force of the majority idea of democracy applied to·intelligence, that there is more light and wisdom in many men reunited than in a single man, about which Tocqueville said, "this doctrine attacks the pride of man in his last asylum." Individual creativeness is just as necessary to a lively and vigorous culture as team or group research. The two *can* exist together, not as a case of the halt leading the blind, but rather of each going side by side and hand in hand.

Will America gird herself to meet the challenge and transcend it into a new stage of intellectual style? Often it seems that every resistance to European culture is hailed as another declaration of independence. Yet borrowing from one culture to enrich another can be effected in two ways; the discreet adaptation into another soil of those cultural ideals and values which may usefully create and stimulate a newer intellectual foliage, or the wholesale transplanting of root and branch into an ill-prepared alien soil. It is the difference between the bee going after the pollen and the beekeeper looting the honeycombs. Herbert Spencer told Americans in 1882 that while Americans possessed an unparalleled fortune in natural resources and had profited by inheriting all the arts and methods of Europe while leaving behind the obstructions, "if along with your material progress there went an equal progress of higher kind, there would remain nothing to be wished." He averred that while nobody could say how things would work out, the United States would have many troubles, but would eventually triumph over them as in the past: "I think that whatever difficulties they may have to surmount, and whatever tribulations they may have to pass through, the Americans may reasonably look forward to a time when they will have produced a civilization grander than any the world has known." [3]

Europe may try to understand the American spirit, which is undoubtedly setting the pattern of the future. Europe cannot, like Lot's wife, look backward. Both shores are not only fully engaged to each other, but fully committed by conjugal bonds. While the wedlock may not be holy, divorce is unthinkable. We are no longer living on cultural islands between which the only communication is by messages in bottles thrown into an ocean with the hope that they will wash on another shore. Like the Mediterranean of ancient times, the Atlantic must become a vast interior lake embracing our common and historic Western civilization. It is true that the center of gravity has changed and that Europe is no longer the fulcrum in the balance of power. If there is any balance of power left, it is in the frightful atomic arsenals outside Europe. This fact dictates a radical change in European ways of looking at things, a change in 2,500 years of conditioned thinking of Europe alone as the center of the world. The "stupid" nineteenth century has given way to the scientifically irrational twentieth. A European change of attitudes means that without too much difficulty Europeans can raise their eyes to the larger horizon of Atlantic integration with few basic assumptions altered:

> Every mass is a peece of the *Continent,* as part of the
> *maine;* if a clod bee washed away by the *Sea, Europe*
> is the lesse, as well as if a *Promentorie* were, as well as
> if a *Mannor* of thy friends or if *thine owne* were;
> any mans *death* diminishes me, because I
> am involved in *Mankinde;* and therefore never send
> to know for whom the *bell* tolls; It tolls for thee.

The transatlantic relation should not be based on a false sentimentality. Nothing is more disgusting than a trumped-up emotion. Let us agree with Stephen Potter when he wrote: "Anglo-American Relation." This chilling phrase is more piercingly destructive of Anglo-American relations than any other spine in the whole prickly pear." [4] Do-gooders on both sides of the

Atlantic try to swathe the sore spots in cotton and deny that there are any festers at all. A real sentiment should be restored to its freshness, truth, and effectiveness. Let us not have florid or hollow sentiments of the phrasemakers who only cloud difficult situations where a direct precise disagreement might be clarified and solved.

What makes American-European understanding difficult? We fail to comprehend the fundamental diversities of the two. Europe has three refrains; the Greco-Latin tradition represented by France and other Latin countries, the Nordic-Germanic of Luther, Kant, and Hegel, and the Anglo-Saxon of empiricism, pragmatism, and utilitarianism. These three strains remain basically separate because of language and customs, but there has always been a cultural interplay to provide a common intellectual life for all Europe.

France best represents the Greco-Latin tradition: it is Thomist and Cartesian, building systematic and rational systems, erecting philosophical edifices sometimes so logical that the tower collapses and the building has to begin anew. What appears to be disordered in the French system is that no one has found or can ever find that perfectly geometrical pattern which the French mind seeks. Thus there is no conventional agreement, and only a few standards are accepted. Pascal said, "All our dignity consists in thought." De Gaulle described the French as the "most mobile and least docile on the earth." Even at its most rebellious and revolutionary moments, French thinking is classical and critical. All students are trained in the critical system of *explication de texte,* and their classic writers are critics: Montaigne, Racine, Corneille, Molière, Voltaire. Rousseau's romanticism is but an antidote, for the French are fundamentally questioning, do not believe that man or his motives are fundamentally good per se, nor that this is the Leibnizian best of all possible worlds. It is constant criticism which refreshes and renews the French intellectual spirit and makes the French *mission civilisatrice* useful. The French go "beyond" national or ethnic thinking in search of a notion or idea valid for all mankind, and this has provided its attraction to all peoples of the earth. It helps explain the saying that everyone has two countries, his own and France, which is fine for everybody except the Frenchman, who is left with only his own to share with everybody else. Victor Hugo's France is a *beau spectacle à ravir la pensée.*

The French think that Americans always try to oversimplify a problem; the American thinks every situation a problem that admits of a solution. All

Frenchmen think of a problem as a situation, which calls not necessarily for a solution, but for clear perception and the hope of a gradual transformation effected more by time than by man. Perhaps this holds for Anglo-Saxons in general. Taine wrote: "An Englishman entering on life, finds to all great questions an answer ready-made. A Frenchman entering on life, finds to all great questions simply suggested doubts." Cartesianism seeks to make all nature bow to French reason. The French will fight ferociously for a principle *(furia francesca)*, where others would seek compromise and accommodation. The French Chamber is a *Tribune* for the exposition of doctrines where legislative work is done with much light and much heat, a conflict of ideas, where adversaries are not convinced but worn down. The President of the Assembly is not an umpire, but a calmer of intellectual passions trying to avoid brickbats. The serious work has already been done in advance in the corridors and committees (as in the United States). This fidelity to intellectual doctrines produces a myriad of strongly held views, and, as a result, compromise is difficult if not impossible. Difficult compromises lead to shifting cabinets, and where compromise is impossible, revolution. Strong individualism, points of honor, principles, all make social and political or any group cooperation difficult. All Gaul is divided, and only a highly developed sense of French manners and forms provide any unity. But if the French are fundamentally anarchical and undisciplined, at the same time they dislike disorder and are constantly sweeping the Augean stables. French intellectual love of abstraction, as De Madariaga said, "separates things thought to think of ideas of things rather things themselves." Unlike Anglo-Saxon "government" or German *Regierung,* France has *l'Administration*. American "administration" comes and goes every four years, French *administration* goes on forever. *Le Droit* is codified and neatly annotated, and any citizen can easily pick up a cheap edition of the particular code when he wants to find out where he stands with the law.

L'Etat stands outside and aloofly above the social system. The French do not cry "Vive l'Etat," but "Vive la République," "Vive la France," or "Vive la Révolution." The *régime* is official and does not stir the same emotions that the British monarchy does. The civic spirit is strong, but not in the cooperative American sense of "service." The French are masters of constitution-writing: the *Légiste* covers all the fine points in doctrine, and even codifies emotion *(crime passionnel,* and so on). Written laws and clear decrees are promulgated without any delusions about human nature, and, unlike England or America, there is no "benefit of doubt," for there is no "reason" for it. If it is not perfectly "clear," the subject should be further explored until it is—"Imperans non intendit persuadere, sed vim habit cogendi." To an Anglo-Saxon eye, the Frenchman may seem less moral, but this is not the case. The Frenchman has no illusions about himself either, and he rationalizes his own and others' actions rather than denying them or covering them up hypocritically. In America and England there is public virtue and private sin; in France it is almost the opposite. In a rational system there is always a place for the irrational, the area of which is delimited but is still acknowledged to be there.

Everything should be thought out beforehand, planned, categorized, theorized. Racine wrote to a friend, "I have finished my tragedy; nothing remains but to write it." The French place intellect before spontaneous or intuitive action. The Frenchman does not like to act before thinking about it, and if an unexpected event arises, he is physically upset. Linné, expatriate Swede, perhaps best shows the French love of ordering nature and classifying it. The French introduced the metric system, the only completely rational system of measurement in the world. The Americans only half-finished their revolution by adopting the decimal system for their coinage, but are still back in the Middle Ages with the English feet, yards, and miles, pints, quarts, and gallons, ounces, pounds, and tons. The English are worse with their stones, rods, and furlongs, florins, half-crowns, and guineas, English gallons and Imperial gallons. French engineering design is wonderfully good. Is it at all unusual that Descartes' greatest work should be on *La Méthode?*

Notions of order imply a strict sense of limits, of never overdoing a thing. Is this not seen in French notions of eating, drinking, and loving, in contrast to others? A *Faschung* is completely different from a carnival *Mardi-Gras.* "Mon verre n'est pas grand, mais je bois dans mon verre" is one of the most typically French expressions. "Colossal" or "super" is not in the French taste, which prefers *rien de trop.* The French rightly worry that they might be submerged in a new mass life not geared to their philosophy. The French do not like big beefsteaks without taste.

For the Frenchman, to know is to see. That was the intellectual vision of the Enlightenment. *La clarté* is the highest expression of French thought. Paris is *la ville lumière,* for luminosity is what the French seek, while obscurity and the shadows of darkness are to be avoided. In the *rayonnement* of French culture of the *mission civilisatrice,* the French see themselves as the torchbearers for the world. They are the genii of the lamp, the radioactive curious Curies. It is true that when ideas are abstracted by the French they become universal. Perhaps that is why the French seldom emigrate; like moths they like to flit about the light. *Le Roi Soleil* found that many others did too. The French have followed Pope John XII's address to them: "While ye have the light, believe in the light, that ye may be the children of light." In *Journeys Between Wars* John Dos Passos wrote:

They embody a stubborn, unfanatical, live-and-let-live habit of mind, a feeling in every man and woman of the worth of personal dignity that is, for better or worse, the unique contribution of Western Europe to the world. . . . It's easy to forget how central the French people are in everything we mean when we say Europe.[5]

∽⌒⌒⌒

While the mind has been primarily the concern of the French, Germans attempt to go beyond the mind alone. Germany is constantly searching its *geist*. Kant criticized pure reason. The Hegelian dialectic, while trying to impose a systematic pattern, winds up in mysticism and false spirituality. In trying to liberate the soul, a strict order must be placed upon the body, leading to an unfortunate split of the German personality. Kant's epistomology never bridged the gap between reality and reason; he provided the idealistic cloak to mask materialist aspirations, wherein any categorical imperative can be raised into universal law. Hegel's idealism taught that history is reason, and reason history. The rationale of history becomes really the actual. Historical determinism thus can be turned to justify national policy. Croce softly indicated, "the unifying force of liberal character was always, in this nation, somewhat rare and intermittent."

In writing of German discipline, André Siegfried said that in the philosophical style of the country of Kant, the state is transcendent: "It is not a question of community as in Anglo-Saxon democracies, but a distinct armature, functioning under experts respected for their competence, and the things they do are not the business of the people, who themselves, moreover, are persuaded of this." [6] During the Berlin uprisings of 1953, the Adenauer government came out with the astonishing statement that *Ruhe ist die erster Burgerflicht*. Neither Brecht nor Grass could commit themselves, although both felt moral pangs of conscience. With Hegel and Marx, with Germany, as well as the Russian system based on the German Marx, morality has no place in politics. If force is necessary to the collective rule, it will be used simply for what it is, with no holds barred, no qualms of conscience, and no excuse necessary. Much German thinking goes along the lines of *post hoc sed non propter hoc*. Luther held that the prince wielded the sword of God, and thus had absolute temporal rule. Prince, king, kaiser, and fuehrer have consequently had no quarrel with Luther. Fichte wrote:

finally, Virtue can be no object of the State. . . . [which] in its essential character of a compulsive power, calculates upon the absence of Good-will, and therefore upon the absence of virtue, and upon the

presence of Evil-will; it supplies the want of the former and represses
the outbreak of the latter by fear of punishment.

Treitschke's 1883 address at Darmstadt, "Luther and the German Nation,"
praised Luther for denying that the "spiritual power is higher than temporal
power" and asserting that "the State is itself ordained by God."

The direct influence of Kant, Fichte, Hegel (who assumed Fichte's chair
of philosophy at Berlin in 1818), and Marx on political and social thought
has been disastrous. For over a hundred years now, Marxians continue to
mime Marx: they come up with dross and are unable to push Marxian ideas,
not ideology, ahead one inch. But then a good Marxian is not supposed to
deviate. "There is an amazing similarity," wrote Oscar Cargill, "when the
verbiage of Fichte, Hegel, and Marx is analyzed, in their essentially German
conception of the word 'freedom.' Practically, it amounts to a spiritual inward delight in an outward powerful order which is completely repressive." [7]
Germans gave themselves up to Hitler because of their incapacity for individual action and their wish to be hierarchically organized. German bureaucracy was supinely followed and obeyed. In the postwar denazification trials,
the defendants (even Adolf Eichmann in Israel) pleaded that they were only
doing their duty by following orders from above. Those who were against
the regime yet did not flee the country made what the Germans call an
innere Emigration, blocking Nazi excesses from their minds in attempt to
protect the integrity of the soul. This *innere Emigration* has been continued
in the postwar years by a number of thoughtful young German writers known
as Gruppe 47, which holds the whole German nation and each individual
German as responsible for Nazism, not just the Nazis themselves.

German methodology in the physical world leads to wonders in science
and technology, as well as to the overordered life found in northern Europe.
Germany has never been paralyzed by great general strikes and should be the
despair of true Marxists who wish to show the power of the working class.
The working class rather aligns itself with the ruling political and economic
class. The German Trade Union building in Cologne is in every way as
luxurious as the capitalist towers of finance in Dusseldorf and Frankfurt.
The other side of the German coin, the spirit, leads to Goethe, Schiller,
Harder, Schelling, and the amazing intellectual flights of Nietzsche.

German thought is often poles apart from French thought. Voltaire was
uncomfortable at the Prussian court. The only way that Germany has been
able to storm the gates of Paris has been by force. Force had proclaimed the
German empire at Versailles. Weimar as a republic was a failure, and force
had again taken its place. The Treaty of Versailles was broken by force, and
force dictated a new surrender at Compiègne. French thought must be ex-

pressable, and expressed in form. Much German thought falls into formless intuition involving subjective "feeling" or *seele* and is cast out in vaguely pseudoscientific terminology; take *Gestalt* or *Weltanschauung*. German thought is supposed to be most profound when it is most obscure. This attitude has unfortunately been adopted by the American disciples of Max Weber and other German theorists.

The German finds words difficult to use to express his soul, finds it hard to exteriorize. His prose is heavy and overcharged, but his poetry and music sing. Here we can feel the German soul transcending and transcendent, as he feels it himself. Bayreuth is not only a Wagnerian spectacle, but also a spectacle of Germans watching Wagner. G. B. Shaw's *The Perfect Wagnerite* describes this emotion.

As a German journalist in the United States has written:

> In the mind of every German when he meditates in his country is a vision—a vision that has been variously called the "other," the "real," the "covert" Germany. It is the Platonic idea of Germany, waiting just below the unsatisfactory and dreary surface to be conjured up to the light: perfect, redeemed, cleansed of all stains of the past and present. This perfectionist vein shows time and again in my compatriots —now as disgust with politics, now as an exuberant chiliastic hope for the millenium. The world around senses this, and is afraid of it.[8]

The lack of interior controls makes German social life difficult, and order too easily accepted from above, or at least outside, the individual. A conscious awareness of this leads to a fundamental streak of pessimism in German breasts of *Schadenfreude* or of *Götterdämmerung*, of which Spengler is an example.

German democracy is not expressed in the Rights of Man, but rather through the rights of groups or corporations, as in the Middle Ages. As an individual, the German feels isolated; as a citizen or member of a group, he feels all powerful. The group is more than the sum of its parts. The Germans love parades, mass sport, huge, smoky beer halls, *Gemeinschaft*. Spengler liked the idea of a contented, reverent peasantry and an aristocratic army, both led by a strong leader. The history of individual liberty in Germany is a short one, conjuring up mainly 1848, while the tradition of oligarchy and militarism is deep seated. Hegel called the Prussian state "in an essential sense the work of God itself." "The State is the rational in itself and for itself. Its substantial unity is an absolute end in itself. To it belongs the supreme right in respect to individuals whose first duty is—just to be members of the State." The Wagnerian *leitmotiv* is repeated in every generation.

It is the Tristan story, the eternal quest, the eternal vision, the Faustian formula, the Holy Grail, the potion necessary for love.

Germans like to think of their government as something transcendent, sometimes divine; at least something outside themselves. Americans, on the other hand, look on their government as a necessary evil, often suspect ("throw the rascals out"), a homespun affair of committees appointed to take care of communal services, and strictly committed by the Constitution not to go beyond its instructions, although Americans will "take the law into their own hands" with posses, vigilante committees, minute men, and deputy sheriffs. The German official *(beampt)* is highly respected; the American official is tolerated, often held in contempt. German government achieves a high degree of efficiency, has "class" in its civil service; America achieves bureaucracy, no "class," and often much inefficiency. Fichte, who translated Machiavelli, gave a good idea of the state in its relation to *Kultur:* the state in its most perfect form becomes the seat of highest culture and promotes the great purpose of the human race.

Perhaps it is significant that Germany has had a very short existence as a nation united; its history is turbulent and with no fixed frontiers. For generations, hundreds of thousands of Germans lived outside its frontiers and great numbers of non-Germans lived within them. Today, Germany is again divided, and it may be that the real "German miracle" will not be the postwar economic boom, but an effective reintegration by democratic means of all the diverse *Gemeinschäften* that are traditionally held to be "Germany." The Germans think of a true Germanic *heimatland,* whether they live there or not, for it is primarily a place of the spirit, of the *Volk,* of a people's tradition, culture, and language. With no frontiers, Germany tends to be imperial-minded and to assert a presumed authority over Slavs and Latins to impose a "higher" German order. The story is not yet finished unless Germany (rather Germans) be fully satisfied that their *geist* can be transcended and integrated with the "higher" order of the Atlantic community. This is asking rather much of the most populous people of Europe when the French, British, Italians, Americans, and all other members of the community have not fully gone beyond their own particular nationalisms.

England compromises between the Greco-Latin and the Germanic tradition. Indeed, all English history and English thought have been successfully built on compromise, of "muddling through." English common sense is intuitive, a compromise between feeling and reason. In economics it is laissez faire, Adam Smith, and Bentham. A massive traditional philosophy has been constructed on the pragmatic basis from Hobbes and Locke through Bentham and Mill, the commonsense philosophy of Reid and the Scottish School, down to contemporary philosophers. The English like to be in constant touch with experience, and, like Americans, fear abstract ideas. A reporter asked an English general what his "general idea" was, and the reply was shot back, "Sir, I am an Englishman, I have no general ideas!" When the English say "that does not matter," it shows an unconcern with the immaterial. To an American it would mean more that it is "inconsequential." Scottish realism is popular (also in America) because it is a restatement of Locke against the skepticism of Hume; it is rational and its theology is comfortably orthodox.

The great monument of common law is pragmatic and utilitarian and is repeated nowhere else in Europe. Continental law is rigid, and makes nature bow to reason; all is set down in rules. *Recht, Diretto,* and *le Droit* have a different sense from English "law," as the terms indicate. English law is "common," and is organic and evolving. Perhaps it is significant that the English "read" law while the continentals "study" it. An Englishman "stands" for political office, while an American "runs" for it. The English constitution is so pragmatic that it has never been set down on paper. The English like to work by rule of thumb. Their cautious liberal politics are found in Burke, Macaulay, and Mill. It is also characteristic that the British national game of cricket seems to have no fixed rules and that the game never ends, except by the cover of nightfall. It seems also significant that the reigning monarch in the United Kingdom is at one and the same time the head of the Anglican Church in England and the head of the Presbyterian Church in Scotland. Neither the monarch nor the ecclesiastics nor the people of each country appear to have the slightest worry over the doctrinal or theological position involved. It has simply been found to be a convenient solution, well tested by time and experience. Henry Adams said that the English mind was "one-sided, systematically unsystematic, and logically illogical. The less one knows of it, the better."

Anthony Trollope tried to sum up the difference between England and America when he wrote:

> The political action of the States is undoubtedly the more logical and the clearer. That indeed of England is so illogical and so little clear that is would be quite impossible for any other nation to assume it, merely by resolving to do so. Whereas the political action of the States might be assumed by any nation tomorrow, and all its strength might be carried across the water in a few written rules as are the prescriptions of a physician or the regulations of an infirmary. With us the thing has

grown of habit, has been fostered by tradition, has crept up uncared for and in some parts unnoticed. It can be written in no book, can be described in no words, can be copied by no statesman, and I almost believe can be understood by no people but that to whose peculiar uses it has been adapted.[9]

The creation of the British Empire was said to be achieved in a fit of absence of mind, showing the pragmatic result: crown colonies, territories, protectorates, mandates, dominions, Indian Empire, and so forth, while France extended itself simply, logically, as *France d'outre-mer.*

British thought is alogical and elastic, unlike the French. The English are not sure enough that ideas are "true." They refrain from dogmatizing or building systems, and all opinion is therefore respected and tolerated. English closeness to practical reality makes their thought paradoxically vague, hedged with reservations, surrounding an expressed idea with, "I should rather think (never believe!) that . . ." which recalls Dickens' Circumlocution Office. English thought is like a spool of thread—it enumerates. French thought is like a series of broken straight lines—it composes out of vectors. English thought is irregular, ever changing position, a constant movement, because the English know that life is ever changing. France prefers an orderly life, but seeking perfection, has constantly to "tidy up" things, often by revolt. Taine, in 1864, compared the political fortunes of England and France: "England is made; she knows it, and they know it. Such as this country is, [it is more] capable than any other people in Europe of transforming itself without recasting, and of devoting itself to its future without renouncing its past."

The difference is easily seen in the free-flowing, natural, and romantic *jardin anglais* and the form-filling, restricted, carefully planned and tailored *jardin à la Française* of such landscape architects as Le Notre, which are formally structured, perpetually frozen in a mold of form and color, where trimmed boxwood and tailored chestnut have not been allowed to grow one inch in two hundred years, and geraniums are aways replaced without anyone's knowing the difference. While Frenchmen are crystalline, Englishmen are more organic. The English are closer to nature than anybody, and could probably beat all, hands down, in a bird-watching contest. The Englishman tends to let nature take its course, the Frenchman will classify and analyze it, and the American will play with its genes to speed it up and to make it bigger and brighter. The English are great gardeners and nature lovers. A look at the nature and garden pages of the English newspapers will easily indicate a higher degree of intelligent interest there than in any other country.

Another element is particularly vital to the English system, and has been transferred to North America, Australia, and New Zealand—no other countries have it, at least in the strict sense—fair play. Essentially it is applied not only in relation to other individuals, or in relation to one's partners in a match (sportive, political, social, economic) but, most important, in regard to the adversary. The loser is helped to his feet with a handshake and with the sincere expression that he fought a good fight. At the same time, the opposition is not always seeking to bring about the downfall of the government, as in France, but is a responsible constructive opposition, and much of the fight is carried on for the simple enjoyment of parry and thrust. Both sides will cheer a point well made. English debate is mostly good humored argument, spiced with much wit, passing the ball back and forth.

Fair play involves consideration for others in the social group, which eventually leads to social discipline and personal self-control. Liberty and authority are not contradictory notions, for both work congruously for the social whole; liberty is not anarchy and authority is not tyranny in the English temper. Is it not significant that an English mother admonishes with "Be a good boy!" while the French mother says "Sois raisonnable!" the German "Brave sind!" and the American "Behave yourself!" All show perceptive national attitudes. British fair play and gentlemanly action, instilled since childhood, lead to personal, self-conscious integrity. A man's word is his honor and is worth any number of contractual signatures. A distinguished Cambridge scientist was working during the War on a highly secret project similar to one on which the Americans were also working. An American brought to London the classified materials of the American project to discuss with the Englishman, but a day after his arrival he was ordered on another mission to North Africa. He excused himself to his British colleague, shoved all the papers into his hands, and said he would return for them when he could. The Cambridge professor hesitated to take the secret American papers, fearful of the responsibility, but the American left confidently, saying, "You're an Englishman, aren't you?" English word of honor, American trustfulness.

Eccentricity is an assertion of the individual will and of private action which spites the public face. Bowlers may be *de rigueur* in the city, but no one bothers turning around to see a toga in the Strand. An Englishman can walk in pouring rain with a closed umbrella. Emerson remarked on the "love of freak which the English delight to indulge, as if to signalize their commanding freedom." Elsewhere he said, "I know not where personal eccentricity is so freely allowed, and no man gives himself any concern with it." Finally, passion and love are a nuisance in Britain. Indeed, it has been intimated that England substitutes hot-water bottles for love. Of course, England has had its full share of Romanticism, typified best by Byron and Shelley, but it has been mostly an escape from the pragmatic position and was best practiced as an escape, as those two poets did, in the warm climates of Italy and Greece. Or as a Lawrence in Arabia. More to English form are Wordsworth and Tennyson who channelized passion into sentimentality. Typical English restraint denies impulsive action. G. K. Chesterton said that the Englishman takes his pleasures sadly (actually it was Froissart who first said it in the fourteenth century) and that the pleasure of despising foreigners he took most sadly of all. Hawthorne noted this and said that while the English valued the American regard toward them, they were "beset by a curious and inevitable infelicity, which compels them, as it were, to keep up what they seem to consider a wholesome bitterness of feeling between themselves and all other nationalities, especially that of America. They will never confess it; nevertheless, it is as essential a tonic to them as their bitter ale." [10]

Europeans fail to understand fully the basic traits of Americans because each of the three great European traditions looks at America from its own angle of vision, from its own origins, and viewed from its own national optic. In effect, America is not a country but a continent embracing all three basic strains. Admittedly, it has less of the Greco-Latin and more of the German-Anglo-Saxon, with the strong element of Puritanism thrown in for good measure. Henry Adams had closely observed the English mind in contact with other minds, especially the American, because:

> [the] limits and defects of the American mind were one of the favorite topics of the Europeans. From the old-world point of view, the American had no mind; he had a economic thinking-machine which could work only on a fixed line. The American mind exasperated the European as a buzz-saw might exasperate a pine forest. The English mind disliked the French mind beause it was antagonistic, unreasonable, perhaps hostile, but recognized it as at least a thought. The American mind was not a thought at all; it was a convention, superficial, narrow, and ignorant; a mere cutting instrument, practical, economical, sharp, and direct. [11]

The English, he concluded, hardly themselves conceived that their minds were sharp, economical, or direct, but what struck Adams was the tremendous waste in eccentricity: "Americans needed and used their whole energy, and applied it with close economy; but English society was eccentric by law and for the sake of eccentricity itself." [12] Fenimore Cooper contrasted the English and American types in much the same way and held that the English had greater independence in their personal characteristics and institutions, while the American had to follow common levels of usage and conform to public opinion.

America is Calvinist, neither Catholic nor Lutheran in mental spirit. The daily preoccupation with predestination, almost messianic, explains the drive to Algerism and the Americanism of the community of the elect. "Increase," in the most material sense, is a Calvinist synonym for benefit, and therefore morally good. Calvinist "abundance" is as much in the American code as it is in the Old Testament. America is the land of milk and honey. But man does not live by bread, even presliced, alone, and the optimistic materialism of America is accompanied by a spiritual nonconfidence. Worldly prosperity has been identified with virtue since the Reformation; in America, wealth is not only evidence of virtue, it *is* virtue. You do not seek the kingdom of God and have wealth added unto you; wealth *is* the kingdom of God. Tocqueville wrote that it was difficult for him to ascertain from the sermons of the American clergy whether the principal object of religion was eternal felicity or prosperity in the world. Americans look at life as if it were a greasy pole with all the prizes at the top. In the mad scramble for Algeresque success one can see the paradise all around, but it vanishes whenever one reaches out to have it for oneself.

In *The American Democracy*, Harold Laski, who had a "deep love" of America, and was a friend of Turner, Channing, Felix Frankfurter, Oliver Wendell Holmes, Louis Brandeis, the Beards, and Franklin Roosevelt, sketched that Puritan strain:

> It thus becomes tempting to argue that the American spirit, in its main outlines, has been until quite recent times the quintessence of a secularized puritanism. The regard for effort, the belief that success depends on it, the suspicion that failure is due to some defect of character, the justification of wealth as a stewardship the obligations of which the public may expect to see fulfilled, the dislike of radical doctrines as a social form of antinomianism, the fear of any ideas which may bring into jeopardy the unity of the commonwealth, all of these seem little more than an adaptation of the religious principles with which the seventeenth century was familiar.[13]

It is reflected in the lack of privacy, of the neighbor's right to know what the other is doing or thinking under threat of whispering campaigns or witch hunting—in sum, the difference between an American smoking car and an English railway carriage. Fenimore Cooper stated crisply: "There can be no doubt that society meddles much more with the private affairs of individuals, and affairs too, over which it properly has no control, in America than in Europe. . . . It is sheer *meddling,* and no casuistry can fitly give it any other name." [14] Puritans all, when aroused they start marching like Cromwell's New Model Army.

The pattern of conformism is likewise basically Calvinist, but Europeans forget the tremendous complexity and diversity of America. There is a centrifugal force constantly trying to shatter its unity, and only well-ingrained myths and traditions hold the vast continent together. America is all of Europe rolled into one, melted down, and recast with new added elements. Some even feel that the pot itself has melted. The uniform social veneer covers a dialectic of conformism and pluralism between federalism and democracy, of a classless social system also torn apart by rivalries between groups. Americans are sorted into "income groups" rather than classes. If Americans are uniformly conformist and basically conservative, it is hard to explain why one-third of the Americans change their residence each year. frequently change their jobs, their wives, their presidents and politicians, their cars, their movie stars and singers, their style. Americans cling to few things with a moral passion.

The restlessness of the American leads to constant experimenting; constantly on the move and more interested in the future than in the present, he is always ready to try something new. Distrustful of the past, he is wary of anything regarded as fixed, absolute, or permanent. The American "beatnik" writers such as Jack Kerouac and Allan Ginsberg express a fundamental American characteristic (which they would undoubtedly deny) in the readiness to hit the open road. The travel theme is reflected not only in the ubiquity of car-trailing "mobile homes" (four million of them), but in a deep strain of American literature itself, from Huck Finn down the Mississippi and the sea of Melville to the international travel of Henry James and the foot-plodding of Lena Grove in *Light in August,* walking from Alabama to Mississippi looking for her lover. Dos Passos' *U.S.A.* is a travel story which ends with the starving young man on the highway watching an airplane passing from New York to Hollywood. *Lolita* is constantly on the move from one motel to another.

America may be English in its cultural descent, but this descent has long since been transformed and permutated. Emerson could say in 1847 that England was the best of actual nations, and that the "American is only the continuation of the English genius into new conditions, more or less propitious," but by then German culture had already begun to make strong inroads in the formation of the American cultural pattern. The Scottish realism introduced by John Witherspoon of Princeton in the 1820's was replaced by a German philosophical idealism which could fall in with the New England transcendentalism of Bronson Alcott and William Torrey

Harris and which spread through the United States. The return of Ticknor and Everett from Göttingen marked the beginning of German cultural interest.

In 1815, George Ticknor at the age of twenty-three took the grand tour of England, France, Germany, Italy, and Spain. He managed to meet such outstanding intellectuals as Scott, Hazlitt, Lamb, Godwin, Talleyrand, Chateaubriand, Constant, Mme de Récamier, Goethe, Humboldt, Schlegel, and was even presented to the Pope. Mme de Staël told him that the Americans were the advance guard of the human race, and Byron told him that he wanted to visit the United States because he was interested in American literature and American universities. Ticknor so charmed Byron that he gave him an autographed copy of his poems, a letter of introduction to the Turkish Pasha, and a pistol to help him get around the Near East. He went to Göttingen with his friend Edward Everett, both under the influence of Mme de Staël's *De l'Allemagne*. While there, he wrote that even though he was having language difficulties and was cut off from many opportunities which the university offered, "the conviction was pressing upon me of the superiority of their instructions and modes of teaching." He confided his enthusiasm for German thought to Edward Channing, for

> that general metaphysical activity and acuteness, and that spirit of philosophical vehemence, which now distinguish Germany from all other nations, I mean that vehement exertion which is now making to have all sciences and knowedge reduced to philosophical systems, which is certainly doing wonders in some respects.

Ticknor returned to Boston in 1819 and established the first modern language studies at Harvard.

Ticknor and Everett were followed by the American intellectual pilgrimages of Bancroft, Motley, Longfellow, G. H. Calvert, J. G. Cogswell, and A. H. Everett. Herbert B. Adams returned from Heidelberg in 1876 with a doctorate *summa cum laude* to set up an historical seminar on the German model at Johns Hopkins. All his students were set to digging up Teutonic antecedents of local institutions and towns. From 1884 to 1900 he led American historical scholarship as secretary of the American Historical Association. Henry Adams introduced the German seminar method in his history courses at Harvard. The Modern Language Association avidly took up the *Quellen-Forschung* of Anglo-Saxon literature, and philology was encouraged by E. A. Freeman's "Race and Language" to go into Icelandic sagas and Sanskrit. E. A. Freeman had come to the United States in 1881 on a joint invitation from Johns Hopkins and the Lowell Institute to spread the

Teutonic gospel that Germany, England, and the United States were all one big family. Oscar Cargill wrote:

> The wolfish pursuit of moronic vocabularies and the goulish unearthing of the kenningsand pennings of the northern barbarians diverted young students from the true historical fount of wisdom—the Greek and Roman classics, which fell into the greatest disuse in Western History. There was treachery, alas, among the teachers of classics themselves. . . . American classical scholars turned away from the teaching of concepts to the venal study of syntax and word origins Before long there were no longer classical scholars in the old sense in America but only philologists, papyri readers, and robbers of tombs. On every front save that of history the triumph of *Kultur* over culture was complete.[15]

By the end of the nineteenth century, most philosophical posts in the universities went to men trained in Germany, the foremost of whom was Josiah Royce. Johns Hopkins University was founded to advance the new German scientific method. Heavy German immigration to American shores, particularly after 1848, accentuated the strong Teutonic influence. Popular American culture has consequently become basically German, as these influences filter through American thinking.

Between 1845 and 1860, over 1,250,000 German peasants streamed to the United States, usually by groups, and poured through the Erie Canal and the Great Lakes into Minnesota, Indiana, Michigan, Missouri, and Iowa. Two hundred thousand Germans arrived during the Civil War, and Anthony Trollope, among others, was astounded at the number of German regiments in the Union army, fiercely loyal to the Union cause. Cincinnati, Ohio, had a German population of 5 per cent in 1830, in 1840 it was 23 per cent, and in 1869, 34 per cent. Milwaukee and St. Louis became almost solidly German, with their beer halls, *Turnverein,* and *Gesängverein.* Some German leaders even called for the establishment of a wholly German state or states in Arkansas, Missouri, Illinois, and Wisconsin, but fortunately American institutions had been established there before the German influx. After 1870 the German immigrants were mainly industrial workers in contrast to the earlier agricultural workers, and they consequently established themselves in the urban-industrial areas. The peak of German immigration was hit in the early eighties but the flood continued until World War I. The Kaiser spoke openly of the loyalty of his German colonies in America.

From the 1840's and 1850's, German philosophy held sway as did German manners. American universities modeled themselves after the German and embraced German methodology as well. When Henry Adams went to teach at Harvard, he said that he "made use of his two lost years of German schooling to inflict their results on his students, and by a happy chance he was in the full tide of fashion." The Germans were crowning their emperor at Versailles, and James Bryce had discovered the Holy Roman Empire. Anthony Trollope noted that New York City was one-third German and that only Berlin and Vienna had a larger German population. He also felt that Germans made better citizens than the Irish. It is not surprising that the American GI felt more at home in Germany than in any other European country. U.S. soldiers quickly forgot their enemy and the ban on fraternization was often broken in favor of sororities. Americans and Germans share a common respect for efficiency and business sense, which is not particularly British. The dollar, let us remember, is a German word.

American intellectual life, its "highbrow" culture, is primarily French, and serious conversation eventually takes French thinking into account. There is a shared intellectual interest in the fate of the individual, and a critical sensibility against the mass pressures of industrial democracy. One can even hazard that the American intellectual's and artist's sympathies lie more with Paris than any other capital, including, at times, his own.

The cultural tie of America to England is still strong, partly because the two countries are separated by a common language, as G. B. Shaw witticized, but Franco-German inroads have been made on the intellectual temper of America, the French mainly highbrow intellectual and artistic, the German largely middlebrow academic and scientific. Americans can still largely agree with Richard Rush's statement regarding the depth of English culture in America in his *A Residence at the Court of London* written in 1883:

> Her fame is constantly before him. He hears of her statesmen, her orators, her scholars, her philosophers, her divines, her patriots. In the nursery he learns her ballads. Her poets train his imagination. Her language is his with its whole intellectual wishes, past and forever newly flowing; a tie, to use Burke's figure, light as air, and unseen; but stronger than links of iron.

Bryce has perhaps done better than others in trying to résumé the American intellectual characteristics. He set out ten points:

1. A desire to be abreast of the best thought and work of the world everywhere, to have every form of literature and art adequately represented, and excellent of its kind, so that America shall be felt to hold her own among the nations.

2. A fondness for bold and striking effects, a preference for large generalizations and theories which have an air of completeness.

3. An absence among the multitude of refined taste and a disposition to be attracted rather by general brilliance than by delicacy of workmanship; a want of mellowness and inadequate perception of the difference between first-rate work in a quiet style and mere flatness.

4. Little respect for canons or traditions accompanied by the notion that new conditions must necessarily produce new ideas.

5. An undervaluing of special knowledge or experience, except perhaps in the sphere of applied science and commerce, an idea that an able man can do one thing pretty much as well as another.

6. An admiration for literary or scientific eminence, an enthusiasm for anything that can be called genius with an over-readiness to discover it.

7. A love of intellectual novelties.

8. An intellectual impatience, and desire for quick and patent results.

9. An over-valuing of the judgments of the multitude, a disposition to judge by "success" work which has not been produced for the sake of success.

10. A tendency to mistake bigness for greatness.

Bryce's estimate remains, in the large, valid for today's America; there is much that is good and some which is bad, some which is true and some which is not wholly false, as with all generalizations.

America as a country is not easy to understand. Jennie Lee, prominent British Socialist wife of Aneurin Bevan, said after five visits to the United States that she despaired of getting "any coherent picture of America . . . and the more Americans explained America to me, the more blurred the picture became." America is more than the sum of its parts.

America is a continent better understood by Europeans as a people of peoples grouped into five or six distinct regions, which could themselves be almost considered nations. "We have so much country that we really have no country at all," Hawthorne wrote. H. G. Wells felt the confusion of many European visitors in trying to comprehend the United States when he compared himself to an ant crawling over the carcass of an elephant. As late as 1906 a French engineer, Georges Moreau, saw America disintegrating into myriad pieces. After a long stay in the United States, he wrote in his *Envers des Etats-Unis:*

Here we are at the end of our voyage. We have crossed the continent, looked at the peaks, examined Uncle Sam and we think we see him as he is: a big and very active man, menaced by alcoholism and the blood of the blacks, who will burst of plethora or succumb, still young, overcome by maladies of old age. We foresee the dismemberment of this great empire into several parts who will fight amongst themselves after the breakup and who will be compelled to pay the same military charges as the antique nations of the Old World. Europe will regard this wreck with an anxious eye and will sigh with relief, happy to see disappear the danger which had so long menaced it.

A decade earlier Bryce wondered the same thing: "No one can travel in the United States without asking himself whether this immense territory will remain united or be split up into a number of independent communities; whether, even if it remains united, diverse types of life and character will spring up within it. . . ."

The last half-century has shown that the opposite has taken place, that within the increasing complexity of the United States there has been an increasing uniformity. Laski brilliantly showed that American federalism can no longer maintain variety within unity, and a most recent serious example in legal and political philosophy (as well as social) has been the clash between Federal Constitutional civil rights and the doctrine of states' rights, particularly that of interposition.

America is Europe's child, resembling the parent, but a different person. Kafka wrote, "America is but Europe writ large and mechanized." As a nation of nations, a people of peoples, factional sectionalism and nullification were settled once and for all by the Civil War. Vastly uniform, America is coincidentally many-sided, pluralist, relativist, assymetric and unsystematic. American philosophy does not tend to system-building or doctrinaire rigidity, and shies away from speculative extremes. It produces rebels rather than revolutionaries. Where Russia provides a uniform direction and social cohesion by force, America achieves its unity by teamwork and by endless haggling between groups. Every foreign visitor to America is amazed that no sooner is a political election over than the politicking for a new one begins, a perpetual political mardi gras. American politics are like the politics of Walpole, comprised of factions, lobbies, groups, constantly conflicting and merging, constantly seeking a new consensus.

The new Atlantic world, beyond capitalism, opens vistas of hope through technology. Group research and individual creativity *may* exist side by side if they respect each other for what they are. There are differences also in life and thought between Europe and America and we should respect this,

but Europe might make an effort to understand Anglo-American pragmatism,
while England and America could stand a strong injection of classicism and
rationalism.

NOTES

1. Burnham, p. 113.

2. Siegfried, p. 352.

3. Cinted in Nevins, pp. 495–96.

4. Sephen Potter, *Potter on America* (New York: Random House, Inc., 1956),
p. 185.

5. John Dos Passos, *Journeys Between Wars* (New York: Harcourt, Brace &
World, Inc., 1938), p. 334.

6. André Siegfried, *L'Ame des Peuples* (Paris: Hachette, 1950), p. 100.

7. Cargill, p. 24.

8. Joseph, p. 116.

9. Anthony Trollope, pp. 204 ff.

10. Cited in Mowat, *Americans in England,* pp. 160–61.

11. Adams, *The Education of Henry Adams,* p. 181.

12. *Ibid.,* p. 183.

13. Laski, p. 42.

14. "National Differences." Cited in Rahv, p. 143.

15. Cargill, p. 521.

⌒ THE AMERICAN STREAM ∽

Row, brothers, row the stream runs fast,
The Rapids are near and the daylight's past.

—Thomas Moore

In the United States, individual self-sufficiency is regarded as technologically crude. The American has to work in a smoothly geared, closely articulated collective cooperation for maximum efficiency. The danger is that little provision has been made for the anarchic or isolated elements necessary to society. The absent-minded professor who forgets schedules and strips social gears is always good for an American laugh. The anarchic individual is coerced into "adjusting" himself. Adjustment in school is regarded as a good sign of the well-integrated individual. Perhaps man should rather adjust himself *against* a social situation; perhaps his taking the opposite direction from the herd may be the more fruitful one. This takes a certain amount of courage, rather than meekly accepting and harmonizing with a situation. Artistic or intellectual creation is not often made by adjustment to life or environment, but more frequently by insurgence and protest. All too often Americans tend to shirk personal responsibilities in favor of collective decisions.

In America the sphere of unanimity grows larger, and the moral unison which swells on the American scene is socially the most coercive. The off-note is unappreciated in the moral harmony, the off-beat is out of tempo. One wonders if the American theme should always be played at *moderato cantibile,* whether America is going to keep any creative drive without more syncopation. "We have thrown away the most valuable asset we have," Mark Twain wrote of his Americans, "the individual right to oppose both flag and country when he (just *he* by himself) believes them to be in the wrong. We have thrown it away; and with it all that was really respectable about that grotesque and laughable word, Patriotism." [1] One sees more and more a passive spirit accepting conformism while at the same time Americans profess to love the now virtually nonexistent pioneer spirit of individuality. One is secretly content to be "in step," to be "one of the gang," to have the same ideas, to dress the same way as others, and to have the same kind of wife as the person next door. The Americans will be friendly with neighbors and strangers but are hostile to strange ideas. American society is chained more and more in the lockstep of "togetherness," and dissent is discouraged. Americans do not like to be alone and must feel accepted. "Don't go without me, I'm coming," is a pathetic cry frequently heard. To Americans "together-ness" is comforting, as it is to all children afraid to be alone in the dark with their own psyches or the bugbear of an individually held idea.

Americans love the idea of equality—social, civic, political, legal—and seem to think intellectual equality should go along with all other equali-ties. Why this should be so is hard to determine, for just as not all can run the four-minute mile, not all can be nuclear physicists or experts in Sanskrit. A requirement of social effectiveness is that envy not be aroused by an unseemly display of intelligence or talent; those heads coming above dead level will be chopped off. Equality in the intellectual sphere means only that everyone has the opportunity of his own chance at bat.

If one has "sense," it should only be horse sense. Intellectuality leads to wickedness, like the story of Faust (Faust, it will be remembered, finally ends up as an engineer), and is satanic like Frankenstein. Braininess is supposed to be bloodless. In America, there was the tragedy of *Arrowsmith*. The com-poser or painter is regarded as unstable, unwholesome, and most probably homosexual. One of the best and freshest American composers, Gian Carlo Menotti, wrote:

It is my contention that the average American has little respect for the creative artist and is apt to consider him as an almost useless member of the community. . . . No wonder that the young American artist is perhaps the most neurotic in the world and for generations has sought in Europe his spiritual home.[2]

This neglect was boldly put by Huntington Cairns: "In the United States we are confronted with the apparent fact that not a single composer is able to subsist by his serious work." The intellectual is regarded as an un-democratic snob, aloof from "real people." Most Americans find it hard to comprehend that the intellectual pursues his profession for disinterested ends. Inventors are regarded as freaks or crackpots until they discover something that pays off; only then do the kudos come. Philip Wylie wrote in his *Opus 21:* "American avarice held in open contempt all culture and all thought, decerebated itself and so died headless,"[3] while E. E. Cummings in *Collected Poems 1923-1954* held of the antiintellectual:

> that you should ever think, may god forbid
> and(in his mercy)your true lover spare:
> for that way knowledge lies,the foetal grave
> called progress,and negation's dead undoom.[4]

College and university professors are also singled out by the mass-encouraged politicians as something suspect, perhaps corrupting our children who have been hesitatingly confided to them. The professor may harbor strange ideas. In Sherwood Anderson's *Hands,* the sensitive and able teacher, well loved by his students, was hounded out of the community by malicious gossip. Professors are obliged in some states to be fingerprinted and to take loyalty oaths not required of other citizens, and their private lives are investigated and subjected to whispering campaigns. The former education editor of *The New York Times,* Benjamin Fine, reported from a survey that teachers should not have dissenting ideas, engage in controversies, wear too much lipstick, drink beer, or go dancing. At Notre Dame, on May 15, 1953, George F. Kennan, who himself had been banished from his official career for being too much of an egghead, deplored

> the powerful strain of our American cast of mind that has little use for the artist or the writer. . . . What is it that causes us to huddle together, herdlike, in tastes and enthusiasms that represent only the common denominator of popular acquiescence rather than to show ourselves receptive to the tremendous flights of creative imagination of which the individual mind has shown itself capable? Is it that we are forgetful of the true source of our moral strength, afraid of ourselves, afraid to look into the chaos of our own breasts, afraid of the bright, penetrating light, of the great teachers? [5]

How often do we need to be told that orthodoxy, uniformity of thought and habit, can easily lead to demagoguery and dictatorship? If free enterprise is so good for business, it should be good for the mind too—for art, literature, and scholarship.

It is unlikely that there would be a *trahison des clercs* in the United States, but there are disturbing signs that the impugned intellectual will no longer be listened to or will be drowned out by the gabble of the rabble and their rousers. The danger lies in the loss of humanistic values of Western culture which the intellectual keeps alive in a half-dead and imitative present and then transmits and translates through his personal contribution to that heritage. The old valued landmarks may be dangerously washed from sight by the shifting sea of the valueless relativism and pragmatism of today's society. The understanding of the living past by thinking people is our life raft in today's ocean of problems.

Compared to Oxford and Cambridge, German universities, or the *Ecole Normale Supérieure,* American universities have played a relatively small role in politics. When party machines see the inevitability of an electoral defeat, they put up as a candidate a professor who will take up arms against the sea of troubles and righteously and indignantly demand reform. Defeated, he again takes up teaching freshmen the intricacies of constitutional government, while the machine publicly preens its political purity. Wilson, the Presbyterian professor from Princeton, surprised the politicos by actually being elected Governor of New Jersey, then surpised Charles Evans Hughes, who went to bed thinking himself president, and awakened to find public preference for the professor in that great unacademic institution called the electoral college. Business distrusted the New Freedom of academic "radicalism," and frothed even more at the New Deal of the brain trust which came down from Columbia's Morningside Heights to Washington. Steel and high finance were distrustful of the New Frontier which had moved Harvard to Washington.

Jefferson saw the future security of American democracy in the individual farmer. Whether it was the physiocratic element of the soil or the frontier, one new ingredient was added: that of opportunity, or its reverse, freedom from economic and social restraints. If the frontier closed, new opportunities arose in the growing industrialized cities. There is an American impatience with any restraint on activity that does not endanger the community, for the free-enterprising individual is face to face with his own fate as with his free-willing Calvinist God. This is the essence of American rugged individualism. But this very freedom of opportunity brought with it a sense of community, of collective self-help. This spirit has been transcended in contemporary America by the concept of human relations in industry, the key to increased production and the mutual interest of all engaged in rationalizing and perfecting the productive process. This ever-increasing production for an expanding consumer market breeds the public relations man to take the pulse of the consumer and to satisfy his every whim. Americans have taken over German methodology and humanized it, not necessarily for the individual, but for the greater interest and well-being of collective society. Individual opportunity becomes, therefore, the gum of social cohesion in America: the American is better off by being the good neighbor by cooperation, by group identification. American freedom for the individual makes cooperation the more justified. No one would be mean enough or short-sighted enough not to "turn a hand," or "give a lift." The American does not ask "what do you want," but rather "what can I do for you?" American politics, wars, and society are run that way.

This is much less true in Europe, which is still stratified by class interest. Where America has produced the organization man, Europe still has the individual entrepreneur. Europe is now in the process of painfully undergoing the managerial revolution, which is often called Americanization. In Europe there are still social islands and hilltop castle retreats for special classes and interests, whereas America is a vast, level prairie with a social skyscraper here and there. Europe is compartmentalized and favors particularism and social conservatism, restricted and confined except in intellectual spirit. America's open frontiers, including two great oceans, offer vistas of imaginative expansion, outward-looking but less conducive to ordered and more introspective activity.

Europeans criticize America in terms of absolutes, as if it were a utopia *manqué*. Europeans judge America by different standards from those by which they judge themselves or other countries. Often in criticizing America they are criticizing a country which does not exist. After all, America is only made up of a lot of men and women, two hundred million of them who are people, not mankind. America has been embraced by many races, peoples, and religions, and altogether this progressive incorporation of vast bodies of immigrants of various bloods makes up as motley a political and social group as has been seen since the late Roman Empire, and even on a greater scale. It has been a case of "horizontal civilizing," of people of all nations running against one another in the race for the exploitation, even plundering, of a vast continent. If there is the ideal brotherhood of man in America, it is again in the Calvinist sense, a brotherhood made practical by good works: the justification is not by faith alone. The running that is done is democratic and classless. The European émigré wanted to get out from under in a society where one class was piled upon another as in a deck of cards. When classes began to form in the Eastern United States, the bottom part of society slid out to pioneer the western states, those very people whom Mrs. Trollope hated in Cincinnati. All Americans belong to the middle masses and, as Dickens noted, America has no tradesmen, only merchants. Janitors are called supervising building engineers, the elevator boy becomes a vertical engineer, and the undertaker in Virginia, if not a Southern planter, is a family funeral consultant. The American worker is not the down-trodden zealot of Jack London's *Iron Heel,* but a middle-class bourgeois with a high income and low cultural content. Actually, the "non-privileged" worker benefits most from American-style capitalism. Those who represent the middle class live much as they live in Europe, and the rich much as they live everywhere.

America is the only nation which is not founded on ethnographic principles or on blood ties. It is based on community ideals embedded in the Constitution. Accept these principles, and you can be an American; reject them, and you are un-American. The real American democracy is to be found in its myths and traditions, which permeate the whole moral and social fabric of the country. To be an American is an act of faith, and this faith presents a solid front against all other and alien ideologies. This helps to clarify the constant tendency to explain international politics in terms of black and white, simplifying all questions into the struggle for the democratic way of life. It helps to explain the American penchant for rhetorical moralizing, the adoption of platforms, charters, and cheers. and the preaching of Americanism as a solution for the world's ills. It sounds perfectly natural to American ears, but obviously strange to Europeans. Americans descend from Mount Sinai with tables: the Monroe Doctrine, the Open Door policy, the Fourteen Points, the Kellogg-Briand Pact, the Atlantic Charter, the United Nations Charter, and the Truman and Eisenhower doctrines. Has there been an adequate defense for them all?

"When we hear that a people have declared their intention of being henceforth better than their neighbors," wrote Anthony Trollope, "and going upon a new theory that shall lead them direct to a terrestrial paradise, we button up our pockets and lock up our spoons. And that is what we have done very much as regards the Americans." [6] However, he felt sure that America was keeping its promise.

If America had never existed, it would have been necessary to invent it, or we never would have seen the European utopias tried out in practice, even imperfectly. America, like Soviet Russia, is a philosophical experiment. Both have ways of life the beauties of which should be extended and shared with all other peoples at whatever cost or effort. We shall know the truth and the truth shall set *you* free, whether you like it or not. The sense of nationality in "Americanism" is different from the European in its mobility and different loyalties.

One thing that hampers the common Atlantic community effort is the missionary attitude of the United States, too often in the pharisitic sense: "Thank God I am not as other men." Dickens has Chollop say to Mark Tapley, "We are the intellect and the virtue of the airth, the cream of human natur', and the flower of moral force." America is now more or less voluntarily recognized as the leader of the Occidental world, but only in the face of the Communist menace, nuclear science, and the conquest of space. This is already a big order. Why then is it necessary for America to take over other domains, including morality? Puritan evangelism? Profit motive? Pride? Americans would realize their ambitions if they had a greater modesty. It is by no means certain that Europeans, or any others for that matter, would agree with Senator Albert J. Beveridge that God has "marked the American people as His chosen nation to finally lead in the regeneration of the world." Americans charge around like medieval knights looking for dragons to slay, fair ladies in distress to save. This is not to underestimate all the good that Americans have done in the world, and with the best intentions in the world. American leaders are more aware of the possible world consequences, however far away, of each action they take.

The United States lives in constant danger of falling in love with itself. As Emerson said in his lecture "The Future of the Republic," "the American eagle is very well. Protect it here and abroad. But beware of the American peacock." Tocqueville picked up the same thing in saying,

> What I reproach most in democratic government as it is organized in the United States is not as most people pretend in Europe its weakness, but on the contrary its inestimable force. What is most repugnant to me in America is not the extreme liberty found there, but the little guarantee one finds against tyranny.

Americans love liberty so much that they sometimes take liberties with her.

Sartre took a negative look at Americanism, but not without an element of truth. He wrote in the review *Les Temps Modernes* that Americanism is a "great external apparatus," remaining essentially outside the Americans. Americanism is an "implacable machine," and "a monstrous complex of myths, values, recipes, slogans, figures, and rites." America is not the Americans, but they are caught in it. "They struggle against it or accept it; they stifle it or reinvent it; they give themselves up to it or make furious efforts to escape from it; in any case it remains outside them, transcendent, because they are men and it is a thing." [7] Sartre shows an America unhappy and bewildered and caught in its myths of bounty, progress, happiness, liberty, and triumphant maternity.

Americans need their idealism in order to retain their creative drive. Americans have an optimistic cult of life in the same manner that Spaniards have a cult of death. Yet optimism can be an atractive sign not only of youth, but also of puerility. Jean Giraudoux, who visited the United States between the wars, saw in America one vast club. It was a luxurious and exclusive club with admission requirements, waiting lists, initiation rites, dues, *bonhomie,* and Puritan social codes to be respected if one wanted to remain a member in good standing; it was *Philistia regnante*. Americans always wonder who they are and are constantly engaged in a process of self-identification. The English and French have long known what was English or French about their countries, as do others, and consequently they are not self-conscious about it. Americans are never sure exactly what it is to be American (although a Congressional committee will define what is un-American), and thus from the very beginning they have asserted loudly and inconclusively that they *were* sure. A favorite pastime of American and foreign writers has been to write strange fiction about what Americans are. The Carnegie Corporation asked "Who Knows America?" and concluded, almost nobody: "Our lawmakers, journalists, civic leaders, diplomats, teachers and others have less than an adequate understanding of their own society."

"The trouble with European judgments of this country," said the American, "is that Europeans don't really know America." The Englishman smiled. "Who knows America?" he said. "I can't claim to. But I seriously doubt that you yourselves do—partly because you are not particularly interested in your own history, partly because you haven't had time to assimilate the turbulent things that have happened to your nation." The opening lines of a memoir written by an English graduate student as he was about to set off on a scholarship to the United States are rather sad for the transatlantic relation:

> I don't know very much about America. I have never been particularly interested in America, so I suppose I am fairly typical of my country-men. Nobody I have met in the past few months has ever heard of the Mid-Western university I am going to and only a few have any idea of where the State of Indiana is. . . . With solemnity I was asked, yes even begged, not to become "Americanized." (This seems to be a warning against adopting childish intellectual standards, loud taste in clothes and ideas, irresponsibility, flamboyance and general unsoundness. Possibly some unmortality; petting at least.)

His account of an unblindfolded initiation into American rites would lead all into a better knowledge of both Europe and America, for if one knows only his own country, he is bound to be less than objective and less than a complete man.

Santayana said in his *Character and Opinion in the United States,* "to be an American is of itself almost a moral condition, an education, and a career." [8] Santayana hated the spirit of Puritanism in America as the enemy of all joy and equilibrium. Puritanism was fine for the pioneer, the colonial, the businessman, but it dried up the intellectual spirit with too many scruples.

In his novel *The Last Puritan,* he contrasted the end of the Puritan Oliver Alden, cold and lost, against the animal vitality of Mario van de Weyer, the wise and cultured product of Europe.

Santayana characterized the American as a split personality: "the American will inhabits the skyscraper; the American intellect inhabits the colonial mansion." America is always complete but never finished. There is no conclusion to Huck Finn, jazz, a skyscraper, a road, a comic strip, or a soap opera. Americans ask, "How are things *going?*" Matter in science is now fluid, not static; economics and philosophy are interested in "process"; modern industry moves automatically on conveyer belts; American society is an open rather than a closed system, and it is devoted to development, not permanence. The American past, like its future, is open—it does not extend down, but across. America is tension rather than serenity, a steel bridge rather than a Pont du Gard. Obsolescence is planned.

It is hard to describe the panorama of American democracy because it is hard to add up all the pieces; in some cases one has to multiply by a couple of million, and in others divide by two. It is more than the sum of its parts. Turner believed that the frontier provided the means of democracy in the nineteenth century, and he was certainly partly right, but the machine made the industrial democracy of the twentieth century. The machine has forced democracy and equality on us all. Marianne Moore wrote in "To a Steam Roller," "You crush all the particles down into close conformity, and then walk back and forth on them." [9] The success of the machine depends upon its being free of the complex emotions of men. This is equally true of the so-called technologization of Europe. Only Americans are "more equal" than others. In an industrial society it raises the old problem of the one and the many. It is not at all odd that the American national motto should be *E pluribus unum.*

Sinclair Lewis, one of the best portrayers of the ideal mass man enjoying his mass habits, mass distractions, and little mass sins and prejudices that become terrifying when multiplied by two million, let loose with an uncharacteristic and Menckenlike sneer at the unintelligent, bumbling, conformist mass.

> The United States of America are peopled by a mighty herd which . . . drives foolishly in whatever direction their noses point—a herd endowed with a tremendous blind power, with big bulldozers, but with minds rarely above their bellies and their dams . . . with a herd power that sweeps majestically onward in a cloud of dust of its own raising, seeming to be lords and masters of a continent. But in fact they are somewhat stupid, feeble in brain and will, stuffed with conceit in their

own excellence, esteeming themselves the great end for which creation has been in travail; with a vast respect for totems and fetishes; purveyors and victims of Bunk—a vast middleman herd that dominates the continent but cannot reduce it to order or decency.[10]

In "Shine, Perishing Republic," Robinson Jeffers also lamented:

While this America settles in the mould
      of its vulgarity, heavily thickening to empire,
And protest, only a bubble in the
      molten mass, pops and sighs out,
      and the mass hardens,[11]

The American drama is written in the mass—it has always been a community enterprise, whether in raising barns, building automobiles, or fighting wars. Yet American crowds are not like indistinct Oriental masses such as we see in the insectivization of Communist China. It is true that Americans have a collective mystique, but individuality is not totally absorbed. Bernard Fay remarked that the sensation of crowds, oppressive elsewhere, is attractive and stimulating in America; the country is exhilarated by its own mass, and the individual person enjoys it. Bryce wrote in his *American Commonwealth* in 1888,

> Democracy has not only taught the Americans . . . how to secure equality, it has also taught them fraternity. That word has gone out of fashion in the Old World. . . . Nevertheless there is in the United States a sort of kindness, a sense of human fellowship, a recognition of the duty of mutual help owed by man to man, stronger than anywhere in the Old World, and certainly stronger than in the upper or middle classes of England, France, or Germany.

In the immense collective American personality, Americans like to be liked, and they are injured by mean interpretations of their goodwill, their mass-produced culture, and materialist ease. An Englishman never thinks about being "liked"; he is even more accustomed to not being liked. In 1500 a Venetian diplomat noted in his *Relation of England,* "The English are great lovers of themselves and of everything belonging to them. They think that there are no other men than themselves and no other world but England." A Frenchman is so convinced in advance that he is appreciated that he is impervious to criticism by the less civilized foreigners. The French and the British, like the Greeks and the Romans, were never surprised at the illogical behavior of the incomprehensible barbarians—they simply left them to their strange habits, or administered, cajoled, or coerced them when necessary. Americans want to liberate peoples and missionize them into the American pursuit of happiness. Whereas Americans woo them it is the other countries who win their favors.

Maritain says that the "unjust" European (and Asian) refusal to recognize the good intentions of America and their cheap and cynical explanation of the immense effort of American goodwill injures the American soul itself. Tocqueville noted the same American sensitivity:

> The American, taking part in everything that is done in his country, believes it necessary to defend everything which we criticze there, for it is not only his country which is thus attacked, it is himself; also one sees his national pride rise to every artifice and descend to all childishness of individual vanity. There is nothing more annoying in their habits than this irritable patriotism of the Americans. The foreigner would willingly agree to praise much in their country, but he would like to be permitted to blame something, and this is absolutely refused. America is thus a country of liberty, where to offend no one, the foreigner should not speak freely of individuals, of the State, of the governors or the governed, of public and private enterprise; of nothing finally, that he encounters, unless perhaps the weather or the soil, and even there one finds Americans ready to defend the one or the other, as if they had collaborated in forming them.

Frances Trollope echoed a similar contemporary theme:

> Other nations have been called thin-skinned, but citizens of the Union have, apparently, no skins at all; they wince if a breeze blows over them, unless it be tempered with adulation. . . . So deep is the conviction of this singular people that they cannot be seen without being admired, that they will not admit the possibility that anyone should honestly and sincerely find aught to disapprove in them, or their country.[12]

Will America be saddled with the limitations of its own perspective? America must look to its contact with Europe to provide that spark of philosophy and grain of relative insight that its own history has denied it. As Van Wyck Brooks has said, America must "come of age." America can transcend itself with the help of Europe. Maritain pointed a philosophical finger at the problem: Americans mistrust ideas; they have too much ideological modesty, which carries a serious risk of intellectual isolation. There is the risk of rendering incommunicable the American reality and its human

and social success to other nations. It is walled in as long as its philosophy
and ideology remain hidden behind its real behavior. Tocqueville announced:

> Up to now America has only a few remarkable writers, has no great
> historians and not one poet. Its inhabitants see literature as such with
> a sort of disfavor and any third-rate city in Europe publishes more literary
> works than the twenty-four states of the Union put together. The
> American mind avoids general ideas and is not directed at all toward
> theoretical discovery. . . . In America they apply with sagacity the in-
> ventions of Europe, and having perfected them, adapt them marvellously
> to the needs of the country.

In his *Democratic Vistas,* Whitman said, "Our New World democracy,
however great a success in uplifting the masses out of their sloughs, in
materialistic developments . . . is an almost complete failure . . . in really
grand religious, moral, literary, and esthetic results," and Matthew Arnold
noted after his American tour, "Of the really beautiful in the other arts, and
in literature, very little has been produced there as yet. . . . The American
artists live chiefly in Europe; all Americans of cultivation and wealth visit
Europe more and more constantly." After critical investigations he asserted,
"in truth, everything is against distinction in America, and against the sense
of elevation to be gained through admiring and respecting it." [13] There was
too much glorification of the average man by newspapers, statesmen, and
publicists, to his mind.

America still needs Europe, just as Europe needs America, and each
should heed the other's voice across the water. On Henry Adams' return
from Europe, he felt that American society was

> always trying, almost blindly like an earthworm, to realize and under-
> stand itself; to catch up with its own head, and to twist about in
> search of its tail. . . . It enjoyed the vast advantage over Europe that
> all seemed for the moment, to move in one direction, while Europe
> wasted most of its energy in trying several contradictory movements at
> once. . . .[14]

Americans might be more open to useful outside criticism and aware
themselves of the problems and dangers involved in their mass culture. This
mass culture tends to reenforce the basic American traits of conformity and
uniformity and the stifling of individual expression in the name of the
general will of Americanism. The black-and-white intellectual backbone
should not be replaced by a technicolored wishbone. Siegfried gives a clue:

American society now appears as a first-class piece of organization; it is a whole nation of workers each with his own job. This nation enjoys a high standard of living, not Germanic in atmosphere, for it contains a greater degree of humanity and a certain measure of unconstraint, but it is nevertheless a society where phantasy and liberty do not reign as they did formerly.[15]

Matthew Arnold saw that the human problem was yet imperfectly solved in the United States, that "a great void exists in the civilization over there; a want of what is elevated and beautiful, of what is interesting," and that the want is greater because it is so little recognized by the mass of Americans, "nay, so loudly denied by them." [16] Arnold regretted that Americans did not want to seek a remedy, but seemed to have agreed to deceive themselves and cover their defects by boasting. With the same apprehension, Arnold Bennett wrote: "Americans never did and never will look in the right quarters for vital art. They are imitative, with no real opinions of their own." [17] Even though both tended to be subjective, it is hard to neglect some element of partisan truth, for it was also expressed by Carlyle and Ruskin. To give a final example, T. H. Huxley frankly told an American audience of his feeling with regard to America:

> I cannot say that I am in the slightest degree impressed by your bigness, or your material resources as such. Size is not grandeur, and territory does not make a nation. The great issue, about which hangs a true sublimity, and the terror of overhanging fate, is what are you going to do with all these things? What is to be the end to which these are to be the means? . . . . Truly America has a great future before her; great in toil, in care, and in responsibility; great in true glory if she be guided in wisdom and righteousness; great in shame if she fail.[18]

An industrial democracy brings up the underside of society to be educated and cultivated, and because this underside is more seen and heard does not mean that a nation as a whole is less cultured or that there is a degrading cultural leveling going on. The "average" American seen in Europe *is* average, not more, not less. The refined American or European who shudders at the bad grammar or the bad spelling of the product of our democratic school system should remember that a generation or so ago many were illiterates, ignored and unheard, recognized only as useful servitors.

The machine, like the blackjack or the bayonet, becomes the great equalizer, and gears us all into its ceaseless revolutions. Frail humans, if we do not obey it, the wheels jam. The machine does not understand us nor care to; it knows only its own uniform motion and takes no account of our individual and tender psyches. The machine must be covered with safety gadgets to make up for our little stupidities, for it is ever ready to bite the hand that oils it. Emerson described that machinery, applied to all work with such perfection that we have only to tend engines and feed furnaces:

> The machine requires punctual service, and as they never tire, they prove too much for their tenders. Mines, forges, mills, breweries, railroads, steam-pump, steam-plough, drill of regiments, drill of police, rule of court and shoprule have operated to give a mechanical regularity to all the habit and action of men. A terrible machine has possessed itself of the ground, the air, the men and women, and hardly even thought is free.

Lewis Mumford pointed out the perils years ago in the *New Republic* (September 7, 1921). It was not industrialism's brutal effect on the worker or the economic concentration of power that was essentially dangerous but the fact that the greater part of labor could be done by a "healthy imbecile," that by nicely adjusted wages and prices and timely, organized luxury campaigns, the worker could be kept docile and servile with new radio sets and vacuum cleaners, literally sold on the pleasure that the chains provided. Personal authority disappeared into anonymity with the distribution of power; "in every large organization the equipment for passing the buck is polished and inspected every day." As for technics and civilization, Mumford later wrote, "lacking a cooperative social intelligence and good will, our most refined technics promises no more for society's improvement than an electric bulb would promise to a monkey in the midst of a jungle."

Daily we push buttons, pull handles, turn dials, stop at the red and go at the green, consciously or unconsciously follow formulas and rules. The curse of Adam has been lifted by the machine. As Frank Lloyd Wright said, man will now "live by the sweat of a push-button-finger." Every toothpaste or soap has a new, miraculous, "scientific" ingredient, and ever new and more powerful formulas fuel the motors of more and more powerful automobiles. Like Walter Mitty, we all dream of being the cool and effective master of machines and techniques, but we wind up like Charlie Chaplin in *Modern Times.*

Sherwood Anderson in *Perhaps Women* felt that man was too enmeshed in the gears of machines to be redeemed, that as a slave to the machines he had been reduced to powerlessness. The only hope he saw was in woman.

The machine might tire her physically but could not paralyze her spirit; a machine could not create children, or take that power away from her. Capek's *R. U. R.,* Rice's *The Adding Machine,* and O'Neill's *The Dynamo* showed how men lose their free will as passive servants of the machine. O'Neill's *The Hairy Ape* portrayed the mechanical slave stoking the boilers of the modern industrial ship, as Sandburg's "Smoke and Steel" put human blood into making man become part of the steel rivet in a skyscraper. There was the legendary Negro John Henry who pitted himself against a steam drill, "de flesh ag'in the steam," who won, but broke a blood vessel and died.

For relaxation, so called, we turn to popular music, which repeats the incessant tom-tom of the machine, and repeated short melodic themes become a sort of narcotic. The mechanically minded hi-fi experts will even put a seventy-piece symphony orchestra in your living room for relaxation. The earlier nineteenth-century industrial revolution with its steam engines and spinning jennies is the Dark Ages compared to Henry Ford, and Henry Ford is a Gutenberg compared to IBM calculators in the present-day chrome-plated jungle of America.

The machine is ambivalent. It will do only what it is told to do. It can be the instrument of liberation or repression. It can serve human purposes as well as destroy them. The machine may be able to do away with man in industry, in which the worker has become no longer an industrial slave but a technical surveyor of instruments, but it cannot do away with man in the arts, liberal and humane. The new technics violate the old weary goddess of culture, and we the people, deprived of critical spirit, kneel down in homage to the expert. Neutral and ambivalent, the machine could be used to increase and perfect man's senses; used otherwise, it will paralyze his will to art and culture. The danger of the machine, Babette Deutsch said, is not that it hurries us along too fast or that it shrinks our horizon or that it robs us of a comprehensive philosophy, but that it forces us to live in a world as empty of emotional values as the algebraic letter. It is man who should be the active agent and the machine the passive. Man must directly feel, touch, sing, and see and smell, rather than passively accept pseudoreality. Le Corbusier made houses "machines for living" and jammed people into his own concepts of the way they should live. His famous Swiss House at the *Cité Universitaire* at Paris was uninhabitable and had to be changed over at great expense. Frank Lloyd Wright, despite his pleas for the "organic," made a beautifully monstrous museum of art for the Guggenheims in New York that shows his architectural pride better than the pictures to be housed. The Bauhaus of Gropius and Mies van der Rohe blessed us with prestressed concrete and glass, tubular chrome and plasticized furniture—all as angular for the human body as a T-square.

Used for good, the scientific machine can clarify and objectify, much like the camera of Stieglitz. The Cubists, Brancusi, Duchamp, and Calder, have made of the machine a functional art, free from ornamentation, and have shown that the machine is not necessarily inherently ugly or undesirable. The machine properly used should refine, simplify, economize. Machines themselves have given up the useless decoration seen on old cash registers, sewing machines, and radiators, and assert their true, functional style. Beginning with Roebling, Eiffel, and Sullivan, structure begins to show honest form. Externals are simplified to indicate internal complications, which is the essence of the machine and perhaps presages our automated life of the future.

The calculator can dangerously dehumanize. You live by numbers; rather you are a series of little holes on a punch card and fall into your proper slot when electronically stimulated. In school the exact mental capacity of your child is measured by figures. If you lose your wallet, you lose the number of your credit cards, draft classification number, passport number, insurance policy numbers, driver's license numbers, automobile registration numbers (which, of course, do not correspond always to those affixed to the car). You are one, and only one, of 200,000,000 Americans or 300,000,000 Europeans. The town meeting of 1,000 changes its function in scale to a city of 1,000,000. The same people are not simply multiplied by a thousand, but are different. A "good" television program is based on a rating of 18,000,000 viewers; if you happen to be one of the only 5,000,000 televiewers who wants to see a particular program that has been abandoned, one can only be sorry for you. What the public is interested in is not often in the public interest. Your "number" may be up: it is even scientifically predicted for you that you may be one of the 47,583 killed over New Year's Eve; four out of five will die of cancer; eight prominent physicians certify that nine out of ten . . . , etc. Women are numerically categorized, such as the "perfect 36," and someone is bound to say, "who was that pretty number I saw you with?" One-third of the marriages contracted in the United States end in divorce in the first ten years, but where does this statistic get anyone? Emerson felt this already in 1884 in stating, "We come to wear one cut of face and figure, and acquire by degrees the gentlest asinine expression."

No wonder modern man feels alienated; no wonder he is lost in the lonely crowd; no wonder he would like to contradict Donne and be an isle unto himself. There is a perpetual malaise among Americans; they are constantly on the move, hopefully sure that there are greener pastures over the next ridge. It may be a healthy dissatisfaction with the status-quo, an impatience with staying put too long. Man needs roots, one hears again and again, yet men are not plants. We live in a fast, mobile society, not in suspended animation, but poised and balanced, one hopes, in motion and time, with fixed points of reference like the stars that also move in our galaxy.

A French woman declared that she would not marry an American because all Americans have "problems." It does seem as if more and more couches are being warmed in the offices of psychologists. The patron saint of the United States is Saint Vitus. Americans are feeling the effects of a highly charged, technoindustrial society. Europeans will shortly have to meet the same "problems," the same frustrations and inhibitions. The characteristic heavy whiskey-drinking in many American sectors is now transferred to chic sets in France, Germany, and Italy and is considered quite snobbish. Can it be that only the Latins have a happy uncomplicated sex life and that the Americans are titillated enough by the movies, but not too much? (The Motion Pictures Association and the League for Decency take out the naughty words but leave all the suggestions in.) The clerk and the shopgirl are offered sensationalism in the newspapers and thrills in the movies, censored just enough to keep their immorality beyond reach, the vicarious sensation of Huxley's "feelies" and Orwell's "Soma" tablets. The joy pills have already arrived in the tranquillizer tablets, and if there are not yet "feelies," there is now "odorama." If the tranquillizer does not work, there are frontal lobotomies. The movies become a neutral womb where man can lose himself, possibly the only place now in modern society outside of church. The cinema helps to "adjust," to excise guilts and transfer sexual and criminal passions. Perhaps the human being needs a little bit of immorality to keep his even balance, instead of a libertarian and then a Victorian swing of the pendulum, of Puritanism and then wild revivalism, of dull dreariness and then carnival and *fasching,* of unrestrained radical jaunts and then Joe McCarthyism. In a highly organized machine life our sense of pleasure becomes lethally weakened, is artificially stimulated by unrewarding sterile entertainment, and consequently becomes further atrophied.

Neither the machine nor science is emotional or subjective, and there is nothing inspirational about either. We need no more expect beauty through a machine than morality from a laboratory. Both are simply utilitarian. Man is not himself outside science, he lives with it and benefits from it, but what he does care most about is outside the realm of science. Anatole France held, "the sciences are beneficient, they keep men from thinking." Science cannot measure or calculate those things which we love, hate, desire, adore, appreciate. Scientific measurement cancels out individual experience and private history. Aquinas gave us a hint when he said that science seeks the truth;

religion has it. In his search for truth Henry Adams found that "modern science offered not a vestige of proof, or theory of connection between its forces, or any scheme of reconciliation between thought and mechanics; while St. Thomas at least locked together the joints of his machine." Science, even social science, takes phenomena at face value. Theology seeks salvation, science manipulation. Science considers the inner life of man as trivial— merely subjective—and annoying and bothersome because it cannot be classified. William James at Harvard was strongly against the new experimental psychology. He saw that when people began measuring for the sake of measuring that they could only measure the small things, and eventually all the greater things would be ignored. Psychology, he thought, had to take in the whole nature of man himself. Psychologists, sociologists, and cultural anthropologists are inevitably bound to be determinists when they use the scientific approach. In doing so they have yet to find any instrument to reveal the human psyche, the soul of the individual. It is manifestly impossible to "find" because it is transcendent and can only be distantly approached through religion or art, perhaps coincidentally by philosophy.

Science tries, but cannot, take in the whole experience. We can learn more about man's nature from Pascal or Spinoza than from the textbooks of modern psychologists. Only subjective experience seen by the poet or philosopher takes in the whole, and science has only a thin slice of life which it can slide into a microscope or tabulate with punch cards. Science can define truth of a kind, but not the whole truth nor a kind of truth. This break from a uniform set of beliefs began with Roger Bacon; instead of evolving a rational universe from a thought, thought was being evolved from the universe. The mind was then forced to follow scientific matter, and man comes to depend more and more on forces other than his own.

Science may be good for everyday material things, but it becomes confused when it comes up against metaphysics and the myths men live by, frequently destroying without replacing. Whitehead, in *Science and the Modern World*, grappled with the problem of relativity, which throws all absolutes out of the window, including moral ones. We now talk about the values we "hold" rather than the values we "believe in." The fact that man can alter nature as he likes brings up the old problem of free will, and in the end, man can only rely on his intuition. Einstein and Bergson, as Wyndham Lewis argued in *Time and Western Man*, have ruined the hope for an ordered and comprehensible world, leaving us uncertain and unhappy at the idea of being caught up in a constant flux. Dewey tried to take account of science to form a more hopeful pragmatic theory, but was he successful?

Medieval man lived by a set of beliefs; modern man attempts to live by a set of facts. The force of the cross for the thirteenth century was as powerful as radium or plutonium for the twentieth century; the same force that raised Santa Sophia raised Chartres. Luther's Bible became a mainspring for German literature, as did the King James version for English. Cross and Gold in Spanish America led Las Casas to suggest the importation of Negro slaves to relieve the poor lot of native Indians, and Puritans found in 1620 the new promised land under the Good Book in New England.

Science being per se neutral, it is man who must set up its values. Neutral science can cure disease or poison populations; atoms can cure cancer and create holocaust. Can there be "science for its own sake," such as "art for art's sake?" The scientist must establish a sense of values within a scientific framework which otherwise is dehumanized. The laboratory worker must be conscious of the world outside, and even "pure" research must in the final analysis justify itself to society. The scientist may develop a dangerous bacteria in his laboratory when his ultimate purpose is the extirpation of a disease. Yet the ultimate social purpose makes the growth of that biological culture a moral act. If there is no such end in view, we should take the scientist's test tubes away from him.

With unselfish devotion the scientist goes into a moral isolation in the laboratory; in his pursuit of scientific truth, he must cast off human frailties —the disinfected man in the white coat, the Child of Light, extracts, abstracts, detracts, and substracts and then emerges with his gift to mankind. Laymen become enslaved to new cures, new products, new scientific language. A different kind of pill each year, and this year we learn the sometimes disastrous side effects of last year's pill, which unintentionally led to hardening of the arteries, palpitations, sterility, deformed children, convulsions, migraines, adhesions, or paralysis. As Voltaire said, "Doctors pour drugs of which they know little to cure diseases of which they know less into human beings of whom they know nothing."

Social tension will increase unless new social directions are found to accompany the perfecting of a machine-science civilization. Fortunately, as we watch the dissolution of the mechanical world picture and find the physical sciences less exact and more relative, the new science is turning to life itself, to the biological organism. The organic concept undermines the authority of the mechanical explanation of physical life.

The prestige of science is almost too popular to attack. In *The Place of Science in Society* Thornstein Veblen wrote: "On any large question which is to be disposed of for good and all, the final appeal is by common consent to the scientist. The solution offered in the name of science is decisive, so long as it is not set aside by a still more searching inquiry." [19] President Truman expressed the utopian scientific dream entertained by many Americans:

> With patience and courage, we shall some day move into a new era— a wonderful golden age—an era when we can use the peaceful tools that science has forged for us to do away with poverty and human misery everywhere. . . . There is no end to what can be done. I can't help but dream out loud a little here.[20]

We may wonder if evil can be conquered by science and more research teams. Man is evidently good and inherently evil, and although science has heightened the possibilities of life, it has also lowered the depths. There is some doubt and disenchantment, even among the scientists. The nuclear physicists declare their gloomy forebodings and we share their *angst* over the letter that Einstein wrote to Roosevelt in the fall of 1939. The scientist has worked in an intellectual vacuum, unaware of the world about him, uneducated in the best sense of the word. As Archibald MacLeish wrote in 1929:

> > > He lies upon his bed
> Exerting on Arcturus and the moon
> Forces proportional inversely to
> The squares of their remoteness and conceives
> The universe.

> Humans are but atoms, and
> > > If they will not speak
> Let them be silent in their particles.

> And everything will
> Sweep over into movement and dissolve
> All differences in the indifferent flux! [21]

The danger is not to be found in science itself but in "scientism," when the scientist puts his authority above inquiry. Ancient Egypt had a scientific priesthood; today we have a priestly sciencehood. The scientist is aggrieved that anyone might question the rightness of his concepts in his special field. The worst offenders are the medical scientists, who seem to continue a medieval monopoly of practicing a mystical cabal. We often hear that the operation was a success, but that the patient died, which reminds us of Dr. Slop in *Tristram Shandy*. The medical hypocrisies of his time have not abated. The doctor is visited only when one is sick, as is the lawyer only when one in trouble, or as the car is brought to the garage when it doesn't work. Unlike garagemen or lawyers, however, many doctors look upon themselves as the high priests of Aesculapius. Perhaps we should adopt the old Chinese tradition of paying the doctor only when we are well and nothing while we are sick.

Are the scientists really controlling nature, as man has been told repeatedly? Maybe the machine has gone into reverse and we are seeing the opposite side of control. We are exploding the forces of nature in each other's faces and needling our own bodies as if they were voodoo dolls. The hurtling machines of science are colliding on road, on rail, in the air, and on the sea, all equipped with the latest "scientific" safety devices. The human casualty becomes simply a statistic. We are crouching on runaway engines, madly pushing on the accelerator with no regard for our destination.

Jacques Barzun brings a bit of humorous sense to the scientific dilemma:

> About the results of science's efforts ranging from ingenuity to genius, we are grateful, gaping, respectful even when we do not understand. We do not even question when the dicta of science contradict each other. Not long ago, between Saturday and Monday, the age of the universe doubled and its size was multiplied by eight. We took it all in stride, as we have done for a century past. It used to be "The world is running down, good people. Get your blankets, the night will be cold." (This was Old Huxley and his friends down to thirty years ago.) After that, it became "Wake up, good people, matter is being created all the time. Off with your winter underwear, into your blue Jeans." (That was the party line after Einstein and the late Sir James.) "Light can rotate matter," says X. "No, it can't," says Y. INVESTIGATION UPSETS ESTABLISHED THEORY, say the morning papers.[22]

Science, after all, is a human enterprise like any other, and it is due only the same respect accorded art or religion. It is not superhuman and its pretensions overshoot its capabilities. Nor is the machine a brain. The machine cannot invent itself. A machine cannot make an individual moral decision, even though it can calculate five million similar moral decisions under similar given situations. It is only the *person* who can make the moral decision, and whether this decision be right or wrong, or disagree with the machine, it makes little difference, for the deciding personality has to live with the de-

cision forever in his conscience, even subconscience. The machine could not
care less: its work done, the plug pulled, the juice runs out of the tubes for
the night.

Nobody wants to turn the clock back. One should have only the perspective to see that science has its limitations and that man has none. Before
science existed there were art and philosophy, morality and religion, sages
and prophets. Indeed, science and art were inseparable until the mid-seven-
teenth century. Michelangelo and Da Vinci were scientists; Vesalius was an
artist. It is pretty clear that science killed off religion more effectively than
deism and that it has been unable to put anything in its place. Science has
enormously expanded man's physical senses, but at great expense to the spirit.
Science has not instructed man, but has only implemented him. Again, this
may be a lesson that the Old World can teach the New. The son may be six
inches taller than his father, but that does not mean he is any wiser. The
headlong rush of an America all geared up for action, all throttles out, con-
sternates a Europe that would like a little time off to think of where we are
being led. America has cause to pause and reflect. C. P. Snow, eminently
involved as much in science as literature, says that the major mistake Americans are making as they judge the world and the truth is not difficult to find,
but it is not pretty: Britain in the nineteenth century and the United States
in the twentieth have let technology go to their heads. Both have become
stupified by a kind of technological conceit, for we have discovered that
technology is rather easy and that any country, given the drive and will, can
carry out a technological revolution. The Russians proved that, and the
Chinese are proving it again. The Japanese miraculously transformed themselves into a modern technological society within forty years after the Meiji
restoration. What the individual may have gained on the one hand by scientific technology, he lost on the other when he was deprived of his personal
initiative. Body and soul are turned over gratefully to the government to be
taken care of, when the state becomes the friend of all and the enemy of
each. Society then becomes menaced by multiple sclerosis, and if society is to
breath freely once more, it must be due to the individual's initiative in finding
a new private balance between himself and his society. The material gain is
nothing unless there is a permanent dividend in the way of durable things
such as art, literature, science, and philosophy. A consumer market is good,
but there are more desirable things that cannot be consumed or exhausted—
in short, a culture that is constantly renewed and which can be transmitted.

The Americans do not have enough of the Greco-Latin tradition to leaven the German-Anglo-Saxon lump, and what Americans have of the classic tradition is better described as Roman-Hebraic. America produces its Catos and Plinys, jurists and proconsuls, and the allusion could even be carried to the vestal virgins. The Greek philosophic spirit and the Latin spirit of Augustine and Aquinas (of a Montaigne, say) is not there to provide that vital spark of insight. Without the Latin tradition, Europe would lose its equilibrium, for its realism brings a counterweight to American dynamism as the United States draws away from the classic tradition. The lack of a classic Latin spirit is already the chief distinguishing mark between America and Europe. In a sense, it is what makes Europe seem mature and America immature, or "old" and "young," if you prefer, even though Europe is not antiquated nor America puerile. Puritanism may have become transcendental, but it remains basically English Puritan, pragmatic, and utilitarian. It made the Yankee practical and inventive, nonrevolutionary on principles or ideas, progressively optimistic, a doer rather than a thinker, guided by common law and common sense with all its checks and balances in private and public life. The absence of a Greco-Latin ingredient, of that classic harmony and sense of measure, goes far to explain the passionate pilgrim and the American expatriate. Henry James might have been a better psychologist than his brother. Here also is the clue to Pound's winding up in a mental asylum, Hemingway's concern with the universals of time and death, and Eliot's becoming an Anglo-Catholic. It is the problem of *Dodsworth*.

If America continues to perfect its industrial technocracy at the expense of humanism, it risks becoming a souless computing machine unworthy of the responsibilities thrust upon it. What is it to gain the earth if America loses its soul? At a crucial moment America's leadership may be questioned; someone is bound to remark that the emperor is wearing no clothes. The air-conditioned nightmare could be turned again into the American dream with a fresh injection of the classic element and by redefining the basic purposes of the American nation. Bryce indicated a conspicuous and dangerous trend in America:

Admiral practical acuteness, admirable ingenuity in inventing and handling machinery, whether of iron and wood or of human beings, coexist in the United States with an aversion to the investigations of general principles as well as trains of systematic reasoning. The liability to be caught by fallacies, the inability to recognize facts which are not seen must be inferentially found to exist, the incapacity to imagine a future which must result from the unchecked operation of present forces.

Americans like to think of their country as an automatic candy dispenser: put a penny in the slot and out come the goodies. If it does not produce, shake it violently, for a scientific gadget *must work,* otherwise the American is frustrated and disillusioned. The American frets if the goal is not reached.

Matthew Arnold found American life culturally uninteresting, as Bryce later believed. The remedy, Arnold thought, was to develop a true sense of criticism that would encourage the really fine and distinguished in the arts and letters. He felt that America was too content with mediocre achievements and quoted Lowell's view that the Americans were "the most common-schooled and least cultured people in the world." The critical spirit is still not highly enough developed in America. Successive waves of literary criticism, for example, wander from the retelling of a story the way the critic would have written it, but probably couldn't, to textual criticism playing with language and structure (a necessary criticism where much American writing is haphazard and imprecise), to psychological and inner criticism, with all the accoutrements of Freudian jargon, often about the book which was never written, but which the critic always hopes to write himself. Malcolm Cowley believed that most works of criticism were so badly written that they revealed a sort of aesthetic deafness. Integral or textual criticism is only interested in pure words; no author, no historical or psychological background, no social message, no relation of the work to anything else. The author's intention is utterly disregarded, and his book is no longer his property, but the property of the critic who feels he can best interpret what the author really meant. The critic imprisons himself more and more in his tangled nets of analyses and is obsessed with the critical process itself as an elaborate sublety understood only by those in the inner circle.

Twentieth-century American literary criticism seems to the outsider like a civil war among the critics themselves rather than an elucidation of literature for the public's deeper appreciation and understanding and clearer judgment; Marxists looking into an impossible future, Southerners looking back to a nonexistent past, classicists like Babbitt, More, and Eliot trying to force newer unorthodox styles into an Alexandrian straitjacket, and textual New Critics dissecting all spirit out of literature.

One reads with relief the critical writing of a person like Edmund Wilson who will tell us clearly what a book is about, the author's motivation and style, and where the message fits in. Wilson puts literature truly into relation with humanity, elucidating in causeries after the manner of Sainte-Beuve. He mastered French and Russian literature, was interested in the American Civil War writers, and learned Hebrew to go to Israel to write about the Dead Sea Scrolls. He translated Pushkin, showed a profound knowledge of Michelet and Marx (*To the Finland Station*), and did a good study of Dickens and Kipling (*The Wound and the Bow*). He was the literary mentor of F. Scott Fitzgerald. With such a catholic taste and personal feeling for getting inside all kinds of writers, Edmund Wilson's criticism bears throughout a deep sense of humanity. Van Wyck Brooks affirms that, unlike the other critics, Wilson "saw literature in terms not of itself alone but of the life of humanity and its chief interests; and he combined the aesthetic with the psychological, social and historical sense, knowing that one must see the writer as a man in order to appreciate him as an artist." [23]

John Crowe Ransom, Tate, Eliot, and Pound, it is true, brought American criticism up to a much higher level. American criticism, like American architecture, became international in style, as Howard Mumford Jones noted, and was based on "Freud, an Austrian; on Joyce, an Irishman; on French poets and critics congenial to T. S. Eliot, a British subject, and to Ezra Pound, whose American connections are those of an expatriate." Allen Tate embraced an older European literary style for Southern writing in his *Reactionary Essays on Poetry and Ideas:* "The South clings blindly to forms of European feeling and conduct that were crushed by the French Revolution and what, in England at any rate, are barely memories." [24] The same idea is reflected in John Crowe Ransom's contribution to the manifesto of the Southern agrarians, *I'll Take My Stand:* "the South is unique on this continent for having founded and defended a culture which was according to European principles of culture, and the European principles had better look to the South if they are to be perpetuated in this country." [25] These traditionalists imagine the South to be a literate aristocratic *ancien régime,* but it is only a symbolic ideal which plantation owners never knew, much as European and American Marxist critics take an idyllic look at Communist Russia, bound to see red through rose-colored glasses.

Americans should welcome, not fear, the critical spirit. A refined criticism does not in the least hamper artistic and literary production; it encourages more and better literary efforts. A liberal criticism is not the destruction of talent, but its midwife.

While the critical spirit is not as yet strongly enough developed, America suffers also from a lack of style. There is almost an indifference to it in many well-known American writers and painters of the neo-realist and expressionist bent, and in spite of all the efforts of Pound, Eliot, and, yes, Hemingway, whose crisp terseness makes an unbeatable style however simple it may look. It is style that provides the nuance of flavor: taste. Much American poetry after the writers abandoned style, is now written without meter or rhyme, and therefore also without reason. It is, as Frost said, like playing tennis with the net down. It is not much fun to look at boxes of tomato soup as serious painting, yet soup is good in its own place. Good American style can often be found in the effectively well-thought-out writing and design in Madison Avenue's advertising where clarity of style is paramount in seeking the immediate impact. Good American style can also be found in industrial design and in beautiful common utensils made for everyday living. If style for "gracious" living has gone unnoticed because it seems so commonplace, we need only look at an old Sears, Roebuck catalog or think of the nineteenth-century sardine can, unevolved and unopenable. The development of style seems less respected by the writers whose business it is to instruct us in the basic element of their art.

The classic tradition never loses sight of criticism and style and constantly seeks to redefine and order a changing world. It may embrace utilitarianism, but for its own sake, and the youth in our universities would do well to follow a broad humanist education, which in the long run "pays off." The student who takes only his bread and butter courses, "practical" courses, may often find himself handicapped. More often than not the career he planned at sixteen or twenty does not turn out the way he thought it would; perhaps he will find a totally different posibility from those of travel, marriage, friends, or acquaintances. The student is only one of many groups of people. Bell Telephone, among others, has found it necessary to send its executives back to the university for the humanist exposure to equip them for higher positions of imagination and responsibility; and businessmen gather at Aspen, Colorado, to work over the great problems of the Western world, fatigued minds pounded into shape at the same time as fatigued bodies.

"One has the impression that this country of vast possibilities, of complete goodwill and intense sincerity requires dosing with a large portion of classicism," says Siegfried. It needed a Montaigne, and what it got was an Emerson. "Dominated by the didactic preoccupation of the age it might risk forgetting that the essential purpose of civilization is not at bottom technique, production, or gadgetry, but man himself." [26] Classicism in style and sensibility, critical spirit, and philosophy can provide the humanist antidote to the common colds of science and business. In one of his many *dictées* on America, Stendhal felt this lack and remarked, "One is inclined to say that the source of sensibility is dried up in this people [the Americans]. They are just, they are reasonable, but they are not happy." Scholars, writers, and artists in their envy of the success of the scientists and businessmen often borrow their techniques, and while they may gain in some elements of objectivity, some provable truth, they may lose sight of the overall truth which neither science nor business can alone embrace.

If classical humanism suffers at the hands of scientific method, so does a sense of history. It is understandable that Americans wanted to break with the past, that immigrants wanted the New Life, pioneering a virgin soil, but this former rejection should not burden twentieth-century thinking. William Dean Howells wrote sadly: "History is an unwilling guest in our unmemoried land." [27] America jumped into the world stream with such vigor that it became convinced that its swift, forward movement made it unnecessary to take an occasional backward glance to see where it had been. Stieglitz said that in every five years in America there is a new generation. Americans need to acquire a relative time sense, to see that their nation developed in the context of Western civilization, not outside it, and that strong historical forces are governing its relation in the Atlantic community with the rest of the world. The professional American historians are only now gradually coming to see this, just as individual European nations have begun rewriting their national histories in a European sense. Americans have the possibility of looking at Europe objectively, as Europeans can look at the United States. However, no American has yet written a great intellectual history of Europe in the way that Tocqueville and Bryce looked at the United States.

Often the social scientists put too much confidence in the borrowed trappings of science—observing, copying, classifying, cataloging, and translating with charts, graphs, and polls—which, however useful, do not tell us the whole story or paint the whole picture. Social scientists produce vast collections of empirical data about particular events or manifestations and end up by saying nothing about behavior or acculturation and make only relativist conclusions. Statistics tell us only where we have been, not where we are, and are often of little use for predicting the future. Generalizations and statistics are the breath of the sociologists. It is ridiculous for "scientific" economists to look at man simply as a consumer of goods and to explain church-building, plagues, and wars by economic motivations. Because they have put "science" on their side, we accept their utterances with faithful credulity, still with the feeling that we are being crowded in on all sides by their statistical analyses. The social scientist would do well to recall the true meaning of science in German, *Wissenschaft,* which, with a more embracing translation into English, would be called knowledge.

Men are doltish and unpredictable, and move by habits, traditions, instincts, and prejudices, mostly scientifically unmeasurable. They are not machines, nor can they be easily forced into a Pavlovian pattern, as the Russians have found out. China's insectivization of its peasants, according to reports, has been a monumental failure covered over by traditional passivity. We might well remember that valuable and different insights are given by what Baudelaire called "passionate partiality," which can also be as true as the objectively impersonal. It may be a consolation to the humanist writer or scholar who tries to discard the scientific crutch to remember that science itself is hardly infallible and has an amazing way of reversing itself every so often, while the classics of great art and great literature go on forever.

America has the resources and the ability to produce a great culture.

Will these resources and ability be squandered? America may find that creative and spiritual impulse necessary to transcend itself. A prerequisite is a growing, stronger, deeper flow of skeptics, experimenters, taste-formers, creators, eggheads. All those concerned with the preservation and advance of Western culture must seek a higher level of discourse. When completing *The American Democracy*, Harold Laski wrote:

> National maturity is marked not merely by the ability to play a significant role on the stage of world history; it is marked, also, by the capacity of a people to recognize that it must be able to laugh at itself, and to reexamine, if necessary, the basic principles on which it is founded. It would be going too far to say that Americans in general have reached out to that second quality with any enthusiasm. But I do not think that it is going too far to argue that . . . a significant group of Americans, growing ever larger, has become aware that it would be necessary to undertake the task.[28]

Elsewhere he remarks more directly that "a fundamental change is needed in the direction of American life; for nothing is more fatal to the greatness of a culture than impotence to translate the mind of man from the relation of a past tradition to the relation of emerging creativeness."

A new human relationship is needed to solve today's problems. American conformity has to respect plurality and individualism which are formally incorporated in its ideals. America is a fluid and upward-moving society which should drive the machine, not be harnessed to it. Science *must* be controlled in man's favor and not to his destruction. The dehumanization of life may be arrested, and man rescued from the "indifferent flux" by healthy doses of art, religion, literature, philosophy, and history, which have always had *man* as their principal inquiry, and from which we learn things most worthwhile to the fruitful life and the pursuit of happiness.

NOTES

1. Paine, *Mark Twain's Notebook*, p. 395.
2. *The New York Times*, June 29, 1952.
3. Philip Wylie, *Opus 21* (New York: Holt, Rinehart & Winston, Inc., 1949), p. 13.

4. E. E. Cummings, "you shall above all things," *Poems 1923–1954* (New York: Harcourt, Brace & World, Inc., 1954), p. 345.

5. Cited in Peyre, p. 249.

6. Anthony Trollope, p. 271.

7. Cited in André Visson, *As Others See Us* (New York: Doubleday & Company, Inc., 1948), pp. 149–50.

8. Santayana, p. 95.

9. Marianne Moore, *Collected Poems* (New York: The Macmillan Company, 1961), p. 90.

10. Cited in Valentine, pp. 190–91.

11. Robinson Jeffers, *The Selected Poetry of Robinson Jeffers* (New York: Random House, Inc., 1959), p. 168.

12. Frances Trollope, p. 355.

13. Cited in Nevins, pp. 509–10.

14. Adams, *The Education of Henry Adams,* p. 237.

15. Siegfried, *America at Mid-Century,* p. 112.

16. Cited in Nevins, p. 512.

17. Cited in Valentine, p. 168.

18. T. H. Huxley, *American Addresses* (New York: Appleton-Century-Crofts, 1877), p. 125.

19. Cited in Valentine, p. 205.

20. Barzini, pp. 63–64.

21. MacLeish, *Poems, 1924–1933,* pp. 73–74.

22. Jacques Barzun, *Gods Country and Mine* (Boston: Little, Brown and Company, 1954), p. 144.

23. Brooks, *From the Shadow of the Mountain,* p. 190.

24. Cited in Kazin, p. 442.

25. *Ibid.,* p. 428.

26. Siegfried, *America at Mid-Century,* p. 356.

27. Cited in Brooks, *From the Shadow of the Mountain,* p. 41.

28. Laski, p. 67.

⊶ ATLANTIC COMMUNITY ⊷

La question que j'ai soulevée n'intéresse pas
seulement les Etats-Unis, mais le monde entier;
non pas une nation, mais tous les hommes.

—Tocqueville

The principal task facing the Western countries today is to make it widely
known that the Atlantic community exists. It has had a real existence for at
least two hundred years and has become more coherent with each generation.
Dominated in the eighteenth and nineteenth centuries by the British Empire
while the European continental land mass was controlled by France, the
Atlantic connection was clearly important in the turgid imperial conflicts for
supremacy. North America, it was realized, was not India. Nor was it to
develop, as Laski noted, like Canada or Australia, nor, as Tocqueville said,
like Latin America. The American relationship to Europe was different and
unique.

America had intrigued Europe since the Renaissance. Richard Hakluyt
stirred the European imagination with the wealth of the New World,
enumerated from precious gems to fine wines and delicious fowl and fish;
he concluded, "all the commodities of our olde decayed and dangerous trades
in all Europe, Africa and Asia haunted by us, may in short space and for
little or nothing, in a manner be had in that part of America which lieth
between 30 and 60 degrees of northerly latitude." [1]

The eighteenth-century struggle for power blurred the picture of the
transfer of Western culture from the Mediterranean to the Atlantic world, a
process beginning with the close of the Renaissance and the emergence of
the new national monarchies. The nineteenth century showed a clearer Atlantic pattern, particularly economically and socially, in the vast migration of
talents and skills to North America, a continuation of the earlier European
Völkerwanderung, greater than the barbarian invasions of the fifth century.
Between 1815 and 1914, over thirty million people left Europe for the
United States. There were closer contacts and quickening communication between the Old World and the New. There developed what Elie Halévy
described as an international mercantile republic. In America there was not

an imperialism of one people over another subject aboriginal people as in Asia and Africa. The American Indian was mostly shoved aside and then ignored, unlike the Incas and Aztecs. It was an effective colonization of virtually empty spaces and virgin land, literally a transfer of peoples to a new world without parallel.

To the solid economic and social bases of earlier centuries, the twentieth century added an increasing political integration, sometimes only reluctantly welcomed on both sides of the water. Today, Europe and America go spiritually and morally together. The tie that binds may not always be blessed, but it is a fact. Some may prefer to nurse parochial or national prejudices rather than accept the transatlantic relation. Once recognized, this relation upsets no basic assumptions common to the Western world.

The most important and common Atlantic task is to break out of the limiting narrow framework of the remaining vestiges of earlier statecraft and particularism and to make the new Atlantic order known for what it is. At this moment, Europeans seem to look on the Atlantic community as a limited partnership with limited risks. Americans seem to want a corporation with the blue-chip shares.

Atlantic tides are strong: it is our job to see that we are not individually stranded by an unexpected ebb tide. It is easier to unite for an immediate and common danger than for the attainment of a remote and disputed common good. At this point the Atlantic community is neither fact nor fiction. Lyndon Johnson in a NATO speech endorsed an Atlantic "confederation . . . a true Atlantic community with common institutions . . . a genuine political as well as economic community," and William Fulbright in *Foreign Affairs* called for the development of supranational institutions for the North Atlantic.

The social revolutions of the twentieth century indicate the need for wider outlooks and stronger regional groupings based on common attitudes and purposes. On both domestic and international planes we are obliged to enter upon vast collective measures, implying an increasing discipline of people, and with the danger that the individual will be crushed into a formless mass man. It is this danger that must be avoided to preserve the Western civilization as the evolving story of human liberty. We must remain captains of our souls.

The reality of the Atlantic community is not incompatible with the aspirations of other peoples: Western goals are identical with those of evolving nations, and the West willingly encourages others in mankind's upward march. The West's purpose is not to dominate, but to set men free with sustained economic and political growth. There is no question that we shall be poorer for the global responsibilities that we increasingly bear. We must likewise realize that no disinterested act of ours is probably to be admitted as completely virtuous by those we aid. The future of the Atlantic community is interwoven in the vast web of destinies of other peoples, often going in oblique directions, but the Atlantic community remains the solid center to provide the strength for the Afro-Asian periphery.

The extension of the Common Market to England and other European countries, and probably one day to Canada and America, with a possible Japanese association, will have enormous economic effects. It will mobilize the resources of the free world, embracing three of the four industrial complexes in the world against Russian or Chinese imperialism, and will certainly assure to us the balance of economic power. It is unthinkable that the wider common market, an Atlantic Market, will not come to pass; otherwise, we would abdicate the challenge, raise isolationist tariff walls, threaten our political and military alliances, and abandon the rest of the world to a communist future. The underdeveloped countries, including the semideveloped ones of Latin America, will not be blocked out of the Atlantic Market, for their development, as well as their sale of raw materials, depends on the West. The Soviet trading system cannot absorb all their raw materials nor give all the technical and economic assistance that the West can afford and encourage.

The new and emerging democracies will be menaced by the old feudal orders, visibly disintegrating under the impatience of masses prone to quick solutions and dictatorial means. This is not an original thing. In spite of 150 years of democratic constitutions, much of Latin America still oscillates between revolution and dictatorship. We must expect that when tehnical and economic aid is introduced to awaken slumbering masses stirring out of an age-old sleep, the social orders will be disrupted for a long time. Social injustices and cultural dislocations will be heightened, as they were in late eighteenth- and nineteenth-century England and France. America did not pass easily from a traditional agrarian society to a modern techno-industrial society, as the Populist revolt showed. We must expect that the development of the emerging countries will often be disorderly and chaotic, and that the new societies will listen equally to those who would help them and those who would use them. We must encourage a self-respecting independence and a self-sustaining rate of economic and political growth.

Western wealth was created by natural resources, inventive genius, ruthless enterprise, and broken workers. It was a costly affair in persons and materials, but there were social gains—such as a more literate society, more children able to remain in schools, a higher standard of living. There are now no more sodden slaves to the factory system such as Marx described, except in Soviet countries. Westernization of the underdeveloped world will bring the bad as well as the good. Democracy is not often relative to old or primitive cultures, which are primarily collective (the family, the tribe, mystic or pantheistic religions). Economic development does not mean that people become more democratic; in fact, state authoritarian controls are more often necessary to bring about a basic change, for changing an archaic agriculture is the basic condition to a changing social order. Whether there are traditional rulers or revolutionary leaders, they find social change difficult and prefer to incite xenophobia to distract popular passions from changing social disturbances.

It would be futile and downright misleading to instill the idea in most underdeveloped countries that prosperity is just around the corner and that their local capitals will soon glisten like Rome, Paris, London, or New York, or their cities hum with industries. It is unlikely that Ghana will become a black Switzerland. It is plain to see that there are parts of the world that will never, never be able to support a highly integrated technical industrial society and will continue, in the main, to supply raw materials to other regional industrial complexes. Making deserts blossom with fresh water made from sea water or making industry turn on a half pound of uranium is a long, very long, and expensive way off. And not least, even if everybody does become middle class, there is no reason to think that his life would have any more significance or value than the middle class has today.

The Atlantic community, to be true to itself, must know itself—its goals reiterated, its tasks constantly defined. Identity of purpose and not necessarily an identical viewpoint should be readily known and accepted by all, rather than airily admitted by a foreseeing few. Conflicts of Atlantic points of view are even necessary. Conflicts are inevitable incidents in any active system of cooperation and may be welcomed because they introduce healthy variations and modifications as the sign of a robust and living Atlantic society. We may expect that progress toward an Atlantic community will not be straightforward or even tangentially upward, but will often be distorted or distracted and subject to fluctuating emotions and momentary experiences.

In the face of a rapidly evolving new world order based on the ever-present and historic factors of race and religion, colored by nationalist or communist ideologies, we cannot forget that it is the West itself which created the tidal wave which threatens to engulf its own civilization. Our present jitters are caused by the fact that we are not sure that we shall now be able to ride the crest. The West must learn to live with itself and others without that hard knot of panic in the stomach, to find its own inner calm against outside pressures. We now seem to be in the winter of our own discontent. Our political chaos appears so real that it seems convincing.

The mantle of Mediterranean civilization has been inherited by our

Atlantic community. The question used to be asked: "What is Europe?" and the frequent answer was that it was but a changing geographic expression. The Atlantic countries are those which embrace this Western tradition. South America, by its geographical situation and by the fact that this Western heritage was highly filtered through Spain and Portugal, may be described as an appendage to the Atlantic community. North America must not be thought of as an Anglo-Saxon-Scotch-Irish lump as it existed until the mid-nineteenth century. The Italian and Greek and Scandinavian and Jewish influences are seen and felt as much as the German. North America is thus the composite of Europe, transformed by differing economic and social conditions but with all the characteristics that the son has of the father. America is Europe once-removed. The return of America to Europe, the so-called "Americanization" of Europe, is more than the return of the prodigal son: Europe's easy acceptance of American ways, accompanied by many European sighs, fortells some characteristis of an entirely new Atlantic society undergoing birth pangs.

It is nothing new to say that the United States now is and will remain the leading Western country in physical and industrial might. Now, when America sneezes, the world catches a cold. Colonel Ferri Pisani, aide to Prince Napoléon in America in 1861, feared this. "Will America someday be Europe's protector and master," he asked, "just as a hundred years ago Europe was America's? Faced with these redoubtable problems our pride and birthright revolt, while the insolent boldness of an ambitious race promises to solve them, to its advantage, before the end of the Twentieth Century." [2] America has not been a bully, as most will admit, but the United States must accept the leadership and the laboring oar. If no other nation will create a workable system of free states, perhaps with the military force necessary to protect them, the arrangements necessary for their economic development, and with a sufficient community of ideas and purposes for their political cohesion, this burden must be assumed.

However, America's undisputed leadership can no longer be what it was yesterday. Europe no longer actually needs to depend on the United States, as America did earlier on Europe, but there must be a reciprocal solidarity. Europe now plays a more respected, autonomous role in the partnership. While military power relationships between Europe and the United States have widened, there is no reason not to have closer political and economic contact.

Can we foresee some stronger institutional framework for the Atlantic community over the next twenty or thirty years? It is certain that NATO will undergo transformations from today's primarily military character,[3] with probably coequal political and economic bodies standing alongside. But it is idle to think of, or rather to discuss with a straight face at this point, the relinquishment of national sovereignties to a nebulous supergovernment. Because no one has adequately described what purely undefiled national sovereignty is, or where it rests, it is adding a doubt to an assumption. Harold Laski said that the real sources of sovereignty are undiscoverable. Great pieces of sovereignty, not to speak of national territory itself, have already been handed over under the elemental exigencies of the possibility of push-button warfare. Other coins of sovereignty (let us think of postal and communication systems) could conceivably be handed up without anyone feeling the difference except, perhaps, the added efficiency, but imagine the hue and cry from each country! Savigny was more correct than Condorcet: institutions are not made, they develop. The architect is necessary, but his blueprints would have little use without the bricklayer and stonemason. Constitution-writing does not get very far without a solid fundament, and chartism is only successful when it shows enough flexibility to be modified by changing circumstances. A law may be legislated, wisely or unwisely, but it is only in its application that it becomes effective law. Let necessity dictate the institutional framework of the Atlantic community.

A principal obstacle to a formal structuring of the Atlantic community is common sense. To paraphrase an old legal dictum, the Atlantic community must not only work, it must be *seen* to work. Then and only then will the doubting Thomas and the man from Missouri join the parade. The ground swell of the new Atlantic energy is still mostly below the surface and still escapes the notice of the average man in the street, although many lie fretfully awake at night worrying about problems that used to concern only statesmen and diplomats. Democratic people must solve problems by themselves and solutions cannot be forced from above. It is a long pull to make people understand what is necessary to be done.

Is this not the Atlantic mission? When the Atlantic peoples realize that some old bonds must be sprung and new and larger ones cast, we can then think of a stronger institutional framework, but not until then. When in the course of human events it becomes necessary to form a more perfect union, we shall do it. But when men do not make up their minds, events decide for them; *any* decision is better than indecision. The Atlantic community must be forged as a reality. The contact between Europe and America is still not automatic nor the exchange of ideas immediate. We must construct a continued cultural effort.

The Atlantic community's relationship to the European community is single and without any evident basic conflict, unlike other international organizations which introduce other interests and other areas. The European community is simply a smaller circle within a larger one, even allowing for momentary economic and political divisions. America, which has encouraged European unity since World War II. will come into one large trading, industrial circle which hopefully will embrace all countries of the non-Communist bloc. A more immediate danger is that the new economic construction of Atlantic peoples must not become so exclusive that it blocks the progress of the Afro-Asian and Latin American countries that will likewise need raw materials themselves as their industrialization increases.

Ruffled technicalities rather than starched principles need ironing out. Europe exists within the Atlantic community, and the two are locked in a perpetual embrace like Dante's lovers. Closer Atlantic assimilation automatically flows from closer European integration. One does not become "un-Atlantic" by becoming more European—an Italian may be "un-American" but pro-American, non-American but pro-Atlantean.

We can fix our objectives and determine our ends by taking into account our respected and different national traditions. We should not be like the caterpillar who bindly takes a new path while effacing the old one. Progress does not go onward in a single file simply for the sake of progress. Our progress should be rational and directed in the sense of organization, integration, and most of all, consolidation. We should keep an eye on the compass when the horizon is not yet completely seen.

The relation of the Atlantic community to other international organizations such as the British Commonwealth, the French system of alliances, and worldwide American commitments have admittedly made political relationships more difficult, bothered moreover by different peoples and differing social attitudes. Any answer can be valid only at a given time; all systems are subjected to strong ideological strains. Each of the principal partners of the Atlantic community is committed to leadership in its own sphere of influence, and all are nominally committed to the United Nations. These commitments may not necessarily be reconciled to the day-by-day purposes of the Atlantic community, and they may even enter into a basic conflict.[4] Each Atlantic country must bear its own responsibilities, imposed or assumed, as courageously and intelligently as possible and with the sympathetic, understanding aid of other members. Those Atlantic countries joined by historic ties to other organizations, it must be asserted, are the transmitters of the Western spirit, of the basic ideals of the community itself. All those in the Atlantic community can and should aid directly in the effort. The two continents are ordained to work together, for the successes and failures of one are those of the others as well. It is only putting on the blinkers of a new splendid isolationism for Europeans to talk of a Third Force, *ohne mich,* unilateralism. "Better Red than dead" is a very poor argument indeed of the "futilitarians."

One accomplishment has been the conversion of the OEEC into the

OECD (including Japan), nicely tying into a combined Atlantic plan all scattered efforts such as Colombo, Constantine, and other French aid, the successors of Point Four, and the growing U.S.-Latin American Alliance for Progress. This is the right pattern for our relation with lesser-developed countries, a scheme of things more acceptable to all. We can concentrate all our productive capacities contained in the Atlantic basin to achieve a total effort, rather than fritter away our immense combined resources in selfish indulgences of the political moment.

Is there a direct conflict or an area of possible conflicts between the United Nations and the Atlantic community? We see the dream of world community established at San Francisco melting into ineffectiveness because of contending and seemingly irreconcilable world factions (similar to the League's). The United Nations seems to be bursting apart with the violence of the atom. We have definitely not been crowning the good with brotherhood from sea to shining sea, but rather witnessing the tortured scrambling of a lobster pot.

People think erroneously that the United Nations can serve as a world tribunal, whereas it is only a world body expressing a parliamentary moral opinion. It has been expanded to include newly independent states the size of Rhode Island, and traditional nation-states are lost in the egalitarian principle. But this egalitarian principle is inconsistent with the present power structure, and will be for years to come. There is no reason for members of the Atlantic community to vote against each other in the United Nations, as has been done frequently. If a common policy has not been found, is it not enough for a particular Atlantic nation to abstain if it finds itself not in agreement? It is hurtful to vote against friends, and the wounds are not quickly healed nor an intimate confidence maintained. We live in glass houses but continue to throw stones at each other for all the world to see. Although it is worthwhile to coordinate allied action in the various parts of the world, we often see that an appeal for coordination is heard most loudly when there is the least allied coherence. A community of civilization does not promise political solidarity any more than cultural differences prevent political alliances. Dean Acheson cogently argues:

> It would be a great and dangerous mistake to mould political and military action out of a fancied necessity of "reconciling" it with the United Nations Charter. . . . To regard ourselves as inhibited by its words because we argue unsuccessfully that others should be so governed, or in order to set an example for those who have not the least intention of following it, seems to me a very bad bargain indeed.[5]

We should not shed tears over the breakdown of a world community, for it was never built up. As in the Kellogg-Briand Pact, sin is legislated against, and all subscribe, but the red-light districts continue. Reinhold Niebuhr neatly put it when he said, "irony is increased by the frantic efforts of some of our idealists to escape this hard reality by dreaming up schemes of an ideal world which have no relevance to our present dangers or our urgent duties." 6 World order is no longer held together by spiritual forces, as it was in the Middle Ages, when a lord might give up the idea of aggression if he were warned that he would roast for eternity. With the lack of a common spirit, United Nations idealists pretend that differences do not exist—because they prefer that they should not exist. People say that war is unthinkable because they do not wish to think about it.

More sensibly, regional organizations are sanctioned by the United Nations Charter. They are not only condoned but encouraged for the strengthening of peace. The successful future of the United Nations now lies in such organizations' mobilizing the basic interests of each world area on a secondary regional level and merging eventually at the summit in the United Nations. The establishment of an Afro-Asian bloc at the United Nations has concerned many, but it is natural and its effective power is felt. Perhaps the consternation is the result of the vagaries of a head without a body; those countries feel a regional pull, but have no solid, thoughtful organization uniting them to avoid the sometimes comic antics we see at the United Nations. The United Nations now has a majority of Afro-Asian members. When acting in concert or aligning with one or another bloc, they can control the Assembly. To some at least, this does not make sense, when many of these countries are smaller and less populated that many states of the United States or of Europe, and who do not have the background of political experience and responsibility developed in the Western world.

We must admit that Soviet Russia has done a good job of building up its regional organization of the "peaceful socialist camp." From the satellite regional periphery, the aim is now a 360-degree constellation. Truly, if this Communist circle is squared, we shall have peace of a sort, the silent peace of the graveyard littered with the tombstones of unfulfilled Western hopes. The East and the West are locked in an embrace like wrestlers, unable to budge, with purple faces, bursting veins, and bulging muscles. There has been a clear shift of traditional power situations. The USSR seeks to impede, frustrate, and confuse the building of any workable international system but its own triumph and dominion. Yet the West still seeks to "test Soviet intentions," wants on every issue to see if they are "sincere." They are "sincere" only insofar as they sincerely believe that they are advancing their own cause. The same may be said for Chinese imperialism. We have no system comparable to the Soviet; we have only loose groupings of nations without concerted leadership.

After World War I we tried to make the world safe for democracy, and since World War II we and the Soviets have tried to build walls to contain it. Now the political and economic counteroffensive must be maintained. We mistakenly tend to believe that all social revolutions are Communist inspired and consequently we create the very climate for Communism. In many ways our Western civilization produces the basic ideas for revolution, of the search for the better life, ending poverty and pestilential scourges, lengthening life and putting off death.

Western unity may be asserted within and without the United Nations, and traditional Western leadership felt by its moral as well as economic and political force. But our ideology will not be made to shine brightly through the use of words only. Otherwise how can the so-called "un-committed" countries be expected to align themselves to something which itself seems divided and querulous? St. Paul said, "if the trumpet give an uncertain sound, who shall prepare himsef to the battle?" It is rather easier to commit hungry and unenlightened peoples to a monolithic Marxian gospel with all its superficial answers in hand. It is an observable fact that Communism has come to pass only in backward countries, unlike the Marxist prediction.

We would prefer to be romantic Tom Sawyers, but that fence needs painting—a drab and dreary fact that the West needs to teach itself as well as others. Yet time is running out; we must get our Atlantic system underway, rather than supinely accepting a Spenglerian decline. We must decide between high consumption and hard work. Capital reinvestment abroad and accelerating international aid may develop a more powerful productive system for the free world. We daily witness private opulence and public squalor. John Gunther squarely addressed himself to the Americans: Is America a serious country? Do Americans really understand deeply enough the stunning irreversible changes that have come to the world in the past quarter century? Do Americans really understand that the world which was accepted so complacently twenty-five years ago is gone forever, and that life can never be the same again? Do Americans realize the basic character of the grim challenges that have come along? Marx may have been right for the wrong reason in saying that capitalism contained the seeds of its own destruction.

The moral influence of the United Nations has taken a terrible beating: who would then say that we should consequently cast off the morals of its presuppositions and ultimate aims? Rather too big a load and perhaps too much faith has been placed in the United Nations. These nations are much less united in purpose than the Holy Alliance which held together more or less as a system for a century, a short time in mankind's history. Because of shared interests in their own community welfare, regional groups such as the Atlantic community should shoulder many of the responsibilities which, for lack of a better place to go, have wound up in the United Nations. The moral impact of the United Nations will be better guarded if it is used as a court of appeal rather than first instance. It will never be a supreme court as long as the system of nation-states exists.

The Atlantic community, when made to realize what it represents, can help to guarantee a world order free and aspiring. We must guard and extend the loyalties of free men. Americans and Europeans should be wary of castles in the air, of fairy-tale organizations, of planification in the eighteenth-century, rationalist-utopian fashion. We must strengthen the real thing, for we need to build a house to relax in, not a fire department. The Atlantic community should know what it stands for and faithfully maintain its long tradition. Respect for its leadership will be acknowledged only when its leaders are able to impress clearly, under always changing circumstances, our familiar Western aims. Above the political shouts we need to reflect on constantly conflicting views, to make sure of our cultural aims, and to be convinced of our purpose. We should examine those things which go without saying to see if they still go. Shall we agree with Pope that:

> In human works, though laboured on with pain,
> A thousand movements scarce one purpose gain?

Each country must take stock of what it is doing in the Atlantic alliance, to regard its own relationship and possible greater contribution. Each country must bring its own individual and freely offered effort. Americans can only contribute to the community as Americans, English as English, and French as French. The Atlantic house must cease to be divided, but it must be a house of many mansions, not an enormous room.

The winds of progress blow fitfully, and our ship will often be becalmed or drift backward, but the Atlantic community, Western civilization, has brought mankind through time and tide further along than any other. We shall respect that civilization by recognizing what it represents not only to ourselves, but to others, thus assuring that the lamps that light our binnacle will be kept burning brightly across the Atlantic thoroughfare.

The consolidation of the Atlantic community goes on. It continues, despite momentary political and economic upheavals, and because its inherent unity of culture and advanced technology sets an example to the world. Yet this should not be an egocentric example. Other cultures have their own values which should be carefully respected while tendering the helpful hand.

NOTES

1. Richard Hakluyt, *The principall navigations, voiages and discoveries of the English nation, made by sea or ouer land, to the most remote and farthest distant quarters of the earth at any time within the compasse of these 1500 yeeres* (1589).

2. Pisani, p. 40.

3. A rose of a vastly different color from CENTO and SEATO, which hardly go further than occasional political conferences and consultations among general staffs.

4. American anticolonialism has had disastrous effects on relationships with European partners and its own strategic power situation: Roosevelt's Anfa meeting with the Sultan of Morocco; American pressure on France and England to surrender Treaty Port Rights in China; American refusal to admit Britain to the ANZUS pact; Grady's encouragement of Mossadegh with the consequent British surrender of Abadan; Caffrey's support of Naguib undermining traditional British influence in Egypt with the unexpected result of Nasserism; lack of consistent support of France in Indo-China and its own consequent involvement; pressure on the Dutch to relinquish the Dutch East Indies too soon; the Suez catastrophe; the bad-mannered "good offices" for Sakiet; weak support of the Goan problem; and so on. It is difficult to see how our Western alliance has been strengthen by such policies.

5. Dean G. Acheson, *Power and Diplomacy* (Cambridge: Harvard University Press, 1958), p. 42.

6. Reinhold Niebuhr, *The Irony of American History* (New York: Charles Scribner's Sons, 1952), p. 2.

◁ WAVES OF THE FUTURE ▷

We are acting all for mankind.

—Jefferson

This is a time that truly tries men's souls. The changes of today's world reflect the kind of changes that took place in the fourth century with the triumph of Christianity or in the seventeenth century with the dawn of modern science. The new world of the twentieth century must be brought into focus, a difficult task in face of Western pluralism and relativism. The Cartesian world view is discredited, but there has been no new synthesis to replace it unless it be the possible exception of a refined structuralism. We are given only philosophies of mathematical analysis, realism, pragmatism, or of despair and resignation.[1]

The existentialists argue only from phenomenology and behaviorism and block out the human psyche, while the "academic" proponents of mathematical analysis or Wittgenstein's linguistic analysis seem to lead us nowhere. An outstanding American philosopher, Lewis M. Feuer, frankly regrets that

> the intellectual history of contemporary America can be written today virtually without mention of its 2,100 or so professional philosophers. . . . They are mostly telling each other privately what a waste of time it all is, that nothing significant is being said and that they don't know what it's all about. . . .

He concludes that "philosophy is far too important to be left in the hands of the academic philosophers" and would prefer that the job be turned over to intellectual historians and scientists.

Contemporary science has crashed the frontiers of seventeenth-century cosmology, but now we are sunk into Einstein's "indifferent flux." Physics has moved so far away from our capacity to imagine things as they are (or were) that we cannot like Humpty Dumpty, put everything back together. In the eighteenth century, Christendom and God himself awaited the verdict of science and philosophers. Now the classical problem of man's philosophical relation to God is ignored, and some theologians and philosophers tell us that God is dead. Such an eminent physicist as the late P. W. Bridgman of Harvard said, "The structure of nature may eventually be such that our processes of thought do not correspond to it sufficiently to permit us to think about it at all. . . . We are confronted with something truly ineffable." Robert Oppenheimer repeated the theme: "Never has our common knowledge been so frail a part of what is known . . . in the world of learning there is mediation in the great dark of ignorance between the areas of light." [2]

We have the same thing offered us by the theologians. The Swiss Karl Barth says there is no longer a straight line from man to God. "What we say breaks apart constantly . . . producing paradoxes which are held together in seeming unity by agile and arduous running to and fro on our part"; in America, Reinhold Niebuhr affirms, "Life is full of contradictions and incongruities. We live our lives in various realms of meaning which do not cohere rationally."

When we cast a look at the world revolution about us we see insecurity everywhere, feel it ourselves, and react to it. We have the atomic strength of a Samson, with the power to bring the temple down on our heads. Adlai Stevenson said that all human society has become plastic and malleable in the flame of social revolution, and that human energies everywhere were seeking to run into new molds. We ask whether we shall always be living with a world out of focus. The unity of the universe is gone for the first time (from the Greeks, to Aquinas, to Descartes), but our natural will to order demands that a new unity be found. We insist on solving problems that cannot be solved. An American thinks that nothing is impossible, except perhaps his wife. But just as there are some things that cannot be understood, we must still believe in them. The humanist and the social scientist insist on tackling the problem of this new world revolution, with the hope that even as a problem is defined, a clue may be found.

The United States experienced the shock of recognition of the world, a new world which has extended our vision and changed our traditional values. Since World War II, America has gone through the biggest geography and history lesson since its establishment. In recent years America has had to take more risks than France and England at the height of their imperial power. Harold Laski wrote that we used a "rough map of the universe, a training in the art of living with other people, a realization of what is meant by a world perpetually in flux, and an insight into the art of self-adaptation to the fact of change." [3] This is a big order, but not an impossible one to fulfill.

Americans used to think that the highest aspiration for a foreigner was to be as American as possible; they believed they were the Gem of the

Ocean. Now, slowly, America is becoming cosmopolitan. Americans are beginning to realize that there are values other than their own, and values which do not often correspond to theirs. It is necessary to understand these other values. Santayana has said that to ignore the world "is ignominious and practically dangerous, because unless you understand and respect things foreign, you will never perceive the special character of things at home or of your own mind." Was it really laughable in 1940 when Senator Kenneth Wherry said, "With God's help, we will lift Shanghai up and up, ever up, until it is just like Kansas City."

In the 1930's, only 400,000 Americans annually visited abroad; today the number is over ten times higher. There are 1,600,000 Americans living abroad, over 21,000 students are enrolled in foreign universities, with Europe attracting about 70 per cent, and 4000 professors are teaching and researching abroad. In the total exchange, Americans abroad represent only 20 per cent, whereas 80 per cent come to the United States as foreign students. Only one-fiftieth as many Americans study in Asia or Africa as come from those areas. At present there are over 110,000 foreign students in the United States. About 9,000 foreign professors are teaching or doing research in American universities, approximately one-half of whom are from Europe.

Thousands cross the ocean to learn something from a new and friendly Atlantic nation and to impart something of their own national cultures, many of them talented enough and sensitive enough to become excellent interpreters of their own countries and the country which they visit. Students and teachers who would never have thought it possible to study abroad or in America now spend a profitable year inquisitively poking around.

The great foundations—Rockefeller, Guggenheim, Harkness, Carnegie, Ford, and others—greatly stimulate the passage of scholars to and fro; artistic treasures of our common heritage are restored, studied, and cataloged. The renewed spirit of *civis praeclarus* becomes basically important to mutual comprehension and intellectual stimulation. Research in art, science, and letters is greatly augmented. Versailles got a new roof, Rheims was renovated, and the American artists and classicists are house in neo-Roman grandeur at the American Academy of Rome. Brightly scrubbed young intellectuals are neatly bedded down at Rhodes House, Oxford, and are wakened to the subtle and deeply penetrating influence of that great university. It is not as Ezra Pound described in his *"Stark Realism":*

> This little American went to Oxford. He rented
> Oscar's late rooms. He talked about the nature
> of the beautiful. He swam in the wake of

Santayana. He had a great cut-glass bowl full of
lilies. He believed in Sin. His life was
immaculate. He was the last convert to Catholicism.[4]

Since the War, Americans have learned that others have something
to say in their own languages, not merely in accented English. At the
same time English, American English if you like, has become the second
language over the world. American institutes have proliferated and American
"studies" have penetrated the staid traditional European curricula. The
many centers established by American universities abroad help to assure
a constant dialogue. A host of "intercultural" publications has sprung up
and on the whole has not fared badly. Our ballets and orchestras cross
back an forth, and the international music festival has replaced the nineteenth-century spas, where people now flock, not to cure testy livers and
gout, but to seek mutual spiritual and intellectual refreshment. *Porgy and
Bess* plays in Vienna, the *Comédie Française* on Broadway, and *West Side
Story* in London, with great success. Kenneth Tynan spends a year "living"
Broadway, Eliot preferred London, Auden and Huxley the States. Lillian
Helman translates Anouilh; Cocteau, Tennessee Williams; Camus, Faulkner;
and Thornton Wilder moves in Germany's intellectual climes, having already
done Paris in the twenties. Giraudoux, Sartre, and De Beauvoir look at the
States through differently colored glasses, as did Duhamel in his *Scènes de la
vie future*.

The *mission civilisatrice* of France shows a much greater effort toward
international training, if taken by population and resources alone, than
any other country in the world. Foreign students in France have increased
greatly in numbers since World War II; a conservatively safe estimate by
the Ministry of Education is thirty thousand students, not including students
from French-speaking Africa. This is less than one-half the number of
foreign students in the United States, but a far greater proportion per-
centagewise. Approximately ten per cent of all foreign students come to
the United States under full or partial governmental auspices. In France,
fifteen per cent are subsidized by the French government.

England, like France, has done yeoman work in international educational
development. The grand total of all foreign students in Engand of every
category is over 55,000.

In contrast to all this effort in England and France (and other European
countries), America has not revised its attitude to new world challenges
and has not trained its own citizens and others in sufficient numbers to meet
effectively the requirements of the second half of the twentieth century
and after. Americans are generally not too interested in what is going on

abroad but live leisurely in one vast barbecue pit extending from coast to coast. America's strength has been so great that it has survived its weaknesses. Too often it is caught up by events rather than anticipating them. America should be on the takeoff rather than the more frequent crash landing.

There is not only a communist ideological threat to be faced by the Western world. In competing with communism the things which we are compelled to do are things which ought to be done anyway. Western Europeans and others often see East-West differences as differences between the United States and Soviet Russia, or equate Russia with the extreme Left, and therefore, the United States with the extreme Right. It is an easy but fallacious reasoning. Communism challenges the West like the earlier rise of Islam and will probaby suffer the same fate after all the crusading has been finished. In our ideological war, as in religious wars, the enemy will be partly pushed back, partly transformed, and partly assimilated. Anticommunism, in fact, is in danger of becoming as doctrinaire, undemocratic, and intolerant as communism itself. The communist menace must be fought with our methods, not theirs, using the techniques of freedom; respect for diversity, unlimited discussion, individualism, and personal liberty. Western free-world institutions should be based on Jefferson's words for the founding of the University of Virginia: "the illimitable freedom of the human mind. For here we are not afraid to follow truth wherever it may lead, nor to tolerate error so long as reason is free to combat it."

Are we gaining the world and losing our soul? As things stand, we are like Conrad's courageous captain who, "tossing aloft, and invisible in the night, gave back yell for yell to an easterly gale." We do not understand why Russia does not play the game according to Hoyle, why there is no "fair play." This is mental myopia. It is like asking Hindus or Muslims to see things as Protestants or Catholics do. Why is it so difficult to understand that countries and races of differing colors and traditional attitudes seek to integrate Western techniques into their own societies while maintaining their own identities?

It is one thing to take Western techniques, which are easily exportable, and another to take Western values such as liberty and individualism, which seem to need a kind of visa to get into other cultures. Jared Sparks told Tocqueville that those who would like to imitate America must remember that there are no precedents for its history. And Tocqueville jotted down, "Only an ambitious or a foolish man could, after seeing America, maintain that in the actual state of the world, American political institutions could be applied elsewhere than there. . . . When I speak of their institutions I mean taken as a whole. There is no people but could usefully adopt some of them." The task of Western leadership is not to allow underdeveloped countries to fall by default, but to give all cultural assistance possible to train those who wish to help themselves. This is the basic purpose that the emerging countries are seeking, and the longest lasting.

Abhorrence of foreign languages is deeply engrained in all people. For years, speaking a foreign language in the United States was the sign of the immigrant and had something "un-American" about it. In 1919, the laws of fifteen American states prohibited instruction in foreign languages. German was suspect and Russian virtually unknown, as were Oriental languages. If anyone wanted to speak to Americans, anything worthwhile should be said in English. This is not true and was never true, as many an American traveler can testify. Languages are the keys to communication and the understanding of other people's psychology and national temper. Henry Peyre, who has educated two generations of Americans in Romance languages at Yale University, stated:

> Too many American scientists, educators, men of affairs, army officers called upon to administer and train oftener than to fight, politicians and diplomats, businessmen and officials of international organizations behave like mute and inglorious cripples when attending meetings where a language other than their own is spoken. Even when simultaneous translation is provided, they lie at the mercy of interpreters; while multilingual foreigners do part of their work in the lobbies, at the bar where truth in wine is revealed, in conversation with wives at which masks might be lifted and playful hints dropped and picked up, monolingual Americans feel out-talked and outwitted.[5]

Language instruction (or, rather, the effective teaching of a *second* or *third* language) meets but one-half of the problem facing youth entering today's world scene. Language is only a tool. Vastly more international education must be included in college and university study in America and abroad. There is a preoccupation with minutiae that blots out the great and tragic outlines of contemporary history. International education should be the ferment to brew a new intellectual environment.

A liberal arts education, humanistic and international minded, has been regarded as a pretty piece of bric-a-brac decorating an "efficient" and "useful" education. When a *Fortune* survey asked parents why they wanted their children to go to college, most replied for "a better job or profession"; only two per cent said for "culture, appreciation of the arts." A liberal arts education is most central to the concept of the dignity and rights of man on both sides of the Atlantic.

"Useful" education for "common" knowledge is not a new thing in American life. The character of the American Philosophical Society for the Promotion of Useful Knowledge, a Jeffersonian as well as New England Puritan idea, was to devote itself to "common purposes of life, by which trade is enlarged, agriculture improved, the arts of living made more easy and comfortable and the increase and happiness of mankind promoted." The Morrell Act projected the same idea during the Civil War in establishing land-grant colleges for Agricultural and mechanical arts. It is a utilitarian concept that taste makes waste. What is needed is a change in intellectual style, for too many academicians have fallen into prolix scholasticism and pedantry. Universities become bigger and bigger haystacks where scholars search for smaller and smaller needles.

Thus the average is seldom exceeded, the intellectual level eventually drops, and too many clods are produced on the horizon. Excellence becomes undemocratic, the uncommon man intolerable, and the mean far from golden. Too many educational institutions remind us of Tennyson's words:

> Where blind and naked Ignorance,
> Delivers brawling judgments, unashamed,
> On all things all day long.

The public image, of absent-minded professors in the halls of ivy sneers at the fine craftsmanship involved in teaching, a diminution of the educative spirit, and acceptance of shoddy standards, a case of the halt leading the bland. Tocqueville perceived this on his American visit:

> With them the tradition of cultivated manners is going. The people be-
> come educated, knowledge spreads, and middling ability becomes com-
> mon. Outstanding talents and great personalities are rare. Society is less
> brilliant and more prosperous. The various effects of the progress of civi-
> lization and enlightenment, about which only Europe is in doubt, can
> be seen as clear as day in America.

Lincoln said that God must have liked the common man because he made so many of them. It is fallacy to hold the common people inherently "good," *vox populi, vox Dei,* for it leads only to Rousseau's General Will, which, when followed to its ultimate limits, provides the basis for popular dictatorship. To speak of the common man must imply that there are uncommon men, either of intellectual ability, physical drive, or wealth. In education as in society, a mass lobotomy is being performed, where students and citizens take cues from "right thinking" people, move by instincts rather than thought, and form the body of "public opinion." The instant formula for every man of the hour is to stir in sixty Minute Men from the convenient, handy package.

Tocqueville asked:

Why, as civilization spreads, do outstanding men become fewer? Why, when attainments are the lot of all, do great intellectual talents become rarer? Why, when there are no longer lower classes, are there no more upper classes? Why, when knowledge of how to rule reaches the masses, is there a lack of great abilities in the direction of society? America clearly poses these questions.

The major portion of our thought is now devoted to substitutions for thought. We get a new model or new song every year, with minor, superficial, shallow changes. This can only lead to faddism and tabloid minds, the common man enthroned in a faceless ruling class without individual affirmation, which is what both Tocqueville and Matthew Arnold feared. Even heroes like Washington, Franklin, and Lincoln are supposed to have the element of greatness because they have the "common touch." It seems clear, at least to me, that high individual performance must depend on a society which exacts it. Now there is too much fat and not enough lean, hard, sinewy meat in our thinking. The challenge is in a new view of international life. Visitor Martin Chuzzlewit was informed: "We are a busy people, Sir . . . and have no time for reading mere notions We don't mind 'em if they come to us in newspapers along with almighty strong stuff of another sort, but darn your books." The highbrow intellectual and the good professor are commonly thought to carry theory beyond practical common sense and therefore are at least mildly suspect. Yet, any new idea is by definition "radical" in applying change to established patterns. Adlai Stevenson urged a reorientation of our ideals and tastes, the extension of mental and artistic talent. He called for an excellence above social approval, and a mental achievement above quick material success: in brief, a new standard of respect and reward for intellect and culture in cooperation with other communities of scholars and creative thinkers in order to share the pursuit of truth with all mankind.

Up to now, there has been too much intellectual waste in an American society which prides itself on efficiency. Americans pay lip service to international cultural life but trifle with it in practice. The most valuable capital today, and worth the highest investment, is the well trained, world-oriented individual. Labor, in the old economic sense, is simply a burden to a new international technological society. William James foresightedly said in 1906, "the world . . . is only beginning to see that the wealth of a nation consists more than anything else in the number of superior men that it harbors," [6] and Alfred North Whitehead reiterated. "in the conditions of modern life, the rule is absolute, the race which does not value trained intelligence is doomed." [7] For the public good, intellectual extension is needed. It is possible to free the intellect from specialized areas of knowledge and offer a wider world view.

Too often America talks and reads about how many youngsters go to the university rather than how much education they get. The increase in university attendance does not necessarily make any country the most intelligent nation, either in special wisdom, aesthetic discrimination, or even spiritual and emotional serenity. Technical efficiency, yes, but quality and recognition of human values, a question mark. America is grinding out skilled but uneducated people. A liberal international education is a prerequisite to intellectual strength. Universities are not simple repositories of learning and a haven for professional misfits who "couldn't make a go in business," but are the vital transmitters of our culture and the shapers of the rational and human attitude necessary to a world view. There is an indispensable minimum of sound knowledge of other countries and other values which must be imparted unless we choose to live even more dangerously than we do at present.

Increasing world responsibility and mature judgment are required in the serious handling of international affairs. Clinton Rossiter bemoans the American situation:

> Let us be honest about it: we have the wealth, and leisure and techniques to make a great culture an essential part of our lives, an inspiration to the world, and a monument to future generations—and we have not even come close to the mark. When will we come to realize that lives without culture are lives half-lived . . .? [8]

The United States likes to think of itself as "realistic," but it is often unaware of reality: international affairs are looked at like a morality play. Statesmen move about like puppets on the world scene, but their strings are too short. America is not in Jackson's time when egalitarianism went so far that trained personnel in public service were considered unnecessary.

Ever since World War II, the United States has shown a remarkable capacity to rationalize losses to communism and to gradual shifts of power.

A merely passive spectatorship of today's uneasy world becomes unethical, given the responsibilities of Western leadership. A nation remaining in inert self-satisfaction has not long to survive, for history is getting ahead of schedule, and the world revolution is every day happening faster than we thought or expected it would. There are no longer effective sea barriers to isolate America from the world, nor old, stable European colonial systems to act as a buffer. Americans must virtually have a direct knowledge of the New Europe, the New Africa, the New Asia, the New Latin America, and, indeed, for that matter the New America. Americans and Europeans must all paint a larger mural on a greater wall to achieve a newer, more creative civilization.

At last count, the United States is committed to defend forty-five nations on five continents. It has economic aid programs in eighty countries. Clearly, America must strip off its illusions and self-indulgence which its own history has until recently permitted. Until twenty years ago, America was consolidated with little sacrifice as a world power. "It is hard for Americans to realize that the survival of their idea for which this nation stands is not inevitable," says John W. Gardner.

> It may survive if enough Americans care enough. . . . All the signs are not encouraging. At just this moment in history when we need all our vitality, we are in danger of losing our bearings, in danger of surrendering to a "cult of easiness." It does not need a carping critic to detect the slackness, slovenliness and bad workmanship in our national life.[9]

International affairs were once regarded as mere formalities to be taken care of by the Secretary of State. "The diplomatic service," *The New York Sun* wrote in 1889, "is a costly humbug and sham. It is a nurse of snobs. It spoils a few Americans every year, and does no good to anybody. Instead of making ambassadors, Congress should wipe out the whole service." Henry Adams lamented in 1906, "The Secretary of State exists only to recognize the existence of a world which Congress would rather ignore." Secretary of State Elihu Root in 1913 summed up the traditional American point of view. "In this country, international law was regarded as a rather antiquated branch of useless learning, diplomacy as a foolish mystery and the foreign service as a superfluous expense." More recently, McCarthy and his followers have relied on the traditional conspiracy theory to describe Americans in international affairs: that diplomats are aristos or homos in striped pants.

In 1793, the United States was out of touch with Europe for three months during the winter. Most Washington officials would welcome that now. In 1896, the State Department numbered thirty-one people, and in 1939, all could pose on the steps of the Old State Department building for a picture with Cordell Hull. Now in the State Department alone there are 13,000 employees and 10,000 local national employees in embassies and consulates. The United States Information Service has 11,000 employees, and the Agency for International Development, 15,000. There are many thousands in the Central Intelligence Agency; their number is not known, but Theodore H. White reported that in many countries the CIA has more agents than the State Department and ten times the spending money. When the Peace Corps and the Disarmament Agency, Treasury, Agriculture, and Labor personnel abroad are also added, the immensity of training these people to be effective representatives abroad becomes abundantly clear.

Now the cushions are gone and the United States will not have anything for nothing. If America comes to any good, it must get there by its own efforts. It can no longer get along with late starts, feeble alliances, and mediocre efforts. The possibiity that its efforts may sometimes fail does not lift the responsibility of finding out what is needed and trying to obtain it. We might harken back to Emerson: "I wish to see America as no country ever was . . . the office of America is to liberate, to abolish kingcraft, priestcraft, castle, monopoly, to pull down the gallows, to burn up the bloody statute-book, to take in the immigrant, to open the doors of the sea and the fields of the earth."

A democratic life in this world requires effort; it is not a comfortable refuge or line of least resistance. Americans have been coasting, but now they are sliding downhill rapidly over the dangerous problems of international life with much veering and lurching from crisis to crisis, wakened from their torpitude to one astonishment after another. Americans have been oscillating rather than fixing definite goals and concentrating on them. American have been speaking loudly and using the big pogo stick. There are signs that America may be in the process of destroying its moral and cultural values while defending them physically, for Americans love to deceive themselves and hate to be shorn of their illusions and myths. Presidents, politicians, and press prefer to reassure the people rather than to disturb their tranquil habits. No one likes to discuss unpopular subjects; most people prefer to sail on a sea of misinformation without getting the "whole story." America runs on headlines only.

Americans have, to their cost, been excessively culture-bound in facing the mammoth tasks of the twentieth century. A new intellectual mobilization and fresh assessment by a wider group of thinking people is required. No one can assume that the new tasks are temporary emergencies: there will be no "return to normalcy." The new tasks must be regarded as new opportunities.

∽≁

Up to now, America has been sailing by old landmarks in new seas, grating over reefs with many a bump and grind. Yesterday's attitudes are today's cherished but useless heirlooms, which are being constantly polished and reverently regarded. American optimism often counts on the future to remedy the failures of the past and the shortcomings of the present. Americans talk too much about living standards and not enough about an art of living. It is clear that the United States is not successfully galvanizing the imagination of friends abroad. The clarion has been muffled, for what the outsider sees is a high standard of low living. Technology and enterprise can produce a higher economic standard but cannot of itself produce a higher culture or standard of life. In the acquisitive society which the West embodies, worth is measured too much in money and symbols of quality (the "biggest"), goods are often mistaken for the Good, which is not what was meant by the American forefathers' "pursuit of happiness." American society hums like a vast, glisteningly smooth machine, but it would be nice to know what we are making. Is a great and glorious society only to be big and glamorous? Will an Atlantic society be written down in history as one representing the Eminent Vulgarians? Before the final act is consummated will the world continue to witness just so many pitfalls and pratfalls? Will it be like *Hamlet,* with corpses spread all over the stage? Our responsibility is to bend every effort to make sure of the outcome.

The perspectives which science and technology hold out for the later twentieth century force us into new individual attitudes and a new attention toward the patterns of a new society. The flux is already seen in the dissatisfaction of our boisterous youth in America and Europe with the old order. Europe and America should listen to them for new ideas. Perhaps through the next international humanistic generation we shall see the rise of the uncommon man.

NOTES

1. Many valuable insights may be gained from Peter F. Drucker, *Landmarks of Tomorrow* (New York: Harper & Row, Publishers, 1957).

2. Robert Oppenheimer, "Atomic Weapons and American Foreign Policy," *Foreign Affairs,* XXXII (July, 1953), 530–32.

3. Laski, p. 333.

4. Pound, *Pavannes and Divagations* (New York: New Directions, 1958), p. 104.

5. Peyre, p. 9.

6. William James, "Stanford's Ideal Destiny," Founders Day Address, 1906 (New York: Longman, Green & Co., 1934).

7. Alfred North Whitehead, *Aims of Education* (New York: The Macmillan Company, 1929).

8. John K. Jessup *et al., The National Purpose* (New York: Holt, Rinehart & Winston, Inc., 1960), p. 87.

9. John W. Gardner, *Excellence* (New York: Harper & Row, Publishers, 1961), p. 147.

☙ BIBLIOGRAPHY ❧

Aaron, Daniel. *Men of Good Hope*, New York: Oxford University, 1951.

Abrams, Irwin. "The American Abroad: A Preface," *The Antioch Review*, Vol. XVIII, No. 4 (1960).

Acheson, Dean. *Power and Diplomacy*. Cambridge: Harvard University Press, 1958.

Acton, Lord. "Lord Acton's American Diaries," *Fortnightly Review*, CX, CXI (London, 1921).

Adams, B. P. (ed.). *You Americans*. New York: Funk & Wagnalls, 1939.

Adams, Charles Francis. *Richard Henry Dana*, 2 vols. Boston: Houghton Mifflin, 1891.

Adams, E. D. *Great Britain and the American Civil War*. New York: Longmans, Green. 1925.

Adams, Henry. *Democracy*. Cambridge: Henry Holt, 1880.

———. *The Education of Henry Adams*. Boston: Houghton Mifflin, 1907.

———. *Mont St. Michel and Chartres*. Boston: Houghton Mifflin, 1904.

Adams, Walter, and Garrity, John. *Is the World our Campus?* East Lansing: Michigan State University Press, 1960.

Aldridge, Alfred O. *Franklin and his French Contemporaries*. New York: New York University Press, 1957.

Algren, Nelson. *Who Lost an American?* New York: Macmillan, 1963.

Allen, H. C. *The Anglo-American Relationship Since 1783*. London: A. C. Black, 1959.

Almond, Gabriel A. *The Struggle for Democracy in Germany*. Chapel Hill: University of North Carolina Press, 1949.

American Historical Association. *Talleyrand in America As a Financial Promoter 1794–96*. Translated and edited by Hans Huth and Wilma J. Pugh, 3 vols. Washington, D.C.: Government Printing Office, 1942.

American Studies Association. *American Perspectives, the National Self-Image in the Twentieth Century*. Edited by Robert E. Spiller and Eric Larrabee. Cambridge: Harvard University Press, 1961.

Amphlett, William. *The Emigrant's Directory to the Western States of North America*. London, 1819.

An American (anonymous). *Rambles in Italy in the Years 1816–1817*. Baltimore, 1818.

Anderson, Carl L. *The Swedish Acceptance of American Literature*. Stockholm: Almquist & Wiksell, 1957.

Anglo-American Yearbook, 1936. Directory and Guide to London, Americans with British Titles and the Anglo-American Who's Who. London, 1913– .

Arendt, Hannah. *On Revolution*. New York: Viking Press, 1963.

Armfield, Maxwell. *An Artist in America*. London: Methuen, 1925.

Armstrong, Emma Kate. "Chateaubriand's America. Arrival in America and First Impressions," Modern Language Association of America, new series, XV, 345–70.

Arnavon, Cyrille. *Histoire littéraire des Etats-Unis*. Paris: Hachette, 1931.

———. *L'Américanisme et nous*. Paris: Editions mondiales Del Duca, 1958.

———. *Les lettres Américaines devant la critique française (1878–1917)*. Lyon: Annales de l'Université de Lyon, 1951.

Arnold, Matthew. *Civilization in the United States: First and Last Impressions of America*. Boston: Cupples & Hurd, 1888.

———. *Discourses in America*. London: Macmillan, 1885.

Aron, Raymond. *France: Steadfast and Changing. The Fourth to the Fifth Republic*. Cambridge: Harvard University Press, 1960.

———. and Heckscher, August. *Diversity of Worlds: France and the United States Look at Their Common Problems*. New York. Reynal, 1957.

Aron, Robert, and Dandieu, Armand. *Le cancer américain*. Paris: Rieder, 1931.

Arvin, Newton. *Longfellow: His Life and Work*. Boston: Little, Brown. 1963.

Asselineau, Roger (ed.). *The Literary Reputation of Hemingway in Europe*. New York: New York University Press, 1965.

Atkinson, Brooks (ed.). *The Complete Essays and other writings of Ralph Waldo Emerson*. New York: Modern Library, 1940.

Atlantic Union. Annual Report for 1906.

Auden, W. H. *The Age of Anxiety*. New York: Random House, 1947.

Augas, W. M. *Rivalry on the Atlantic*. New York: Furman, 1939.

Babbitt, Irving. *Criticism in America*. New York: Harcourt, Brace, 1924.

———. *Democracy and Leadership*. Boston: Houghton Mifflin, 1924.

———. *Masters of Modern French Criticism*. New York: Noonday Press, 1963.

Baker, Paul R. *The Fortunate Pilgrims: Americans in Italy, 1800–1860*. Cambridge: Harvard University Press, 1964.

Baldensperger, Fernand. *Le mouvement des idées dans l'émigration française, 1789–1815*. 2 vols. Paris: Plon-Nourrit, 1924.

————. "Le séjour de Brillat-Savarin aux Etats-Unis," *Revue de la littérature comparée* (Paris, 1922.)

Barrett, E. W. *Truth is Our Weapon.* New York: Funk & Wagnalls, 1953.

Barth, Alan. *The Loyalty of Free Men.* New York: Viking Press, 1951.

Barzini, Luigi, Jr. *Gli Americani sono soli al mondo.* Milan: A.Mondadori, 1952.

Barzun, Jacques. *God's Country and Mine.* Boston: Little, Brown, 1954.

————. *The House of Intellect.* New York: Harper & Row, 1959.

————, and Graff, Henry F. *The Modern Researcher.* New York: Harcourt, Brace and World, 1957.

Baur, John I. H. *Revolution and Tradition in Modern American Art.* Cambridge: Harvard University Press, 1951.

Beach, Joseph Warren. *American Fiction, 1920–1940.* New York: Macmillan, 1941.

Beals, Ralph L., and Humphrey, Norman D. *No Frontier to Learning.* Minneapolis: University of Minneapolis Press, 1957.

Beard, James Franklin (ed.). *The Letters and Journals of James Fenimore Cooper.* Cambridge, Belknap Press, 1960.

Becker, Carl L. *The Declaration of Independence.* New York: Harcourt, Brace & World, 1922.

————. *Freedom and Responsibility in the American Way of Life.* New York: Alfred A .Knopf, 1945.

————. *New Liberties for Old.* New Haven: Yale University Press, 1941.

Beer, Thomas. *The Mauve Decade, American Life at the End of the Nineteenth Century.* New York: Alfred A. Knopf, 1926.

Bell, Daniel (ed.), *The New American Right.* New York: Criterion, 1955.

Belloc, Hillaire. *The Contrast.* New York: R. M. McBride & Co., 1924.

Beloff, Max. *The United States and the Unity of Europe.* Washington: The Brookings Institution, 1963.

Bennett, Arnold. *Your United States.* New York: Harper & Row, 1912.

Benton, T. H. *An Artist in America.* New York: R. M. McBride & Co., 1937.

Berger, Max. *The British Traveller in America, 1836–1860.* New York: Columbia University Press, 1943.

Bernays, Edward L. *Crystallizing Public Opinion.* New York: Boni & Liveright, 1923.

Bernhard, Duke of Saxe-Weimar Eisenach. *Travels through North-America, 1825–26.* Philadelphia: Carey, Lea and Carey, 1828.

Berryman, John. *Stephen Crane.* New York: William Sloane Associates, 1950.

Berthoff, Rowland T. *British Immigrants in Industrial America, 1789–1950.* Cambridge: Harvard University Press, 1953.

Bestor, Arthur E., Jr. *Backwoods Utopias.* Philadelphia: University of Pennsylvania Press, 1950.

Beyle, Henri (Stendhal). *De l'Amour.* Paris: Michel Lévy, 1853.

Bigelow, John. *Retrospections of an Active Life.* 5 vols. New York: Baker & Taylor, Co., 1909.

Billington, Ray Allen. *The Protestant Crusade, 1800–1860: A Study of the Origins of American Nativism.* New York: Macmillan, 1938.

Birdsall, Paul. *Versailles Twenty Years After.* Hamden, Conn.: The Shoe String Press, Inc., 1941.

Birkenhead, F E., *America Revisited.* Boston: Little, Brown, 1924.

———. *My American Visit.* London: Hutchinson & Co., 1918.

Blodgett, Harold. *Walt Whitman in England.* Ithaca, Cornell University Press, 1934.

Blouet, Paul. *A Frenchman in America.* New York: Cassell, 1891.

Blowe's Emigrants Directory. Geographical, historical, commercial, and agricultural view of the United States of America; forming a complete emigrant's directory through every part of the republic. London: Edward & Knibb, 1820.

Blum, John Morton. *The Promise of America.* Boston: Houghton Mifflin, 1966.

———. *Woodrow Wilson and the Politics of Morality.* Boston: Little, Brown, 1956.

Bok, Edward. *The Americanization of Edward Bok.* New York: Scribner's, 1920.

Boorstin, Daniel J. *America and the Image of Europe.* New York: Meridian, 1960.

———. *The Image, or, What Happened to the American Dream?* New York, Atheneum, 1962.

Boulding, Kenneth. *Organizational Revolution, a Study in the Ethics of Economic Organization.* New York: Harper & Row, 1953.

Bourget, Paul. *Outre-Mer, Impressions of America.* New York: Scribner's, 1895.

Bowers, Claude G. *The Spanish Adventures of Washington Irving.* Boston: Houghton Mifflin, 1940.

Bowers, David F. *Foreign Influences in American Life.* Princeton: Princeton University Press, 1944.

Bowle, John. *Politics and Opinion in the Nineteenth Century.* New York: Oxford University Press, 1954.

Boyesen, H. H. "Amerca in European Literature," *Literary and Social Silhouettes.* New York: Harper, 1894.

Bright, John. *A Friendly Voice from England on American Affairs.* New York: William C. Bryant & Co., 1862.

Brillat-Savarin, Anthelme. *Physiologie du gout.* Paris: A. Sautelet, 1826.

Brinton, Crane. *The Lives of Talleyrand.* New York: W. W. Norton, 1936.

Brodin, Pierre. *Ecrivains Américains du vingtième siècle.* Paris: Horizons de France, 1946.

Brogan, Denis W. *The American Character.* New York: Alfred A. Knopf, 1941.

————. *The American Problem.* London: Hamish Hamilton, 1944.

————. *American Themes.* New York: Harper, 1949.

Broglie, Albert, duc de (ed.). *Memoirs of the Prince de Talleyrand.* Paris: The Napoleon Society, 1895.

Brooke, Rupert. *Letters from America.* New York: Scribner's, 1916.

Brooke-Cunningham, C. A. *Anglo-Saxon Unity and Other Essays,* London: Selwyn & Blount, 1925.

Brooks, John Graham. *As Others See Us, A Study of Progress in the United States.* New York, Macmillan, 1910.

Brooks, Robert C. (ed.). *Bryce's "American Commonwealth": Fiftieth Anniversary.* New York: Macmillan, 1939.

Brooks, Van Wyck. *America's Coming-of-age.* New York: B. W. Huebsch, 1914.

————. *The Confident Years 1885–1915.* New York: Dutton, 1955.

————. *Days of the Phoenix.* New York: Dutton, 1957.

————. *The Dream of Arcadia: American Writers and Artists in Italy, 1790–1915.* New York: Dutton, 1958.

————. *Emerson and Others.* New York: Dutton, 1927.

————. *From the Shadow of the Mountain.* New York: Dutton, 1961.

————. *Howells: His Life and World.* New York: Dutton, 1959.

————. *New England Indian Summer, 1865–1915.* New York: Dutton, 1940.

————. *The Ordeal of Mark Twain.* New York: Dutton, 1933.

————. *The Pilgrimage of Henry James.* New York: Dutton, 1925.

————. *Three Essays on America: America's Coming of Age, Letters and Leadership, The Literary Life in America.* New York: Dutton, 1934.

————. *The Wine of the Puritans.* London: Sisley Ltd., 1908.

Brooks-Wright Foundation. *Aspects of Anglo-American Relations.* New Haven: Yale University Press, 1928.

Brown, Stuart Gerry. *Memo for Overseas Americans: The Many Meanings of American Civilization.* Syracuse: Syracuse University Press, 1960.

Browning, Elizabeth B. *Letters of Elizabeth Barrett Browning.* 2 vols. New York: Macmillan, 1897.

Bruckberger, Raymond Léopold. *La république américaine*. Paris: Gallimard, 1958.

Bryant, Arthur. *The American Ideal*. New York: Longmans, Green, 1936.

Bryce, James. *The American Commonwealth*. 2 vols. London: Macmillan, 1893–95.

Bryson, Lyman. *The Next America: Prophecy and Faith*. New York: Harper & Row, 1952.

Buchan, Alastair. *NATO in the 1960s: The Implications of Interdependence*. New York: Praeger, 1963.

Burnham, James. *The Managerial Revolution*. New York: John Day, 1941.

————. (ed.). *What Europe Thinks of America*. New York: John Day, 1953.

Cairns, William B. "British Criticisms of American Writings, 1793–1815," *University of Wisconsin Studies in Language and Literature*, No. 1, Madison: University of Wisconsin Press, 1918.

————. "British Criticisms of American Writings, 1815–1833," *University of Wisconsin Studies in Language and Literature*, No. 14, Madison: University of Wisconsin Press, 1922.

Callaghan, Morley. *That Summer in Paris*. Toronto: Macmillan, 1963.

Cambiaire, C. P. *The Influence of Edgar Allen Poe in France*. New York: G. E. Stechert & Co., 1927.

Canby, Henry Seidel. *Turn West, Turn East: Mark Twain and Henry James*. Boston: Houghton Mifflin, 1951.

Canfield, Dorothy. *The Deepening Stream*. New York: Harcourt, Brace, 1930.

Cantril, Hadley. *Public Opinion, 1935–1946*. Princeton: Princeton University Press, 1951.

Cargill, Oscar. *Intellectual America: Ideas on the March*. New York: Macmillan, 1941.

Carlier, Auguste. *La république américaine*. 4 vols. Paris: Guillaumin & Cie, 1890.

Carnegie, Andrew. *The Empire of Business*. New York: Doubleday, 1902.

Case, Lynn M. *French Opinion on the United States and Mexico, 1860–1867*. New York: Appleton-Century, 1936.

Cerami, Charles A. *Alliance Born of Danger: America, The Common Market and the Atlantic Partnership*. New York: Harcourt, Brace, 1963.

Chadourne, Marc. *Quand Dieu se fit américain*. Paris: Fayard, 1950.

Chambrun, Adolphe, marquis de. *Impressions of Lincoln and the Civil War*. New York: Random House, 1952.

Chasles, Philarète. *Etudes sur la littérature et les moeurs des Anglo-Américains au XIXe siècle*. Paris: Amyot, 1851.

Chastellux, François Jean, marquis de. *Voyages dans l'Amérique septen-tionale dans les années 1790, 1791 et 1792*. 2 vols. Paris: Prault, 1788–1791.

Chester, Edward W. *Europe Views America: A Critical Evaluation*. Washington: Public Affairs Press, 1962.

Chesterton, G. K. *What I Saw in America*. New York: Dodd, Mead, 1923.

Chevalier, Michel. *Letters sur l'Amérique du Nord*. 2 vols. Paris: Gosselin, 1837.

Cheyney, Edward Potts. *European Background of American History, 1300–1600*. New York: Harper & Row, 1904.

Child, Frances S. *French Refugee Life in the United States, 1790–1800*, 1940.

Chinard, Gilbert. *L'Amérique et le rêve exotique dans la littérature française au XVIIe XVIIIe siècles*. Paris: Hachette, 1913.

———. *La Doctrine de l'Américanisme*. Paris: Hachette, 1918.

———. *George Washington as the French Knew Him*. Princeton: Princeton University Press, 1940.

———. *Honest John Adams*. Boston: Little, Brown, 1933.

Clay, Lucius D. *Decision in Germany*. New York: Doubleday, 1950.

Cleveland Harlan. "The Real International World and the Academic Lag," *New Viewpoints in the Social Sciences*, National Council for the Social Studies, Washington, D.C.: National Education Association, 1958.

———, and Mangone, Gerald J. *The Art of Overseamanship*. Syracuse: Syracuse University Press, 1957.

———, and Adams, John Clarke. *The Overseas Americans*. New York: McGraw-Hill, 1960.

Cobb, Irwin S. *Paths of Glory—Impressions of War Written at and near the Front*. New York: Dutton, 1915.

Cobbett, William. *The Emigrant's Guide*. London: The Author, 1829.

———. *Observations on the Emigration of a Martyr to the Cause of Liberty*. (Peter Porcupine, 1794).

———. *A Year's Residence in the United States of America*. 3 vols. London, Sherwood, Nedy, and Jones, 1818–19.

Cocteau, Jean. *Lettres aux Américains*. Paris: Grasset, 1949.

———. *La fin du Potomak*. Paris: Gallimard, 1940.

———. *Le Potomak*. Paris: Stock, 1924.

Coindreau, M. E. *Aperçus de la littérature américaine*. Paris: Gallimard, 1946.

Commager, Henry Steele (ed.). *America in Perspective, the United States seen through Foreign Eyes*. New York: Random House, 1947.

————. *The American Mind: An Interpretation of American Thought and Character since the 1880's.* New Haven: Yale University Press, 1950.

Committee on International Interchange Policy. *Expanding University Enrollments and the Foreign Student: A Case for Foreign Students at U.S. Colleges and Universities.* New York: Institute of International Education, February 1957.

————. *The Foreign Student: Exchangee or Immigrant?* New York: Institute of International Education, May 1958.

————. *The Goals of Student Exchanges: An Analysis of Goals of Programs for Foreign Students.* New York: Institute of International Education, January 1955.

————. *Twenty Years of United States Government Programs in Cultural Relations.* New York: Institute of International Education, September 1959.

Conference Board of Associated Research Councils. *Educational Exchanges: Aspects of the American Experience.* Report of a Conference, Princeton, N.J., 1954. Princeton: National Academy of Sciences, 1956.

Conway, J. J. *Footprints of Famous Americans in Paris.* New York: John Lane, 1912.

Cooke, Alistair. *One Man's America.* New York: Alfred A. Knopf, 1952.

Coombs, Edith I. (ed.). *America Visited.* New York: Book League of America, n.d.

Cooper, James Fenimore. *Correspondence of James Fenimore Cooper.* 2 vols. New Haven: Yale University Press, 1922.

————. *England, with Sketches of Society in the Metropolis.* London: Bentley, 1837.

————. *Gleanings in Europe.* New York: Oxford University Press, 1928.

————. *Letter to his Countrymen.* New York: Wiley, 1843.

————. *Notions of the Americans.* London: Colburn, 1828.

————. *Recollections of Europe.* Paris: Baudry, 1837.

Cowley, Malcolm. *Exile's Return.* New York: Norton, 1934.

Crane, Werner W. *The Legend of the Founding Fathers.* New York: New York University Press, 1956.

Crawford, Rex (ed.). *The Cultural Migration. The European Scholar in America.* Philadelphia: University of Pennsylvania Press, 1953.

Crevecoeur, St. John. *Letters of An American Farmer.* London: T. Davies, 1782.

Croce, Benedetto. *Politics and Morals.* New York: Philosophical Library, 1945.

Croly, Herbert D. *Les promesses de la vie américaine.* Translation and introduction by Firmin Roz. Paris: F. Alcan, 1913.

Crook, David Paul. *American Democracy and English Politics, 1815–1850.*
New York: Oxford University Press, 1965.

Cunliffe, Marcus. *The Literature of the United States.* Harmondsworth, England: Penguin, 1955.

Curti, Merle. *American Philanthropy Abroad: A History.* New Brunswick, N.J.: Rutgers University Press, 1963.

———. *The Growth of American Thought.* New York: Harper & Row, 1943.

Daiches, David. *Willa Cather.* Ithaca, N. Y.: Cornell University Press, 1951.

D'Andrea, Ugo. *La rivoluzione moderna si chiama America.* Bologna: Capelli, 1956.

Davis, K., BREDEMEIR, H., and LEVY, M. *Modern American Society.* New York: Rinehart 1949.

Dermigny, Louis. *U.S.A. Essai de mythologie américaine.* Paris: Presses Universitaires, 1955.

Deutsch, Karl W. *Nationalism and Social Communication.* New York: Wiley, 1953.

DeVoto, Bernard. *The Literary Fallacy.* Boston: Little, Brown, 1944.

———. *Mark Twain's America.* Boston: Little, Brown, 1932.

Dewey, John. *Freedom and Culture.* New York: Putnam, 1939.

———. *German Philosophy and Politics.* New York: Henry Holt, 1915 and 1939.

———. *Influence of Darwin on Philosophy.* New York: Henry Holt, 1910.

Dicey, Edward. *Six Months in the Federal States.* London: Macmillan, 1863.

Dickens, Charles. *American Notes, and Pictures from Italy.* London: Chapman, 1907.

Dickinson, G. Lowes. *Appearances.* New York: Doubleday, 1915.

Divine, Robert A. *American Immigration Policy, 1924–1952.* New Haven: Yale University Press, 1957.

———. *The Reluctant Belligerent, American Entry into World War II.* New York: Wiley, 1965.

Dobert, Zitel Wolf. *Deutsche Demokraten in Amerika, Die Achtundvierziger und ihre Schriften.* Göttingen: Vandenhoek und Ruprecht, 1958.

Dobbs, John W. *American Memoir.* New York: Holt, Rinehart and Winston, 1959.

Dollot, Louis. *Les Relations Culturelles Internationales.* Paris: Presses Universitaires de France, 1964.

Dommergues, Pierre. *Les Ecrivains américains d'aujourd'hui.* Paris: Presses Universitaires de France, 1965.

Donald, David. *Charles Sumner and the Coming of the Civil War.* New York: Alfred A. Knopf, 1960.

Dos Passos, John. *The Grand Design.* New York: Harcourt, Brace and World, 1949.

———. *The Ground We Stand On.* New York: Harcourt, Brace and World, 1941.

———. *Journeys between Wars.* New York: Harcourt, Brace and World, 1922.

———. *Mr. Wilson's War.* New York: Doubleday, 1962.

———. *State of a Nation.* Boston: Houghton Mifflin, 1944.

Dreiser, Theodore. *Tragic America.* New York: Liveright, 1931.

———. *A Traveller at Forty.* New York: Century, 1913.

Drucker, Peter F. *Landmarks of Tomorrow.* New York: Harper & Row, 1957.

———. *The Myth of American Uniformity.* New York: Harper & Row, 1952.

Duberman, Martin D. *Charles Francis Adams, 1807–1886.* New York: Houghton Mifflin, 1961.

Dunbar, Seymour. *History of Travel in America.* Indianapolis: Bobbs-Merrill, 1915.

Eastman, William A. *Artists in Uniform.* London: Allen & Unwin, 1934.

Echevarria, Durand. *Mirage in the West: A History of the French Image of America to 1815.* Princeton: Princeton University Press, 1957.

Edel, Leon. *Henry James,* Philadelphia: Lippincott, 1953–.

——— (ed.). *Henry James and H. G. Wells.* Urbana: University of Illinois Press, 1958.

Eggleston, Edward. *The Transit of Civilization from England to America in the Seventeenth Century.* New York: Appleton, 1901.

Errmann, Henry W., *et al. European Views of America: Problems of Communication in the Atlantic World.* Edited by Gene M. Lyons and Michael O'Leary. Hanover, N.H.: Dartmouth College, 1965.

Einstein, L. *Divided Loyalties.* Boston: Houghton Mifflin, 1933.

Emerson, Ralph Waldo. *English Traits.* Boston: Phillips Sampson, 1856.

Everett, William. *On the Cam.* London: Ward, 1869.

Fairchild, Henry Pratt. *The Melting Pot Mistake.* Boston: Little, Brown, 1926.

Fay, Bernard. *The American Experiment.* New York: Harcourt, Brace and World, 1929.

———. *Franklin, the Apostle of Modern Times.* Boston: Little, Brown, 1929.

Ferguson, John Delancey. *American Literature in Spain.* New York: Columbia University Press, 1916.

Ferrero, Gugliemo. *La fin des aventures: guerre et paix.* Paris: Rieder, 1931.

Fiedler, Leslie A. *An End to Innocence.* Boston: Beacon Press, 1955.

Finletter, Thomas K. *Foreign Policy: The Next Phase.* New York: Harper & Row, 1958.

Fisher, Henry W. *Abroad with Mark Twain and Eugene Field.* New York: N. L. Brown, 1922.

Fishwick, Marshall W. *American Heroes: Myth and Reality.* Washington, D.C.: Public Affairs Press, 1954.

———. *American Studies in Transition.* Philadelphia: University of Pennsylvania Press, 1964.

Fiske, John. *American Political Ideas Viewed from the Standpoint of Universal History.* Boston: Houghton Mifflin, 1911.

Foerster, Norman (ed.). *Humanism and America.* New York: Farrar and Rinehart, 1930.

Foerster, Robert F. *The Italian Emigration of Our Times.* Cambridge: Harvard University, 1919.

Ford, Madox Ford. *Henry James.* New York: Boni, 1915.

Fraenkel, Ernst. *Amerika im Spiegel des deutschen politischen Denken.* Cologne: Opladen, Westdeutscher Verlag, 1959.

Frankel, Charles. *The Neglected Aspects of Foreign Affairs.* Washington, D.C.: The Brookings Institution, 1966.

Franklin, Benjamin. *Correspondance inédite et secrète du Docteur B. Franklin depuis l'année 1753 jusqu'en 1790.* Paris: Janet père, 1817.

Fullbright, J. William. *Prospects for the West.* Cambridge: Harvard University Press, 1963.

Gabriel, Ralph H. *The Course of American Democratic Thought.* New York: Ronald, 1940.

Galbraith, John Kenneth. *The Affluent Society.* Boston: Houghton Mifflin, 1958.

———. *The Liberal Hour.* Boston: Houghton Mifflin, 1960.

Gallup, George, and Rae, Saul Forbes. *The Pulse of Democracy: The Public-Opinion and How It Works.* New York: Simon & Schuster, 1940.

Gardner, John W. *Excellence.* New York: Harper & Row, 1961.

Garnier, Marie Reine. *Henry James et la France.* Paris: Honoré Champion, 1927.

Garrity, John A., and Adams, Walter. *From Main Street to the Left Bank.* East Lansing: Michigan State University Press, 1959.

Gasparin, Count Agénor de. *America Before Europe.* New York: Scribner's, 1862.

Getlein, Frank, and Gardiner, Harold C. *Movies, Morals, and Arts.* New York: Sheed and Ward, 1961.

Giedion, Siegfried. *Mechanization Takes Command.* New York: Oxford University Press, 1948.

Glazer, Nathan, and Moynihan, Daniel. *Beyond the Melting Pot.* Cambridge: Harvard University Press, 1963.

Godechot, Jacques. *France and the Atlantic Revolution of the Eighteenth Century, 1770–1789.* Translated by Herbert H. Rowen. New York: Free Press, 1965.

Gohdes, Clarence. *Ameican Literature in Nineteenth-Century England.* New York: Columbia University Press, 1944.

Goldman, Eric F. *The Crucial Decade.* New York: Alfred Knopf, 1956.

———. *Rendezvous with Destiny.* New York: Alfred A. Knopf, 1952.

Goodfriend, Arthur. *The Twisted Image.* New York: St. Martin's Press, 1963.

Gorer, Geoffrey. *The American People. A Study in National Character.* New York: W. W. Norton, 1964.

Greene, Edward J. H. *T. S. Eliot et la France.* Paris: Boivin, 1951.

Guérard, Albert. *Beyond Hatred, the Democratic Ideal in France and America.* New York: Scribners, 1925.

———. *Personal Equation.* New York: W. W. Norton, 1948.

Gullahorn, John, and Jeanne E. "American Fulbrighters Back Home," *News Bulletin,* New York: Institute of International Education, Vol. XXXIV, No. 8 (April, 1959).

———. "American Students Abroad: A French Perspective," *The Midwest Sociologist,* Vol. XX, No. 1 (December, 1957).

Gurko, Leo. *The Angry Decade.* New York: Dodd, Mead, 1947.

———. *Heroes, Highbrows, and the Popular Mind.* New York: Bobbs-Merrill, 1953.

Guttmann, Allen. *The Wound in the Heart, America and the Spanish Civil War.* New York: The Free Press, 1962.

Guttridge, G. H. "English Whiggism and the American Revolution," *University of California Publications in History,* Vol. XXVIII, Berkeley, Calf.: University of California Press, 1942.

Hackett, Alice Payne. *Sixty Years of Best-Sellers, 1895–1955.* New York: R. R. Bowker, 1956.

Handlin, Oscar. *The American People in the Twentieth Century.* Cambridge: Harvard University Press, 1954.

———. (ed.). *American Principles and Issues, The National Purpose*. New York: Holt, Rinehart and Winston, 1961.

———. *Immigration as a Factor in American History*. Englewood Cliffs, N. J.: Prentice-Hall, 1959.

———. *Race and Nationality in American Life*. Boston: Little, Brown, 1957.

———. *The Uprooted*. Boston: Little, Brown, 1951.

———, and Handlin, Mary. *The Dimensions of Liberty*. Cambridge: Harvard University Press, 1961.

Hansen, Marcus Lee. *The Atlantic Migration, 1607–1860*. Cambridge: Harvard University Press, 1940.

———. *The Immigrant in American History*. New York: Harper Torchbooks, 1940.

Harley, John Edgar. *World-Wide Influences of the Cinema*. Los Angeles: University of Southern California Press, 1940.

Hartz, Louis. *The Liberal Tradition in America*. New York: Harcourt, Brace, 1955.

Hawthorne, Julian. *Hawthorne and his Circle*. New York: Harper & Row, 1903.

———. *Nathaniel Hawthorne and His Wife*. 2 vols. Boston: Osgood, 1884.

Hawthorne, Nathaniel. *The English Notebooks*. Edited by Randall Stewart. New York: Oxford University Press, 1941.

———. *The Marble Faun*. Boston: Ticknor & Fields, 1860.

———. *Our Old Home*. Boston: Houghton Mifflin, 1907.

———. *Passages from the French and Italian Note-Books*. Boston: Houghton Mifflin, 1871.

Hayakawa, S. I. *Language in Action*. New York: Harcourt, Brace, 1941.

Heindel, Richard H. *The American Impact on Great Britain, 1898–1914. A Study of the United States in World History*. Philadelphia: University of Pennsylvania, 1940.

Heiney, Donald. *America in Modern Italian Literature*. New Brunswick, N. J.: Rutgers University Press, 1965.

Hellman, George S. *Washington Irving, Esquire, Ambassador at Large from the New World to the Old*. New York: Alfred A. Knopf, 1925.

Hemminghaus, Edgar Hugo. *Mark Twain in Germany*. New York: Columbia University Press, 1939.

Henry, Jules. *Culture Against Men*. New York: Random House, 1963.

Herbst, Jurgen. *The German Historical School in America: A Study in the Transfer of Culture*. Ithaca, N. Y.: Cornell University Press, 1965.

Hermant, Abel. *Les Transatlantiques*. Paris: Larousse, n.d.

Herter, Christian. *Toward An Atlantic Community.* New York: Harper & Row, 1963.

Hibbert, Christopher. *Garibaldi and His Enemies.* Boston: Little, Brown, 1966.

Hicks, Granville. *The Great Tradition.* New York: Macmillan, 1933.

Hobson, J. A. *Richard Cobden, The International Man.* London: Ernest Benn, Ltd., 1918.

Hoffer, Eric. *The Ordeal of Change.* New York: Harper & Row, 1963.

Hoffman, Frederick J. *The Twenties.* New York: Viking Press, 1953.

Hofstadter, Richard. *Anti-Intellectualism in American Life.* New York: Alfred A. Knopf, 1963.

————, Miller, William, and Aaron, Daniel. *The United States.* New York: Prentice-Hall, 1957.

Hoover, Robert C. *The Challenge to Liberty.* New York: Scribner's, 1934.

Hornstein, Simon. *Mark Twain, la faillite d'un idéal.* Paris: R. Lacoste, 1950.

Houle, Cyril O., and Nelson, Charles A. *The University, The Citizen, and World Affairs.* Washington, D.C.: American Council on Education, 1956.

Hovland, Carl I. *Experiments in Mass Communication.* Princeton: Princeton University Press, 1949.

Howells, William Dean. *Italian Journeys.* New York: Hurd & Houghton, 1867.

————. *Venetian Life.* New York: Hurd & Houghton, 1867.

Huberman, Leo M. *America, Incorporated.* New York: Viking Press, 1940.

Huxley, Aldous. *Literature and Science.* New York: Harper, 1964.

Huxley, T. H. *American Addresses.* New York: Appleton, 1877.

Institute of Research on Overseas Programs. *The International Programs of American Universities.* East Lansing: Michigan State University Press, 1958.

Irving, Pierre M. *The Life and Letters of Washington Irving.* 4 vols. New York: Putnam, 1862–64.

Irving, Washington. *Tour in Scotland, 1817, and Other Manuscript Notes.* Edited by Stanley T. Williams. New Haven: Yale University Press, 1927.

Jacobs, Lewis. *The Rise of the American Films.* New York: Brace & Co., 1939.

Jäckh, Ernst. *Amerika und Wir, 1926–51. Amerikanisch-deutsches Ideenbundnis.* Stuttgart: Deutsche Verlagsanstalt, 1951.

James, Henry. *Parisian Sketches, Letters to the New York Tribune 1875–76.* New York: New York University Press, 1957.

————. *Transatlantic Sketches.* Boston: Osgood, 1875.

————. *William Wetmore Story and His Friends.* Edinburgh: William Blackwood & Sons, 1903.

James, Leslie. *Americans in Glasshouses.* New York: Henry Schuman, 1951.

Janson, Florence E. *The Background of Swedish Immigration, 1840–1930.* Chicago: University of Chicago Press, 1931.

Jantz, Harold. "Amerika im deutschen Dichten und Denken," in Wolfgang Stammler (ed.), *Deutsche Philologie im Aufriss,* No. 24 (revised edition, Berlin, 1960).

Jaspers, Karl. *The Future of Germany.* Chicago: University of Chicago Press, 1967.

Jeanne, René, and Ford, Charles. *Histoire du cinéma,* Tome III, *Histoire du cinéma américain.* Paris: Laffont, 1956.

Jessup, John K., Stevenson, Adlai, MacLeish, Archibald, Sarnoff, David, Graham, Billy, Gardner, John W., Rossiter, Clinton, Wohlstetter, Albert, Reston, James, and Lippmann, Walter. *The National Purpose.* New York: Holt, Rinehart and Winston, 1960.

Joinville, Prince de. *Guerre d'Amérique—Campagne du Potomac.* Paris: Michel-Lévy frères, 1863.

Jones, Howard Mumford. *America and French Culture, 1750–1848.* Chapel Hill: University of North Carolina Press, 1927.

————. *Ideas in America.* Cambridge: Harvard University Press, 1944.

————. *O Strange New World.* New York: Viking Press, 1964.

Jordan, Donaldson, and Pratt, Edwin J. *Europe and the American Civil War.* Boston, New York: Houghton Mifflin, 1931.

Joseph, Franz M. (ed.) *As Others See Us: The United States Through Foreign Eyes.* Princeton: Princeton University Press, 1959.

Jungk, Robert. *Tomorrow is Already Here.* London: R. Hart-Davis, 1954.

Kallen, Horace. *Culture and Democracy in the United States.* New York: Boni and Liveright, 1924.

Kates, George W. (ed.). *Willa Cather in Europe.* New York: Alfred A. Knopf, 1956.

Kazin, Alfred. *On Native Grounds.* New York: Harcourt, Brace and World, 1942.

Kent, Donald P. *The Refugee Intellectual: The Americanization of the Immigrant of 1939–41.* New York: Columbia University Press. 1953.

Kimball, Marie. *Jefferson: The Scene of Europe, 1784–1789.* New York: Coward-McCann, 1950.

Kipling, Rudyard. *American Notes.* London, New York: Standard Book Co., 1930.

————. "The Walking Delegate," in *The Day's Work,* New York: Doubleday & McClure Co., 1898.

Kirk, Grayson. *The Study of International Relations in American Colleges and Universities.* New York: Harper & Row, 1947.

Klapper, Joseph T. *The Effects of Mass Communication: An Analysis of Research* . . . . New York: The Free Press, 1960.

Klein, Roger M. (ed.). *Young Americans Abroad.* New York: Harper & Row, 1963.

Knaplund, Paul, and Clewes, Carolyn M. (ed.). "Private Letters from the British Embassy in Washington . . . 1880–1885," *Annual Report of the American Historical Association for the Year 1941,* Washington, D.C.: Government Printing Office, 1942.

Koht, Halvdan. *American Spirit in Europe.* Philadelphia: University of Pennsylvania Press, 1949.

Kraus, Michael. *The Atlantic Civilization.* Ithaca, N.Y.: Cornell University Press, 1949.

Krutch, Joseph Wood, *et al. Is the Common Man Too Common?* Norman: University of Oklahoma Press, 1954.

Kubly, Herbert. *American in Italy.* New York: Simon & Schuster, 1955.

Künzig, Ferdinand. *Washington Irving und seine Beziehungen zur englischen Literatur des 18. Jahrhunderts.* Heidelberg: Buchdruckerei Carl Pfeiffer, 1911.

Lafayette, Marie Joseph, marquis de. *Mémoires, correspondance et manuscrits du Général Lafayette.* Publiés par sa famille, Bruxelles, 1837.

Langer, William L. and Gleason, S. Everett. *The Challenge to Isolation.* New York: Harper & Row, 1952.

———. *The Undeclared War,* New York: Harper and Row, 1953.

Larkin, Oliver W. *Art and Life in America.* New York: Rinehart, 1949.

Laski, Harold J. *The American Democracy.* New York: Viking Press, 1948.

———. *The American Presidency.* New York. Harper & Row, 1940.

Laun, Adolf. *Washington Irving: Ein Lebens und Charakterbild.* 2 vols. Berlin: Robert Oppenheim, 1870.

Lawrence, D. H. *Studies in Classic American Literature.* New York: T. Seltzer, 1923.

Law-Robertson, Harry. *Walt Whitman in Deutschland.* Giessen: Giessener Beitrage zur deutschen Philologie, XLII, 1935.

Le Breton, Maurice. "Henry Adams et la France," in *Harvard et la France.* Paris: Revue d'Histoire Moderne, 1936.

Le Clair, Robert Charles. *Three American Travellers in England, James Russell Lowell, Henry Adams, Henry James.* Unpublished Ph.D. dissertation, University of Pennsylvania, 1945.

Leclerc, Max. *Choses d'Amérique: les crises économiques et religieuses aux Etats-Unis.* Paris: E. Plon, 1895.

Lehman, Lucien. *"Ces cochons d'Américains!!" Essai sur l'orgueil, l'égoisme et l'ignorance des Français.* Paris: Maisonneuve, 1954.

Leonard, C. H. *Arnold in America: A Study of Matthew Arnold's Literary Relations with America and of his Visits to this Country in 1883 and 1886.* Unpublished Ph.D. dissertation, Yale University, 1932.

Lerner, Daniel, and Aron, Raymond. *La Querelle de la C. E. D.* Paris: Armand Colin, 1956.

Lewis, Wyndham. *America and Cosmic Man.* London: Nicholson, 1948.

———. *The Mysterious Mr. Bull.* London: R. Hale, 1938.

———. *Time and Western Man.* London: Chatto and Windus, 1927.

Ley, J. W. T. *The Dickens Circle.* London: Chapman and Hall, 1919.

Lichtheim, George. *The New Europe: Today—and Tomorrow.* New York: Praeger, 1963.

Lillibridge, G. D. *Beacon of Freedom: The Impact of Democracy upon Great Britain, 1830–1870.* Philadelphia: University of Pennsylvania Press, 1955.

Lind, Edward (ed.). *S. F. B. Morse; His Letters and Journal.* Boston: Houghton Mifflin, 1914.

Lippitt, Ronald, and Watson, Jeanne. *Learning Across Cultures: A Study of Germans Visiting America.* East Lansing: State University of Michigan Press, 1955.

Lippmann, Walter. *Inquiry into Principles of the Good Society.* Boston: Atlantic Monthly Press, 1937.

———. *The Phantom Public.* New York: Harcourt, Brace and World, 1925.

———. *Public Opinion.* New York: Macmillan, 1922.

Lipset, Seymour M. *The First Nation: The United States in Historical and Comparative Perspective.* New York: Basic Books, 1963.

Long, Orie W. *Literary Pioneers—Early American Explorers of European Culture.* Cambridge: Harvard University Press, 1935.

Lonn, Ella. *Foreigners in the Confederacy.* Chapel Hill: University of North Carolina Press, 1940.

———. *Foreigners in the Union Army and Navy.* Baton Rouge: Louisiana State University Press, 1951.

Lowell, Amy. *Six French Poets: Studies in Contemporary Literature.* Boston: Houghton Mifflin, 1921.

Lowell, James Russell. *Fireside Travels.* Boston: Houghton Mifflin, 1904.

Lubock, Percy (ed.). *The Letters of Henry James.* New York: Macmillan, 1920.

Lucas, Henry S. *Netherlanders in America: Dutch Immigration to the United States and Canada, 1789–1950.* Ann Arbor: University of Michigan Press, 1955.

Lyell, Sir Charles. *A Second Visit to the United States of North America.* 2 vols. New York: Harper & Row, 1868.

Lynd, Robert Staughton, and Lynd, Helen Merrell. *Middletown, A Study in Contemporary American Culture.* New York: Harcourt, Brace and World, 1929.

——. *Middletown in Transition.* New York: Harcourt, Brace and World, 1937.

Lynes, Russell. *The Domesticated Americans.* New York: Harper and Row, 1963.

——. *The Taste-makers.* New York: Harper & Row, 1954.

MacDonald, Dwight. *Against the American Grain.* New York, Random House, 1962.

McElroy, Robert. *American History as an International Study.* Oxford: Clarendon Press, 1926.

MacKay, Alexander. *The Western World.* 2 vols. Philadelphia: Lea and Blanchard, 1849.

MacLeish, Archibald. *The American Cause.* New York: Duell, Sloan & Pearce, 1941.

Madariaga, Salvador de. *Americans.* London: Oxford University Press, 1930.

——. *Englishmen, Frenchmen, Spaniards.* London: Oxford University Press, 1928.

——. *Portrait of Europe.* London: Hollis and Carter, 1952.

Mann, Golo. *Vom Geist Amerikas. Eine Einführung in amerikanisches Denken und Handel in 20 Jahrhundert.* Zurich: Europa Verlag, 1954.

Mantoux, Etienne. *The Carthaginian Peace, or the Economic Consequences of Mr. Keynes.* London: Oxford University Press, 1946.

Maritain, Jacques. *Man and the State.* Chicago: Chicago University Press, 1951.

——. *Réflections sur l'Amérique.* Paris: Fayard, 1958.

Markel, Lester, *et al. Public Opinion and Foreign Policy.* New York: Harper & Row, 1949.

Marx, Karl, and Engels, Frederick. *The Civil War in the United States.* New York: International Publishers, 1937.

Martineau, Harriet. *A History of the American Compromises.* London: J. Chapman, 1856.

——. *The Manifest Destiny of the American Union.* New York: Anti-Slavery Society, 1857.

——. *A Retrospect of Western Travel.* 3 vols. London: Saunders & Otley, 1838.

——. *Society in America.* 3 vols. New York: Saunders & Otley, 1837.

Matthews, T. S. *O My America!.* New York: Simon & Schuster, 1962.

Maurois, André. *Adrienne ou Madame LaFayette*. Paris: Hachette, 1960.

————. *Chantiers américains*. Paris: Gallimard, 1933.

————. *Chateaubriand*. Paris: Grasset, 1938.

————. *Conseils à un jeune Français partant pour les Etats-Unis*. Paris: La Jeune Parque, 1947.

————. *En Amérique*. Paris: Flammarion, 1933.

————. *Etats-Unis 39*. Paris: Les Editions de France, 1939.

————. *Histoire des Etats-Unis, 1492–1944*. New York: Editions de la Maison Française, 1944.

May, Ernest R. *Imperial Democracy, The Emergence of America as a Great Power*. New York: Harcourt, Brace and World, 1961

May, Henry F. *The End of American Innocence*. New York: Alfred A. Knopf, 1959.

Mayer, J. P. *Prophet of the Mass Age*. London: Dent and Sons, 1939.

Mayes, Herbert R. *Alger; a Biography without a Hero*. New York: Macy-Macius, 1928.

Melville, Herman. *Journal of a Visit to Europe and the Levant, October 11, 1856–May 6, 1857*. Edited by Howard C. Horsford. Princeton: Princeton University Press, 1955.

————. *Journal of a Visit to London and the Continent, 1849–50*. Edited by Eleanor Melville Metcalf. Cambridge: Harvard University Press, 1948.

Mesick, Jane Louise. *The English Traveller in America, 1785–1835*. New York: Columbia University Press, 1922.

Meyer, Hildegard. *Nord-Amerika im Urteil des deutschen Schrifttums bis zur Mitte des 19. Jahrhunderts*. Hamburg: Friedrichsen, de Gruyter & Co., 1929.

Michaux, Régis. *Autour d'Emerson*. Paris: Brossard, 1924.

————. *Ce qu'il faut connaître de l'âme américaine*. Paris: Boivin et Cie, 1929.

————. *A French Friend and Inspirer of Emerson*. Berkeley: University of California Press, 1921.

Mills, C. Wright. *The Power Elite*. New York: Oxford University Press, 1956.

————. *White Collar: The American Middle Class*. New York: Oxford University Press, 1951.

Moltke, Otto, Graf von. *Nord-Amerika: Beiträge zum Verständnis seiner Wirtschaft und Politik*. Berlin: E. S. Mittler, 1903.

Monaghan, Frank. *French Travellers in the United States, 1765–1932: A Bibliography*. New York: The New York Public Library, 1933.

Montalembert, Comte de. *La Victoire du Nord aux Etats-Unis*. Paris: E. Dentu, 1866.

Moore, Ben T. *N.A.T.O. and the Future of Europe*. New York: Harper & Row, 1958.

Morison, Elting E. *The American Style: Essays in Value and Performance*. New York: Harper & Row, 1958.

———. *Men, Machines and Modern Times*. Cambridge: M.I.T. Press, 1966.

Morley, Charles (ed.). *Portrait of America. Letters of Henry Sienkiewicz*. New York: Columbia University Press, 1959.

Morris, Lloyd R. *The Rebellious Puritan* (Hawthorne). New York: Harcourt, Brace and World, 1929.

Morris, Richard T. and Davidsen, Oluf M. *Two-Way Mirror*. Minneapolis: University of Minnesota Press, 1960.

Morse, J. T. *Life and Letters of O. W. Holmes*. 2 vols. New York: Houghton Mifflin, 1896.

Mosse, George L. *The Culture of Western Europe: Nineteenth and Twentieth Centuries*. Chicago: Rand McNally, 1961.

Mott, Frank Luther. *Golden Multitudes: The Story of Best Sellers in the United States*. New York: Macmillan, 1947.

Mowat, R. B. *Americans in England*. Boston: Houghton Mifflin, 1935.

———. *The American Entente*. London: E. Arnold, 1939.

———. *The American Venture*. London: A. Dakers, 1942.

Mulder, William. *Homeward to Zion: The Mormon Migration from Scandinavia*. Minneapolis: University of Minnesota Press, 1957.

Mumford, Lewis. *The Brown Decades, a Study of the Arts in America, 1865–1895* (rev. ed.). New York: Dover, 1955.

———. *The Culture of Two Cities*. New York: Harcourt, Brace and World, 1938.

———. *The Golden Day*. New York: Boni & Liveright, 1926.

———. *Herman Melville*. New York: Literary Guild of America, 1929.

———. *The Highway and the City*. New York: Harcourt, Brace and World, 1963.

———. *Sticks and Stones: A Study of American Architecture and Civilization*. New York: Boni & Liveright, 1924.

———. *The Story of Utopias*. New York: Boni & Liveright, 1922.

———. *Technics and Civilization*. New York: Harcourt, Brace and World, 1934.

Murat, Achille. *A moral and Political Sketch of the United States of North America*. London: E. Wilson, 1833.

Myers, Andrew Breen (ed.). "Washington Irving Madrid Journal 1827–1828 and Related Letters," *Bulletin of the New York Public Library*, LII (May–September, 1958), 219–471.

Myers, Gustavus. *America Strikes Back*. New York: I. Washburn, 1935.

Myrdal, Gunnar. *An American Dilemma*. New York: Harper & Row, 1944.

Namier, L. B. *England in the Age of the American Revolution*. New York: St. Martin's Press, 1962.

Neago, Peter. *Americans Abroad*. The Hague: The Servire Press, 1932.

Nef, John U. *The United States and Civilization*. Chicago: University of Chicago Press, 1942.

Nevins, Allan. *American Social History as recorded by British Travellers*. New York. Holt, Rinehart and Winston, 1923.

Nicol, Eric, and Whalley, Peter. *Say, Uncle*. New York: Harper & Row, 1961.

Niebuhr, Reinhold. *The Irony of American History*. New York: Scribner's, 1952.

Norton, Charles Eliot. *Letters of Charles Eliot Norton*. Edited by Sara Norton and M. A. DeWolfe Howe. 2 vols. Boston: Houghton Mifflin, 1913.

Nye, Russel Blaine. *The Cultural Life of the New Nation, 1776–1830*. New York: Harper & Row, 1960.

Ogburn, W. F. (ed.). *American Society in Wartime*. Chicago: University of Chicago Press, 1943.

Olmsted, F. L. *Walks and Talks of An American Farmer in England*. New York: Putnam, 1852.

Ortega y Gasset, J. *The Revolt of the Masses*. New York: W. W. Norton, 1957.

Orth, Samuel P. *Our Foreigners*. New Haven: Yale University Press, 1920.

Ostrogorski, M. Y. *Democracy and the Organization of Political Parties*. New York: Macmillan, 1902.

Owen, Collinson. *The American Illusion*. London: E. Benn, 1929.

Packard, Vance. *The Hidden Persuaders*. New York: D. McKay, 1957.

Paine, Albert Bigelow (ed.). *Mark Twain's Notebook*. New York: Harper & Row, 1935.

Papa, Dario, and Fontana, Fernandino. *New York*. Milan: G. Galli, 1884.

Park, Julian (ed.). *The Culture of France in Our Time*. Ithaca, N.Y.: Cornell University Press, 1954.

Park, Robert E., and Miller, Herbert A. *Old World Traits Transplanted*. New York: Harper & Row, 1921.

Park, Rev. Roswell. *Handbook for American Travellers in Europe*. Putnam, 1853.

Parrington, V. L. *Main Currents of American Thought.* 3 vols. New York: Harcourt, Brace, 1927–30.

Paul, Elliot. *The Last Time I Saw Paris.* New York: Random House, 1942.

Payne, G. H. *England: Her Treatment of America.* New York: Sears Publishing Co., 1931.

Pease, Otis. *The Responsibilities of American Advertising.* New Haven: Yale University Press, 1958.

Pelling, Henry. *America and the British Left from Bright to Bevan.* London: A. & C. Black, 1956.

Pennell, E., and Pennell, J. *The Life of Whistler,* Philadelphia: Modern Library, 1908.

Penney, Clara Louisa (ed.). *Washington Irving Diary, Spain 1828–1829.* New York: The Hispanic Society of America, 1926.

Perry, Bliss. *The American Mind and American Idealism.* Boston: Houghton Mifflin, 1913.

———. *The American Spirit in Literature.* New Haven: Yale University Press, 1918.

———. *The Heart of Emerson's Journals.* Boston: Houghton Mifflin, 1926.

Perry, Ralph Barton. *Characteristically American.* New York: Alfred A. Knopf, 1949.

———. *Puritanism and Democracy.* New York: Vanguard, 1944.

Peterson, Theodore. *Magazines in the Twentieth Century.* Urbana: University of Illinois Press, 1956.

Peyre, Henri. *Literature and Sincerity.* New Haven: Yale University Press, 1963.

———. *Observations on Life, Literature and Learning in America.* Carbondale: Southern Illinois University Press, 1961.

Pierson, George. *Tocqueville and Beaumont in America.* New York: Oxford University Press, 1938.

Pisani, Camille Ferri. *Prince Napoleon in America, 1881.* Translated by George J. Joyaux. Bloomington: University of Indiana Press, 1959.

Pitt, Barrie. *1918: The Last Act.* London: Cassell, 1962.

Polenz, Wilhelm. *Das Land der Zukunft.* Berlin: F. Fontane, 1905.

Pollard, A. F. *Factors in American History.* Cambridge: Harvard University Press, 1925.

Poniatowski, Michel. *Talleyrand aux Etats-Unis.* Paris: Perrin, 1967.

Potter, David M. *People of Plenty.* Chicago: University of Chicago Press, 1964.

Potter, Stephen. *Potter on America.* New York: Random House, 1957.

Pound, Ezra L. *Impact: Essay on Ignorance and the Decline of American Civilization.* Chicago: H. Regnery Co., 1960.

———. *Letters, 1907–1941*. Edited by D. D. Paige. New York: Harcourt, Brace, 1950.

———. *Patria Mia*. Chicago: R. F. Seymour, 1950.

Pross, Helge. *Die deutche akademische Emigration nach den Vereinigten Staaten, 1933–1941*. Berlin: Duncker & Humblot, 1955.

Putnam, Samuel. *Paris Was Our Mistress*. New York: Viking Press, 1947.

Putt, S. Gorley. *Cousins and Strangers. Comments on Americans by Commonwealth Fund Fellows from Britain, 1946–52*. Cambridge: Harvard University Press, 1956.

———. *Henry James, A Reader Guide*. Ithaca: Cornell University Press, 1966.

———. *View from Atlantis*. London: Constable, 1955.

Rahv, P. (ed.). *The Discovery of Europe*. Boston: Houghton Mifflin, 1947.

Ray, Gordon (ed.). *Letters and Private Papers of William Makepeace Thackeray*. Cambridge: Harvard University Press, 1945.

Reed, E. B. (ed.). *Commonwealth Fund Fellows and Their Impressions of America*. New York: The Commonwealth Fund, 1932.

Reichart, Walter A. *Washington Irving and Germany*. Ann Arbor, Mich.: University of Michigan Press, 1957.

Reid, T. Wemyss. *The Life, Letters and Friendships of Richard Monckton-Milnes*. 2 vols. London: Cassell & Co. 1890.

Riesman, David. *Individualism Reconsidered, and Other Essays*. New York: The Free Press, 1954.

———. *The Lonely Crowd; A Study of the Changing American Character*. New Haven: Yale University Press, 1950.

Roberts, Cecil. *And so to America*. New York: Doubleday, 1947.

Roberts, Henry L., and Wilson, Paul A. *Britain and the United States: Problems in Cooperation*. New York: Harper & Row, 1953.

Romains, Jules. *Salsette Discovers America*. Translated by Lewis Galantière. New York: Alfred A. Knopf, 1942.

———. *Visites aux Américains*. Paris: Flammarion, 1937.

Roosevelt, Theodore. *American Ideal, and Other Essays, Social and Political*. New York and London: Putnam, 1897.

Rorty, James. *Where Life is Better*. New York: Reynal and Hitchcock, 1936.

Rosenberg, Bernard, and White, David M. (eds.). *Mass Culture: The Popular Arts in America*. New York: The Free Press, 1958.

Ross, Murray. *Stars and Strikes*. New York: Columbia University Press, 1941.

Rossi, Joseph. *The Image of America in Mazzini's Writings*. Madison, Wis.: University of Wisconsin Press, 1954.

Rostow, Walter W. *The United States in the World Arena: An Essay in Recent History*. New York: Harper & Row, 1960.

Rousiers, Paul de. *American Life*. Translated from the French by A. J. Herbertson. Paris: Firmin-Didot, 1892.

Roz, Firmin. *Les Américains vus par leurs romanciers*. Monaco: Société des Conférences, 1926–28.

―――. *L'Amérique et nous*. Brussels: Globe, 1946.

―――. *L'Amérique nouvelle*. Paris: Flammarion, 1923.

―――. *Comment faire connaitre la France à l'étranger*. Paris: Plon-Nourrit, 1922.

―――. *L'Energie américaine*. Paris: Flammarion, 1910.

―――. *L'Evolution des idées et des moeurs américaines*. Paris: Flammarion, 1951.

Rush, Richard. *A Residence at the Court of London*. Philadelphia: Lea & Blanchard, 1845.

Rusk, Dean. *The Winds of Freedom*. Boston: Beacon Press, 1963.

Russell, Bertrand. *The Impact of Science on Society*. New York: Simon & Schuster, 1953.

Sahl, Hans. *The Few and the Many*. New York: Harcourt, Brace & World, 1962.

Salin, Edgar. *Amerikanische Impressionen*. Tübingen: J. L. B. Mohr, 1953.

Samuels, Ernest. *Henry Adams: The Major Phase*. Cambridge: Harvard University Press, 1964.

―――. *Henry Adams: The Middle Years*. Cambridge: Harvard University Press, 1958.

Sand, Maurice. *Six Mille Lieues à Toute Vapeur*. Paris: M. Lévy frères, 1862.

Sandburg, Carl. *The People, Yes*. New York: Harcourt, Brace, 1936.

Santayana, George. *Character and Opinion in the United States*. New York: Doubleday, 1956.

―――. *Egotism in German Philosophy*. London: J. M. Dent, 1960.

―――. *The Last Puritan*. New York: Scribner's, 1925.

―――. *Soliloquies in England and Later Soliloquies*. New York: Scribner's, 1922.

Savelle, Max. *Seeds of Liberty: The Genesis of the American Mind*. New York: Alfred A. Knopf, 1948.

Schafer, Joseph. *Carl Schurz, Militant Liberal*. Evansville, Wis.: The Antes Press, 1930.

Schorer, Mark. *Sinclair Lewis*. New York: McGraw-Hill, 1961.

Schumpeter, Joseph A. *Capitalism, Socialism, and Democracy*. New York: Harper & Row, 1942.

Schuyler, Eugene. *Italian Influences*. New York: Scribner's, 1901.

Schwab, Arnold T. *James Gibbons Huneker, Critic of the Seven Arts*. Stanford: Stanford University Press, 1963.

Seldes, Gilbert. *The Great Audience*. New York: Viking Press, 1950.

————. *The Public Arts.* New York: Simon & Schuster, 1956.

————. *The Seven Lively Arts.* New York: Harper and Row, 1924.

Senior, Nassau W. *Conversations with M. Thiers, M. Guizot, and other distinguished persons during the Second Empire.* London: Hurst & Blackett, 1878.

Shannon, David (ed.). *Beatrice Webb's American Diary, 1898.* Madison, University of Wisconsin Press, 1963.

Sheean, Vincent. *Dorothy and Red.* Boston: Houghton Mifflin, 1963.

Shepperson, Wilbur S. *Emigration and Disenchantment: Portraits of Englishmen Rapatriated from The United States.* Norman: University of Oklahoma Press, 1965.

Sherrill, Charles H. *French Memories of Eighteenth Century America.* New York: Scribner's, 1915.

Siegfried, André. *L'Ame des Peuples.* Paris: Hachette, 1950.

————. *America at Mid-century.* New York. Harcourt, Brace and World, 1955.

————. *America Comes of Age.* New York: Harcourt, Brace and World, 1927.

————. *Tableau des Etats-Unis.* Paris: A. Colin, 1954.

Simon, Julius, R. W. *Emerson in Deutschland, 1851–1932.* Berlin: Junker und Dünnhaupt, 1937.

Sinclair, Upton. *Mammonart.* Pasadena, Calif.: The Author, 1925.

Skard, Sigmund. *American Studies in Europe.* 2 vols. Philadelphia: University of Pennsylvania Press, 1958.

Skinner, Cornelia Otis. *Elegant Wits and Grand Horizontals.* Boston: Houghton Mifflin, 1962.

Smalley, George Washburn. *Anglo-American Memoirs.* London: Putnam, 1912.

————. *London Letters.* 2 vols. New York: Harper & Row, 1891.

Smith, Bradford. *Why We Behave Like Americans.* Philadelphia: Lippincott, 1957.

Smith, E. F. *Priestley in America, 1794–1804.* Philadelphia: P. Blakiston's Son & Co. 1920.

Smith, Francis Prescott. *Washington Irving and France.* Unpublished Ph.D. dissertation, Harvard University, 1937.

Smith, Henry Nash. *Virgin Land; the American West as Symbol and Myth.* New York: Vintage Books, 1957.

Smith, Huston C. (ed.). *The Search for America.* Englewood Cliffs, N.J.: Prentice-Hall, 1959.

Smith, Thelma M., and Miner, Ward L. *Transatlantic Migration: The Contemporary American Novel in France.* Durham, N.C.: Duke University Press. 1955.

Smyth, Albert H. (ed.). *The Writings of Benjamin Franklin.* New York: Macmillan, 1905–1907.

Soldati, Mario. *America primo amoro.* Milan: A. Mondadori, 1959.

Southard, Frank A., Jr. *American Industry in Europe.* Boston: Houghton Mifflin, 1931.

Spender, Stephen. *European Witness.* London: H. Hamilton, 1946.

Spiller, Robert E. *The American in England during the First Half-Century of Independence.* New York: Holt, 1926.

————, et. al. *Literary History of the United States.* 3 vols. New York: Macmillan, 1948.

Stallman, R. W., *Stephen Crane,* New York: Braziller, 1968.

Stead, William T. *The Americanization of the World.* New York: H. Markley, 1902.

Stearns, Harold E. *America Now.* New York: Scribner's, 1938.

———— (ed.). *America: a Reappraisal.* New York: Hillman-Curl. 1937.

————. *Civilization in the United States, an Inquiry by Thirty Americans.* New York: Harcourt, Brace, 1922.

————. *America and the Young Intellectual.* New York: George H. Doran, 1921.

————. *Rediscovering America.* New York: Liveright, 1934.

Stein, Gertrude. "The Making of Americans," in *In Lectures in America.* New York: Random House, 1935.

Stephenson, George M. *A History of American Immigration, 1820–1924.* New York: Russell & Russell, 1964.

Stolberg-Wernigerode, Otto, Count zu. *Germany and the United States of America during the Era of Bismarck.* Reading, Pa.: Carl Schurz Foundation, 1937.

Strausz-Hupe, Robert. *A Forward Strategy for America.* New York: Harper & Row, 1961.

Strout, Cushing. *The American Image of the Old World.* New York: Harper & Row, 1963.

Sulzberger, C. L. *What's Wrong with U.S. Foreign Policy.* New York: Harcourt, Brace and World, 1959.

Swift, Richard N. *World Affairs and the College Curriculum.* Washington, D.C.: American Council on Education, 1959.

Taupin, René. *L'influence du symbolisme français sur la poésie américaine de 1910 à 1920.* Paris: H. Champion, 1929.

Thistlethwaite, Frank. *The Anglo-American Connection in the Early Nineteenth Century.* Philadelphia: University of Pennsylvania Press, 1959.

Thomason, Charles A., and Laves, Walter H. C. *Cultural Relations and U.S. Foreign Policy.* Bloomington: University of Indiana Press, 1963.

Thornberg, E. H. *Sverige i Amerika, Amerika i Sverige*. Stockholm: A. Bonnier, 1938.

Thornton, J. E. (ed.). *Science and Social Change*. Washington, D.C.: The Brookings Institution, 1939.

Thwaite, B. H. *The American Invasion: or England's Commercial Danger and the Triumphal Progress of the U.S.* London: Hugh MacHugh, 1902.

Ticknor, George. *Life, Letters, and Journals of George Ticknor*. Boston: Osgood, 1876.

Tocqueville, Alexis de. *Democracy in America*. Translated by Henry Reeve. London: Saunders and Otley, 1835.

————. *Journey to America*. Edited by J. P. Mayer. New Haven: Yale University Press, 1960.

Torrielli, Andrew J. *Italian Opinion on America as Revealed by Italian Travellers, 1850–1900*. Cambridge: Harvard University Press, 1941.

Toynbee, Arnold J. *America and the World Revolution*. New York: Oxford University Press, 1962.

Trent, William P., and Hellman, George S. (eds.). *The Journals of Washington Irving*. Boston: The Bibliophile Society, 1919.

Trollope, Anthony. *North America*. New York: Lippincott, 1862.

Trollope, Frances. *Domestic Manners of the Americans*. London: Whittaker, Treacher, 1832.

Tunnard, Christopher, and Reed, Henry H. *American Sky-Line*. New York: Houghton Mifflin, 1956.

Twain, Mark. *The American Claimont*. New York: Charles Webster Co., 1892.

————. *Europe and Elsewhere*. New York: Harper & Row, 1923.

————. *Literary Essays*. New York: Harper & Row, 1899.

————. *Mark Twain in Eruption*. Edited by Bernard DeVoto. New York: Harper & Row, 1922.

Ulich, Robert. *The Education of Nations*. Cambridge: Harvard University Press, 1961.

United States Department of State, Bureau of Intelligence and Research, External Research Division. "Area Study Programs in American Universities," Washington, D.C.: Government Printing Office, 1959.

United States Senate. "The American Overseas, Hearings before the Committee on Foreign Relations, February 18, 1959," Washington, D.C.: Government Printing Office, 1959.

Uri, Pierre. *A Partnership for Progress: A Program for Tansatlantic Action*. New York: Harper & Row, 1963.

Urzidil, Johannes. *Das Glück der Gegenwart; Goethes Amerikabild*. Zurich: Artemis Verlag, 1958.

Vacher, Léon. *Le Homestead aux Etats-Unis.* Paris: Guillaumin et Cie, 1895.

Valentine, A. *The Age of Conformity.* Chicago: H. Requery Co., 1954.

————. *1913.* New York: Macmillan, 1962.

Vandenberg, Arthur H., Jr. (ed.). *The Private Papers of Senator Vandenberg.* Boston: Houghton Mifflin, 1952.

Veblen, Thorstein. *The Theory of the Leisure Class.* New York: Macmillan, 1899.

Viatte, Auguste. *Histoire Littéraire de l'Amérique française des origines à 1950.* Québec: Presses Universitaires Laval, 1954.

Visson, André (ed). *As Others See Us.* New York: Doubleday, 1948.

Wagenknecht, Edward C. *Henry Wadsworth Longfellow.* New York: Oxford University Press, 1966.

————. *The Man Charles Dickens.* Boston: Houghton Mifflin, 1929.

————. *Washington Irving: Moderation Displayed.* New York: Oxford University Press, 1962.

Waithman, Robert. *The Day before Tomorrow.* New York: Scribner's, 1951.

————. *Report on America.* London: F. Muller Ltd., 1940.

————. *Understanding the English.* London: F. Muller Ltd., 1953.

Walker, Mack. *Germany and the Emigration, 1816–1855.* Cambridge: Harvard University Press, 1964.

Wanson, Léon. *Les Américains et nous.* Paris: Julliard, 1950.

Watson, Elkanah. *Men and Times of the Revolution, including Journals of Travels in Europe and America from 1777 to 1842.* New York: Dane and Co, 1856.

Wecter, Dixon. *The Age of the Great Depression.* New York: Macmillan, 1948.

Wegelin, Christof. *The Image of Europe in Henry James.* Dallas: Southern Methodist University Press, 1958.

Weidner, Edward W. *The World Role of Universities.* New York: McGraw-Hill, 1963.

Wellek, René. *Confrontations: Studies in the Intellectual and Literary Relations between Germany, England, and the United States during the Nineteenth Century.* Princeton: Princeton University Press, 1965.

Wells, H. G. *An Englishman Looks at the World.* London: Cassell, 1914.

————. *The Future in America: a Search after Realities.* New York: Harper & Row, 1906.

————. *The New America.* London: Macmillan, 1953.

————. *Social Forces in England and America.* New York: Harper & Row, 1914.

Wescott, Glenway. *Fear and Trembling.* New York: Harper and Row, 1932.

Wharton, Edith. *A Backward Glance.* New York: Appleton Century, 1934.

————. *Fighting France*. New York: Scribner's, 1915.
————. *French Ways and their Meanings*. New York: Appleton-Century, 1919.
Whelpley, James D. *British-American Relations*. Boston: Little, Brown, 1924.
White, Morton. *Social Thought in America: the Revolt against Formalism*. Boston: Beacon Press, 1957.
Whitehead, Alfred N. *Adventures of Ideas*. New York: Macmillan, 1933.
————. *Science and the Modern World*. New York: Macmillan, 1925.
Whitman, Walt. *Democratic Vistas*. Washington, D.C.: J. S. Redfield, 1871.
Whyte, William H., Jr. *The Organization Man*. New York: Simon & Schuster, 1956.
Wickersham, George W. *Report on Law Observance and Enforcement*. Washington, D.C.: Government Printing Office, 1930–31.
Wilcox, Francis O., and Haviland, H. Field, Jr. (eds.). *The Atlantic Community: Progress and Prospects*. New York: Praeger, 1963.
Williams, Francis. *The American Invasion*. London: A. Bloud, 1962.
Williams, Stanley T. (ed.). *Journal of Washington Irving (1823–1824)*. Cambridge: Harvard University Press, 1931.
————. *The Life of Washington Irving*. New York: Oxford University Press, 1935.
————. *The Spanish Background of American Literature*. New Haven: Yale University Press, 1955.
————. *Washington Irving: Notes While Preparing Sketch Book, etc, 1817*. New Haven: Yale University Press, 1927.
Willson, Beckles. *America's Ambassadors to England, 1785–1929*. New York: Frederick A. Stokes, 1929.
————. *America's Ambassadors to France, 1777–1927*. London: J. Murray, 1928.
————. *John Slidell and the Confederates in Paris*. New York: Milton, Balch, Co., 1932.
Wilson Edmund. *The American Jitters*. New York: Scribner's, 1932.
————. *Europe without Baedeker*. New York: Doubleday, 1947.
————. *The Shock of Recognition*. New York: Doubleday, 1943.
————. *Travels in Two Democracies*. New York: Harcourt, Brace and World, 1936.
Wilson, Howard E. *American College Life as Education in World Outlook*. Washington, D.C.: American Council on Education, 1956.
————. *Universities and World Affairs*. New York: Carnegie Endowment for International Peace, 1951.
Winterich, John T. *An American Friend of Dickens* (Washington Irving). New York: T. F. Madigan, 1933.

Wish, Harvey. *Society and Thought in America.* 2 vols. New York: Longmans, Green, 1950–52.

Wittke, Carl F. *The Irish in America.* Baton Rouge: Louisiana State University Press, 1956.

———. *Refugees of Revolution, the German Forty-Eighters in America.*
Philadelphia: University of Pennsylvania Press, 1952.

———. *We Who Built America: The Saga of the Emigrant.* New York:
Prentice-Hall, 1939.

Wright, Frances. *Views of Society and Manners in America.* Edited by Paul
R. Baker. Cambridge: Harvard University Press, 1963.

Wright, Louis B. *The Atlantic Frontier, Colonial American Civilization
1607–1763.* New York: Alfred A. Knopf, 1947.

———. *The Cultural Life of the American Colonies, 1601–1763.* New
York: Harper & Row, 1957.

Wright, Natalia. *Horatio Greenhough: The First American Sculptor.* Philadelphia: University of Pennsylvania, 1953.

Wrong, G. M. *The Conquest of New France.* New Haven: Yale University
Press, 1918.

Wyllie, Irwin C. *The Self-Made Man in America: The Myth of Rags to
Riches.* New Brunswick, N. J.: Rutgers University Press, 1954.

ᑲ INDEX ᑭ

Abbey, Edwin Austin, 110, 121–22
Acheson, Dean, quoted, 286
Acton, Lord, quoted, 15
Adams, Abigail (Mrs. John), quoted, 30, 197
Adams, Brooks, 126
Adams, Charles Francis, 39, 123
Adams, Charles Francis, Jr., 123
Adams, Henry, 39, 46, 53, 68, 99, 105, 110, 122–27 (quoted), 131, 161, 164, 228, 243; quoted, 9, 35, 85, 108, 197, 198, 237, 240, 244–45, 260, 266, 300
Adams, Mrs. Henry, 120
Adams, Herbert B., 243
Adams, John, 7, 12, 21, 40, 210; quoted, 10, 15, 20, 30, 31, 32
Adams, John Quincy, 60
Adams, Samuel, 9
Adler, Mortimer, 93, 179
Agassiz, Louis, 87
Ain (France), 159
Albany, New York, 12, 82
Albert Hall (London), 186
Alcott, A. Bronson, 242
Alden, John and Priscilla, 45
Aldington, Richard, 135
Alfieri, 32
Alger, Horatio, 86
Allegheny, Pennsylvania, 119, 159
Allston, Washington, 7, 40, 42, 45
Alsace, 158
American Academy (Rome), 121, 293
Amiens, 125, 126
Anderson, Sherwood, 160, 163, 168, 191, 251, 262; quoted, 160
André, Major John, 7
Angell, Norman, 157
Anglesey, fourth Marquess of, 100
Anne (England), 6
Anouilh, Jean, 294
Ansermet, Ernest, 91
Antheil, George, 135, 164
Anville, Duchesse d', 21

Appleton, Frances (Mrs. Henry W. Longfellow), 45
Appolinaire, Guillaume, 159
Aquinas, St. Thomas, 265, 271, 292
Aragon, Louis, 93
Arkansas, 244
Arnauld, Abbé, 21
Arnold, Matthew, 47, 51, 104–105 (quoted), 115, 123, 134, 272, 298; quoted, 96–97, 260, 261
Aron, Raymond, quoted, 203
Aspen, Colorado, 274
Astor, Lord, 100
Astor, Elizabeth, 99
Astor, John Jacob, 99
Atherton, Gertrude, 101; quoted, 200
Auden, W. H., 294
Augustine, St., 168, 271
Aurelius, Marcus, see Marcus Aurelius

Babeuf, Gracchus, 17
Babbit, Irving, 134, 172, 272
Bach, 130
Bacon, Roger, 18, 266
Badenweiller, 117
Baer, George F., quoted, 85
Bagot, Lord, 100
Bahaus, 91
Baldwin, Stanley, 181
Baltimore, 22, 41, 57
Balzac, 43, 48
Bancroft, George, 14, 33, 37, 45, 105, 243
Barbès, 48
Barbusse, Henri, 182
Baring, Alexander (Lord Ashburton), 99
Barlow, Joel, 17, 31, 40; quoted, 200
Barnard, Fred, 110
Barnes, Harry Elmer, quoted, 140
Barney, Nathalie, 161
Barrès, Maurice, 118
Barth, Karl, 208; quoted, 292